handbook

Physics

1 Value Points
2 Competition Insight
3 Knowledge Booster
4 Knowledge Library

Highly useful for XI-XII, Engg., Medical & Other Competitions

handbook

Physics

With

Fantastic 4

1 Value Points
2 Competition Insight
3 Knowledge Booster
4 Knowledge Library

Highly useful for XI-XII, Engg., Medical & Other Competitions

Keshav Mohan

Supported by

Dharmendra Singh

Avinash Kumar

ARIHANT PRAKASHAN, (SERIES) MEERUT

卐 **Administrative & Production Offices**

Regd. Office

'Ramchhaya' 4577/15, Agarwal Road, Darya Ganj, New Delhi -110002
Tele: 011- 47630600, 43518550

卐 **Head Office**

Kalindi, TP Nagar, Meerut (UP) - 250002
Tel: 0121-7156203, 7156204

卐 **Sales & Support Offices**

Agra, Ahmedabad, Bengaluru, Bareilly, Chennai, Delhi, Guwahati, Hyderabad, Jaipur, Jhansi, Kolkata, Lucknow, Nagpur & Pune.

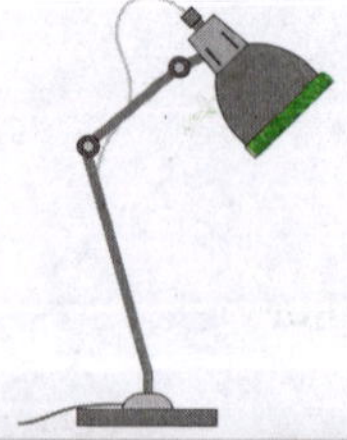

卐 **PRICE ₹395.00**

PO No. : TXT-59-T067891-11-25

Published by Arihant Publications (India) Ltd.

For further information about the books published by Arihant, log on to www.arihantbooks.com or e-mail at info@arihantbooks.com

Follow us on   

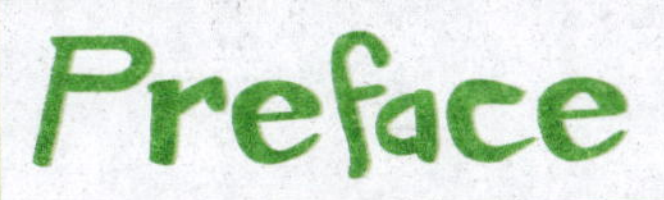

Preface

This Arihant handbook is unique multipurpose Revision book, developed to facilitate quick and powerpacked revision of various **keyNotes, Terms, Definitions & Formulae**.

The book is equally useful for revision before board exam and all relevant competitions like **JEE, NEET, NDA, CDS, UPSC** etc.

The handful nature of book help in quick revision anytime from anywhere even between the exam shifts or while travelling as well.

This revised edition of Arihant handbook Physics is now even more powerful with Fantastic 4

1. **Value Points** Assorted pointers with enhanced info for more impactful revision.
2. **Competition Insight** Most valuable competition related concepts segregated to create more focus.
3. **Knowledge Booster** Concept enhancers to elevate knowledge sphere outline
4. **Knowledge Library** Unique compendium of indispensable facts excluded from Rationalised NCERT.

However, we have put our best efforts in preparing this book, but if any error or what so ever has been skipped out, we will by heart welcome your suggestions. A part from all those who helped in the compilation of this book a special note of thanks goes to Ms. Yojna Sharma of Arihant Publications.

Author

CONTENTS

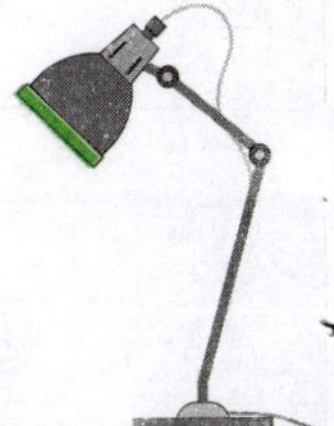

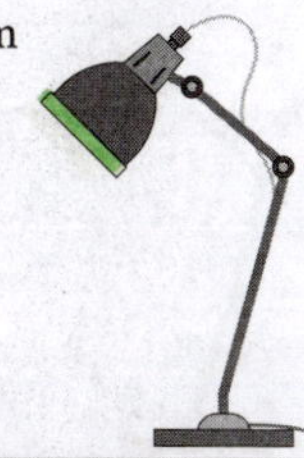

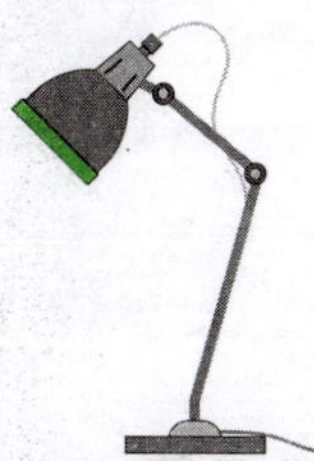

Chapter 01

Units and Measurement

The comparison of any physical quantity with its standard unit is called **measurement**.

Physical Quantities

All the quantities which can be measured directly or indirectly and in terms of which the laws of Physics are described are called physical quantities.

Units

A standard amount of a physical quantity chosen to measure the physical quantity of the same kind is called a physical unit. It should be easily reproducible, internationally accepted.

Fundamental Quantities and Their Units

Those physical quantities which are independent of other physical quantities are called **fundamental quantities** and their units are called **fundamental units.**

Fundamental quantities	Fundamental units		
	Name	**Symbol**	**Definition**
Length	Metre	m	The metre is the length of the path travelled by light in vacuum during a time interval of 1/299,792,458 of a second. (1983)
Mass	Kilogram	kg	The kilogram is equal to the mass of the International prototype of the kilogram (a platinum-iridium alloy cylinder) kept at International Bureau of Weights and Measures at Sevres, near Paris, France. (1889)
Time	Second	s	The second is the duration of 9,192,631,770 periods of the radiation corresponding to the transition between the two hyperfine levels of the ground state of the cesium-133 atom. (1967)

Fundamental quantities	Fundamental units		
	Name	Symbol	Definition
Electric current	Ampere	A	The ampere is that constant current which, if maintained in two straight parallel conductors of infinite length, of negligible circular cross-section and placed 1 m apart in vacuum, would produce a force between these conductors equal to 2×10^{-7} N/m of length. (1948)
Thermodynamic temperature	Kelvin	K	The kelvin is the fraction 1/273.16 of the thermodynamic temperature of the triple point of water. (1967)
Amount of substance	Mole	mol	The mole is the amount of substance of a system which contains as many elementary entities as there are atoms in 0.012 kg of carbon-12. (1971)
Luminous intensity	Candela	cd	The candela is the luminous intensity in a given direction of a source that emits monochromatic radiation of frequency 540×10^{12} Hz and that has a radiant intensity in that direction of 1/683 watt per steradian. (1979)

Supplementary Fundamental Quantities and Their Units

Radian and steradian are two supplementary fundamental units. They measure plane angle and solid angle, respectively.

Supplementary fundamental quantities	Supplementary units		
	Name	Symbol	Definition
Plane angle (figure labels: ds, dθ, O, r)	Radian	rad	One radian is the angle subtended at the centre of a circle by an arc equal in length to the radius of the circle. *i.e.* $d\theta = \frac{ds}{r}$
Solid angle (figure labels: r, dΩ, O, dA)	Steradian	sr	One steradian is the solid angle subtended at the centre of a sphere, by that surface of the sphere, which is equal in area, to the square of radius of the sphere. *i.e.* $d\Omega = \frac{dA}{r^2}$

Derived Quantities and Their Units

Those physical quantities which are derived from fundamental quantities are called **derived quantities** and their units are called **derived units** *e.g.* velocity, acceleration, force, work, etc.

System of Units

A system of units is the complete set of units, both fundamental and derived, for all kinds of physical quantities. The common system of units which is used in mechanics are given below:

(i) **CGS System** In this system, the unit of length is centimetre, the unit of mass is gram and the unit of time is second.

(ii) **FPS System** In this system, the unit of length is foot, the unit of mass is pound and the unit of time is second.

(iii) **MKS System** In this system, the unit of length is metre, the unit of mass is kilogram and the unit of time is second.

(iv) **SI System** The system of units, which is accepted internationally for measurement is the International System of Units abbreviated as SI. This system contains seven fundamental units and two supplementary fundamental units.

Relationship between Some Mechanical SI Unit and Commonly Used Units

S.No.	Physical Quantities		Units
1.	Length	(a)	1 micrometre = 10^{-6} m
		(b)	1 nanometre = 10^{-9} m
		(c)	1 angstrom = 10^{-10} m
2.	Mass	(a)	1 metric ton = 10^{3} kg
		(b)	1 pound = 0.4537 kg
		(c)	1 amu = 1.66×10^{-27} kg
3.	Volume		1 litre = 10^{-3} m^3
4.	Force	(a)	1 dyne = 10^{-5} N
		(b)	1 kgf = 9.81 N
5.	Pressure	(a)	1 kgf-m^2 = 9.81 Nm^{-2}
		(b)	1 mm of Hg = 133 Nm^{-2}
		(c)	1 pascal = 1 Nm^{-2}
		(d)	1 atmosphere pressure = 76 cm of Hg = 1.01×10^{5} pascal
6.	Work and energy	(a)	1 erg = 10^{-7} J
		(b)	1 kgf-m = 9.81 J

S.No.	Physical Quantities		Units
		(c)	1 kWh = 3.6×10^6 J
		(d)	1 eV = 1.6×10^{-19} J
7.	Power	(a)	1 kgf- ms^{-1} = 9.81 W
		(b)	1 horse power = 746 W

Knowledge Booster

Some Practical Units of Length

(i) 1 fermi = 10^{-15} m

(ii) 1 X-ray unit = 10^{-13} m

(iii) 1 astronomical unit = 1.49×10^{11}m (average distance between sun and earth)

(iv) 1 light year = 9.46×10^{15} m

(v) 1 parsec = 3.08×10^{16} m = 3.26 light year

Dimensions

Dimensions of any physical quantity are those powers to which the fundamental quantities are raised to express that quantity. The expression of a physical quantity in terms of its dimensions, is called its **dimensional formula.**

Dimensional Formula of Some Physical Quantities

S.No.	Physical Quantities	Dimensional Formula	MKS Units
1.	Area	$[L^2]$	m^2
2.	Volume	$[L^3]$	m^3
3.	Velocity	$[LT^{-1}]$	ms^{-1}
4.	Acceleration	$[LT^{-2}]$	ms^{-2}
5.	Force	$[MLT^{-2}]$	newton (N)
6.	Work or energy	$[ML^2T^{-2}]$	joule (J)
7.	Power	$[ML^2T^{-3}]$	J s^{-1} or W (watt)
8.	Pressure or stress	$[ML^{-1}T^{-2}]$	Nm^{-2}
9.	Linear momentum or impulse	$[MLT^{-1}]$	kg ms^{-1}
10.	Density	$[ML^{-3}]$	kg m^{-3}
11.	Strain	dimensionless	unitless
12.	Modulus of elasticity	$[ML^{-1}T^{-2}]$	Nm^{-2}
13.	Surface tension	$[MT^{-2}]$	Nm^{-1}

S.No.	Physical Quantities	Dimensional Formula	MKS Units
14.	Velocity gradient	$[T^{-1}]$	s^{-1}
15.	Coefficient of viscosity	$[ML^{-1}T^{-1}]$	$kg\ m^{-1}s^{-1}$
16.	Gravitational constant	$[M^{-1}L^3T^{-2}]$	Nm^2/kg^2
17.	Moment of inertia	$[ML^2]$	$kg\text{-}m^2$
18.	Angular velocity	$[T^{-1}]$	rad/s
19.	Angular acceleration	$[T^{-2}]$	rad/s^2
20.	Angular momentum	$[ML^2\ T^{-1}]$	$kg\ m^2s^{-1}$
21.	Specific heat	$[L^2T^{-2}\ \theta^{-1}]$	$Jkg^{-1}K^{-1}$
22.	Latent heat	$[L^2T^{-2}]$	J/kg
23.	Planck's constant	$[ML^2T^{-1}]$	J-s
24.	Universal gas constant	$[ML^2T^{-2}\ \theta^{-1}]$	J/mol-K

Value Points

The physical quantities separated by the symbols +, –, =, >, <, etc. have the same dimensions.

Homogeneity Principle

If the dimensions of left hand side of an equation are equal to the dimensions of right hand side of that equation, then the equation is dimensionally correct. This is known as **homogeneity principle**.

Mathematically, [LHS] = [RHS].

Applications of Dimensions

(i) To check the accuracy of physical equations.

(ii) To change a physical quantity from one system of units to another system of units.

(iii) To obtain a relation between different physical quantities.

Significant Figures

In the measured value of a physical quantity, the number of digits about the correctness of which we are sure plus the next doubtful digit, are called the significant figures.

Rules for Finding Significant Figures

(i) All non-zero digits are significant figures, *e.g.* 4362 has 4 significant figures.

(ii) All zeros occuring between non-zero digits are significant figures, *e.g.* 1005 has 4 significant figures.

(iii) All zeros to the right of the last non-zero digit are not significant, *e.g.* 6250 has only 3 significant figures.

(iv) All zeros to the right of the last non-zero digit are significant, if they come from a measurement, *e.g.* 5080 m. It has four significant figures.

(v) In a digit less than one, all zeros to the right of the decimal point and to the left of a non-zero digit are not significant, *e.g.* 0.00325 has only 3 significant figures.

(vi) All zeros to the right of a non-zero digit in the decimal part are significant, *e.g.* 1.4750 has 5 significant figures.

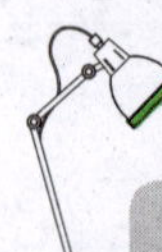

EXPERT Scale Up

Significant figures do not change, if we measure a physical quantity in different units, e.g. 5.608 cm, 56.08 mm and 0.05608 m, all have four significant figures.

Significant Figures in Algebraic Operations

(i) **In Addition or Subtraction** In addition or subtraction of the numerical values, the final result should retain as many decimal places as there are in the number with the least places. *e.g.*

If $l_1 = 4.326$ m and $l_2 = 1.50$ m,

then, $l_1 + l_2 = (4.326 + 1.50)\text{ m} = 5.826\text{ m}$

As l_2 has measured upto two decimal places, therefore

$$l_1 + l_2 = 5.83\text{ m}$$

(ii) **In Multiplication or Division** In multiplication or division of the numerical values, the final result should retain as many significant figures as there are in the original number with the least significant figures. *e.g.* If length $l = 12.5$ m and breadth $b = 4.125$ m,

then, area $A = l \times b = 12.5 \times 4.125 = 51.5625\text{ m}^2$

As l has only 3 significant figures, therefore

$$A = 51.6\text{ m}^2$$

Rounding Off

The process of omitting the non-significant digits and retaining only the desired number of significant digits, incorporating the required modifications to the last significant digit is called rounding off the number.

Rules for Rounding off a Measurement

(i) If the digit to be dropped is less than 5, then the preceding digit is left unchanged. *e.g.* 1.54 is rounded off to 1.5.

(ii) If the digit to be dropped is greater than 5, then the preceding digit is raised by one. *e.g.* 2.49 is rounded off to 2.5.

(iii) If the digit to be dropped is 5 followed by digit other than zero, then the preceding digit is raised by one. *e.g.* 3.55 is rounded off to 3.6.

(iv) If the digit to be dropped is 5 or 5 followed by zeros, then the preceding digit is raised by one, if it is odd and left unchanged if it is even. *e.g.* 3.750 is rounded off to 3.8 and 4.650 is rounded off to 4.6.

Competition Insight

Error

The lack in accuracy in the measurement due to the limit of accuracy of the measuring instrument or due to any other cause is called an error. The difference between the measured value and the true value of a quantity is known as the error in the measurement.

$$\text{Error} = \text{True value} - \text{Measured value}$$

Errors are usually classified as

1. Absolute Error

The difference between the true value and the measured value of a quantity is called absolute error.

If $a_1, a_2, a_3, \ldots, a_n$ are the measured values of any quantity a in an experiment performed n times, then the arithmetic mean of these values is called the true value (a_m) of the quantity.

$$a_m = \frac{a_1 + a_2 + a_3 + \ldots + a_n}{n}$$

The absolute error in measured values is given by

$$\Delta a_1 = a_m - a_1$$

$$\Delta a_2 = a_m - a_2$$

....

$$\Delta a_n = a_m - a_n$$

2. Mean Absolute Error

The arithmetic mean of the magnitude of absolute errors in all the measurement is called mean absolute error.

$$\overline{\Delta a} = \frac{|\Delta a_1| + |\Delta a_2| + \ldots + |\Delta a_n|}{n}$$

3. Relative Error or Fractional Error

The ratio of mean absolute error to the true value is called relative error.

$$\text{Relative error} = \frac{\text{Mean absolute error}}{\text{True value}} = \frac{\overline{\Delta a}}{a_m}$$

4. Percentage Error

The relative error expressed in percentage is called percentage error.

$$\text{Percentage error} = \frac{\overline{\Delta a}}{a_m} \times 100\%$$

- **Least Count Error** The smallest value that can be measured by the measuring instrument is called its least count and error arises due to the limitation imposed by the least count of the measuring instrument is called least count error.
- **Random Error** The error which occurs irregularly and at random, in magnitude and direction are called random error.

Combinations of Errors

(i) **Error in Addition or Subtraction** Let $x = a + b$ or $x = a - b$

If the measured values of two quantities a and b are $(a \pm \Delta a)$ and $(b \pm \Delta b)$, then maximum absolute error in their addition or subtraction is

$$\Delta x = \pm (\Delta a + \Delta b)$$

(ii) **Error in Multiplication or Division** Let $x = a \times b$ or $x = \frac{a}{b}$

If the measured values of a and b are $(a \pm \Delta a)$ and $(b \pm \Delta b)$, then maximum relative error

$$\frac{\Delta x}{x} = \pm \left(\frac{\Delta a}{a} + \frac{\Delta b}{b} \right)$$

(iii) **Error in Raised to a Power** Let $z = a^p b^q / c^r$

If the measured values of a, b and c are $(a \pm \Delta a)$, $(b \pm \Delta b)$ and $(c \pm \Delta c)$, then maximum error $\frac{\Delta z}{z} = \pm \left[p\left(\frac{\Delta a}{a}\right) + q\left(\frac{\Delta b}{b}\right) + r\left(\frac{\Delta c}{c}\right) \right]$

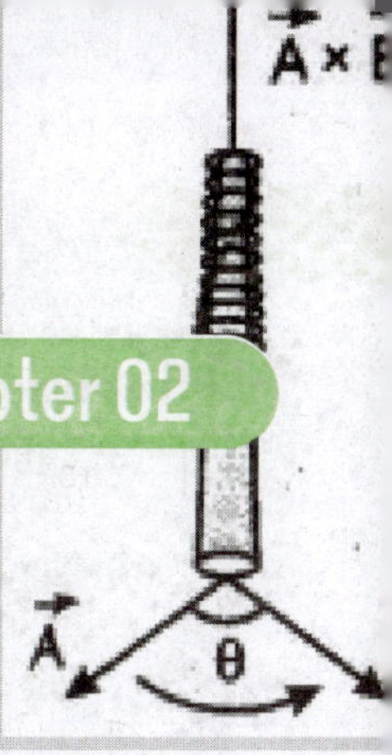

Chapter 02

Scalars and Vectors

Scalar Quantities

Those physical quantities which require only magnitude but no direction for their complete representation are called **scalar quantities.**

Distance, speed, work, mass, density, etc. are the examples of scalars. Scalars can be added, subtracted, multiplied or divided by simple algebraic laws.

Vector Quantities

Those physical quantities which require magnitude as well as direction for their complete representation and follows vector laws are called **vector quantities.**

e.g., Displacement, acceleration, velocity, momentum, force, etc.

Vectors can be mainly classified into following two types

1. Polar Vectors

These vectors have a starting point or a point of application such as displacement, force, etc.

2. Axial Vectors

These vectors represent rotational effect and act along the axis of rotation in accordance with right hand screw rule, such as angular velocity, torque, angular momentum, etc.

Tensors

Tensors are those physical quantities which have different values in different directions at the same point.

Moment of inertia, radius of gyration, modulus of elasticity, pressure, stress, conductivity, resistivity, refractive index, wave velocity, density etc. are the examples of tensors. Magnitude of tensor is not unique.

Other Types of Vectors

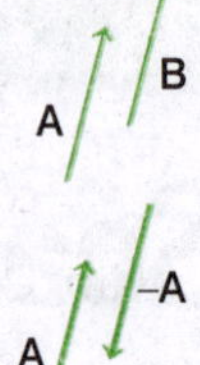

(i) **Equal Vectors** Two vectors of equal magnitude and having same direction are called equal vectors.

(ii) **Negative Vectors** Two vectors of equal magnitude but having opposite directions are called negative vectors.

The negative vector of $\mathbf{A}$ is represented as $-\mathbf{A}$.

(iii) **Zero Vector or Null Vector** A vector whose magnitude is zero, known as a zero or null vector. Its direction is not defined. It is denoted by $\mathbf{0}$.

Velocity of a stationary object, acceleration of an object moving with uniform velocity and resultant of two equal and opposite vectors are the examples of null vector.

(iv) **Unit Vector** A vector having unit magnitude is called a unit vector.

A unit vector in the direction of vector $\mathbf{A}$ is given by

$$\hat{\mathbf{A}} = \frac{\mathbf{A}}{|\mathbf{A}|}$$

A unit vector is unitless and dimensionless vector and represents direction only.

(v) **Orthogonal Unit Vectors** The unit vectors along the direction of orthogonal axis, i.e. X-axis, Y-axis and Z-axis are called orthogonal unit vectors.

They are represented by $\hat{\mathbf{i}}$, $\hat{\mathbf{j}}$ and $\hat{\mathbf{k}}$.

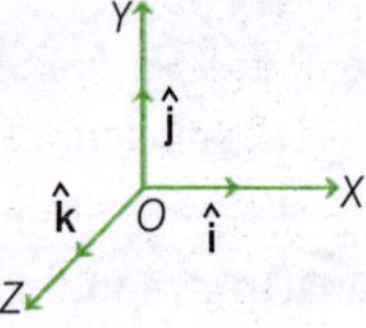

(vi) **Co-initial Vectors** Vectors having a common initial point, are called co-initial vectors.

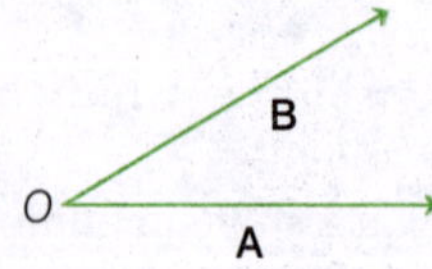

(vii) **Parallel Vectors** Two vectors are said to parallel vectors if both vectors have same direction or exactly in the opposite direction. If **A** and **B** are parallel vectors, then $\mathbf{A} = \pm m\mathbf{B}$, where m is constant number.

(viii) **Collinear Vectors** Vectors having equal or unequal magnitudes but acting along the same or parallel lines are called collinear vectors.

(ix) **Coplanar Vectors** Vectors acting in the same plane are called coplanar vectors.

(x) **Localised Vector** A vector whose initial point is fixed, is called a localised vector.

(xi) **Non-localised or Free Vector** A vector whose initial point is not fixed is called a non-localised or a free vector.

(xii) **Position Vector** A vector which gives position of an object with reference to the origin of a coordinate system is called position vector. It is represented by a symbol **r**.

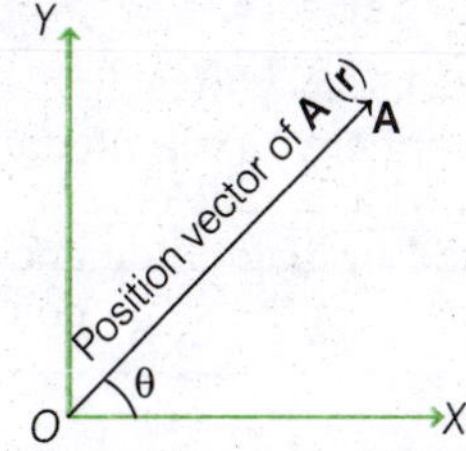

(xiii) **Displacement Vector** The vector which tells how much and in which direction an object has changed its position in a given interval of time is called **displacement vector.**

Displacement vector is the straight line joining the initial and final positions and does not depend on the actual path undertaken by the object between the two positions.

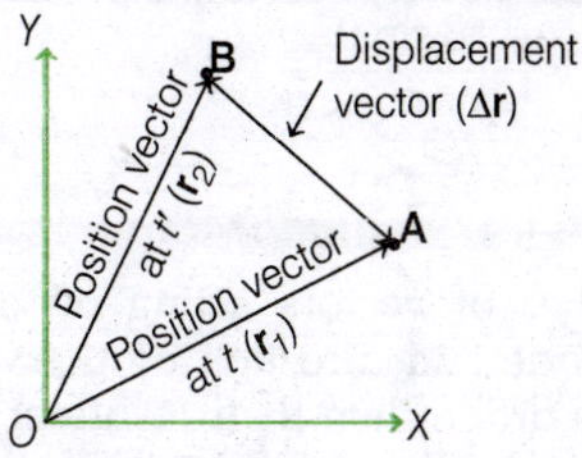

The displacement vector for **AB** is $\Delta\mathbf{r} = \mathbf{r}_2 - \mathbf{r}_1$

Addition of Vectors

1. Triangle Law of Vectors Addition

If two vectors acting at a point are represented in magnitude and direction by the two sides of a triangle taken in one order, then their resultant is represented by the third side of the triangle taken in the opposite order.

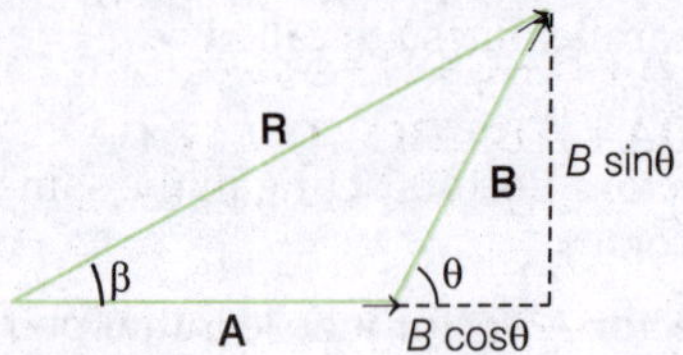

If two vectors **A** and **B** acting at a point are inclined at an angle θ, then their resultant, $R = \sqrt{A^2 + B^2 + 2AB\cos\theta}$

If the resultant vector **R** subtends an angle β with vector **A**, then

$$\tan\beta = \frac{B\sin\theta}{A + B\cos\theta}$$

2. Parallelogram Law of Vectors Addition

If two vectors acting at a point are represented in magnitude and direction by the two adjacent sides of a parallelogram drawn from a point, then their resultant is represented in magnitude and direction by the diagonal of the parallelogram drawn from the same point.

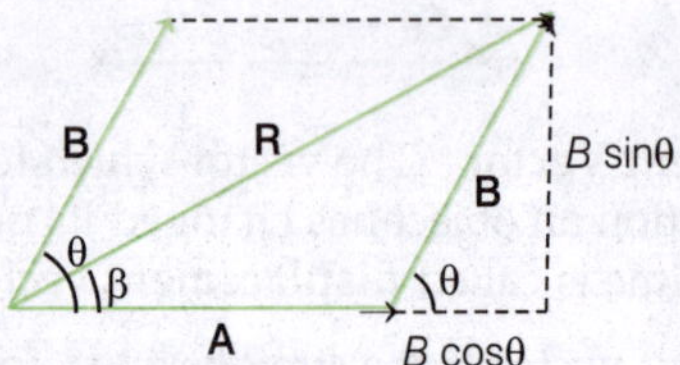

Resultant of vectors **A** and **B** is given by $R = \sqrt{A^2 + B^2 + 2AB\cos\theta}$

If the resultant vector **R** subtends an angle β with vector **A**, then

$$\tan\beta = \frac{B\sin\theta}{A + B\cos\theta}$$

3. Polygon Law of Vectors Addition

It states that, if number of vectors acting on a particle at a time are represented in magnitude and direction by the various sides of an open polygon taken in same order, then their resultant vector is represented in magnitude and direction by the closing side of polygon taken in opposite order. In fact, polygon law of vectors is the outcome of triangle law of vectors.

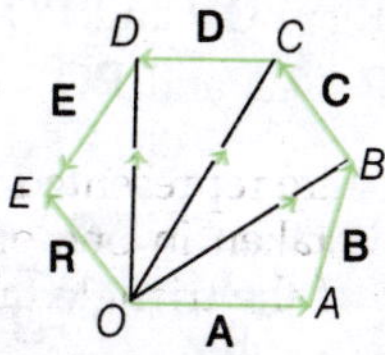

$$\mathbf{R} = \mathbf{A} + \mathbf{B} + \mathbf{C} + \mathbf{D} + \mathbf{E}$$

$$\mathbf{OE} = \mathbf{OA} + \mathbf{AB} + \mathbf{BC} + \mathbf{CD} + \mathbf{DE}$$

Properties of Vector Addition

(i) Vector addition is commutative, *i.e.* $\mathbf{A} + \mathbf{B} = \mathbf{B} + \mathbf{A}$

(ii) Vector addition is associative, *i.e.*

$$\mathbf{A} + (\mathbf{B} + \mathbf{C}) = \mathbf{B} + (\mathbf{C} + \mathbf{A}) = \mathbf{C} + (\mathbf{A} + \mathbf{B})$$

(iii) Vector addition is distributive, *i.e.* $m(\mathbf{A} + \mathbf{B}) = m\mathbf{A} + m\mathbf{B}$

(iv) $\mathbf{A} + \mathbf{0} = \mathbf{A}$

Subtraction of Vectors

Subtraction of a vector **B** from a vector **A** is defined as the addition of vector $-\mathbf{B}$ (negative of vector **B**) to vector **A**.

Thus, $$\mathbf{A} - \mathbf{B} = \mathbf{A} + (-\mathbf{B})$$

Value Points

- If vectors are of unequal magnitude, then minimum three coplanar vectors are required for zero resultant.
- If the magnitude of sum of two vectors is equal to the magnitude of difference of the two vectors, then the angle between these vectors will be 90°.
- Resultant of two vectors is always located in their common plane.

Rotation of a Vector

(i) If a vector is rotated through an angle θ, which is not an integral multiple of 2π, the vector changes.

(ii) If the frame of reference is rotated or translated, the given vector does not change. The components of the vector may, however, change.

Resolution of Vectors into Two Components

If two component vectors of **R** are **OP** and **PQ** in the direction of **A** and **B** respectively, and suppose **OP** = λ**A** and **PQ** = μ**B**, where λ and μ are two real numbers.

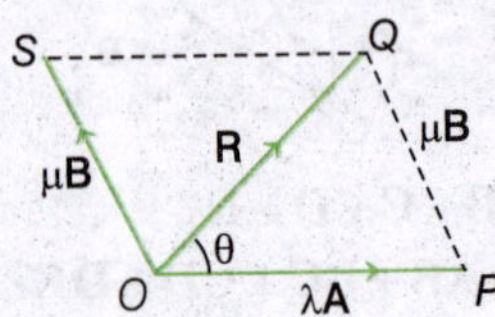

Then, resultant vector, $\mathbf{R} = \lambda\mathbf{A} + \mu\mathbf{B}$

Resolution of a Vector into Rectangular Components

If any vector **A** subtends an angle θ with X-axis, then its

horizontal component, $A_x = A\cos\theta$

and vertical component, $A_y = A\sin\theta$

Magnitude of vector, $A = \sqrt{A_x^2 + A_y^2}$

$$\tan\theta = \frac{A_y}{A_x}$$

$$\text{Angle, } \theta = \tan^{-1}\left(\frac{A_y}{A_x}\right)$$

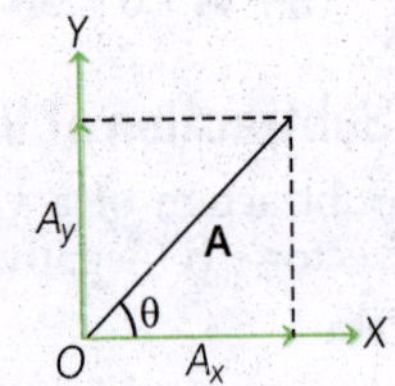

Direction Cosines of a Vector

If any vector **A** subtends angles α, β and γ with *X*-axis, *Y*-axis and *Z*-axis respectively, and its components along these axes are A_x, A_y and A_z, then

$$\cos\alpha = \frac{A_x}{A}, \quad \cos\beta = \frac{A_y}{A}, \quad \cos\gamma = \frac{A_z}{A}$$

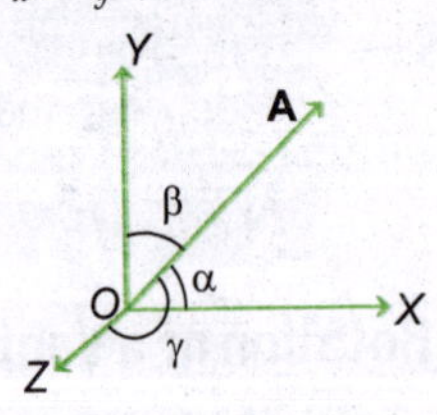

Then, $$\cos^2\alpha + \cos^2\beta + \cos^2\gamma = 1$$

Knowledge Booster

Multiplication of a Vector

1. **By a Real Number** When a vector **A** is multiplied by a real number *n*, then its magnitude becomes *n* times but direction and unit remains unchanged.
2. **By a Scalar** When a vector **A** is multiplied by a scalar *S*, then its magnitude becomes *S* times and unit is the product of units of **A** and *S* but direction remains same as that of vector **A**.

Division of Vectors by Scalars The division of vector **A** by a non-zero scalar *m* is defined as the multiplication of **A** by 1*m*. In this, the unit of resultant vector is the division of unit **A** and *m*.

Scalar or Dot Product of Two Vectors

The scalar product of two vectors is equal to the product of their magnitudes and the cosine of the smaller angle between them. It is denoted by · (dot).

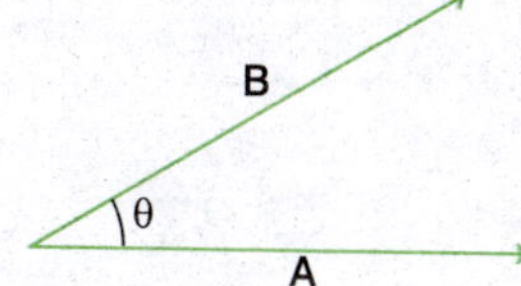

$$\mathbf{A} \cdot \mathbf{B} = AB \cos \theta$$

The scalar or dot product of two vectors is a scalar.

Properties of Scalar Product

(i) Scalar product is commutative,

i.e. $$\mathbf{A} \cdot \mathbf{B} = \mathbf{B} \cdot \mathbf{A}$$

(ii) Scalar product is distributive,

i.e. $$\mathbf{A} \cdot (\mathbf{B} + \mathbf{C}) = \mathbf{A} \cdot \mathbf{B} + \mathbf{A} \cdot \mathbf{C}$$

(iii) Scalar product of two perpendicular vectors is zero,

i.e. $$\mathbf{A} \cdot \mathbf{B} = AB \cos 90^\circ = 0$$

(iv) Scalar product of two parallel vectors or anti-parallel vectors is equal to the product of their magnitudes,

i.e. $\mathbf{A} \cdot \mathbf{B} = AB \cos 0^\circ = AB$ (for parallel)

$\mathbf{A} \cdot \mathbf{B} = AB \cos 180^\circ = -AB$ (for anti-parallel)

(v) Scalar product of a vector with itself is equal to the square of its magnitude,

i.e. $$\mathbf{A} \cdot \mathbf{A} = AA \cos 0^\circ = A^2$$

(vi) Scalar product of orthogonal unit vectors,

$$\hat{\mathbf{i}} \cdot \hat{\mathbf{i}} = \hat{\mathbf{j}} \cdot \hat{\mathbf{j}} = \hat{\mathbf{k}} \cdot \hat{\mathbf{k}} = 1$$

and
$$\hat{\mathbf{i}} \cdot \hat{\mathbf{j}} = \hat{\mathbf{j}} \cdot \hat{\mathbf{k}} = \hat{\mathbf{k}} \cdot \hat{\mathbf{i}} = 0$$

(vii) Scalar product in cartesian coordinates

$$\mathbf{A} \cdot \mathbf{B} = (A_x\hat{\mathbf{i}} + A_y\hat{\mathbf{j}} + A_z\hat{\mathbf{k}}) \cdot (B_x\hat{\mathbf{i}} + B_y\hat{\mathbf{j}} + B_z\hat{\mathbf{k}})$$
$$= A_x B_x + A_y B_y + A_z B_z$$

Vector or Cross Product of Two Vectors

The vector product of two vectors is equal to the product of their magnitudes and the sine of the smaller angle between them. It is denoted by × (cross).

$$\mathbf{A} \times \mathbf{B} = AB \sin\theta \, \hat{\mathbf{n}}$$

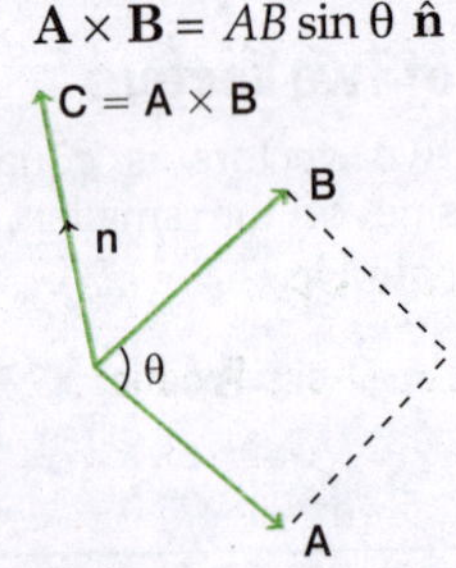

Properties of Vector Product

(i) Vector product is not commutative, *i.e.*

$$\mathbf{A} \times \mathbf{B} \neq \mathbf{B} \times \mathbf{A} \qquad [\because (\mathbf{A} \times \mathbf{B}) = -(\mathbf{B} \times \mathbf{A})]$$

(ii) Vector product is distributive, *i.e.*

$$\mathbf{A} \times (\mathbf{B} + \mathbf{C}) = \mathbf{A} \times \mathbf{B} + \mathbf{A} \times \mathbf{C}$$

(iii) Vector product of two parallel vectors is zero, *i.e.*

$$\mathbf{A} \times \mathbf{B} = AB \sin 0^\circ = 0$$

(iv) Vector product of any vector with itself is zero.

$$\mathbf{A} \times \mathbf{A} = AA \sin 0^\circ = 0$$

(v) Vector product of orthogonal unit vectors

$$\hat{\mathbf{i}} \times \hat{\mathbf{i}} = \hat{\mathbf{j}} \times \hat{\mathbf{j}} = \hat{\mathbf{k}} \times \hat{\mathbf{k}} = 0 \text{ and } \hat{\mathbf{i}} \times \hat{\mathbf{j}} = -\hat{\mathbf{j}} \times \hat{\mathbf{i}} = \hat{\mathbf{k}}$$
$$\hat{\mathbf{j}} \times \hat{\mathbf{k}} = -\hat{\mathbf{k}} \times \hat{\mathbf{j}} = \hat{\mathbf{i}}, \; \hat{\mathbf{k}} \times \hat{\mathbf{i}} = -\hat{\mathbf{i}} \times \hat{\mathbf{k}} = \hat{\mathbf{j}}$$

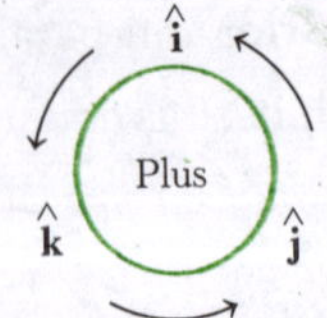

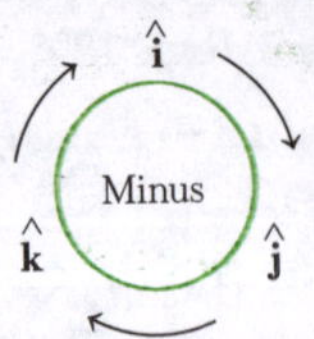

(vi) Vector product in cartesian coordinates

$$\mathbf{A} \times \mathbf{B} = (A_x\hat{\mathbf{i}} + A_y\hat{\mathbf{j}} + A_z\hat{\mathbf{k}}) \times (B_x\hat{\mathbf{i}} + B_y\hat{\mathbf{j}} + B_z\hat{\mathbf{k}})$$

$$= \begin{vmatrix} \hat{\mathbf{i}} & \hat{\mathbf{j}} & \hat{\mathbf{k}} \\ A_x & A_y & A_z \\ B_x & B_y & B_z \end{vmatrix}$$

$$= (A_yB_z - A_zB_y)\,\hat{\mathbf{i}} - (A_xB_z - B_xA_z)\,\hat{\mathbf{j}} + (A_xB_y - A_yB_x)\,\hat{\mathbf{k}}$$

(vii) A unit vector $(\hat{\mathbf{n}})$ perpendicular to **A** as well as **B** is given by

$$\hat{\mathbf{n}} = \frac{\mathbf{A} \times \mathbf{B}}{|\mathbf{A} \times \mathbf{B}|}$$

(viii) If **A, B** and **C** are co planar, then $[\mathbf{A} \cdot (\mathbf{B} \times \mathbf{C})] = 0$

(ix) Angle between $(\mathbf{A} + \mathbf{B})$ and $(\mathbf{A} \times \mathbf{B})$ is 90°.

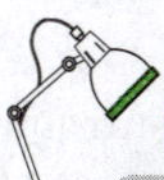

EXPERT Scale Up

Direction of Vector Cross Product

When $\mathbf{C} = \mathbf{A} \times \mathbf{B}$, the direction of **C** is at right angle to the plane containing the vectors **A** and **B**. The direction is determined by the right hand screw rule and right hand thumb rule.

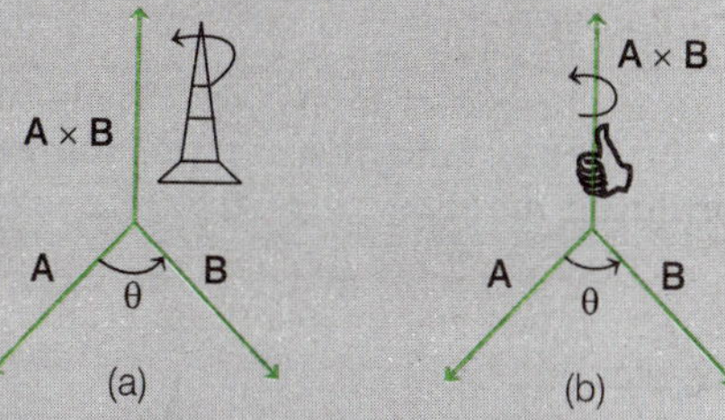

(i) **Right Hand Screw Rule** Rotate a right handed screw from first vector (**A**) towards second vector (**B**). The direction in which the right handed screw moves gives the direction of vector (**C**).

(ii) **Right Hand Thumb Rule** Curl the fingers of your right hand from **A** to **B**. Then, the direction of the erect thumb will point in the direction of $\mathbf{A} \times \mathbf{B}$.

Chapter 03

Motion in a Straight Line

Motion

If an object changes its position with respect to its surroundings with time, then it is called in motion.

Rest

If an object does not change its position with respect to its surroundings with time, then it is called at rest.

Point Object An object can be considered as a point object, if the distance travelled by it is very large in comparison to its dimensions.

Types of Motion

1. One Dimensional Motion

If only one out of three coordinates specifying the position of the object changes with respect to time, then the motion is called one dimensional motion or rectilinear motion.

For instance, motion of a block in a straight line, motion of a train along a straight track, a man walking on a level and narrow road and object falling under gravity, etc.

2. Two Dimensional Motion

If only two out of three coordinates specifying the position of the object change with respect to time, then the motion is called two dimensional motion.

A circular motion is an instance of two dimensional motion.

3. Three Dimensional Motion

If all the three coordinates specifying the position of the object change with respect to time, then the motion is called three dimensional motion. A few instances of three dimensional motion are flying bird, a flying kite, the random motion of gas molecule, etc.

Frame of Reference

The most convenient system is a rectangular coordinate system of three mutually perpendicular axes as X, Y, and Z. The point of intersection of these three axes is called origin (O) and considered as the reference point. The x,y,z-coordinates describe the position of an object w.r.t. the coordinate system. This coordinate system along with a clock constitutes a frame of reference.

Value Points

> Rest and motion are relative states. It means an object which is at rest in one frame of reference can be in motion in another frame of reference at the same time.

Distance or Path Length Covered

The length of the actual path covered by an object is called the distance. It is a scalar quantity and it can never be zero or negative during the motion of an object. Its SI unit is metre.

Displacement

The shortest distance between the initial and final positions of any object during motion is called displacement. The displacement of an object in a given time can be positive, zero or negative.

Displacement, $\Delta x = x_2 - x_1$

where, x_1 and x_2 are the initial and final positions of object, respectively. It is a vector quantity. Its SI unit is metre.

Speed

The time rate of change of position of the object in any direction is called speed of the object.

$$\text{Speed } (v) = \frac{\text{Distance travelled } (s)}{\text{Time taken } (t)}$$

Its SI unit is m/s.

It is a scalar quantity.

Its dimensional formula is $[M^0LT^{-1}]$.

Uniform Speed

If an object covers equal distances in equal intervals of time, then its speed is called uniform speed.

Non-uniform or Variable Speed

If an object covers unequal distances in equal intervals of time and *vice-versa,* then its speed is called non-uniform or variable speed.

Average Speed

The ratio of the total distance travelled by the object to the total time taken is called average speed.

$$\text{Average speed} = \frac{\text{Total distance travelled}}{\text{Total time taken}}$$

If a particle travels distances $s_1, s_2, s_3, \ldots$ with speeds $v_1, v_2, v_3, \ldots$, then

$$\text{Average speed} = \frac{s_1 + s_2 + s_3 + \ldots}{\left(\frac{s_1}{v_1} + \frac{s_2}{v_2} + \frac{s_3}{v_3} + \ldots\right)}$$

If a particle travels equal distances $(s_1 = s_2 = s)$ with velocities v_1 and v_2, then

$$\text{Average speed} = \frac{2v_1v_2}{(v_1 + v_2)}$$

If a particle travels with speeds $v_1, v_2, v_3, \ldots$ during time intervals $t_1, t_2, t_3, \ldots$, then

$$\text{Average speed} = \frac{v_1t_1 + v_2t_2 + v_3t_3 + \ldots}{t_1 + t_2 + t_3 + \ldots}$$

If aparticle travels with speeds v_1 and v_2 for equal time intervals, i.e. $t_1 = t_2 = t$, then

$$\text{Average speed} = \frac{v_1 + v_2}{2}$$

Knowledge Booster

- When a body travels equal distance with speeds v_1 and v_2, the average speed (v) is the harmonic mean of the two speeds, i.e.

$$\frac{2}{v} = \frac{1}{v_1} + \frac{1}{v_2}$$

- If speed is continuously changing with time, $v_{av} = \frac{\int v\,dt}{\int dt}$
- If speed is continuously changing with position, $v_{av} = \frac{\int v\,dx}{\int dx}$

Instantaneous Speed

When an object is travelling with variable speed, then its speed at a given instant of time is called its instantaneous speed.

$$\text{Instantaneous speed} = \lim_{\Delta t \to 0} \frac{\Delta s}{\Delta t} = \frac{ds}{dt}$$

Velocity

The time rate of change of displacement of an object in a particular direction is called its velocity.

$$\text{Velocity} = \frac{\text{Displacement}}{\text{Time taken}}$$

Its SI unit is m/s.

Its dimensional formula is $[M^0LT^{-1}]$.

It is a vector quantity, as it has the both, magnitude and direction.

The velocity of an object can be positive, zero or negative.

Uniform Velocity

If an object undergoes equal displacements in equal intervals of time, then it is said to be moving with a uniform velocity.

Non-uniform or Variable Velocity

If an object undergoes unequal displacements in equal intervals of time, then it is said to be moving with a non-uniform or variable velocity.

Average Velocity

The ratio of the total displacement to the total time taken is called average velocity.

$$\text{Average velocity} = \frac{\text{Total displacement}}{\text{Total time taken}}$$

Instantaneous Velocity

The velocity of a particle at an instant of time t is known as instantaneous velocity.

$$\text{Instantaneous velocity} = \lim_{\Delta t \to 0} \frac{\Delta x}{\Delta t} = \frac{dx}{dt}$$

Competition Insight

Relative Velocity

Relative velocity of one object with respect to another object is the time rate of change of relative position of one object with respect to another object.

Relative velocity of object A with respect to object B

$$\mathbf{v}_{AB} = \mathbf{v}_A - \mathbf{v}_B$$

If it is in one dimensional motion, we can treat vectors as scalars just by assigning the positive sign to one direction and negative to others.

When two objects are moving in the same direction, then

$$\mathbf{v}_{AB} = \mathbf{v}_A - \mathbf{v}_B$$

or

$$v_{AB} = v_A - v_B$$

When two objects are moving in opposite direction, then

$$\mathbf{v}_{AB} = \mathbf{v}_A + \mathbf{v}_B$$

or

$$v_{AB} = v_A + v_B$$

When two objects are moving at an angle θ, then

$$v_{AB} = \sqrt{v_A^2 + v_B^2 - 2v_A v_B \cos\theta}$$

and

$$\tan\beta = \frac{v_B \sin\theta}{v_A - v_B \cos\theta}$$

Acceleration

The rate of change of velocity with time is called acceleration.

$$\text{Acceleration } (a) = \frac{\text{Change in velocity } (\Delta v)}{\text{Time interval } (\Delta t)}$$

Its SI unit is m/s^2.

Its dimensional formula is $[M^0LT^{-2}]$.

It is a vector quantity.

Value Points

- Acceleration can be positive, zero or negative.
- **Positive acceleration** means velocity is increasing with time.
- **Zero acceleration** means velocity is uniform.
- **Negative acceleration** (retardation) means velocity is decreasing with time.

Uniform Acceleration

If an object is moving with uniform acceleration, it means that the change in velocity is equal for equal interval of time.

Non-uniform Acceleration

If an object is moving with non-uniform acceleration, it means that the change in velocity is unequal for equal interval of time.

Average Acceleration

If a particle is accelerated for a time t_1 with acceleration a_1 and for a time t_2 with acceleration a_2, then average acceleration,

$$a_{av} = \frac{a_1 t_1 + a_2 t_2}{t_1 + t_2}$$

Instantaneous Acceleration

It is defined as the acceleration of object at any instant of time.

$$a_{inst} = \lim_{\Delta t \to 0} \frac{\Delta v}{\Delta t} = \frac{dv}{dt}$$

EXPERT Scale Up

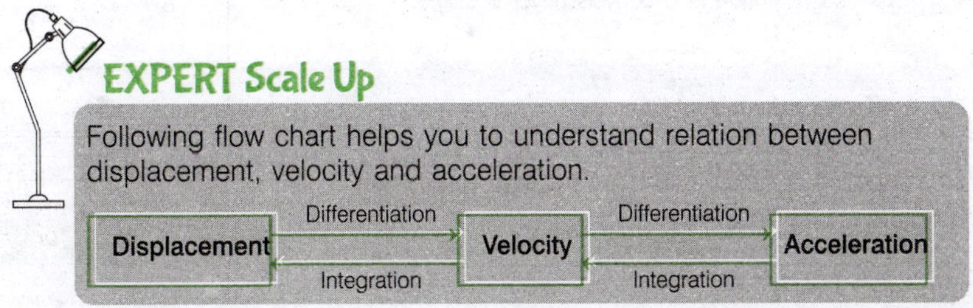

Uniform Motion

If an object moving along the straight line covers equal distance in equal interval of time, it is said to be in uniform motion along a straight line.

Different Graphs of Motion

Displacement-Time Graph

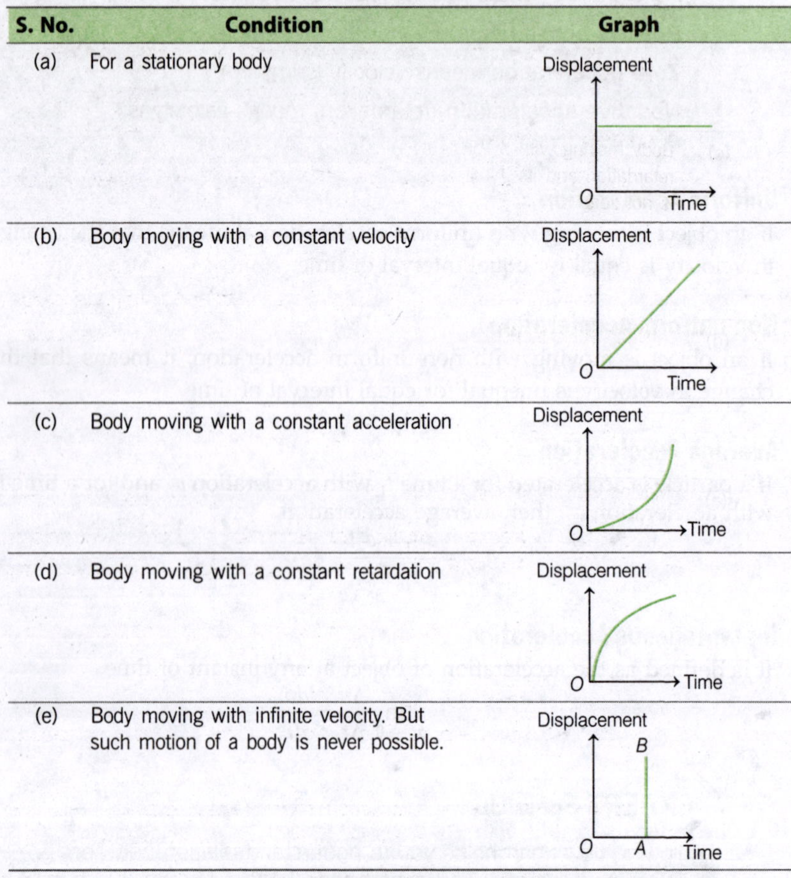

S. No.	Condition	Graph
(a)	For a stationary body	Displacement, O, Time
(b)	Body moving with a constant velocity	Displacement, O, Time
(c)	Body moving with a constant acceleration	Displacement, O, Time
(d)	Body moving with a constant retardation	Displacement, O, Time
(e)	Body moving with infinite velocity. But such motion of a body is never possible.	Displacement, B, O, A, Time

Velocity-Time Graph

S. No.	Condition	Graph
(a)	Moving with a constant velocity	Velocity, O, Time

S. No.	Condition	Graph
(b)	Moving with a constant acceleration having zero initial velocity	Velocity, O, Time
(c)	Body moving with a constant retardation and its initial velocity is not zero	Velocity, A, B, O, Time
(d)	Moving with a constant retardation with zero initial velocity	Velocity, O, Time
(e)	Moving with increasing acceleration	Velocity, O, Time
(f)	Moving with decreasing acceleration	Velocity, O, Time

Acceleration-Time Graph

S. No.	Condition	Graph
(a)	When object is moving with constant acceleration	Acceleration, O, Time

S. No.	Condition	Graph
(b)	When object is moving with uniformly increasing acceleration	Acceleration, O, Time
(c)	When object is moving with uniformly decreasing acceleration	Acceleration, O, Time

Value Points

Slope of displacement-time graph gives average velocity.

Slope of velocity-time graph gives average acceleration.

Equations of Uniformly Accelerated Motion

If a body starts with velocity u and after time t its velocity changes to v, if the uniform acceleration is a and the distance travelled in time t is s, then the following relations are obtained, which are called equations of uniformly accelerated motion :

(i) $v = u + at$ (ii) $s = ut + \frac{1}{2}at^2$

(iii) $v^2 = u^2 + 2as$

- Distance travelled in nth second,

$$s_n = u + \frac{a}{2}(2n - 1)$$

- If a body moves with uniform acceleration and velocity changes from u to v in a time interval, then the velocity at the mid-point of its path,

$$V_{\text{mid}} = \frac{\sqrt{u^2 + v^2}}{2}$$

Non-Uniformly Accelerated Motion

When change in velocity is unequal for equal interval of time, then motion is called non-uniformlly accelerated motion.

For one dimensional motion,

$$v = \lim_{\Delta t \to 0} \frac{\Delta s}{\Delta t} = \frac{ds}{dt}$$

$$a = \lim_{\Delta t \to 0} \frac{\Delta v}{\Delta t} = \frac{dv}{dt}$$

$$= v \cdot \frac{dv}{ds} = \frac{d^2 s}{dt^2}$$

where, Δs is displacement in time Δt, Δv is velocity in time Δt and a is instantaneous acceleration.

In component form,

$$\mathbf{a} = a_x \cdot \hat{\mathbf{i}} + a_y \cdot \hat{\mathbf{j}} + a_z \cdot \hat{\mathbf{k}}$$

where, $a_x = \frac{dv_x}{dt}$, $a_y = \frac{dv_y}{dt}$ and $a_z = \frac{dv_z}{dt}$

Motion Under Gravity

If an object is falling freely ($u = 0$) under gravity, then equations of motion becomes

(i) $v = u + gt$ (ii) $h = ut + \frac{1}{2} gt^2$ (iii) $v^2 = u^2 + 2gh$

- If an object is thrown upward, then g is replaced by $-g$ in above three equations.

It thus follows that:

(i) Time taken to reach maximum height, $t_A = \frac{u}{g} = \sqrt{\frac{2h}{g}}$

(ii) Maximum height reached by the body, $h_{max} = \frac{u^2}{2g}$

(iii) A ball is dropped from a building of height h and it reaches after t seconds on the earth. From the same building, if two balls are thrown (one upwards and other downwards) with the same velocity u and they reach the earth surface after t_1 and t_2 seconds respectively, then

$$t = \sqrt{t_1 t_2}$$

(iv) When a body is dropped freely from the top of a tower and another body is projected horizontally from the same point, both will reach the ground at the same time.

Chapter 04

Motion in a Plane

(Projectile and Circular Motion)

Motion in a Plane

Motion in plane is called as motion in two dimensions, *e.g.* Projectile motion, circular motion. For the analysis of such motions, our reference will be made of an origin and two coordinate axes X and Y.

Terms Related to Motion in a Plane

Few terms related to motion in a plane are given below

1. Position Vector

A vector that extends from a reference point to the point at which particle is located is called position vector.

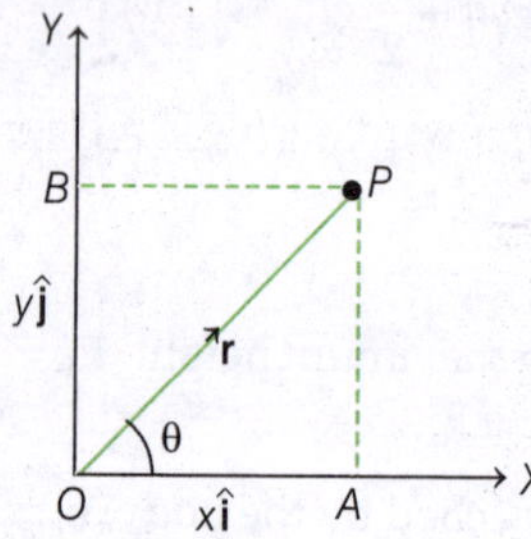

Position vector is given by $\mathbf{r} = x\hat{\mathbf{i}} + y\hat{\mathbf{j}}$

Direction of this position vector $\mathbf{r}$ is given by the angle θ with X-axis where, $\tan\theta = \dfrac{y}{x}$

In three dimensions, the position vector is represented as

$$\mathbf{r} = x\hat{\mathbf{i}} + y\hat{\mathbf{j}} + z\hat{\mathbf{k}}$$

2. Displacement Vector

The displacement vector is a vector which gives the position of a point with reference to a point other than the origin of the coordinate system.

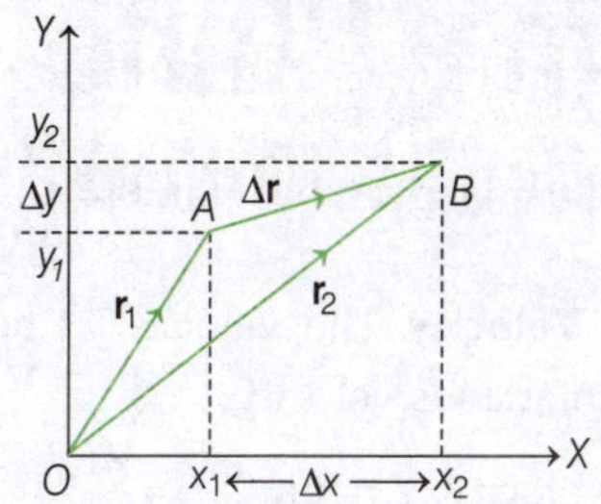

Displacement vector is given by

$$\Delta r = (x_2 - x_1)\hat{\mathbf{i}} + (y_2 - y_1)\hat{\mathbf{j}}$$

Magnitude of displacement vector

$$|\Delta \mathbf{r}| = \sqrt{(\Delta x)^2 + (\Delta y)^2}$$

$$= \sqrt{(x_2 - x_1)^2 + (y_2 - y_1)^2}$$

Direction of the displacement vector $\Delta \mathbf{r}$ is given by

$$\tan\theta = \frac{\Delta y}{\Delta x}$$

 **Value Point**

In three dimensions, the displacement vector can be represented as

$$\Delta \mathbf{r} = (x_2 - x_1)\hat{\mathbf{i}} + (y_2 - y_1)\hat{\mathbf{j}} + (z_2 - z_1)\hat{\mathbf{k}}$$

3. Velocity Vector

Velocity of an object in motion is defined as the ratio of displacement and the corresponding time interval taken by the object.

(i) **Average Velocity** It is defined as the ratio of the displacement and the corresponding time interval.

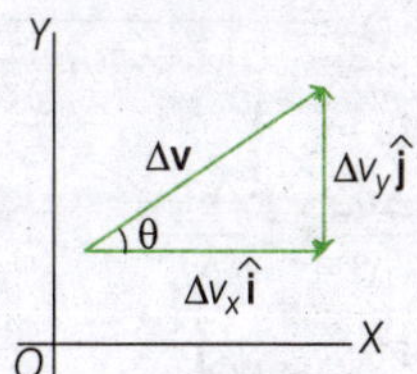

Average velocity, $\mathbf{v}_{\text{av}} = \dfrac{\Delta \mathbf{r}}{\Delta t} = \dfrac{r_2 - r_1}{t_2 - t_1}$

Average velocity can be expressed in the component forms as

$$\mathbf{v}_{\text{av}} = \frac{\Delta x}{\Delta t}\hat{\mathbf{i}} + \frac{\Delta y}{\Delta t}\hat{\mathbf{j}} = \Delta v_x \hat{\mathbf{i}} + \Delta v_y \hat{\mathbf{j}}$$

The direction of v_{av} is given by $\tan\theta = \dfrac{\Delta v_y}{\Delta v_x}$

(ii) **Instantaneous Velocity** The velocity at an instant of time (t) is known as instantaneous velocity.

Instantaneous velocity, $\mathbf{v} = \lim_{\Delta t \to 0} \dfrac{\Delta r}{\Delta t} = \dfrac{dr}{dt}$

$$\mathbf{v} = \frac{dx}{dt}\hat{\mathbf{i}} + \frac{dy}{dt}\hat{\mathbf{j}}$$

$$\mathbf{v} = v_x \hat{\mathbf{i}} + v_y \hat{\mathbf{j}}$$

Magnitude of instantaneous velocity,

$$|\mathbf{v}| = \sqrt{v_x^2 + v_y^2}$$

Direction of $\mathbf{v}$ is given by $\tan\theta = \left(\dfrac{v_y}{v_x}\right)$

4. Acceleration Vector

It is defined as the rate of change of velocity.

(i) **Average Acceleration** It is defined as the change in velocity (Δv) divided by the corresponding time interval (Δt).

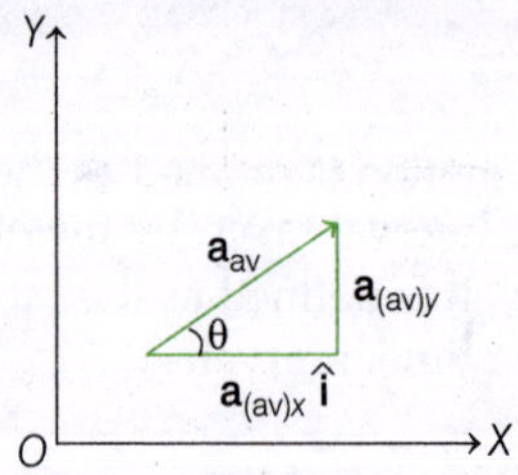

Average acceleration,

$$\mathbf{a}_{\text{av}} = \frac{\Delta v}{\Delta t} = \frac{\Delta v_x}{\Delta t}\hat{\mathbf{i}} + \frac{\Delta v_y}{\Delta t}\hat{\mathbf{j}}$$

$$\mathbf{a}_{\text{av}} = a_{(\text{av})x}\hat{\mathbf{i}} + a_{(\text{av})y}\hat{\mathbf{j}}$$

Magnitude of average acceleration is given by

$$|\mathbf{a}_{av}| = \sqrt{(a_{(av)\,x})^2 + (a_{(av)\,y})^2}$$

Angle θ made by average acceleration with X-axis is

$$\tan\theta = \frac{a_{(av)y}}{a_{(av)x}}$$

(ii) **Instantaneous Acceleration** It is defined as the limiting value of the average acceleration as the time interval approaches to zero.

Instantaneous acceleration, $\mathbf{a} = \lim\limits_{\Delta t \to 0} \dfrac{d\mathbf{v}}{dt}$

$$\mathbf{a} = a_x\hat{\mathbf{i}} + a_y\hat{\mathbf{j}}$$

If acceleration a makes an angle θ with X-axis then, $\tan\theta = \left(\dfrac{a_y}{a_x}\right)$

Value Points

Angle between a and v	Speed of the particle
0° to 90°	Increases
90° to 180°	Decreases
Equal to 90°	Remains constant

Motion in a Plane with Uniform Acceleration

A body is said to be moving with uniform acceleration, if its velocity vector suffers the same change in the same interval of time (however small).

According to definition of average acceleration, we have

$$\mathbf{a} = \frac{\mathbf{v} - \mathbf{v}_0}{t - 0} = \frac{\mathbf{v} - \mathbf{v}_0}{t}$$

$$\mathbf{v} = \mathbf{v}_0 + at$$

In terms of rectangular component, we can express it as

$$\mathbf{v}_x = \mathbf{v}_{0x} + \mathbf{a}_x t \quad \text{and} \quad \mathbf{v}_y = \mathbf{v}_{0y} + \mathbf{a}_y t$$

Path of Particle Under Constant Acceleration

Now, we can also find the position vector (**r**). Let $\mathbf{r}_0$ and **r** be the position vectors of the particle at time $t = 0$ and $t = t$ and their velocities at these instants be $\mathbf{v}_0$ and **v**, respectively. Then, the average velocity is given by

$$\mathbf{v}_{av} = \frac{\mathbf{v}_0 + \mathbf{v}}{2}$$

Displacement is the product of average velocity and time interval.

It is expressed as

$$\mathbf{r}-\mathbf{r}_0=\left(\frac{\mathbf{v}+\mathbf{v}_0}{2}\right)t=\left[\frac{(\mathbf{v}_0+\mathbf{a}t)+\mathbf{v}_0}{2}\right]t$$

$$\Rightarrow \qquad \mathbf{r}-\mathbf{r}_0=\mathbf{v}_0\,t+\frac{1}{2}\,\mathbf{a}t^2$$

$$\Rightarrow \qquad \mathbf{r}=\mathbf{r}_0+\mathbf{v}_0\,t+\frac{1}{2}\,\mathbf{a}t^2$$

In terms of rectangular components, we have

$$x\hat{\mathbf{i}}+y\hat{\mathbf{j}}=x_0\hat{\mathbf{i}}+y_0\hat{\mathbf{j}}+(v_{0x}\hat{\mathbf{i}}+v_{0y}\hat{\mathbf{j}})\,t+\frac{1}{2}(a_x\hat{\mathbf{i}}+a_y\hat{\mathbf{j}})t^2$$

Now, equating the coefficients of $\hat{\mathbf{i}}$ and $\hat{\mathbf{j}}$,

$$x=x_0+v_{0x}t+\frac{1}{2}a_xt^2 \text{ .... along } X\text{-axis}$$

and $$y=y_0+v_{0y}t+\frac{1}{2}a_yt^2 \text{....... along } Y\text{-axis}$$

EXPERT Scale Up

Motion in a plane (two-dimensional motion) can be treated as two separate simultaneous one-dimensional motions with constant acceleration along two perpendicular directions.

Projectile Motion and Circular Motion

Projectile Motion

When an object is thrown from horizontal at an angle θ except 90°, then it moves on a parabolic path known as its **trajectory,** the object is called **projectile** and its motion is called **projectile motion.** If any object is thrown with velocity u, making an angle θ from horizontal, then

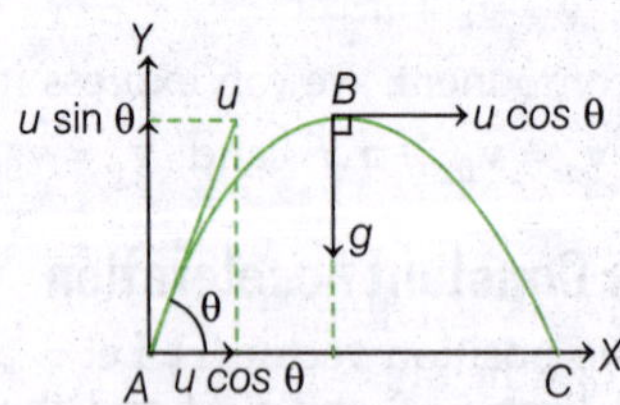

Horizontal component of initial velocity = u cos θ.

Vertical component of initial velocity = u sin θ.

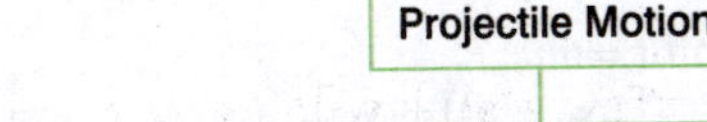

Projectile Motion

Time of Flight

Total time for which projectile is in flight, i.e. time during the motion of projectile is from A to C

Total time of flight,

$$T = \frac{2u \sin\theta}{g}$$

Maximum Height

The maximum vertical height attained by an object above the point of projection during its flight.

Maximum height,

$$H = \frac{u^2 \sin^2\theta}{2g}$$

Horizontal Range

The horizontal range is the horizontal distance covered by the projectile during its time of flight.

Horizontal range, $R = \frac{u^2 \sin 2\theta}{g}$

Here, maximum horizontal range,

$$R_{max} = \frac{u^2}{g} \qquad [\because \theta = 45°]$$

Value Points

- Horizontal component of velocity ($u \cos \theta$) remains same during the whole journey as no force is acting horizontally.
- Vertical component of velocity ($u \sin \theta$) decreases gradually and becomes zero at highest point of the path.
- At highest point, the velocity of the body is $u \cos \theta$ in horizontal direction and the angle between the velocity and acceleration is 90°.

Important Points and Formulae of Projectile Motion

(i) At highest point, the linear momentum is $mu \cos \theta$ and the kinetic energy is $\frac{1}{2} m(u \cos \theta)^2$.

(ii) The horizontal displacement of the projectile after t seconds,

$$x = (u \cos \theta)t$$

(iii) The vertical displacement of the projectile after t seconds,

$$y = (u \sin \theta)t - \frac{1}{2} gt^2$$

(iv) Equation of the path of projectile,

$$y = x \tan \theta - \frac{g}{2u^2 \cos^2 \theta} x^2$$

(v) The path of a projectile is parabolic.

(vi) Velocity of the projectile at any instant t,

$$|\mathbf{v}| = \sqrt{u^2 + g^2t^2 - 2ugt \sin \theta}$$

(vii) Kinetic energy at the lowest point $= \frac{1}{2} mu^2$

(viii) Linear momentum at lowest point $= mu$

(ix) Acceleration of projectile is constant throughout the motion and it acts vertically downwards being equal to g.

(x) Angular momentum of projectile about origin $= mu \cos \theta \times H$, where H denotes the maximum height.

(xi) In case of angular projection, the angle between velocity and acceleration varies from $0° < \theta < 180°$.

EXPERT Scale Up

- The projectile attains maximum height when it covers a horizontal distance equal to half of the horizontal range, *i.e.* at (R/2).
- When the maximum range of projectile is R, then its maximum height is R/4.
- Horizontal range is maximum when it is thrown at an angle of 45° from the horizontal, *i.e.* $R_{max} = \frac{u^2}{g}$
- For angle of projection θ and (90° – θ), the horizontal range is same.
- The shape of trajectory of the motion of particle does not depend onlyon acceleration but also depends on initial condition of motion (initial position and initial velocity).

Projectile Projected at an Angle θ with the Vertical

Let a particle be projected vertically with an angle θ with vertical and speed of projection is u.

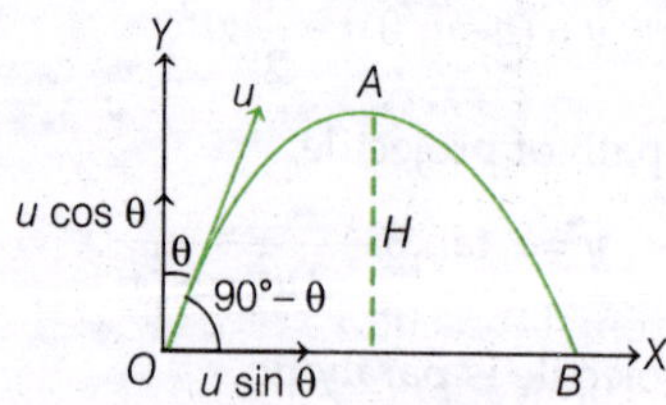

Time of flight, $T = \frac{2u \sin (90° - \theta)}{g} = \frac{2u \cos \theta}{g}$

Maximum height, $H = \frac{u^2 \sin^2 (90° - \theta)}{2g} = \frac{u^2 \cos^2 \theta}{2g}$

Horizontal range, $R = \dfrac{u^2 \sin(180^\circ - 2\theta)}{g} = \dfrac{u^2 \sin 2\theta}{g}$

Equation of the path of projectile, $y = x \cot\theta - \dfrac{gx^2}{2u^2 \sin^2\theta}$

Projectile Projected from Some Height

1. When Projectile Projected Horizontally

Initial velocity in vertical direction $= 0$

Time of flight, $T = \sqrt{\dfrac{2H}{g}}$

Horizontal range, $x = uT = u\sqrt{\dfrac{2H}{g}}$

Vertical velocity after t seconds,

$$v_y = gt \qquad (\because u_y = 0)$$

Velocity of projectile after t seconds,

$$v = \sqrt{v_x^2 + v_y^2} = \sqrt{u^2 + (gt)^2}$$

If velocity makes an angle ϕ from horizontal, then

$$\tan\phi = \frac{v_y}{v_x} = \frac{gt}{u}$$

Equation of the path of projectile, $y = \dfrac{g}{2u^2} x^2$

2. When Projectile Projected Downward at an Angle θ with Horizontal

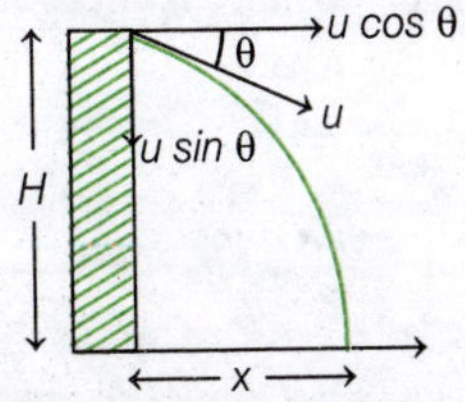

Initial velocity in horizontal direction $= u \cos\theta$

Initial velocity in vertical direction $= -u \sin\theta$

$$\text{Time of flight, } T = -\frac{2u \sin\theta}{2g} \pm \frac{\sqrt{4u^2 \sin^2\theta + 8gh}}{2g}$$

Horizontal range, $x = (u \cos \theta) T$

Vertical velocity after t seconds, $v_y = u \sin \theta + gt$

Velocity of projectile after t seconds,

$$v = \sqrt{v_x^2 + v_y^2} = \sqrt{(u \cos \theta)^2 + (u \sin \theta + gt)^2}$$

$$= \sqrt{u^2 + (gt)^2 + 2ugt \sin \theta}$$

3. When Projectile Projected Upward at an Angle θ with Horizontal

Initial velocity in horizontal direction $= u \cos \theta$

Initial velocity in vertical direction $= u \sin \theta$

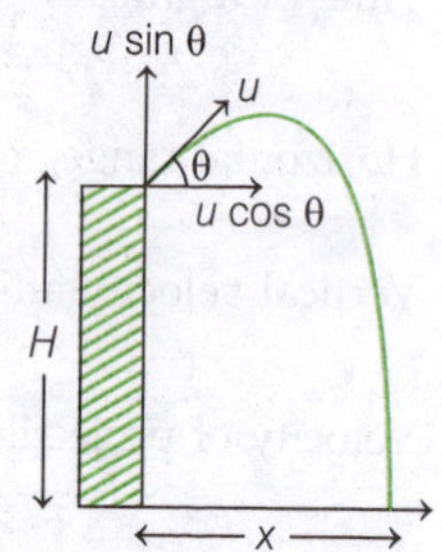

Time of flight, $T = \dfrac{u \sin \theta}{g} \pm \sqrt{\dfrac{u^2 \sin^2 \theta}{g^2} + \dfrac{2h}{g}}$

Horizontal range, $x = (u \cos \theta) T$

Vertical velocity after t seconds, $v_y = (-u \sin \theta) + gt$

Velocity of projectile after t seconds,

$$v = \sqrt{v_x^2 + v_y^2} = \sqrt{(u \cos \theta)^2 + (gt - u \sin \theta)^2}$$

$$= \sqrt{u^2 + (gt)^2 - 2ugt \sin \theta}$$

Knowledge Booster

Projectile Motion on an Inclined Plane

- When an object is thrown with velocity u making an angle α from horizontal, at a plane inclined at an angle β from horizontal, then

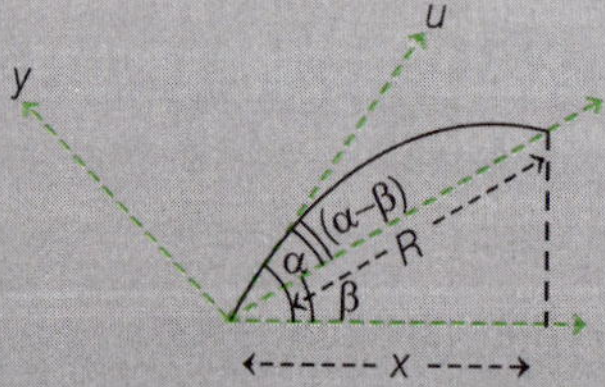

- Initial velocity along the inclined plane $= u \cos (\alpha - \beta)$
- Initial velocity perpendicular to the inclined plane $= u \sin (\alpha - \beta)$
- Acceleration along the inclined plane $= g \sin \beta$
- Acceleration perpendicular to the inclined plane $= g \cos \beta$

- Time of flight, $T = \dfrac{2u \sin(\alpha - \beta)}{g \cos \beta}$
- Maximum height, $H = \dfrac{u^2 \sin^2(\alpha - \beta)}{2g \cos \beta}$
- Horizontal range, $x = \dfrac{2u^2 \sin(\alpha - \beta)\cos \alpha}{g \cos \beta}$
- Range on inclined plane, $R = \dfrac{x}{\cos \beta} = \dfrac{2u^2 \sin(\alpha - \beta)\cos \alpha}{g \cos^2 \beta}$
- Range on inclined plane will be maximum, when $\alpha = 45° + \dfrac{\beta}{2}$

$$R_{max} = \frac{u^2}{g(1 + \sin \beta)}$$

- For angle of projections α and $(90° - \alpha + \beta)$, the range on inclined plane are same.
- If the projectile is thrown downwards, then maximum range is

$$R_{max} = \frac{u^2}{g(1 - \sin \beta)}$$

Circular Motion

Circular motion is the movement of an object in a circular path.

(i) **Uniform Circular Motion** If the magnitude of the velocity of a particle in circular motion remains constant, then it is called uniform circular motion.

(ii) **Non-uniform Circular Motion** If the magnitude of the velocity of a particle in circular motion is not constant, then it is called non-uniform circular motion.

Value Points

A special kind of circular motion where an object rotates around itself is called as **spinning motion.**

Variables in Circular Motion

(i) **Angular Displacement** Angular displacement $\Delta\theta$ is the angle subtended by the position vector at the centre of the circular path.

$$\text{Angular displacement } (\Delta\theta) = \frac{\Delta s}{r}$$

where, Δs is the linear displacement and r is the radius.
Its SI unit is radian.

(ii) **Angular Velocity** The time rate of change of angular displacement $(\Delta\theta)$ is called angular velocity ω.

$$\text{Angular velocity } (\omega) = \frac{\Delta\theta}{\Delta t}$$

Angular velocity is a vector quantity and its SI unit is rad/s.

Relation between linear velocity (v) and angular velocity (ω) is given by

$$v = r\omega$$

(iii) **Angular Acceleration**The rate of change of angular velocity ω is called angular acceleration α.

$$\text{Angular acceleration } (\alpha) = \lim_{\Delta t \to 0} \frac{\Delta\omega}{\Delta t} = \frac{d\omega}{dt} = \frac{d^2\theta}{dt^2}$$

Its SI unit is rad/s^2 and dimensional formula is $[T^{-2}]$.

Relation between linear acceleration (a) and angular acceleration (α),

$$a = r\alpha$$

where, r = radius.

Relation between angular acceleration and linear velocity, $\alpha = \dfrac{v^2}{r}$

Non-uniform Horizontal Circular Motion

In non-uniform horizontal circular motion, the magnitude of the velocity of the body changes with time.

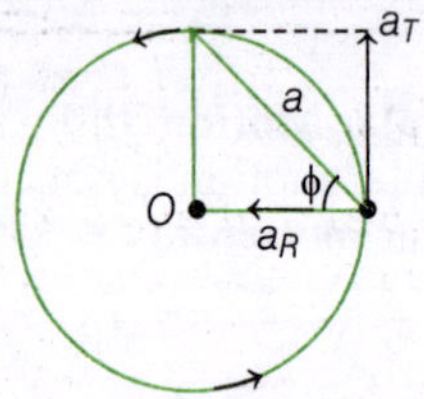

In this condition, a centripetal (radial) acceleration (a_R) acts towards centre and a tangential acceleration (a_T) acts towards tangent.

Both accelerations act perpendicular to each other.

$$\text{Resultant acceleration, } a = \sqrt{a_R^2 + a_T^2} = \sqrt{\left(\frac{v^2}{r}\right)^2 + (r\alpha)^2}$$

and $\tan\phi = \frac{a_T}{a_R} = \frac{r^2\alpha}{v^2}$

where, α is the angular acceleration, r is the radius and v is the velocity.

Kinematic Equations in Circular Motion

Relations between different variables for an object executing circular motion are called kinematic equations in circular motion.

(i) $\omega = \omega_0 + \alpha t$

(ii) $\theta = \omega_0 t + \frac{1}{2}\alpha t^2$

(iii) $\omega^2 = \omega_0^2 + 2\alpha\theta$

(iv) $\theta_t = \omega_0 + \frac{1}{2}\alpha(2t-1)$

(v) $\theta = \left(\frac{\omega + \omega_0}{2}\right)t$

where, ω_0 = initial angular velocity, ω = final angular velocity,
α = angular acceleration, θ = angular displacement,
θ_t = angular displacement at t seconds and t = time.

Centripetal Acceleration

In circular motion, an acceleration acts on the body, whose direction is always towards the centre of the path. This acceleration is called centripetal acceleration.

Centripetal acceleration, $a = \frac{v^2}{r} = r\omega^2$

Centripetal acceleration is also called radial acceleration as it acts along radius of circle.

Its unit is m/s^2 and it is a vector quantity.

Relative Velocity in Two-dimensions

If two objects A and B are moving with velocities $\mathbf{v}_A$ and $\mathbf{v}_B$ respectively (each with respect to some common frame of reference, say ground), then velocity of object A relative to that of B is

$$\mathbf{v}_{AB} = -\mathbf{v}_{BA}$$

If θ be the angle between $\mathbf{v}_A$ and $\mathbf{v}_B$, then

$$\mathbf{v}_{AB} = \sqrt{v_A^2 + v_B^2 - 2v_A v_B \cos\theta}$$

If the relative velocity v_{AB} makes an angle β with v_B, then

$$\beta = \tan^{-1}\left(\frac{v_B \sin\theta}{v_A - v_B \cos\theta}\right)$$

Rain-man Problems

If rain falls with velocity $\mathbf{v}_r$ relative to ground at an angle θ with vertical, the velocity of man relative to ground is $\mathbf{v}_m$, then the man should hold his umbrella in the direction of velocity of rain relative to man $\mathbf{v}_{rm}$, so that he may not get wet as shown in figure.

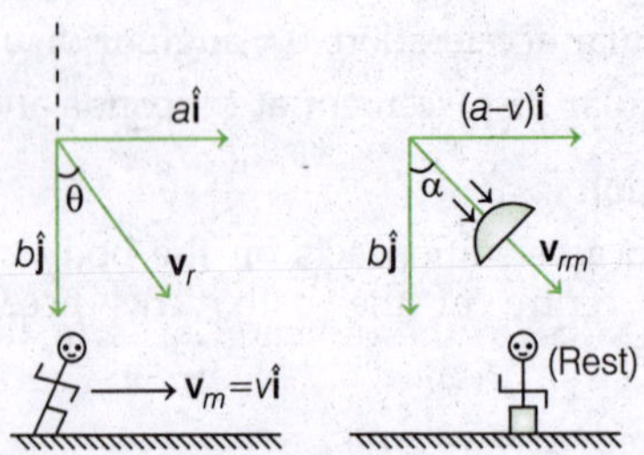

The velocity of rain with respect to man,

$$\mathbf{v}_{rm} = (a - v)\hat{\mathbf{i}} - b\hat{\mathbf{j}}$$

$\Rightarrow$

$$v_{rm} = \sqrt{(a - v)^2 + b^2}$$

The direction of umbrella is α given in the following table

$a > v$	$a = v$	$a < v$
$\tan\alpha = \dfrac{a-v}{b}$ 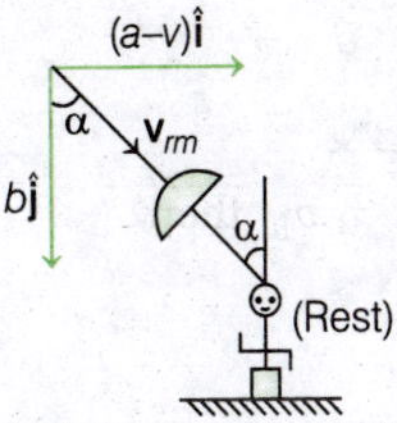 $(a-v)\hat{\mathbf{i}}$, α, $\mathbf{v}_{rm}$, $b\hat{\mathbf{j}}$, α, (Rest)	$\tan\alpha = 0$ $\Rightarrow \alpha = 0°$ ∴ Rain appears to fall vertically  $b\hat{\mathbf{j}}$	$\tan\alpha = \dfrac{v-a}{b}$ 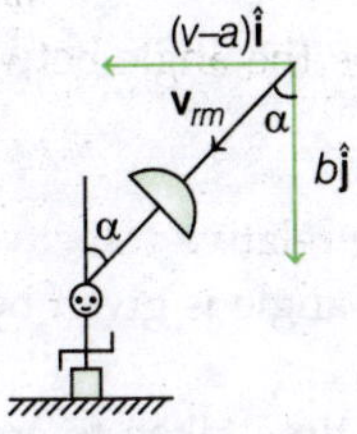 $(v-a)\hat{\mathbf{i}}$, $\mathbf{v}_{rm}$, α, $b\hat{\mathbf{j}}$, α

Swimmer-river Problems

If a swimmer swims in a river with velocity relative to river flow $\mathbf{v}_{sr}$ and the velocity of river is $\mathbf{v}_r$, then the velocity of swimmer with respect to ground,

$$\mathbf{v}_s = \mathbf{v}_{sr} + \mathbf{v}_r$$

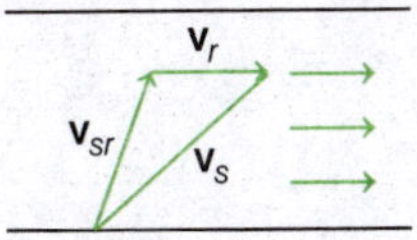

If a swimmer wants to cross a river with minimum possible time, then he should swim perpendicular to the direction of river flow such that the swimmer reaches at point C along the path AC shown in figure below.

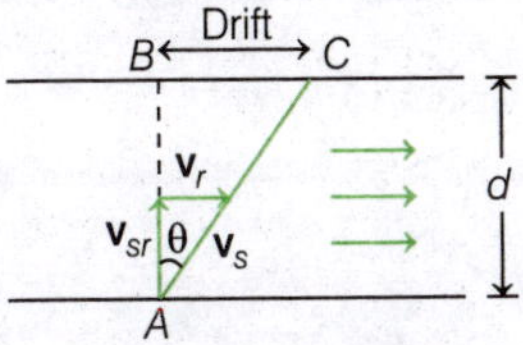

The minimum time required to cross the river, $t_{\min} = \dfrac{d}{v_{sr}}$

The drift BC is given by

$$\text{Drift} = BC = v_r \cdot t_{\min} = \left(\frac{v_r}{v_{sr}}\right) d$$

If a swimmer wants to cross a river along shortest possible path AB as shown in figure below, then he should swim at an angle $(90°+\theta)$ with the direction of river flow.

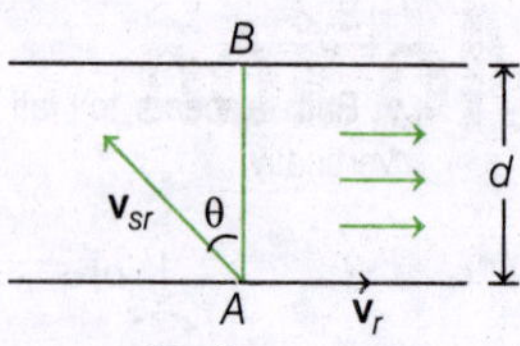

The angle is given by $\theta = \sin^{-1}\left(\frac{v_r}{v_{sr}}\right)$

The time taken to cross the river is given by

$$t = \frac{d}{v_{sr}\cos\theta} = \frac{d}{\sqrt{v_{sr}^2 - v_r^2}}$$

where, $\mathbf{v}_r$ = velocity of river flow,

$\mathbf{v}_{sr}$ = velocity of swimmer with respect to river or velocity of swimmer in still water and d = width of the river.

Chapter 05

Laws of Motion

Aristotle's Fallacy

Aristotelian law of motion is flawed, and it may be concluded as, An external force is required to keep a body in motion.

The opposing forces such as friction (in solids) and viscous force (in fluids) are always present in the natural world, so external forces are required to keep bodies in uniform motion.

Inertia

The property of an object by virtue of which it cannot change its state of rest or of uniform motion along a straight line on its own, is called **inertia**. Greater the mass of a body greater will be its inertia and *vice-versa.* Inertia is of three types

(i) **Inertia of rest** It is defined as the tendency of a body to remain in its position of rest. i.e. A body at rest remains at rest and can not start moving on its own.

(ii) **Inertia of motion** It is defined as the tendency of a body to remain in its state of uniform motion along a straight line, i.e., a body in uniform motion can neither gets accelerated nor gets retarded on its own, also it cannot stop on its own.

(iii) **Inertia of direction** It is defined as inability of a body to change its direction of motion by itself.

Force

Force is a push or pull which changes or tries to change the state of rest, the state of uniform motion, size or shape of a body.

Its SI unit is newton (N) and its dimensional formula is $[MLT^{-2}]$.

Forces can be categorised into two types:

(i) **Contact Forces** Frictional force, tensional force, spring force, normal force, etc. are the contact forces.

(ii) **Distant Forces** (Field Forces) Electrostatic force, gravitational force, magnetic force, etc. are action at a distant forces.

Types of force

- **Balance force** Forces that act on an object in such a way that they do not change the object's state of motion or rest.
- **Unbalanced force** Forces that act on an object in such a way that they do cause a change in the object's state of motion or rest.
- **Pseudo force** When an object is observed from a non-inertial frame, force observed on object due to acceleration of reference frame is called pseudo force.
- **Impulsive force** A force which acts on a body for a short interval of time and produces a large change in momentum is called an impulsive force.

Linear Momentum

The total amount of motion present in a body is called its momentum. Linear momentum of a body is equal to the product of its mass and velocity. It is denoted by p.

Linear momentum, $p = mv$.

Its SI unit is kg-m/s and dimensional formula is $[MLT^{-1}]$.

It is a vector quantity and its direction is in the direction of velocity of the body.

Law of Conservation of Linear Momentum

The total momentum of an isolated system (a system having no external force acting on it) of constant mass remains constant or conserved and does not change with time.

$$F_{\text{ext}} = 0 \Rightarrow \Delta p = 0 \quad \text{or} \quad p_i = p_f$$

Initial momentum = Final momentum

This principle is a consequence of Newton's second and third law of motion.

Linear momentum depends on the frame of reference but law of conservation of linear momentum is independent from frame of reference.

Newton's laws of motion are valid only in inertial frame of reference.

Impulse

The product of impulsive force and time for which it acts is called impulse.

Impulse = Force × Time = Change in momentum (Δp)

$$I = F\Delta t \quad \text{or} \quad I = \int_{t_1}^{t_2} F dt$$

Its SI unit is newton-second (N-S) or kg-m/s and its dimensional formula is $[MLT^{-1}]$. Impulse is also equal to change in momentum of the object. It is a vector quantity and its direction is in the direction of force.

Total impulse for the force applied during period t_1 to t_2 = Area under the F- t curve from t_1 to t_2.

Newton's Laws of Motion

(i) **Newton's First Law of Motion** A body continues to be in its state of rest or in uniform motion along a straight line unless an external force is applied on it.

This law is also called as **law of inertia**.

Examples

- When a carpet or a blanket is beaten with a stick, then the dust particles separate out from it.
- If a moving vehicle suddenly stops, then the passengers inside the vehicle bend outward.

(ii) **Newton's Second Law of Motion** The rate of change of linear momentum is proportional to the applied force and change in momentum takes place in the direction of applied force.

Mathematically, $\mathbf{F} \propto \frac{d\mathbf{p}}{dt} \Rightarrow \mathbf{F} = k\frac{d}{dt}(m\mathbf{v})$

where, k is a constant of proportionality and its value is one in SI and CGS system.

$$\mathbf{F} = \frac{md\mathbf{v}}{dt} = m\mathbf{a}$$

The second law of motion is a vector law. It is equivalent to three equations. One for each component of the vectors

$$F_x = \frac{dp_x}{dt} = m \cdot a_x$$

$$F_y = \frac{dp_y}{dt} = m \cdot a_y$$

$$F_z = \frac{dp_z}{dt} = m \cdot a_z$$

Examples

- It is easier for a strong adult to push a full shopping cart than it is for a baby to push the same cart (this is depending on the net force acting on the object)..

- It is easier for a person to push an empty shopping cart than a full one (this is depending on the mass of the object).

Value Points

Newton's second law of motion is called real law of motion because first and third laws of motion can be obtained from it.

(iii) **Newton's Third Law of Motion** For every action there is an equal and opposite reaction and both acts on two different bodies.

Forces always occur in pairs. If body *A* exerts a force on body *B*, an equal but opposite force is exerted by body *B* on body *A*.

Mathematically, $\mathbf{F}_{AB} = -\mathbf{F}_{BA}$

Examples

- Swimming becomes possible because of third law of motion.

$\mathbf{F}_{AB}$ $\mathbf{F}_{BA}$ (A → ← B)

- Jumping of a man from a boat onto the bank of a river.
- Jerk is produced in a gun when bullet is fired from it.
- Pulling of cart by a horse.

EXPERT Scale Up

The following caution points will help you in solving problems related to force.

- Force can have different directions relative to motion but is always parallel to acceleration.
- A body being momentarily at rest ($v = 0$) doesn't mean force or acceleration are necessarily zero.
- Force acting on a body depends on its current situation, not its past motion. It's not carried from earlier motion.

Rocket Rocket is an example of variable mass following law of conservation of momentum.

- **Thrust on the rocket at any instant,** $F = -u\dfrac{dM}{dt}$

where, u = exhaust speed of the burnt gases and $\dfrac{dM}{dt}$ = rate of combustion of fuel.

- **Velocity of rocket at any instant is given by** $v = v_0 + u \log_e \left(\frac{M_0}{M}\right)$

where, v_0 = initial velocity of the rocket,
M_0 = initial mass of the rocket
and M = present mass of the rocket.

- **If effect of gravity is taken into account, then speed of rocket,**

$$v = v_0 + u \log_e \left(\frac{M_0}{M}\right) - gt$$

Equilibrium of a Particle

When the vector sum of the forces acting on a body is zero, then the body is said to be in equilibrium.

If two forces $\mathbf{F}_1$ and $\mathbf{F}_2$ act on a particle, then they will be in equilibrium if $\mathbf{F}_1 + \mathbf{F}_2 = 0$.

Lami's Theorem

It states that, if three forces act on a particle in equilibrium, then each force is proportional to the sine of the angle between the other two forces.

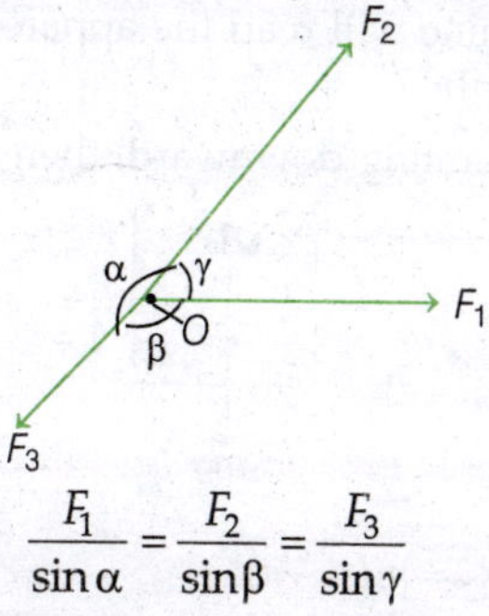

$$\frac{F_1}{\sin\alpha} = \frac{F_2}{\sin\beta} = \frac{F_3}{\sin\gamma}$$

Common Forces in Mechanics

Some of the common forces that we come across in mechanics are given as,

Weight (w)

It is a field force. It is the force with which a body is pulled towards the centre of the earth due to gravity. It has the magnitude mg, where m is the mass of the body and g is the acceleration due to gravity.

$$w = mg$$

Apparent Weight in a Lift

- When a lift is at rest or moving with a constant speed, then

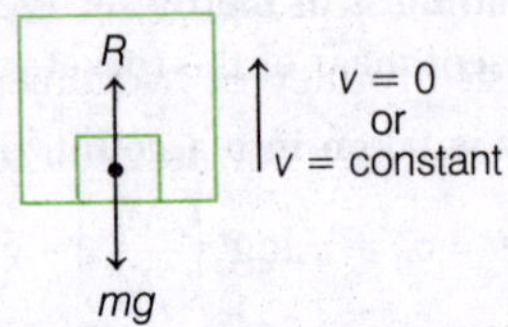

$$R = mg$$

The weighing machine will read the actual weight.

- When a lift is accelerating upward, then apparent weight,

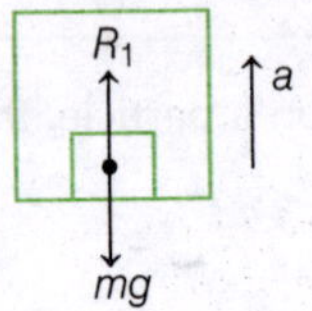

$$R_1 = m(g + a)$$

The weighing machine will read the apparent weight, which is more than the actual weight.

- When a lift is accelerating downward, then apparent weight,

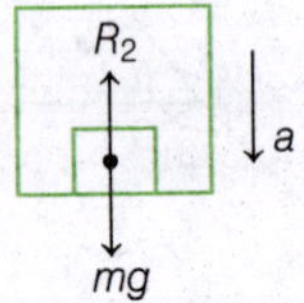

$$R_2 = m(g - a)$$

The weighing machine will read the apparent weight, which is less than the actual weight.

- When lift is falling freely under gravity, then

$$R_2 = m(g - g) = 0$$

The apparent weight of the body becomes zero.

- If lift is accelerating downward with an acceleration greater than g, then body will be lifted from floor to the ceiling of the lift.

Normal Reaction

It is a contact force. It is the force between two surfaces in contact, which is always perpendicular to the surfaces in contact.

Tension

Tension force always pulls a body.

Tension is a reactive force. It is not an active force.

Tension across a massless pulley or frictionless pulley remains constant.

Rope becomes slack when tension force becomes zero.

Spring Force

The resistive force developed in a spring when its length is changed, is called spring force.

$\therefore$ Spring force, $F = -kx$

where, x = change in length of the spring

and k = spring constant.

Friction

A force acting on the point of contact of the objects, which opposes the relative motion is called friction.

It acts parallel to the contact surfaces.

Frictional forces are produced due to intermolecular interactions acting between the molecules of the bodies in contact.

Friction is of three types:

1. Static Friction

It is an opposing force which comes into play when one body tends to move over the surface of the other body but actual motion is not taking place.

Static friction is a self-adjusting force which increases as the applied force is increased. Static friction opposes impending motion.

2. Limiting Friction

It is the maximum value of static friction when body is at the verge of starting motion.

$$\text{Limiting friction, } f_{s(\max)} = \mu_l R$$

where, μ_l = coefficient of limiting friction and R = normal reaction.

Limiting friction does not depend on area of contact surfaces but depends on their nature, *i.e.* smoothness or roughness.

Angle of Friction

It is the angle which the resultant of the force of limiting friction and the normal reaction(N) makes with the direction of N.

$$\mu_l = \tan\theta$$

Angle of Repose or Angle of Sliding

It is the minimum angle of inclination of a plane with the horizontal, such that a body placed on it, just begins to slide down.

If angle of repose is α and coefficient of limiting friction is μ_l, then

$$\mu_l = \tan\alpha$$

3. Kinetic Friction

It is an opposing force that comes into existence when one object is actually moving over the surface of other object.

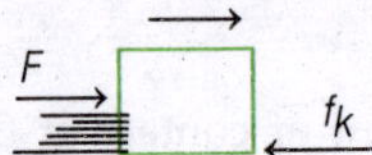

$$\text{Kinetic friction } (f_K) = \mu_K R$$

where, μ_K = coefficient of kinetic friction and R=normal reaction.

Kinetic friction is of two types:

(a) Sliding friction

(b) Rolling friction

As, rolling friction < sliding friction, therefore it is easier to roll a body than to slide.

Variation of friction force with applied force

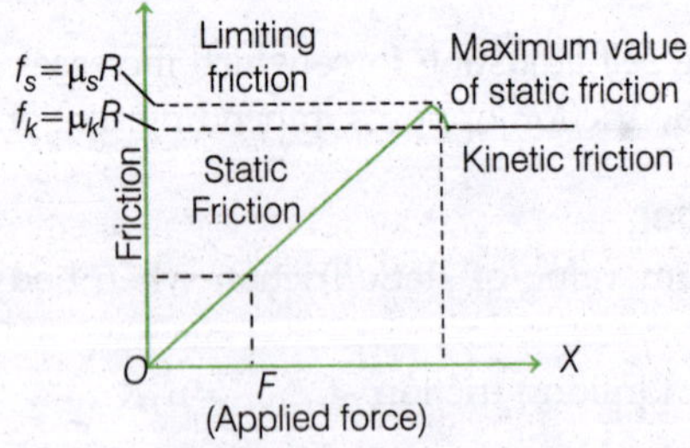

Motion on a Rough Inclined Plane

When an object moves along an inclined plane, then different forces act on it like normal reaction of plane, friction force acting in opposite direction of motion, etc.

Different relations for the motion are given below.

Normal reaction of plane, $R = mg \cos\theta$

and net force acting downward on the block, $F = mg \sin\theta - f$

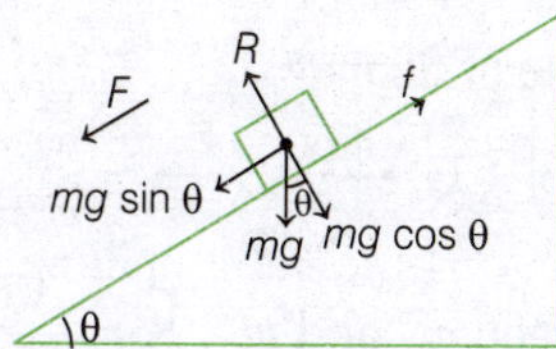

Acceleration on inclined plane, $a = g(\sin\theta - \mu \cos\theta)$

Value Points

When angle of inclination of the plane from horizontal is less than the angle of repose (α), then

- minimum force required to move the body up the inclined plane

$$F_1 = mg(\sin\theta + \mu\cos\theta)$$

- minimum force required to push the body down the inclined plane

$$F_2 = mg(\mu\cos\theta - \sin\theta)$$

Motion of Bodies in Contact

1. Two Bodies in Contact

If force F is applied on an object of mass m_1, then acceleration of the bodies,

$$a = \frac{F}{(m_1 + m_2)}$$

Contact force on $m_1 = m_1 a = \dfrac{m_1 F}{(m_1 + m_2)}$

Contact force on $m_2 = m_2 a = \dfrac{m_2 F}{(m_1 + m_2)}$

2. Three Bodies in Contact

If force F is applied on an object of mass m_1, then acceleration of the bodies, $a = \dfrac{F}{(m_1 + m_2 + m_3)}$

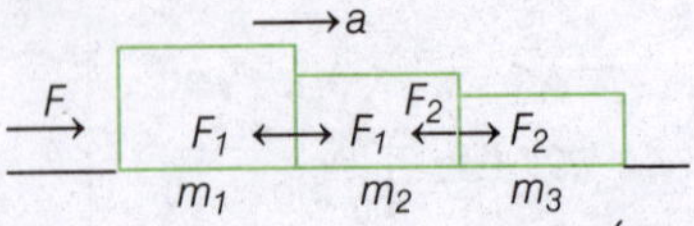

Contact force between m_1 and m_2, $F_1 = \dfrac{(m_2 + m_3)F}{(m_1 + m_2 + m_3)}$

Contact force between m_2 and m_3, $F_2 = \dfrac{m_3 F}{(m_1 + m_2 + m_3)}$

3. Motion of Two Bodies, One Resting on the Other

(a) The coefficient of friction between surface of A and B be μ. If a force F is applied on the lower body A, then common acceleration of two bodies

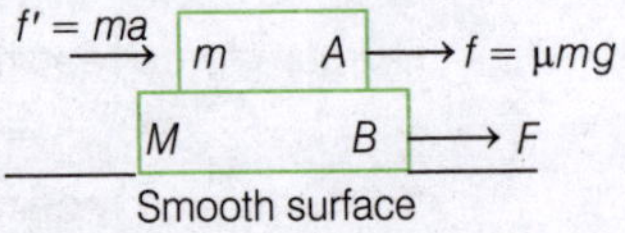

$$a = \frac{F}{(M + m)}$$

Pseudo force acting on block B due to the accelerated motion,

$$f' = ma$$

The pseudo force tends to produce a relative motion between bodies A and B and consequently a frictional force

$f = \mu N = \mu mg$ is developed.

For equilibrium, $ma \le \mu mg$ or $a \le \mu g$

(b) Let friction is also present between the ground surface and body A. Let the coefficient of friction between the given surface and body A is μ_1 and the coefficient of friction between the surfaces of bodies A and B is μ_2. If a force F is applied on the lower body A.

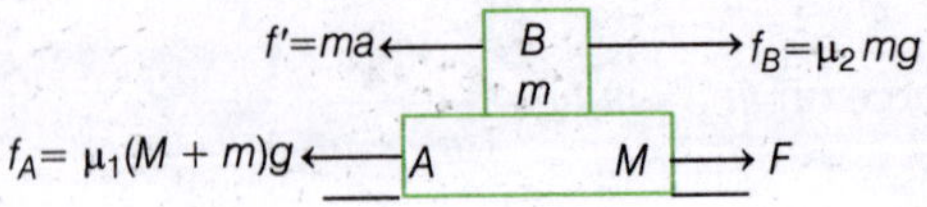

Net accelerating force, $F - f_A = F - \mu_1 (M + m)g$

$\therefore$ Net acceleration, $a = \dfrac{F - \mu_1 (M + m)g}{(M + m)} = \dfrac{F}{(M + m)} - \mu_1 g$

Pseudo force acting on the block B,

$$f' = ma$$

The pseudo force tends to produce a relative motion between the bodies A and B are consequently a frictional force $f_B = \mu_2 mg$ is developed. For equilibrium

$$ma \le \mu_2 mg \text{ or } a \le \mu_2 g$$

If acceleration produced under the the effect of force F is more than $\mu_2 g$, then two bodies will not move together.

4. Motion of Bodies Connected by Strings

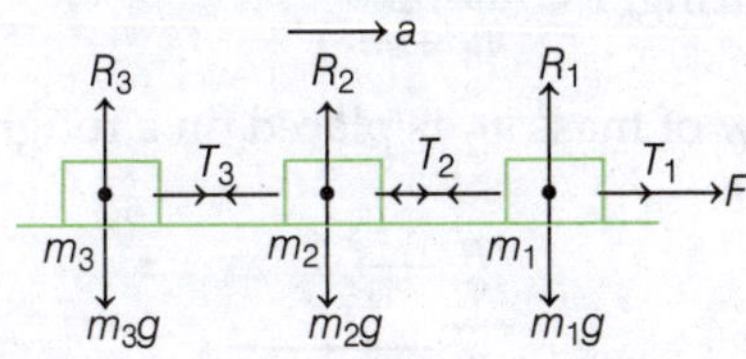

Acceleration of the system, $a = \dfrac{F}{(m_1 + m_2 + m_3)}$

Tension in string, $T_1 = F$

$$T_2 = (m_2 + m_3)\, a = \frac{(m_2 + m_3)\, F}{(m_1 + m_2 + m_3)}$$

$$T_3 = m_3 a = \frac{m_3 F}{(m_1 + m_2 + m_3)}$$

Pulley Mass System

(i) When unequal masses m_1 and m_2 are suspended from a pulley $(m_1 > m_2)$

$m_1 g - T = m_1 a$, and $T - m_2 g = m_2 a$

On solving these equations, we get

$$a = \frac{(m_1 - m_2)}{(m_1 + m_2)} g,$$

$$T = \frac{2 m_1 m_2}{(m_1 + m_2)} g$$

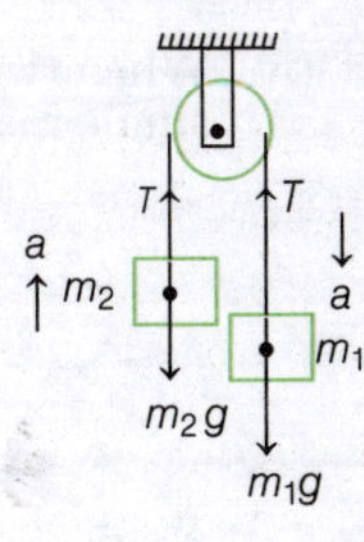

(ii) When a body of mass m_2 is placed on a frictionless horizontal surface, then

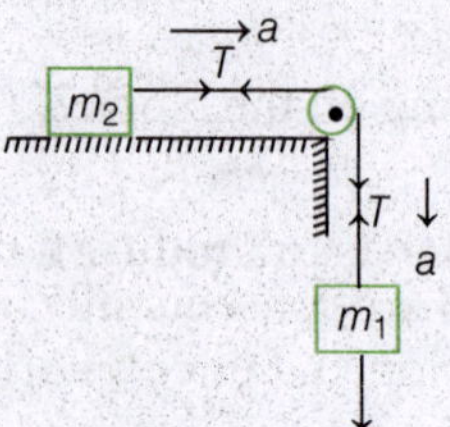

Acceleration, $a = \frac{m_1 g}{(m_1 m_1 + m_2)}$z

Tension in string, $T = \frac{m_1 m_2 g}{(m_1 + m_2)}$

(iii) When a body of mass m_2 is placed on a rough horizontal surface, then

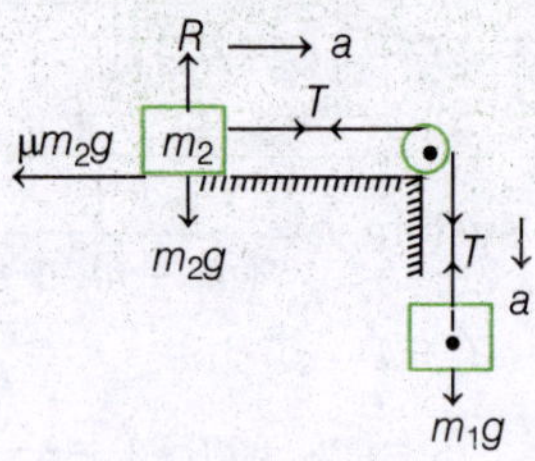

Acceleration, $a = \frac{(m_1 - \mu m_2) g}{(m_1 + m_2)}$

Tension, $T = \frac{m_1 m_2 (1 + \mu) g}{(m_1 + m_2)}$

(iv) When two masses m_1 and m_2 $(m_1 > m_2)$ are connected to a single mass M as shown in figure, then

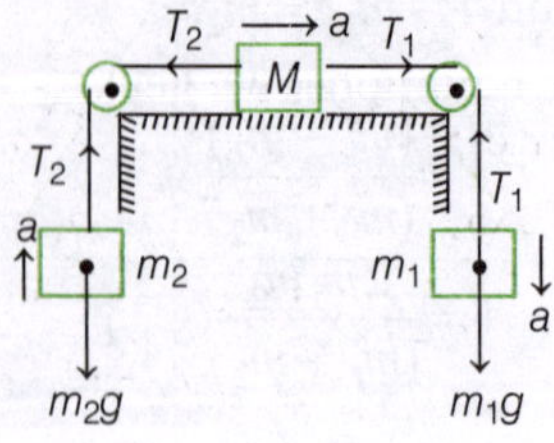

$$m_1 g - T_1 = m_1 a \quad \text{...(i)}$$

$$T_2 - m_2 g = m_2 a \quad \text{...(ii)}$$

$$T_1 - T_2 = Ma \quad \text{...(iii)}$$

Acceleration, $a = \dfrac{(m_1 - m_2)g}{(m_1 + m_2 + M)}$

Tension, $T_1 = \left(\dfrac{2m_2 + M}{m_1 + m_2 + M}\right) m_1 g,$

$$T_2 = \left(\dfrac{2m_1 + M}{m_1 + m_2 + M}\right) m_2 g$$

(v) Motion on a smooth inclined plane, then

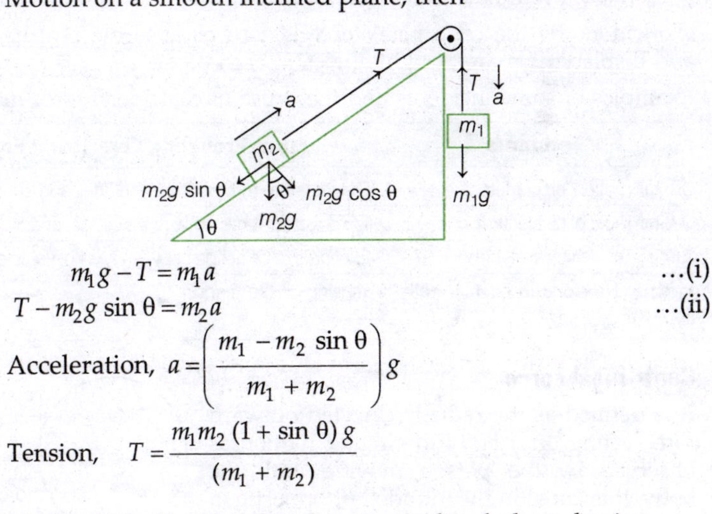

$$m_1 g - T = m_1 a \quad \text{...(i)}$$

$$T - m_2 g \sin\theta = m_2 a \quad \text{...(ii)}$$

Acceleration, $a = \left(\dfrac{m_1 - m_2 \sin\theta}{m_1 + m_2}\right) g$

Tension, $T = \dfrac{m_1 m_2 (1 + \sin\theta) g}{(m_1 + m_2)}$

(vi) Motion of two bodies placed on two inclined planes having different angle of inclination, then

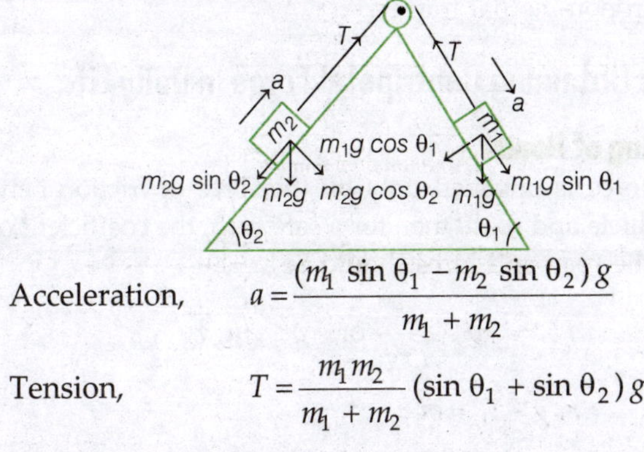

Acceleration, $a = \dfrac{(m_1 \sin\theta_1 - m_2 \sin\theta_2)g}{m_1 + m_2}$

Tension, $T = \dfrac{m_1 m_2}{m_1 + m_2}(\sin\theta_1 + \sin\theta_2)g$

Uniform Circular Motion

When a body moves on circular path with constant speed, then its motion is called uniform circular motion.

Centripetal Force

It is that force which comes into play when a body moves on a circular path. It is directed along the radius of the circle towards its centre.

Centripetal force, $$F = \frac{mv^2}{r} = mr\omega^2$$

where, m = mass of the body, v = linear velocity,

ω = angular velocity and r = radius.

Work done by the centripetal force is zero because the centripetal force and displacement are at right angles to each other.

Examples of some incidents and the cause of centripetal force involved.

Incidents	Force Providing Centripetal Force
Orbital motion of planets.	Gravitational force between planet and sun.
Orbital motion of electron.	Electrostatic force between electron and nucleus.
Turning of vehicles at turn.	Frictional force acting between tyres of vehicle and road.
Motion of a stone in circular path, tied with a string.	Tension in the string.

Centrifugal Force

It is defined as the radially directed outward force acting on a body in circular motion as observed by the person moving with the body. It is equal in magnitude but opposite in direction to centripetal force.

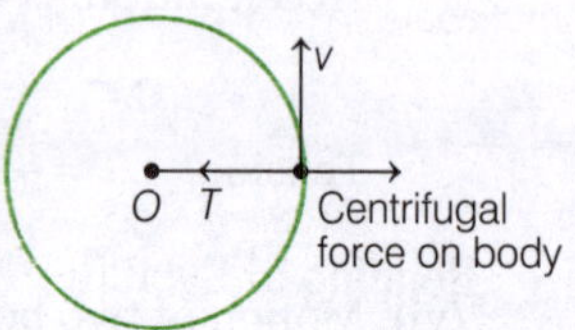

Centrifugal force does not act on the body in an inertial frame but arises as pseudo force in non-inertial frames.

Examples for Obtaining Centripetal Force in Daily Life

Circular Turning of Roads

If centripetal force is obtained only by the force of friction between the tyres of the vehicle and road, then for a safe turn, the coefficient of friction (μ_s) between the road and tyres should be

$$\mu_s \geq \frac{v^2}{rg} \quad \text{or} \quad v \leq \sqrt{\mu_s rg}$$

where, v is the velocity of the vehicle and r is the radius of the circular path.

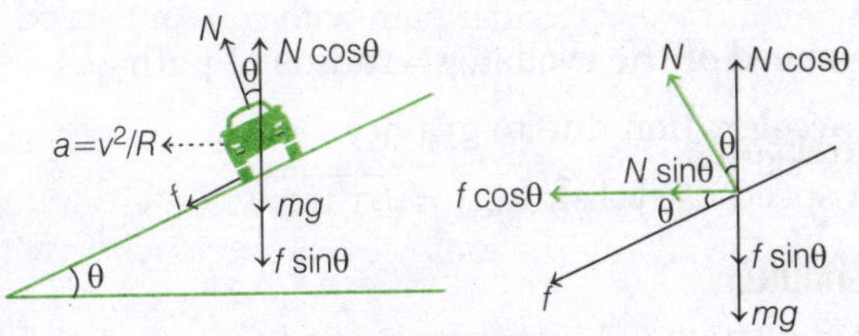

Maximum velocity for no skidding or slipping is $v_{max} = \sqrt{\mu r g}$

If centripetal force is obtained only by the banking of roads, then the maximum speed (v_{max}) of the vehicle for a safe turn

$$v_{max} = \sqrt{rg \tan \theta}$$

If speed of the vehicle is less than $\sqrt{rg \tan \theta}$, then it will move inward (down) and r will decrease and if speed is more than $\sqrt{rg \tan \theta}$, then it will move outward (up) and r will increase.

In normal life, the centripetal force is obtained by the friction force between the road and tyres as well as by the banking of the roads.

Therefore, the maximum permissible speed for the vehicle is much greater than the optimum value of the speed on a banked road.

When centripetal force is obtained from friction force as well as banking of roads, then maximum safe value of speed of vehicle

$$v_{max} = \sqrt{\frac{rg(\tan \theta + \mu_s)}{(1 - \mu_s \tan \theta)}}$$

Bending of Cyclist

When a cyclist takes turn at road, he inclines himself from the vertical, slows down his speed and moves on a circular path of larger radius.

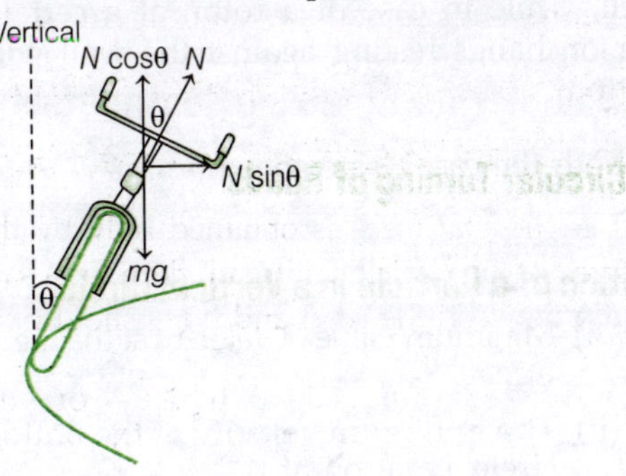

If a cyclist is inclined at an angle θ, then $\tan\theta = \frac{v^2}{rg}$

where, v = speed of the cyclist, r = radius of path

and g = acceleration due to gravity.

Maximum speed of cyclist, $v_{max} = \sqrt{rg\tan\theta}$

Conical Pendulum

It consists of a string OA whose upper end O is fixed and bob is tied at the other free end.

The string is whirled in a horizontal circle, then the arrangement is called a conical pendulum.

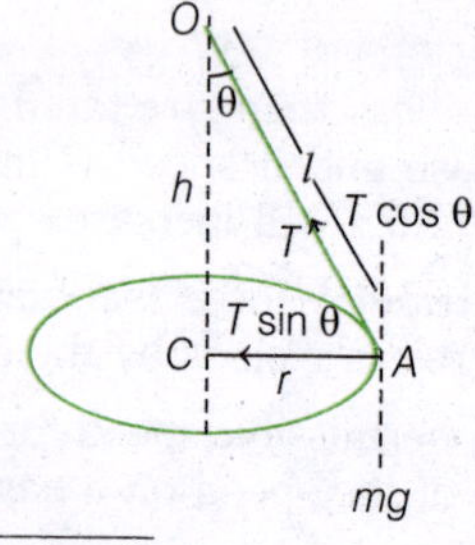

Angular speed, $\omega = \frac{v}{r} = \sqrt{\frac{g\tan\theta}{r}}$

Time period of conical pendulum, $T = 2\pi\sqrt{\frac{l\cos\theta}{g}}$

Death Well or Rotor

In this, a person drives a bicycle on a vertical surface of large wooden well, while in case of a rotor, at a certain angular speed of rotor, a person hangs resting against the wall without any support from the bottom.

In both the cases, safe speed, $v = \sqrt{\frac{gr}{\mu}}$

Motion of a Particle in a Vertical Circle

(i) Minimum value of velocity at the highest point (*i.e.* at point C) is $\sqrt{gr}$.

(ii) The minimum velocity at the bottom required to complete the circle, *i.e.* at point A.

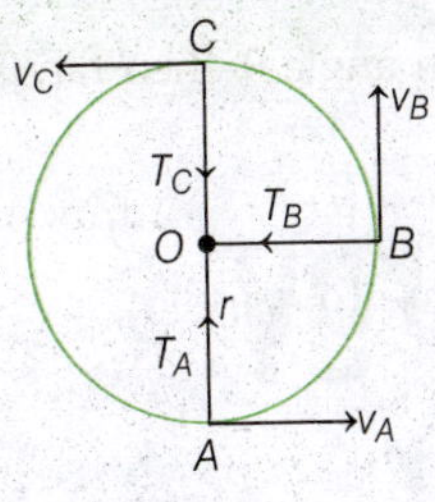

$$v_A = \sqrt{5gr}$$

(iii) Velocity of the body when string is in horizontal position, *i.e.* at point *B*,

$$v_B = \sqrt{3gr}$$

(iv) **Tension in the string**

At the top, $T_C = 0$,

At the bottom, $T_A = 6\,mg$

When string is horizontal, $T_B = 3\,mg$

Knowledge Booster

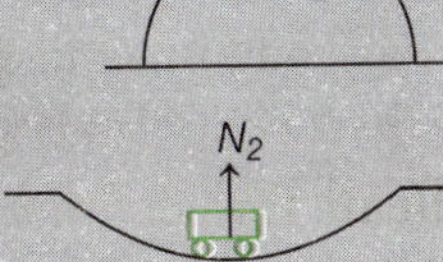

- When a vehicle is moving over a convex bridge, then at the maximum height, reaction (N_1) is $N_1 = mg - \frac{mv^2}{r}$
- When a vehicle is moving over a concave bridge, then at the lowest point, reaction (N_2) is $N_2 = mg + \frac{mv^2}{r}$
- When a car takes a turn, sometimes it overturns. During the overturning, it is the inner wheel which leaves the ground first.

Chapter 06

Work, Energy and Power

Work

When a force acts on an object such that it displaces through some distance in the direction of applied force, then the work is said to be done by the force. Work done by the force is equal to the product of the force and the displacement of the object in the direction of force.

If under a constant force **F**, the object is displaced through a distance **s**, then work done by the force is given by

$$W = \mathbf{F} \cdot \mathbf{s} = Fs \cos \theta$$

where, θ is the smaller angle between **F** and **s**.

Work is a scalar quantity. Its SI unit is joule and CGS unit is erg.

$$\therefore \quad 1 \text{ joule} = 10^7 \text{ erg}$$

Its dimensional formula is $[ML^2T^{-2}]$.

Work done by a force is zero, if

(a) body is not displaced actually, *i.e.* $\mathbf{s} = 0$.

(b) body is displaced perpendicular to the direction of force, *i.e.* $\theta = 90°$.

Value Points

- Work done by a force is **positive**, if angle between **F** and **s** is acute angle.
- Work done by a force is **negative**, if angle between **F** and **s** is obtuse angle.
- Work done by a constant force depends only on the initial and final positions of the object and not on the actual path followed between initial and final positions.

Work done in different conditions

(i) Work done by a variable force is given by $W = \int_{s_1}^{s_2} \mathbf{F} \cdot ds$

It is equal to the area under the force-displacement curve, along with proper sign.

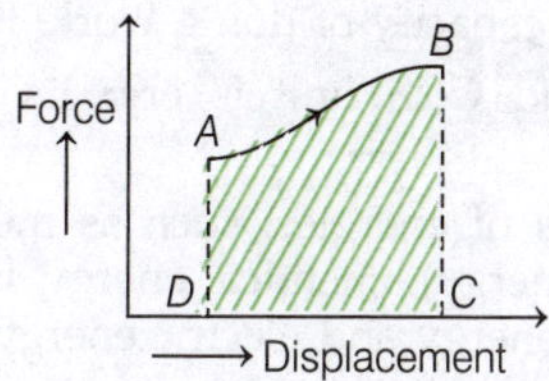

Work done = Area $ABCDA$

(ii) Work done in displacing any body under the action of a number of forces is equal to the work done by the resultant force.

(iii) In equilibrium (static or dynamic), the resultant force is zero, therefore resultant work done is zero.

(iv) If work done by a force during a round trip of a system is zero, then the force is **conservative,** otherwise it is called **non-conservative** force.

- Gravitational force, electrostatic force, magnetic force, etc. are conservative forces. All the central forces are conservative forces.
- Frictional force, viscous force etc are non-conservative forces.

(v) Work done by the force of gravity on a particle of mass m is given by $W = mgh$

where, g is acceleration due to gravity and h is height through which the particle is displaced.

(vi) Work done in compressing or stretching a spring is given by

$$W = -\frac{1}{2}kx^2$$

where, k is spring constant and x is displacement from mean position.

(vii) When one end of a spring is attached to a fixed vertical support and a block attached to the free end moves on a horizontal table from $x = x_1$ to $x = x_2$, then $W = \frac{1}{2}k(x_2^2 - x_1^2)$.

(viii) Work done by the couple for an angular displacement θ is given by $W = \tau \cdot \theta$, where τ is the torque of the couple.

(ix) Work done by a variable force, $W = \int_{r_1}^{r_2} \mathbf{F} \cdot d\mathbf{r}$

where, $d\mathbf{r}$ is the position vector of the particle.

Energy

Energy of a body is its capacity of doing work. It is a scalar quantity.

Its SI unit is joule and CGS unit is erg. Its dimensional formula is $[ML^2T^{-2}]$.

There are several types of energies, such as mechanical energy (kinetic energy and potential energy), chemical energy, light energy, heat energy, sound energy, nuclear energy and electric energy, etc.

Mechanical Energy

The sum of kinetic and potential energy is known as mechanical energy. Mechanical energy is of two types

1. Kinetic Energy

The energy possessed by an object by virtue of its motion is called its kinetic energy.

Kinetic energy of an object is given by $K = \frac{1}{2} mv^2 = \frac{p^2}{2m}$

where, m = mass of the object, v = velocity of the object

and $p = mv$ = momentum of the object.

EXPERT Scale Up

Following description can help you to improve your understanding of kinetic energy.

Since, both m and v^2 are always positive, hence kinetic energy is always positive and does not depend on the direction of motion of the body.

2. Potential Energy

The energy possessed by an object by virtue of its position or configuration is called its potential energy. In one-dimensional motion, potential energy $U(x)$ is defined if force $F(x)$ can be written as

$$F(x) = -\frac{dU}{dx} \quad \text{or} \quad F(x) \cdot dx = -dU$$

or

$$\int_{x_i}^{x_f} F(x) \cdot dx = -\int_{U_i}^{U_f} dU = U_i - U_f$$

Potential energy is defined only for conservative forces. It does not exist for non-conservative forces.

Potential energy depends upon frame of reference.

There are two important types of potential energies

(i) Gravitational Potential Energy

If a body of mass m is raised through a height h against gravity, then its gravitational potential energy $= mgh$.

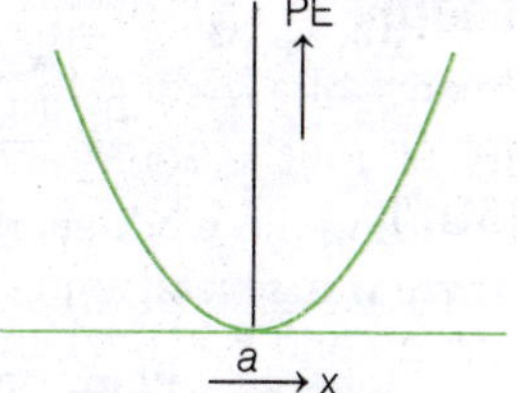

(ii) Elastic Potential Energy

If a spring of spring constant k is stretched through a distance x, then elastic potential energy of the spring $= \frac{1}{2}kx^2$.

The variation of potential energy with distance is shown in figure.

Equilibrium

If the forces acting on the object are conservative and it is in equilibrium, then

$$F_{\text{net}} = 0 \Rightarrow \frac{-dU}{dr} = 0 \text{ or } \frac{dU}{dr} = 0$$

Knowledge Booster

Equilibrium of an object or system can be divided into three types

(i) **Stable equilibrium** An object is said to be in stable equilibrium, if on slight displacement from equilibrium position, it has the tendency to come back to equilibrium position.

Here, $\frac{d^2U}{dr^2} = \text{positive}$

(ii) **Unstable equilibrium** An object is said to be in unstable equilibrium, if on slight displacement from equilibrium position, it moves in the direction of displacement.

Here, $\frac{d^2U}{dr^2} = \text{negative}$

(iii) **Neutral equilibrium** An object is said to be in neutral equilibrium, if on displacement from its equilibrium position, it has neither the tendency to move in direction of displacement nor to come back to equilibrium position.

Here, $\frac{d^2U}{dr^2} = 0$

Work-Energy Theorem

Work done by a force in displacing a body is equal to change in its kinetic energy.

$$W = \int_{v_1}^{v_2} F \cdot ds = \frac{1}{2} mv_2^2 - \frac{1}{2} mv_1^2 = K_f - K_i = \Delta \text{KE}$$

where, K_i = initial kinetic energy

and K_f = final kinetic energy.

Regarding the work-energy theorem, it is worth noting that

(i) If W_{net} is positive, then $K_f - K_i$ = positive, *i.e.* $K_f > K_i$ or kinetic energy will increase and *vice-versa*.

(ii) This theorem can be applied to non-inertial frames also. In a non-inertial frame it can be written as

Work done by all the forces (including the Pseudo force) = Change in kinetic energy in non-inertial frame.

Competition Insight

Other Forms of Energy

Heat Energy

A body possesses heat energy due to the disorderly motion of its molecules. Heat energy is also related to the internal energy of the body.

Chemical Energy

Chemical energy is stored in the chemical bonds of atoms and molecules. If the total energy of the reactants is more than the product of the reaction, then heat is released and the reaction is said to be an **exothermic reaction.** If the reverse is true, then heat is absorbed and the reaction is **endothermic**.

Electrical Energy

It is the energy which is associated with the flow of electric current or with charging or discharging of a body.

Nuclear Energy

It is the binding energy of the nucleus of an atom. It is used in nuclear reactors, nuclear fission, etc.

Mass-Energy Equivalence

According to Einstein, the mass can be transformed into energy and *vice-versa*.

When Δm mass disappears, then produced energy, $E = \Delta mc^2$

where, c is the speed of light in vacuum.

Principle of Conservation of Energy

Energy can neither be created nor be destroyed, it can only be transferred from one form to another form.

Principle of Conservation of Mechanical Energy

For conservative forces, the total mechanical energy (sum of kinetic and potential energies) of an object remains constant.

Power

The rate at which work is done by a body or energy is transferred is called its power.

$$\text{Power} = \text{Rate of doing work} = \frac{\text{Work done}}{\text{Time taken}}$$

If under a constant force **F**, a body is displaced through a distance **s** in time t, then the power $P = \frac{W}{t} = \frac{\mathbf{F} \cdot \mathbf{s}}{t}$

But $\frac{\mathbf{s}}{t} = \mathbf{v}$, uniform velocity with which body is displaced.

$$\therefore \quad P = \mathbf{F} \cdot \mathbf{v} = F v \cos \theta$$

where, θ is the smaller angle between **F** and **v**.

Power is a scalar quantity. Its SI unit is watt and its dimensional formula is $[ML^2T^{-3}]$.

Its other units are kilowatt and horse power,

$$1 \text{ kilowatt} = 1000 \text{ watt}$$
$$1 \text{ horse power} = 746 \text{ watt}$$
$$1 \text{ kWh} = 3.6 \times 10^6 \text{ J}$$

Collisions

Collision between two or more particles is the interaction for a short interval of time in which they apply relatively strong forces on each other.

In a collision, physical contact of two bodies is not necessary.

There are two types of collisions

1. Elastic Collision

The collisions in which both the momentum and the kinetic energy of the system remain conserved are called elastic collisions.

In an elastic collision, all the involved forces are conservative forces and total energy remains conserved.

2. Inelastic Collision

The collisions in which only the momentum remains conserved but kinetic energy does not remain conserved are called inelastic collisions.

The collision in which two particles move together after the collision is called a completely inelastic collision.

In an inelastic collision, some or all the involved forces are non-conservative forces. Total energy of the system remains conserved. If after the collision, two bodies stick to each other, then the collision is said to be perfectly inelastic.

Coefficient of Restitution or Resilience (e)

The ratio of relative velocity of separation after collision to the relative velocity of approach before collision is called coefficient of restitution or resilience. It is represented by *e* and it depends upon the material of the colliding bodies.

Value Points

For a perfectly elastic collision, $e = 1$
For a perfectly inelastic collision, $e = 0$
For all other collisions, $0 < e < 1$

One Dimensional or Head-on Collision

If the initial and final velocities of colliding bodies lie along the same line, then the collision is called one dimensional or head-on collision.

Perfectly Elastic One Dimensional Collision

Applying Newton's experimental law, we have

$$v_2 - v_1 = u_1 - u_2$$

m_1 $\xrightarrow{u_1}$ m_2 $\xrightarrow{u_2}$ | m_1 $\xrightarrow{v_1}$ m_2 $\xrightarrow{v_2}$

Before collision | After collision

Velocities after collision

$$v_1 = \frac{(m_1 - m_2)\,u_1 + 2m_2u_2}{(m_1 + m_2)} \text{ and } v_2 = \frac{(m_2 - m_1)\,u_2 + 2m_1u_1}{(m_1 + m_2)}$$

Important Points Related to Perfectly Elastic One-Dimensional Collision

- When masses of two colliding bodies are equal, then after the collision, the bodies exchange their velocities.

$$v_1 = u_2 \quad \text{and} \quad v_2 = u_1$$

- If second body of same mass ($m_1 = m_2$) is at rest, then after collision first body comes to rest and second body starts moving with the initial velocity of first body.

$$v_1 = 0 \quad \text{and} \quad v_2 = u_1$$

- If a light body of mass m_1 collides with a very heavy body of mass m_2 at rest, then after collision,

$$v_1 = -u_1 \quad \text{and} \quad v_2 = 0$$

It means light body will rebound with its own velocity and heavy body will continue to be at rest.

- If a very heavy body of mass m_1 collides with a light body of mass $m_2 (m_1 >> m_2)$ at rest, then after collision

$$v_1 = u_1 \quad \text{and} \quad v_2 = 2u_1$$

For One-Dimensional Inelastic Collision

Loss of kinetic energy

$$\Delta K = \frac{m_1 m_2}{2(m_1 + m_2)} (u_1 - u_2)^2 (1 - e^2)$$

For Perfectly Inelastic One-Dimensional Collision

Velocity of separation after collision $= 0$.

$$\text{Loss of kinetic energy} = \frac{m_1 m_2 (u_1 - u_2)^2}{2(m_1 + m_2)}$$

If a body is dropped from a height h_0 and it strikes the ground with velocity v_0 and after inelastic collision, it rebounds with velocity v_1 and rises to a height h_1, then

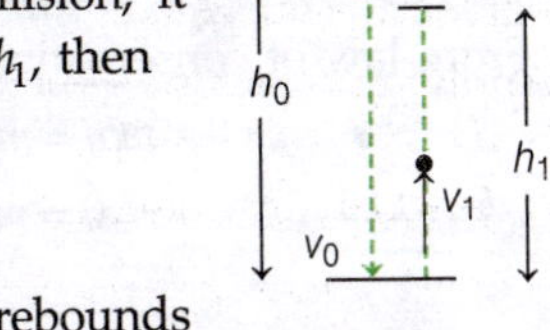

$$e = \frac{v_1}{v_0} = \sqrt{\frac{2gh_1}{2gh_0}} = \sqrt{\frac{h_1}{h_0}}$$

If after n collisions with the ground, the body rebounds with a velocity v_n and rises to a height h_n, then

$$e^n = \frac{v_n}{v_0} = \sqrt{\frac{h_n}{h_0}}$$

Height covered by the body after nth rebound, $h_n = e^{2n} h_o$

Two-Dimensional or Oblique Collision

If the initial and final velocities of colliding bodies do not lie along the same line, then the collision is called two-dimensional or oblique collision.

In horizontal direction,

$$m_1 u_1 \cos \alpha_1 + m_2 u_2 \cos \alpha_2 = m_1 v_1 \cos \beta_1 + m_2 v_2 \cos \beta_2$$

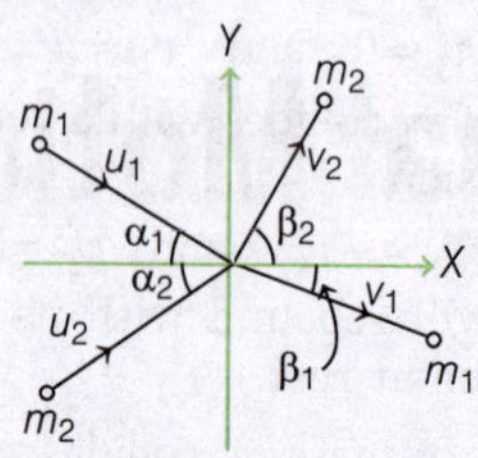

In vertical direction,

$$-m_1 u_1 \sin \alpha_1 + m_2 u_2 \sin \alpha_2 = m_1 v_1 \sin \beta_1 - m_2 v_2 \sin \beta_2$$

If $m_1 = m_2$ and $\alpha_1 + \alpha_2 = 90°$

then $\beta_1 + \beta_2 = 90°$

If a particle A of mass m_1 is moving along X-axis with a speed u and makes an elastic collision with another stationary body B of mass m_2, then

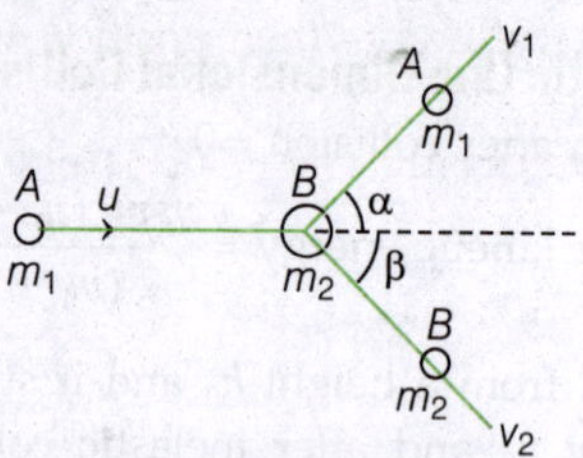

From law of conservation of momentum,

$$m_1 u = m_1 v_1 \cos \alpha + m_2 v_2 \cos \beta$$

$$0 = m_1 v_1 \sin \alpha - m_2 v_2 \sin \beta$$

Chapter 07

Rotational Motion

Centre of Mass

Centre of mass of a system is the point that behaves as whole mass of the system is concentrated on it and all external forces are acting on it. For rigid bodies, centre of mass is independent of the state of the body, *i.e.* whether it is in rest or in accelerated motion, centre of mass will remain same.

Centre of Mass of a System Containing *n* Particles

If a system consists of n particles of masses $m_1, m_2, m_3, \ldots, m_n$ having position vectors $\mathbf{r}_1, \mathbf{r}_2, \mathbf{r}_3, \ldots, \mathbf{r}_n$, then position vector of centre of mass of the system, $\mathbf{r}_{CM} = \dfrac{m_1\mathbf{r}_1 + m_2\mathbf{r}_2 + m_3\mathbf{r}_3 + \ldots + m_n\mathbf{r}_n}{m_1 + m_2 + m_3 + \ldots + m_n} = \dfrac{\sum_{i=1}^{n} m_i\mathbf{r}_i}{\sum m_i}$

In terms of coordinates,

$$\mathbf{x}_{CM} = \frac{m_1\mathbf{x}_1 + m_2\mathbf{x}_2 + \ldots + m_n\mathbf{x}_n}{m_1 + m_2 + \ldots + m_n} = \frac{\sum_{i=1}^{n} m_i\mathbf{x}_i}{\sum m_i}$$

$$\mathbf{y}_{CM} = \frac{m_1\mathbf{y}_1 + m_2\mathbf{y}_2 + \ldots + m_n\mathbf{y}_n}{m_1 + m_2 + \ldots + m_n} = \frac{\sum_{i=1}^{n} m_i\mathbf{y}_i}{\sum m_i}$$

$$\mathbf{z}_{CM} = \frac{m_1\mathbf{z}_1 + m_2\mathbf{z}_2 + \ldots + m_n\mathbf{z}_n}{m_1 + m_2 + \ldots + m_n} = \frac{\sum_{i=1}^{n} m_i\mathbf{z}_i}{\sum m_i}$$

Centre of Mass of Two Particles System

Choosing O as origin of the coordinate axis.

(i) Then, position of centre of mass from $m_1 = \dfrac{m_2 d}{m_1 + m_2}$

m_1 m_2

$O \longleftarrow d \longrightarrow P$

(ii) Position of centre of mass from $m_2 = \dfrac{m_1 d}{m_1 + m_2}$

(iii) If position vectors of particles of masses m_1 and m_2 are $\mathbf{r}_1$ and $\mathbf{r}_2$ respectively, then

$$\mathbf{r}_{CM} = \frac{m_1\mathbf{r}_1 + m_2\mathbf{r}_2}{m_1 + m_2}$$

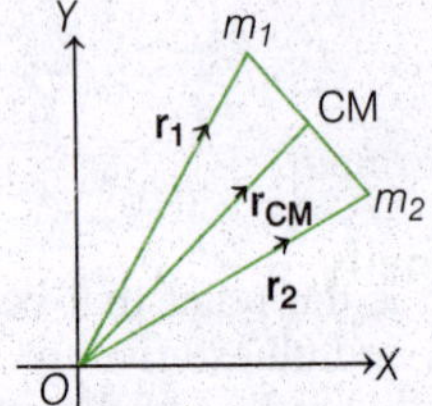

(iv) If particles of masses m_1 and m_2 are moving with velocities $\mathbf{v}_1$ and $\mathbf{v}_2$ respectively, then velocity of the centre of mass,

$$\mathbf{v}_{CM} = \frac{m_1\mathbf{v}_1 + m_2\mathbf{v}_2}{m_1 + m_2}$$

(v) If accelerations of the particles of masses m_1 and m_2 are $\mathbf{a}_1$ and $\mathbf{a}_2$ respectively, then acceleration of the centre of mass,

$$\mathbf{a}_{CM} = \frac{m_1\mathbf{a}_1 + m_2\mathbf{a}_2}{m_1 + m_2}$$

(vi) Centre of mass of an isolated system has a constant velocity. It means, isolated system will remain at rest, if it is initially at rest or will move with the same velocity, if it is in motion initially.

(vii) The position of centre of mass depends upon the shape, size and distribution of the mass of the body.

(viii) The centre of mass of an object need not to lie within the object.

(ix) In symmetrical bodies having homogeneous distribution of mass, the centre of mass coincides with the geometrical centre of the body.

(x) The position of centre of mass of an object changes in translatory motion but remains unchanged in rotatory motion.

Linear Momentum of a System of Particles

For a system of n particles, the total momentum of a system of particles is equal to the product of the total mass and velocity of its centre of mass.

$$\mathbf{p} = M\mathbf{v}_{CM}$$

According to Newton's second law for system of particles

Net external force, $F_{\text{ext}} = \dfrac{dp}{dt}$.

Angular Velocity and its Relation with Linear Velocity

The **average angular velocity** of the particle over the interval Δt is $\dfrac{\Delta\theta}{\Delta t}$, i.e.

$$\overline{\omega} = \frac{\Delta\theta}{\Delta t}$$

where, $\Delta\theta$ is angular displacement.

Instantaneous angular velocity,

$$\omega = \lim_{\Delta t \to 0} \frac{\Delta\theta}{\Delta t} = \frac{d\theta}{dt}$$

The relation between angular velocity (ω) and linear velocity (v) is given by the relation, $v = \omega r$

where, r is the radius of circular path.

At any given instant, the relation $v = \omega r$ applies to all particles of the rotating rigid body.

Angular Acceleration

Angular acceleration (α) is defined as the rate of change of angular velocity, i.e. $\alpha = \dfrac{d\omega}{dt}$. If the axis of rotationis fixed, the direction of ω and α is also fixed.

Rigid Body

A body is said to be a rigid body, when it has perfectly definite shape and size. The distance between all points of particles of such a body do not change, while applying any force on it. General motion of a rigid body consists of both the translational motion and the rotational motion.

Translational Motion

A rigid body performs a pure translational motion, if each particle of the body undergoes the same displacement in the same direction in a given interval of time.

Rotational Motion

A rigid body performs a pure rotational motion, if each particle of the body moves in a circle, and the centre of all the circles lie on a straight line called the axes of rotation.

Equations of Rotational Motion

(i) $\omega = \omega_0 + \alpha t$ (ii) $\theta = \omega_0 t + \frac{1}{2}\alpha t^2$ (iii) $\omega^2 = \omega_0^2 + 2\,\alpha\,\theta$

where, θ is displacement in rotational motion, ω_0 is initial velocity, ω is final velocity and α is acceleration.

Moment of Inertia

The inertia of rotational motion is called **moment of inertia**. It is denoted by *I*.

Moment of inertia is the property of an object by virtue of which it opposes any change in its state of rotation about an axis.

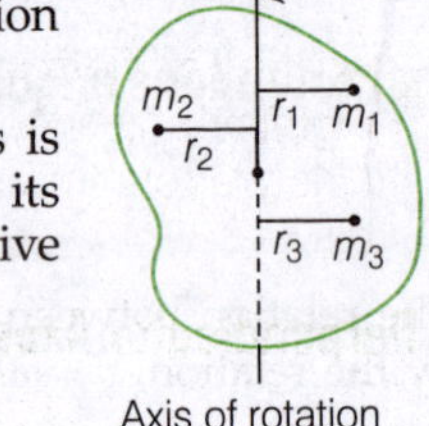

The moment of inertia of a body about a given axis is equal to the sum of the products of the masses of its constituent particles and the square of their respective distances from the axis of rotation.

Moment of inertia of a body,

$$I = m_1 r_1^2 + m_2 r_2^2 + m_3 r_3^2 + \ldots = \sum_{i=1}^{n} m_i r_i^2$$

Its SI unit is kg-m^2 and its dimensional formula is $[ML^2]$.

The moment of inertia of a body depends upon

(a) position of the axis of rotation.
(b) orientation of the axis of rotation.
(c) shape and size of the body.
(d) distribution of mass of the body about the axis of rotation.

Value Points

The physical significance of the moment of inertia in rotational motion is analogous to mass in linear motion.

The Radius of Gyration

The root mean square distance of its constituent particles from the axis of rotation is called the radius of gyration of a body.

It is denoted by *K*.

Radius of gyration, $K = \sqrt{\dfrac{r_1^2 + r_2^2 + \ldots + r_n^2}{n}}$

The product of the mass of the body (*M*) and square of its radius of gyration (*K*) gives the same moment of inertia of the body about the rotational axis.

Therefore, moment of inertia, $I = MK^2 \Rightarrow K = \sqrt{\dfrac{I}{M}}$

Competition Insight

Parallel Axes Theorem

- The moment of inertia of any object about any arbitrary axis is equal to the sum of moment of inertia about a parallel axis passing through the centre of mass and the product of mass of the body and the square of the perpendicular distance between the two axes.

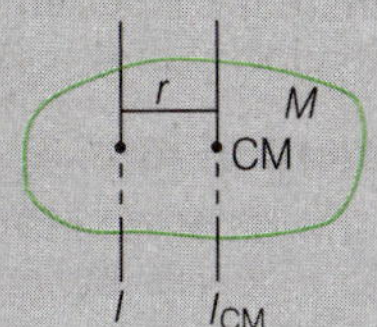

- Mathematically, $I = I_{CM} + Mr^2$

  where, I is the moment of inertia about the arbitrary axis, I_{CM} is the moment of inertia about the parallel axis through the centre of mass, M is the total mass of the object and r is the perpendicular distance between the axes.

Perpendicular Axes Theorem

- The moment of inertia of any two-dimensional body about an axis perpendicular to its plane (I_Z) is equal to the sum of moments of inertia of the body about two mutually perpendicular axes lying in its own plane and intersecting each other at a point, where the perpendicular axis passes through it.

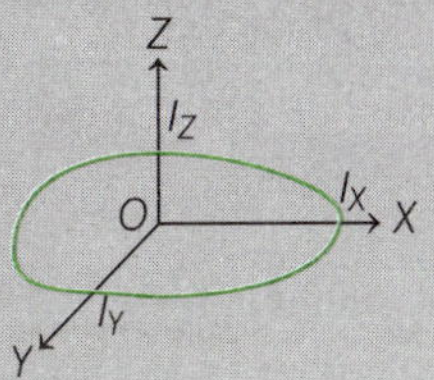

- Mathematically, $I_Z = I_X + I_Y$

  where, I_X and I_Y are the moments of inertia of plane lamina about the perpendicular axes X and Y respectively, which lie in the plane of lamina and intersect each other.

- Theorem of parallel axes is applicable for any type of rigid body whether it is a two-dimensional or three-dimensional, while the theorem of perpendicular axes is applicable for laminar type or two-dimensional bodies only.

Moment of Inertia of Homogeneous Rigid Bodies

For a Thin Circular Ring

S. No.	Axis of Rotation	Moment of Inertia	Formula
(a)	About an axis passing through its centre and perpendicular to its plane	O, R, M, I	$I = MR^2$

S. No.	Axis of Rotation	Moment of Inertia	Formula
(b)	About a tangent perpendicular to its plane	O, R, M, I_T	$I_T = 2MR^2$
(c)	About a diameter	O, R, M, I_D	$I_D = \frac{1}{2}MR^2$
(d)	About a tangent in its plane	O, R, $I_{T'}$	$I_{T'} = \frac{3}{2}MR^2$

For a Circular Disc

S. No.	Axis of Rotation	Moment of Inertia	Formula
(a)	About an axis passing through its centre and perpendicular to its plane	O, R, M, I	$I = \frac{1}{2}MR^2$
(b)	About a tangent perpendicular to its plane	O, R, M, I_T	$I_T = \frac{3}{2}MR^2$
(c)	About a diameter	R, O, M, I_D	$I_D = \frac{1}{4}MR^2$
(d)	About a tangent in its plane	R, $I_{T'}$	$I_{T'} = \frac{5}{4}MR^2$

For a Thin Rod

S. No.	Axis of Rotation	Moment of Inertia	Formula
(a)	About an axis passing through its centre and perpendicular to its length		$I = \frac{ML^2}{12}$
(b)	About an axis passing through its one end and perpendicular to its length		$I = \frac{ML^2}{3}$

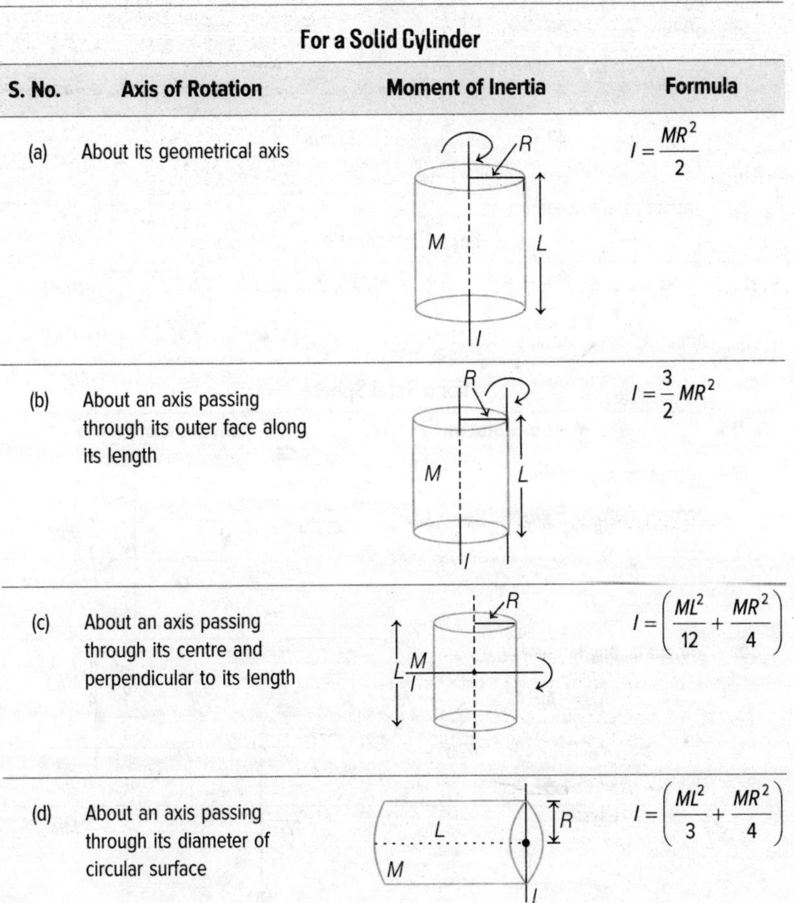

For a Solid Cylinder

S. No.	Axis of Rotation	Moment of Inertia	Formula
(a)	About its geometrical axis		$I = \frac{MR^2}{2}$
(b)	About an axis passing through its outer face along its length		$I = \frac{3}{2}MR^2$
(c)	About an axis passing through its centre and perpendicular to its length		$I = \left(\frac{ML^2}{12} + \frac{MR^2}{4}\right)$
(d)	About an axis passing through its diameter of circular surface		$I = \left(\frac{ML^2}{3} + \frac{MR^2}{4}\right)$

For a Rectangular Plate

Axis of Rotation	Moment of Inertia
About an axis passing through its centre and perpendicular to its plane $I = \frac{M(l^2 + b^2)}{12}$	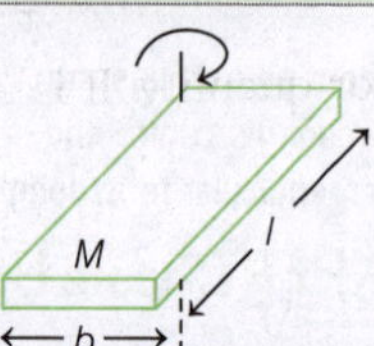

For a Thin Spherical Shell

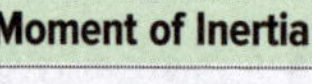

S. No.	Axis of Rotation	Moment of Inertia
(a)	About its any diameter $I_D = \frac{2}{3} MR^2$	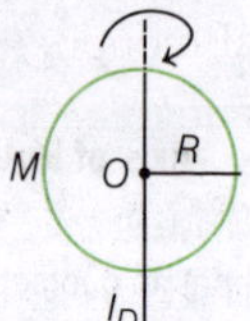
(b)	About its any tangent $I_T = \frac{5}{3} MR^2$	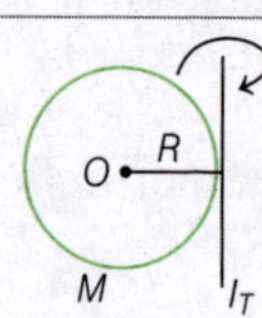

For a Solid Sphere

S. No.	Axis of Rotation	Moment of Inertia
(a)	About its any diameter $I_D = \frac{2}{5} MR^2$	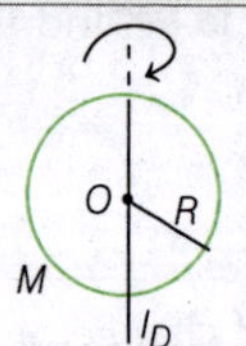
(b)	About its any tangent $I_T = \frac{7}{5} MR^2$	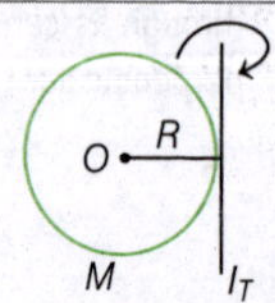

Torque

Torque or moment of a force about the axis of rotation

$$\tau = \mathbf{r} \times \mathbf{F} = rF \sin\theta\, \hat{\mathbf{n}}$$

It is a vector quantity. It is also known as moment of force or couple.

EXPERT Scale Up

While solving torque related problems, torque is taken negative if force rotates the object clockwise and it is taken as positive, if force rotates the object anti-clockwise.

Its SI unit is N-m and its dimensional formula is $[ML^2 T^{-2}]$.

In rotational motion, torque, $\tau = I\alpha$

where, α is angular acceleration and I is moment of inertia.

Principle of Moment

When an object is in rotational equilibrium, then algebraic sum of all torques acting on it is zero. Clockwise torques are taken negative and anti-clockwise torques are taken positive.

Angular Momentum

The moment of linear momentum is called angular momentum.

It is denoted by L

Angular momentum, $L = I\omega = mvr$

In vector form, $L = I\omega = \mathbf{r} \times m\mathbf{v}$

Its SI unit is J-s and its dimensional formula is $[ML^2 T^{-1}]$.

Torque, $\tau = \dfrac{d\mathbf{L}}{dt}$

Torque and Angular Momentum for a System of Particles

The rate of change of the total angular momentum of a system of particles about a point is equal to the sum of the external torques acting on the system taken about the same point.

$$\frac{d\mathbf{L}}{dt} = \tau_{ext}$$

Conservation of Angular Momentum

If the external torque acting on a system is zero, then its angular momentum remains conserved.

If $\tau_{ext} = 0$, then $L = I\omega = \text{constant} \Rightarrow I_1\omega_1 = I_2\omega_2$

Equilibrium of Rigid Body

A rigid body is said to be in equilibrium, if both of its linear momentum and angular momentum are not changing with time.

Thus, for equilibrium, body does not possess linear acceleration or angular acceleration.

(i) When the net force on the object is zero, $F_{net} = 0$, then it is in translational equilibrium.

(ii) When the net torque on the object is zero, $\tau_{net} = 0$, then it is in rotational equilibrium.

Couple

A pair of equal and opposite forces with parallel lines of action is called couple. It produces rotation without translation.

 Knowledge Booster

Centre of Gravity

If a body is supported on a point such that total gravitational torque about this point is zero, then this point is called centre of gravity of the body.

Centre of gravity coincides with centre of mass, if g is constant. But for large objects g will vary, hence centre of gravity does not coincide with centre of mass.

Angular Impulse

Total effect of a torque applied on a rotating body in a given time is called angular impulse. Angular impulse is equal to total change in angular momentum of the system in given time. Thus, angular impulse

$$J = \int_{t_i}^{t_f} \tau \, dt = L_f - L_i$$

Rotational Kinetic Energy

Rotational kinetic energy of a body is equal to the sum of kinetic energies of its constituent particles.

Rotational kinetic energy, $K = \frac{1}{2} I\omega^2$

Competition Insight

Motion of a Body Rolling Down without Slipping on an Inclined Plane

- Acceleration of the body,

$$a = \frac{mg \sin \theta}{m + \frac{I}{r^2}} = \frac{g \sin \theta}{1 + \frac{K^2}{r^2}}$$

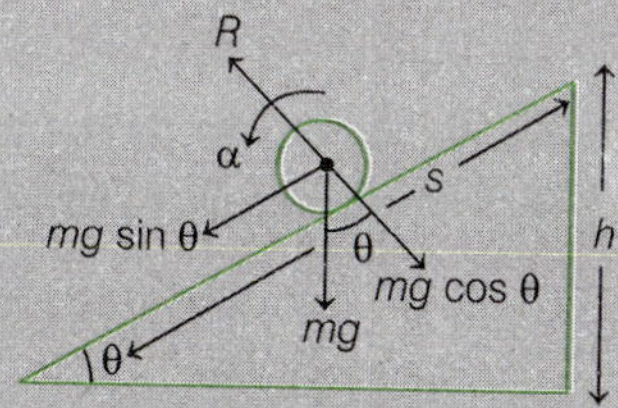

where, K = radius of gyration, m = mass of the body, r = radius of the body and θ = inclination of the plane.

Velocity attained at the bottom,

$$v = \sqrt{\frac{2gh}{1 + \frac{K^2}{r^2}}} = \sqrt{\frac{2gs \sin \theta}{1 + \frac{K^2}{r^2}}} \qquad \left(\because s = \frac{h}{\sin \theta}\right)$$

where, h = height of slope and s = length of slope.

$$\text{Time} = \sqrt{\frac{2s\left(1 + \frac{k^2}{r^2}\right)}{g \sin \theta}}$$

where, s = length of slope and r = radius of rolling body.

- If a cylinder, ring, disc and sphere rolls on an inclined plane, then the sphere will reach the bottom first with greater velocity while ring will reach the bottom with least velocity.
- If a solid and hollow body of same shape are allowed to roll down on an inclined plane, then solid body will reach the bottom first with greater velocity.
- For rolling without slipping, the minimum value of coefficient of friction,

$$\mu = \frac{F}{R} = \frac{(Ia / r^2)}{mg \cos \theta}$$

- **Total kinetic energy of a rolling object**

  = Kinetic energy of translation + Kinetic energy of rotation.

  $$= \frac{1}{2}mv^2 + \frac{1}{2}I\omega^2$$

- **Power delivered by torque** $P = \tau \cdot \omega$
- **Work done by torque** $W = \int_{\theta_1}^{\theta_2} \tau d\theta$
- If τ is constant, then $W = \tau(\theta_2 - \theta_1)$

  or $W = \tau \times$ Angle moved by the particle.
- In rolling motion, all points of the body have same angular speed but different linear speeds.

  In pure translational motion

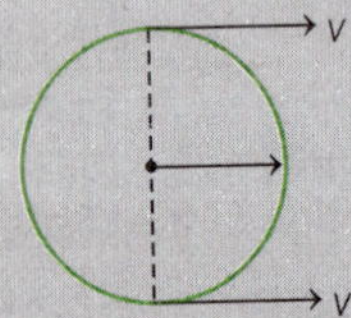

In pure rotational motion

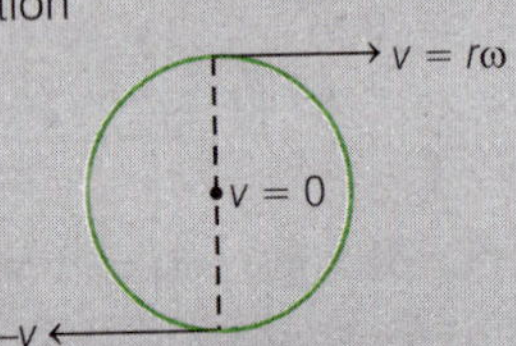

In combined motion, *i.e.* translational as well as rotational motion.

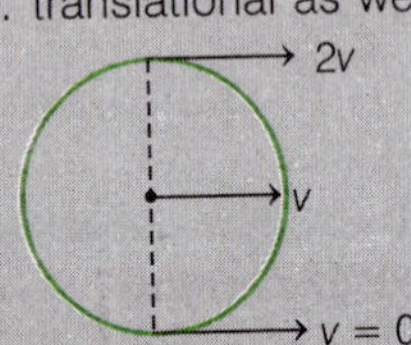

Chapter 08

Gravitation

Each object in the universe attracts every other object with a force, which is called the force of **gravitation.**

Gravitation is one of the four classes of interactions found in nature. These are

(i) the gravitational force
(ii) the electromagnetic force
(iii) the strong nuclear force (also called the hadronic force).
(iv) the weak nuclear forces.

Gravity is the force by which the earth attracts a body towards its centre. Although, of negligible importance in the interactions of elementary particles, gravity is of primary importance in the interactions of large objects. It is gravity that holds the universe together.

Newton's Law of Gravitation

Gravitational force is an attractive force between two masses m_1 and m_2 separated by a distance r.

The gravitational force acting between two point objects is directly proportional to the product of their masses and inversely proportional to the square of the distance between them.

m_1 ———— r ———— m_2

Gravitational force, $F = \frac{Gm_1 m_2}{r^2}$

where, G is universal gravitational constant.

The value of G is 6.67×10^{-11} N-m^2 kg^{-2} and is same throughout the universe.
Dimensional formula of G is $[M^{-1}L^3T^{-2}]$.

Value Points

- The value of G is independent of the nature and size of the bodies as well as the nature of the medium between them.
- Newton's law of gravitation holds good for object lying at very large distances and also at very short distances. It fails when the distance between the objects is less than 10^{-9} m, i.e. of the order of intermolecular distances.

Important Points about Gravitational Force

(i) Gravitational force is a central as well as conservative force.

(ii) It is the weakest force in nature.

(iii) It is 10^{36} times smaller than electrostatic force and 10^{38} times smaller than nuclear force.

(iv) The law of gravitation is applicable for all bodies, irrespective of their size, shape and position.

(v) Gravitational force acting between the sun and planets provides it centripetal force for orbital motion.

(vi) Newton's third law of motion holds good for the force of gravitation. It means that the gravitational forces between two bodies are action-reaction pairs.

(vii) Unlike the electrostatic force, it is independent of the medium between the particles.

(viii) It expresses the force between two point masses (of negligible volume). However, for external points of spherical bodies the whole mass can be assumed to be concentrated at its centre of mass.

Central Forces

Central force is that force which acts along the line joining towards the centres of two interacting bodies. A central force is always directed towards the centre as away from a fixed point.

Acceleration Due to Gravity

The uniform acceleration produced in a freely falling object due to the gravitational pull of the earth is known as **acceleration due to gravity**. It is denoted by g and its SI unit is m/s^2. It is a vector quantity and its direction is towards the centre of the earth.

The value of g is independent of the mass of the object which is falling freely under gravity.

The value of g changes slightly from place to place. The value of g is taken to be 9.8 m/ s^2 for all practical purposes. The value of acceleration due to gravity on the moon is about one-sixth of that on the earth and on the sun is about 27 times of that on the earth.

Among the planets, the acceleration due to gravity is minimum on the mercury.

Relation between g and G is given by, $g = \frac{GM}{R^2}$

where, M = mass of the earth = 6.4×10^{24} kg

and R = radius of the earth = 6.38×10^6 m.

Inertial Mass and Gravitational Mass

(a) Inertial mass $= \frac{\text{Force}}{\text{Acceleration}}$

(b) Gravitational mass $= \frac{\text{Weight of body}}{\text{Acceleration due to gravity}}$

(c) Gravitational mass of a body is affected by the presence of other bodies near it. Inertial mass of a body remains unaffected by the presence of other bodies near it.

Gravitational mass M_g is defined by Newton's law of gravitation.

$$M_g = \frac{F_g}{g} = \frac{w}{g} = \frac{\text{Weight of body}}{\text{Acceleration due to gravity}}$$

$$\therefore \quad \frac{(M_1)_g}{(M_2)_g} = \frac{F_{g_1} g_2}{F_{g_2} g_1}$$

Inertial mass and gravitational mass are equal to each other in magnitude.

Factors Affecting Acceleration Due to Gravity

(i) Shape of the Earth

Acceleration due to gravity $g \propto \frac{1}{R^2}$.

Earth is elliptical in shape. Its diameter at poles is approximately 42 km less than its diameter at equator.

Therefore, g is minimum at equator and maximum at poles.

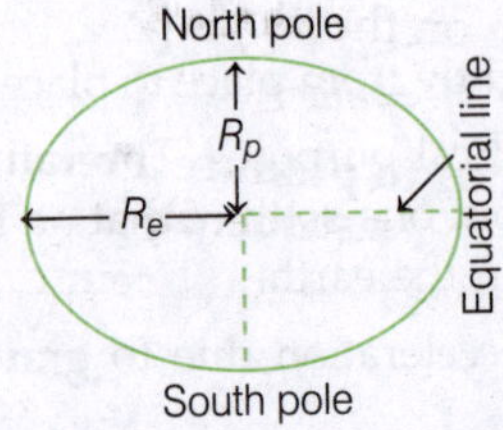

(ii) Rotation of Earth about Its Own Axis

If ω is the angular velocity of rotation of earth about its own axis, then acceleration due to gravity at a place having latitude λ is given by

$$g' = g - R\omega^2 \cos^2 \lambda$$

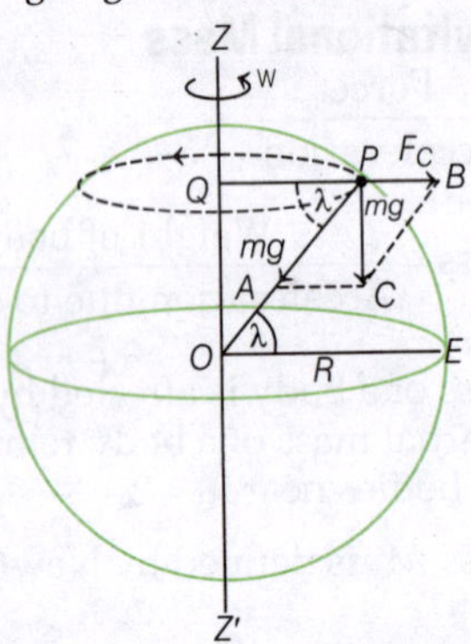

At poles, $\lambda = 90°$ and $g' = g$.
Therefore, there is no effect of rotation of earth about its own axis at poles.
At equator, $\lambda = 0°$ and $g' = g - R\omega^2$
The value of g is minimum at equator. If earth stops its rotation about its own axis, then g will remain unchanged at poles but increases by $R\omega^2$ at equator.

(iii) Effect of Altitude

The value of g at height h from earth's surface

$$g' = \frac{g}{\left(1 + \frac{h}{R}\right)^2}$$

For $h << R$,

$$g' = g\left(1 - \frac{2h}{R}\right)$$

Therefore, g decreases with altitude.

(iv) Effect of Depth

The value of g at depth d from earth's surface

$$g' = g\left(1 - \frac{d}{R}\right)$$

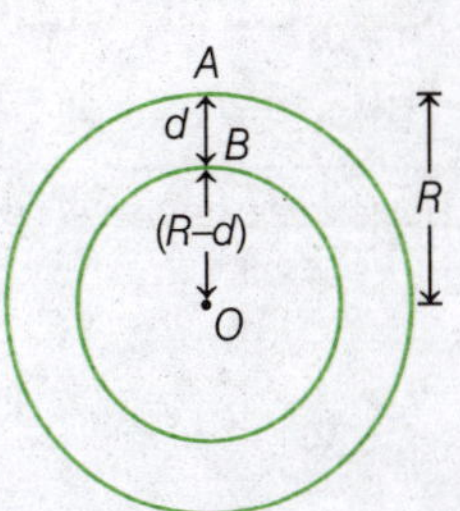

Therefore, g decreases with depth from earth's surface.

The value of g becomes zero at earth's centre.

Gravitational Field

The space in the surrounding of any body in which its gravitational pull can be experienced by other bodies is called gravitational field.

Intensity of Gravitational Field

The gravitational force acting per unit mass at any point in gravitational field is called intensity of gravitational field at that point.

It is denoted by E_g or I.

$$E_g \quad \text{or} \quad I = \frac{F}{m}$$

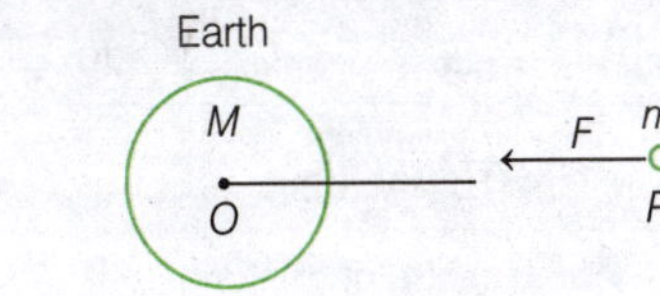

r

Intensity of gravitational field at a distance r from a body of mass M is given by

$$E_g \quad \text{or} \quad I = \frac{GM}{r^2}$$

It is a vector quantity and its direction is towards the centre of gravity of the body. Its SI unit is N/m and its dimensional formula is $[LT^{-2}]$.

Intensity due to a Point Mass

Suppose a point mass M is placed at point O, then gravitational field intensity due to this point mass at point P is given by

M F P
O r

$$I = \frac{GM}{r^2}$$

Competition Insight

- **Intensity due to Uniform Solid Sphere**

Outside the surface $r > R$	On the surface $r = R$	Inside the surface $r < R$
$I = \frac{GM}{r^2}$	$I = \frac{GM}{R^2}$	$I = \frac{GMr}{R^3}$

- **Intensity due to Hollow Spherical Shell**

Outside the surface $r > R$	On the surface $r = R$	Inside the surface $r < R$
$I = \frac{GM}{r^2}$	$I = \frac{GM}{R^2}$	$I = 0$

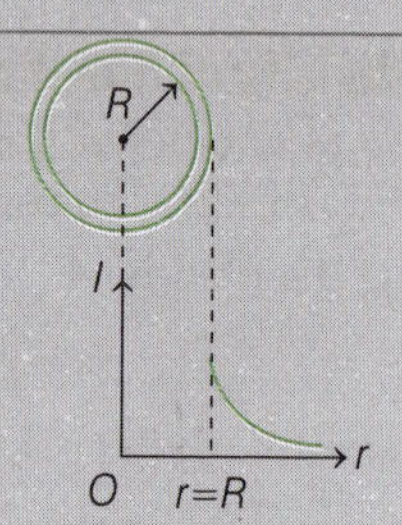

- **Intensity due to Uniform Circular ring**

At a point on its axis	At the centre of the Ring
$I = \frac{GMr}{(a^2 + r^2)^{3/2}}$	$I = 0$

Gravitational Potential

Gravitational potential at any point in gravitational field is equal to the work done per unit mass in bringing a very light body from infinity to that point. It is denoted by V_g.

Gravitational potential, $V_g = \frac{W}{m} = -\frac{GM}{r}$

Its SI unit is J/kg and it is a scalar quantity.

Its dimensional formula is $[L^2T^{-2}]$.

Since, work W is obtained, *i.e.* it is negative, the gravitational potential is always negative.

Potential due to a Point Mass

Suppose a point mass M is situated at a point O, the gravitational potential due to this mass at point P is given by $V = -\frac{GM}{r}$

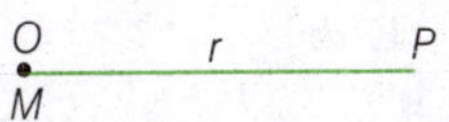

Competition Insight

- **Potential due to Uniform Ring**

At a point on its axis	At the centre
$V = -\frac{GM}{\sqrt{a^2 + r^2}}$	$V = -\frac{GM}{a}$

- **Potential due to Spherical Shell**

Outside the surface $r > R$	On the surface $r = R$	Inside the surface $r < R$
$V = \frac{-GM}{r}$	$V = \frac{-GM}{R}$	$V = \frac{-GM}{R}$

- **Potential due to Uniform Solid Sphere**

Outside the surface $r > R$	On the surface $r = R$	Inside the surface $r < R$
$V = \frac{-GM}{r}$	$V_{surface} = \frac{-GM}{R}$	$V = \frac{-GM}{2R}\left[3 - \left(\frac{r}{R}\right)^2\right]$

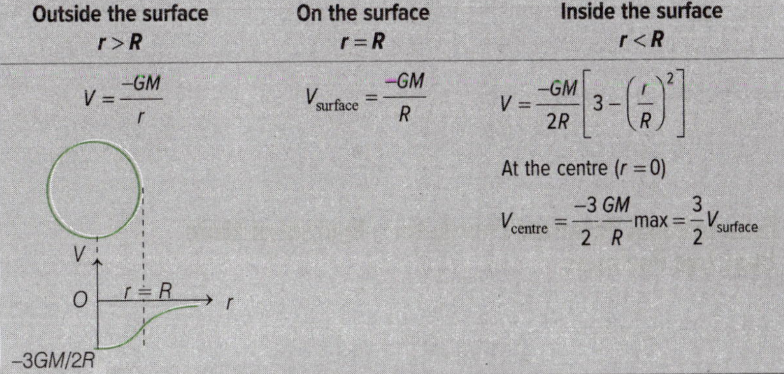

At the centre ($r = 0$)

$$V_{centre} = \frac{-3}{2}\frac{GM}{R} \max = \frac{3}{2} V_{surface}$$

Relation between Gravitational Field and Potential

If change in gravitation potential at a points is dV, gravitational field intensity is E, then during displacement $d\mathbf{r}$ in the field,

$$dV = -\mathbf{E} \cdot d\mathbf{r}$$

where, $\mathbf{E} = E_x\hat{\mathbf{i}} + E_y\hat{\mathbf{j}} + E_z\hat{\mathbf{k}}$

$d\mathbf{r} = dx\,\hat{\mathbf{i}} + dy\,\hat{\mathbf{j}} + dz\,\hat{\mathbf{k}}$

$\therefore \quad dV = -E_x dx - E_y dy - E_z dz$

Also we can write $\quad E_x = \dfrac{-\partial V}{\partial x},\ E_y = \dfrac{-\partial V}{\partial y}$ and $E_z = \dfrac{-\partial V}{\partial z}$

Gravitational Potential Energy

Gravitational potential energy of any object at any point in gravitational field is equal to the work done in bringing it from infinity to that point. It is denoted by U.

Gravitational potential energy, $U = -\dfrac{GMm}{r}$

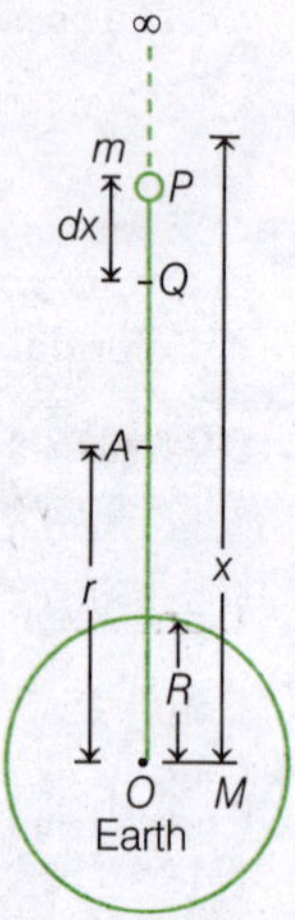

The negative sign shows that the gravitational potential energy decreases with increase in distance.

Gravitational potential energy at height h from the surface of the earth,

$$U_h = -\frac{GMm}{R+h} = \frac{-mgR}{1+\dfrac{h}{R}}$$

Gravitational Potential Energy of a Two Particles System

The gravitational potential energy of two particles of masses m_1 and m_2 separated by a distance r is given by

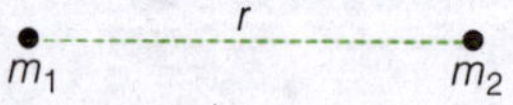

$$U = -\frac{Gm_1m_2}{r}$$

Gravitational Potential Energy for a System of More than Two Particles

The gravitational potential energy for a system of particles (say m_1, m_2, m_3 and m_4) is given by

$$U = -G\left[\frac{m_4m_3}{r_{43}} + \frac{m_4m_2}{r_{42}} + \frac{m_4m_1}{r_{41}} + \frac{m_3m_2}{r_{32}} + \frac{m_3m_1}{r_{31}} + \frac{m_2m_1}{r_{21}}\right]$$

Thus, for an n particle system there are $\frac{n(n-1)}{2}$ pairs and the potential energy is calculated for each pair and added to get the total potential energy of the system.

Kepler's Laws of Planetary Motion

(i) Law of orbit

Every planet revolves around the sun in an elliptical orbit and the sun is at its one focus.

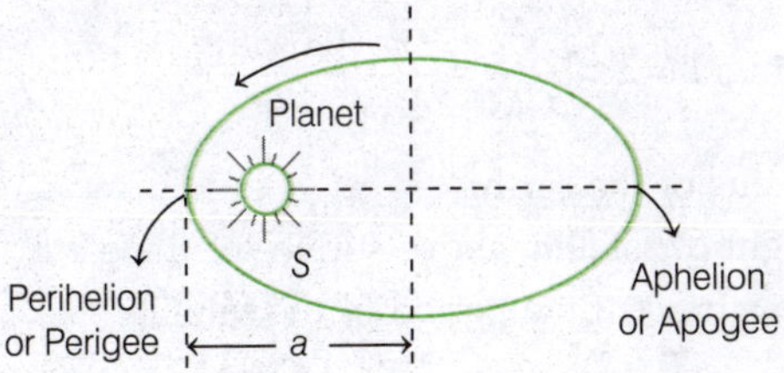

(ii) Law of area

The radius vector drawn from the sun to a planet sweeps out equal areas in equal intervals of time, i.e. the areal velocity of the planet around the sun is constant.

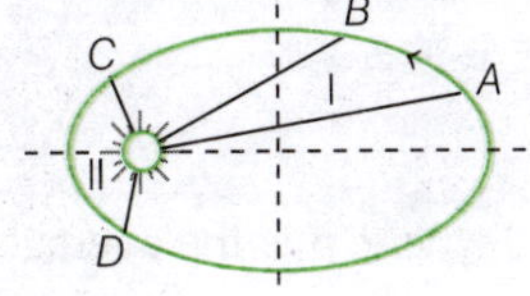

Areal velocity of a planet, $\frac{d\mathbf{A}}{dt} = \frac{\mathbf{L}}{2m}$ = constant

where, L = angular momentum and m = mass of the planet.

(iii) Law of period

The square of the time period of revolution of a planet around the sun is directly proportional to the cube of semi-major axis of its elliptical orbit.

$$T^2 \propto a^3 \quad \text{or} \quad \left(\frac{T_1}{T_2}\right)^2 = \left(\frac{a_1}{a_2}\right)^3$$

where, a = semi-major axis of the elliptical orbit.

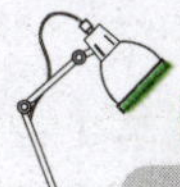

EXPERT Scale Up

Following tip is helpful in understanding the movements of satellites and celestial body.

Kepler's laws are applicable not only to the solar system but also to artificial satellites as well as to the moon revolving around the planets.

Satellite

A heavenly object which revolves around a planet is called a satellite.

Natural satellites are those heavenly objects which are not man-made and revolves around the earth.

Time period of satellite, $T = \dfrac{2\pi r}{\sqrt{\dfrac{GM}{r}}}$,

Here, r = orbital radius of satellite

After simplifying, $T = 2\pi\sqrt{\dfrac{r^3}{GM}} = \dfrac{2\pi}{R}\sqrt{\dfrac{(R+h)^3}{g}}$ $\left[\because g = \dfrac{GM}{R^2}\right]$

where, R = radius of the earth,

and h = height of satellite above surface of the earth.

Near the earth surface, time period of the satellite

$$T = 2\pi\sqrt{\frac{R^3}{GM}} = \sqrt{\frac{3\pi}{G\rho}}$$

$$T = 2\pi\sqrt{\frac{R}{g}} = 5.08 \times 10^3\text{ s} = 84\text{ min} \approx 1.4\text{ h}$$

where, ρ is the average density of the earth.

Knowledge Booster

Artificial satellites are those heavenly objects which are man made and launched for some purposes and revolve around the earth.

Artificial satellites are of two types

Geostationary or Parking Satellites These are those satellites which appear to be at a fixed position at a definite height to an observer on the earth is called geostationary or parking satellites.

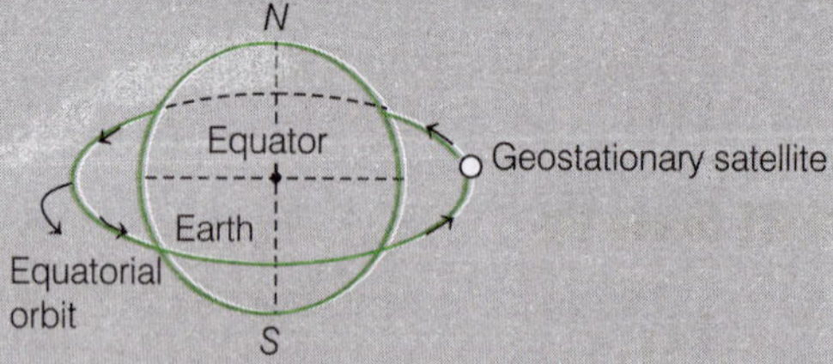

Height, from the earth's surface = 36000 km

Radius of orbit = 42400 km

Time period = 24 h

Orbital velocity = 3.1 km/s

$$\text{Angular velocity} = \frac{2\pi}{24} = \frac{\pi}{12} \text{ rad/h}$$

These satellites revolve around the earth in equatorial orbits.

The angular velocity of the satellites is same in magnitude and direction as that of angular velocity of the earth about its own axis.

These satellites are used in communication purpose.

INSAT 2B and INSAT 2C are geostationary satellites of India.

Polar Satellites These are those satellites which revolve in polar orbits around the earth. A polar orbit is that orbit whose angle of inclination with equatorial plane of the earth is 90°.

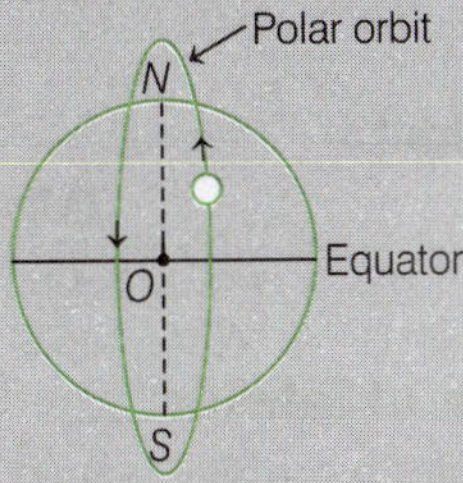

Height from the earth's surface ≈ 880 km

Time period ≈ 84 min

Orbital velocity = 8 km/s

$$\text{Angular velocity} = \frac{2\pi}{84} = \frac{\pi}{42} \text{ rad/min}$$

These satellites revolve around the earth in polar orbits.

These satellites are used in forecasting weather, studying the upper region of the atmosphere, in mapping, etc.

PSLV series satellites are polar satellites of India.

Orbital Velocity

Orbital velocity of a satellite is the minimum velocity required to put the satellite into a given orbit around the earth.

Orbital velocity of a satellite is given by

$$v_o = \sqrt{\frac{GM}{r}} = R\sqrt{\frac{g}{R+h}}$$

where, M = mass of the planet, R = radius of the planet and h = height of the satellite from planet's surface.

If satellite is revolving near the earth's surface, then $r = (R + h) \approx R$.

Now, orbital velocity, $v_o = \sqrt{gR} \approx 7.92 \text{km/s}$

If v is the speed of a satellite in its orbit and v_o is the required orbital velocity to move in the orbit, then

(i) If $v < v_o$, then satellite will move on a parabolic path and satellite will fall back to the earth.

(ii) If $v = v_o$, then satellite will revolve in circular path/orbit around the earth.

(iii) If $v_o < v < v_e$, then satellite will revolve around earth in elliptical orbit.

- The orbital velocity of jupiter is less than the orbital velocity of the earth.

Energy of a Satellite in Orbit

Total energy of a satellite, $E = \text{KE} + \text{PE} = \frac{GMm}{2r} + \left(-\frac{GMm}{r}\right) = -\frac{GMm}{2r}$

Time Period of Revolution of Satellite

The time taken by a satellite to complete one revolution around the earth, is known as time period of revolution of satellite.

The period of revolution (T) is given by

$$T = \frac{2\pi r}{\sqrt{\frac{GM}{r}}} = \frac{2\pi(R+h)}{v_0}$$

Height of Satellite

As it is known that the time period of satellite,

$$T = 2\pi\sqrt{\frac{r^3}{GM}} = 2\pi\sqrt{\frac{(R+h)^3}{gR^2}} \quad \text{...(i)}$$

By squaring on both sides of Eq. (i), we get

$$T^2 = 4\pi^2 \frac{(R+h)^3}{gR^2}$$

$$\Rightarrow \quad \frac{gR^2T^2}{4\pi^2} = (R+h)^3$$

$$\Rightarrow \quad h = \left(\frac{T^2gR^2}{4\pi^2}\right)^{1/3} - R$$

By knowing the value of time period, the height of the satellite from the earth surface can be calculated.

Binding Energy

The energy required by a satellite to leave its orbit around the earth (planet) and escape to infinity is called **binding energy** of the satellite. Binding energy of the satellite of mass m is given by

$$\text{BE} = + \frac{GMm}{2r}$$

Escape Velocity

Escape velocity on the earth is the minimum velocity with which a body has to be projected vertically upwards from the earth's surface, so that it just crosses the earth's gravitational field and never returns.

Escape velocity of any object (the earth's surface),

$$v_e = \sqrt{\frac{2GM}{R}} = \sqrt{2gR} = \sqrt{\frac{8\pi\rho GR^2}{3}} = R\sqrt{\frac{8}{3}\pi GP}$$

Escape velocity does not depend upon the mass or shape or size of the body as well as the direction of projection of the body. Escape velocity at earth is 11.2 km/s.

Some Important Escape Velocities

Heavenly body	Escape velocity
Moon	2.3 km/s
Mercury	4.28 km/s
Earth	11.2 km/s
Jupiter	60 km/s
Sun	618 km/s
Neutron star	2×10^5 km/s

Relation between escape velocity and orbital velocity of the satellite

$$v_e = \sqrt{2}\, v_o$$

A missile is launched with a velocity less than the escape velocity. The sum of its kinetic energy and potential energy will be negative.

Escape Energy Minimum energy given to a particle in form of kinetic energy, so that it can escape from earth's gravitational field, is called escape energy.

$$\text{Escape energy} = \frac{GMm}{R}$$

If escape velocity is v_e, then

$$\text{Escape energy} = \frac{1}{2} m v_e^2$$

Maximum Height Attained by a Particle

When a body is projected vertically upwards from the earth's surface,

$$h = \frac{v^2}{2g - v^2 / R}$$

(i) If velocity of projection v is equal the escape velocity ($v = v_e$), then body will attain maximum height ($h = \infty$).

(ii) If velocity of projection v of satellite is greater than the escape velocity ($v > v_e$), then the satellite will escape away following a hyperbolic path in interplanetary or interstellary space.

(iii) If $v < v_e$, the body will attain certain maximum height and then may move around the planet or may fall down back to the planet.

Knowledge Booster

Weightlessness

It is a situation in which the effective weight of the body becomes zero.

Weightlessness is achieved

(i) during freely falling body under gravity.

(ii) inside a spacecraft or satellite.

(iii) at the centre of the earth.

(iv) when a body is lying in a freely falling lift.

Chapter 09

Elasticity

Deforming Force

A force which produces a change in configuration of the object on applying it, is called a deforming force.

Elasticity

Elasticity is that property of an object by virtue of which it regains its original configuration after the removal of the deforming force.

Elastic Limit

Elastic limit is the upper limit of deforming force upto which a body regains its original form completely when the deforming force is removed, and beyond which if deforming force is increased, the body loses its property of elasticity and gets permanently deformed.

Perfectly Elastic Bodies

Those bodies which regain its original configuration immediately and completely after the removal of deforming force are called perfectly elastic bodies. *e.g.* Quartz, phospher bronze, etc.

Perfectly Plastic Bodies

Those bodies which does not regain its original configuration at all on the removal of deforming force, are called perfectly plastic bodies. *e.g.* Putty, paraffin, wax, etc.

Stress

The internal restoring force acting per unit area of a deformed body is called stress.

$$\text{Stress} = \frac{\text{Restoring force}}{\text{Area}}$$

Its SI unit is N/m^2 or pascal and dimensional formula is $[ML^{-1}T^{-2}]$.

Stress is a tensor quantity.

Stress is of three types :

(i) **Normal Stress** If deforming force is applied normally to an object, then the stress is called normal stress.

If there is an increase in length, then stress is called **tensile stress.**

If there is a decrease in length, then stress is called **compressive stress.**

(ii) **Volumetric Stress** If deforming force is applied normally on an object all over its surface, that changes its volume, then the stress is called volumetric stress.

(iii) **Tangential Stress** If deforming force is applied tangentially to an object, then the stress is called tangential stress. It changes the shape of the object.

Strain

The fractional change in configuration is called strain.

$$\text{Strain} = \frac{\text{Change in configuration}}{\text{Original configuration}}$$

It has no unit and it is a dimensionless quantity.

According to the change in configuration, the strain is of three types

(i) $\text{Longitudinal strain} = \dfrac{\text{Change in length}}{\text{Original length}}$

(ii) $\text{Volumetric strain} = \dfrac{\text{Change in volume}}{\text{Original volume}}$

(iii) Shearing strain = Angular displacement of the plane perpendicular to the fixed surface.

Hooke's Law

Within the limit of elasticity, the stress is proportional to the strain.

$$\text{Stress} \propto \text{Strain}$$

or

$$\text{Stress} = E \times \text{Strain}$$

where, E is the **modulus of elasticity** of the material of the body.

Elastic Modulii

The ratio of stress and strain, called modulus of elasticity or elastic moduli.

Types of Modulus of Elasticity

Modulus of elasticity is of three types

1. Young's Modulus of Elasticity

It is defined as the ratio of normal stress to the longitudinal strain within the elastic limit.

$$Y = \frac{\text{Normal stress}}{\text{Longitudinal strain}}$$

$$Y = \frac{Fl}{A\Delta l} = \frac{Mg\,l}{\pi r^2 \Delta l}$$

Its SI unit is N/m^2 or pascal and its dimensional formula is $[ML^{-1}T^{-2}]$.

Force Constant of Wire

Force required to produce unit elongation in a wire is called force constant of a material of wire. It is denoted by k.

$$k = \frac{YA}{l}$$

where, Y = Young's modulus of elasticity

and A = cross-sectional area of wire.

2. Bulk Modulus of Elasticity

It is defined as the ratio of volumetric stress to the volumetric strain within the elastic limit.

$$K = \frac{\text{Volumetric stress}}{\text{Volumetric strain}}$$

$$K = -\frac{FV}{A\Delta V} = -\frac{\Delta p V}{\Delta V}$$

where, $\Delta p = F / A$ = change in pressure.

Negative sign implies that when the pressure increases, volume decreases and *vice-versa*.

Its SI unit is N/m^2 or pascal and its dimensional formula is $[ML^{-1}T^{-2}]$.

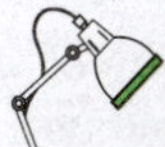

EXPERT Scale Up

Following tip helps you to evaluate the variation in radius of a spherical object in given condition.

- If the bulk modulus of spherical object is K and it is subjected to uniform pressure p, then the fractional decrease in radius will be $\frac{p}{3K}$.

Compressibility

Compressibility of a material is the reciprocal of its bulk modulus of elasticity.

$$\text{Compressibility } (C) = \frac{1}{K}$$

Its SI unit is $N^{-1}m^2$ and CGS unit is $dyne^{-1}\ cm^2$.

3. Modulus of Rigidity (η) (Shear Modulus)

It is defined as the ratio of tangential stress to the shearing strain, within the elastic limit.

$$\eta = \frac{\text{Tangential stress}}{\text{Shearing strain}}$$

$$\eta = \frac{F}{A\,\theta}$$

Its SI unit is N/m^2 or pascal and its dimensional formula is $[ML^{-1}T^{-2}]$.

Factors affecting Elasticity

(i) Modulus of elasticity of materials decreases with the rise in temperature, except for invar.

(ii) By annealing, elasticity of materials decreases.

(iii) By hammering or rolling elasticity, of materials increases.

(iv) Addition of impurities affects elastic properties depending on whether impurities are themselves more or less elastic.

Value Points

- For liquids, modulus of rigidity is zero.
- Young's modulus (Y) and modulus of rigidity (η) are possessed by solid materials only.
- Bulk modulus is relevant for solids, liquids and gases.

$$K_{\text{solid}} > K_{\text{liquid}} > K_{\text{gas}}$$

Poisson's Ratio

When a deforming force is applied at the free end of a suspended wire of length l and radius R, then its length increases by dl but its radius decreases by dR. Now, two types of strain are produced by a single force.

(i) Longitudinal strain $= \Delta l / l$

(ii) Lateral strain $= -\Delta R / R$

$$\therefore \text{ Poisson's ratio } (\sigma) = \frac{\text{Lateral strain}}{\text{Longitudinal strain}} = \frac{-\Delta R/R}{\Delta l/l}$$

Relation between Y, K, η and σ

(i) $Y = 3K(1-2\sigma)$ (ii) $Y = 2\eta(1+\sigma)$

(iii) $\sigma = \dfrac{3K-2\eta}{2\eta+6K}$ (iv) $\dfrac{9}{Y} = \dfrac{1}{K} + \dfrac{3}{\eta}$ or $Y = \dfrac{9K\eta}{\eta+3K}$

Competition Insight

- The theoretical value of Poisson's ratio lies between -1 and 0.5.
- Its practical value lies between 0 and 0.5.
- For the same material, the three coefficients of elasticity γ, η and K have different magnitudes.
- Isothermal elasticity of a gas $E_T = p$, where p = pressure of the gas.
- Adiabatic elasticity of a gas $E_S = \gamma p$
  where, $\gamma = \dfrac{C_p}{C_V}$, ratio of specific heats at constant pressure and at constant volume.
- Ratio between isothermal elasticity and adiabatic elasticity

$$\frac{E_S}{E_T} = \gamma = \frac{C_p}{C_V}$$

Stress and Strain Curve

When a wire is stretched by a load as shown in Fig. (a), it is seen that for small value of load, the extension produced in the wire is proportional to the load as shown in Fig. (b). Hence,

Stress $\propto$ Strain

Beyond the limit of elasticity, the stress and strain are not proportional to each other, on increasing the load further, the wire breaks at point D, known as fracture point.

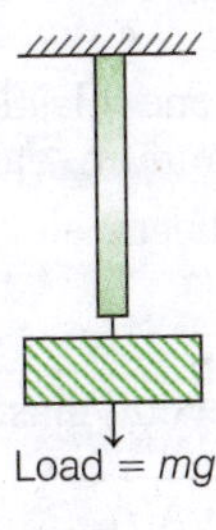

Fig.(a)

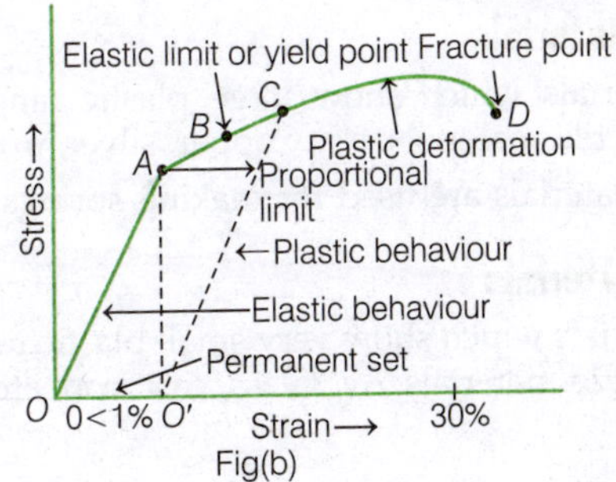

Fig(b)

Breaking Stress

The minimum value of stress required to break a wire, is called breaking stress. Breaking stress is fixed for a material but breaking force varies with area of cross-section of the wire.

$$\text{Safety factor} = \frac{\text{Breaking stress}}{\text{Working stress}}$$

Elastic Relaxation Time

The time delay in restoring the original configuration after removal of deforming force is called elastic relaxation time.

For quartz and phospher bronze, this time is negligible.

Elastic After Effect

The temporary delay in regaining the original configuration by the elastic body after the removal of deforming force is called elastic after effect.

Elastic Fatigue

The property of an elastic body by virtue of which its behaviour becomes less elastic under the action of repeated alternating deforming force is called elastic fatigue.

Elastomers

The materials for which strain produced is much larger than the stress applied, within the limit of elasticity are called elastomers. *e.g.* Rubber, the elastic tissue of arota, the large vessel carrying blood from heart, etc. Elastomers have no plastic range.

Elastic Hysteresis

As a natural consequence of the elastic after-effect, the strain in the body tends to lag behind the stress applied to the body so that during a rapidly changing stress, the strain is greater for the same value of stress. This lag of strain behind the stress is called elastic hysteresis.

Ductile Materials

The materials which show large plastic range beyond elastic limit are called ductile materials. *e.g.* Copper, silver, iron, aluminum, etc.

Ductile materials are used for making springs and sheets.

Brittle Materials

The materials which show very small plastic range beyond elastic limit are called brittle materials. *e.g.* Glass, cast iron, etc.

Malleability

The property of metals by which they can be beaten into thin sheets is called malleability. This is a characteristic property of metals.
e.g., gold, silver, lead etc.

Elastic Potential Energy in a Stretched Wire

The work done in stretching a wire is stored in the form of potential energy of the wire.
Potential energy,

$$U = \text{Average force} \times \text{Increase in length} = \frac{1}{2} F\Delta l$$

$$= \frac{1}{2} \text{Stress} \times \text{Strain} \times \text{Volume of the wire}$$

Elastic potential energy per unit volume,

$$U = \frac{1}{2} \times \text{Stress} \times \text{Strain} = \frac{1}{2} \text{(Young's modulus)} \times (\text{Strain})^2$$

Elastic potential energy of a stretched spring $= \frac{1}{2} kx^2$

where, k = force constant of spring and x = change in length.

Thermal Stress

When temperature of a rod fixed at its both ends is changed, then the produced stress is called thermal stress.

$$\text{Thermal stress} = \frac{F}{A} = Y\alpha\Delta\theta$$

where, α = coefficient of linear expansion of the material of the rod.

When temperature of a gas enclosed in a vessel is changed, then the thermal stress produced is equal to change in pressure (Δp) of the gas.

$$\text{Thermal stress} = \Delta p = K\gamma\, \Delta\theta$$

where, K = bulk modulus of elasticity

and γ = coefficient of cubical expansion of the gas.

Competition Insight

Cantilever

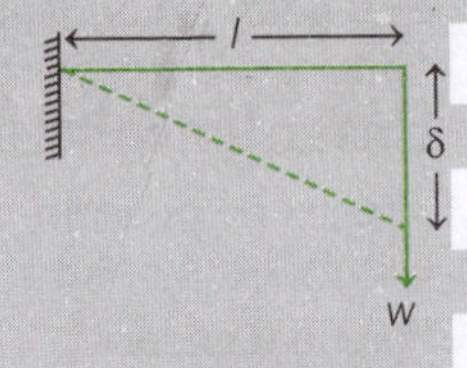

A beam clamped at one end and loaded at free end is called a cantilever. Depression (δ) at the free end of a cantilever is given by $\delta = \dfrac{wl^3}{3YI_G}$

where, w = load, l = length of the cantilever,
Y = Young's modulus of elasticity and
I_G = geometrical moment of inertia.

- For a beam of rectangular cross-section having breadth b and depth or length d, $I_G = \dfrac{bd^3}{12}$
- For a beam of circular cross-section area having radius r, $I_G = \dfrac{\pi r^4}{4}$

Beam Supported at Two Ends and Loaded at the Middle

Depression at middle, $\delta = \dfrac{wl^3}{48YI_G}$

The area of cross-section (A) of a rope required to lift a given load without breaking,

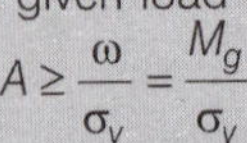

$$A \geq \frac{\omega}{\sigma_y} = \frac{M_g}{\sigma_y}$$

where, σ_y is yield strength of rope.

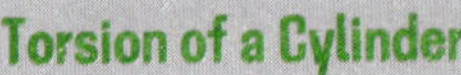

Torsion of a Cylinder

If the upper end of a cylinder is clamped and a torque is applied at the lower end, the cylinder gets twisted by angle θ, then

Couple per unit twist, $C = \dfrac{\pi\eta r^4}{2l}$

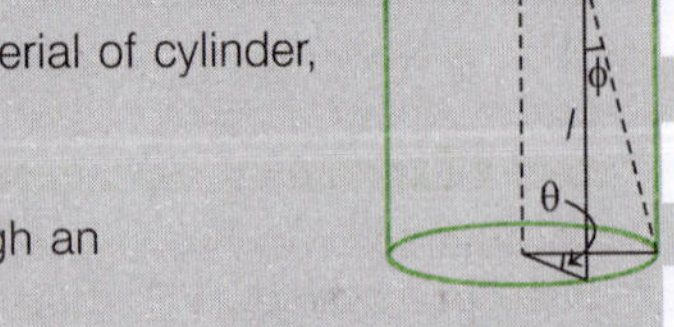

where, η = modulus of rigidity of the material of cylinder,
r = radius of cylinder,
and l = length of cylinder.

Work done in twisting the cylinder through an angle θ,

$$W = \frac{1}{2}C\theta^2$$

Relation between angle of twist (θ) and angle of shear (ϕ),

$$r\theta = l\phi \quad \text{or} \quad \phi = \frac{r}{l}\theta$$

Chapter 10

Hydrostatics

Fluids

Fluids are those substances which can flow when an external force is applied on them.

Liquids and gases are fluids.

The key property of fluids is that they offer very little resistance to shear stress. Hence, fluids do not have finite shape but takes the shape of the containing vessel. Liquids have a fixed volume, whereas a gas fills the entire volume of its container.

In fluid mechanics, the following properties of fluid would be considered

(i) When the fluid is at rest– **hydrostatics**

(ii) When the fluid is in motion– **hydrodynamics**

Thrust

The total normal force exerted by liquid at rest on a given surface is called **thrust** of liquid.

The SI unit of thrust is Newton.

Pressure

Pressure of liquid at a point is $p = \frac{\text{Thrust}}{\text{Area}} = \frac{F}{A}$.

Pressure is a scalar quantity, SI unit is Nm^{-2} and its dimensional formula $[ML^{-1}T^{-2}]$.

Pressure Exerted by the Liquid

The normal force exerted by a liquid per unit area of the surface in contact is called **pressure of liquid** or **hydrostatic pressure.**

Pressure exerted by a liquid column, $p = h\rho g$

where, h = height of liquid column, ρ = density of liquid
and g = acceleration due to gravity.

Mean pressure on the walls of a vessel containing liquid upto height h is $\left(\frac{h\rho g}{2}\right)$.

Variation of Pressure with Depth

Consider a fluid at rest having density ρ contained in a cylindrical vessel as shown in figure. Let the two points A and B separated by a vertical distance h.

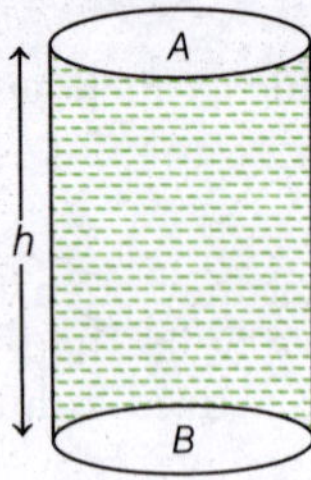

The pressure p at depth h below the surface of a liquid open to atmosphere is given by

$$p = p_a + h\rho g$$

where, ρ = density of liquid and g = acceleration due to gravity.

Atmospheric Pressure

The pressure exerted by the atmosphere on earth is called **atmospheric pressure.**

It is equivalent to a weight of 10 tones on 1 m^2.

At sea level, atmospheric pressure is equal to 76 cm of mercury column. Then, atmospheric pressure

$$= hdg = 76 \times 13.6 \times 980 \text{ dyne/cm}^2$$
$$= 0.76 \times 13.6 \times 10^3 \times 9.8 \text{ N/m}^2$$

Thus, 1 atm $= 1.013 \times 10^5$ Nm^{-2} (or Pa)

 **Value Points**

The atmospheric pressure does not crush our body because the pressure of the blood flowing through our circulatory system is balanced by this pressure.

Atmospheric pressure is also measured in torr and bar.

1 torr = 1 mm of mercury column

1 bar $= 10^5$ Pa

Aneroid barometer is used to measure atmospheric pressure.

Pressure measuring devices are open tube manometer, tyre pressure gauge, sphygmomanometer etc.

Gauge Pressure

Gauge pressure at a point in a fluid is the difference of total pressure (absolute pressure) at that point and atmospheric pressure.

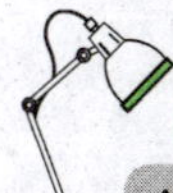

EXPERT Scale Up

Absolute pressure is always greater than or equal to zero. While, gauge pressure can be negative also.

Hydrostatic Paradox

The liquid pressure at a point is independent of the quantity of liquid but depends upon the depth of point below the liquid surface. This is known as hydrostatic paradox.

Important Points Related with Fluid Pressure

Important points related with fluid pressure are given below

(i) At a point in the liquid column, the pressure applied on it is same in all directions.

(ii) In a liquid, pressure will be same at all points at the same level.

(iii) The pressure exerted by a liquid depends only on the height of fluid column and is independent of the shape of the vessel containing liquid.

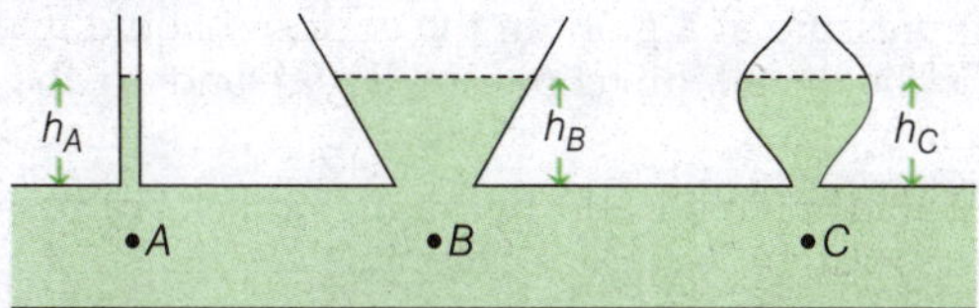

If $h_A = h_B = h_C$, then $p_A = p_B = p_C$

(iv) Consider following shapes of vessels

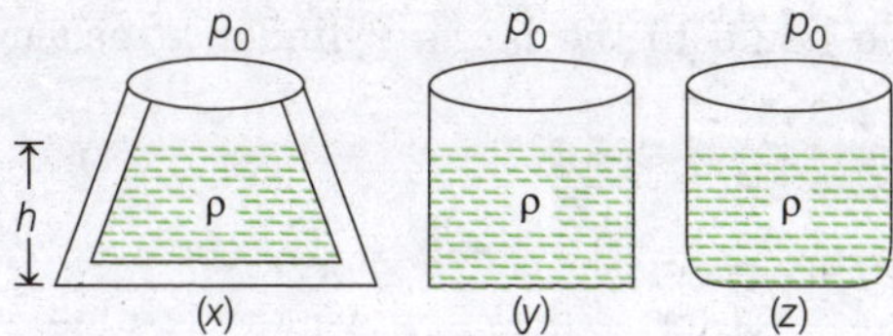

Pressure at the base of each vessel

$$p_x = p_y = p_z = p_0 + \rho gh \text{ but } w_x \neq w_y \neq w_z$$

where, ρ = density of liquid in each vessel,

h = height of liquid in each vessel

and p_0 = atmospheric pressure.

(v) In the figure, a block of mass 'm' floats over a fluid surface

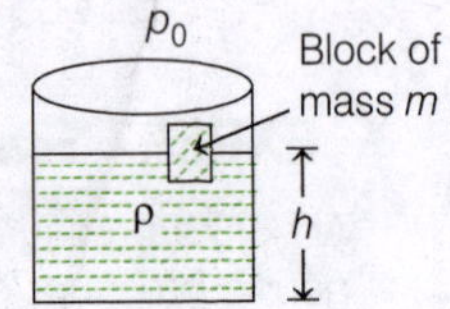

If ρ = density of the liquid

A = area of the block

Pressure at the base of the vessel in

$$p = p_0 + \rho gh + \frac{mg}{A}$$

Buoyancy

When a body is partially or fully immersed in a fluid, an upward force acts on it, which is called buoyant force, the phenomena is called buoyancy.

The buoyant force acts at the centre of gravity of the liquid displaced by the immersed part of the body and this point is called the centre of buoyancy. The magnitude of buoyant force, $F = V\rho g$.

where, V = immersed volume of solid,

s = density of liquid g = acceleration due to gravity.

Pascal's Law

The increase in pressure at a point in the enclosed liquid in equilibrium is transmitted equally in all directions in liquid and to the walls of the container.

The working of hydraulic lift and hydraulic brakes are based on Pascal's law.

- In a hydraulic lift, two pistons are separated by the space filled with a liquid. A piston of small cross-section A_1 is used to exert a force F_1 directly on the liquid. The pressure $p = \dfrac{F_1}{A_1}$ is transmitted throughout the liquid to the larger cylinder attached with a large piston of area A_2,

$$F_2 = pA_2 = \frac{F_1 A_2}{A_1}.$$

Competition Insight

Archimedes' Principle

When a body is partially or fully immersed in a liquid, it loses some of its weight and it is equal to the weight of the liquid displaced by the immersed part of the body. If a is loss of weight of a body in water and b is loss of weight in another liquid, then

$$\frac{a}{b}=\frac{w_{\text{air}}-w_{\text{liquid}}}{w_{\text{air}}-w_{\text{water}}}$$

If T is the observed weight of a body of density σ when it is fully immersed in a liquid of density ρ, then real weight of the body

$$w=\frac{T}{\left(1-\frac{\rho}{\sigma}\right)}$$

If w_1 = weight of body in air, w_2 = weight of body in liquid,

V_i = immersed of volume of solid,

ρ_L = density of liquid and g = acceleration due to gravity

$$\Rightarrow \quad V_i=\frac{w_1-w_2}{\rho_L g}$$

Laws of Floatation

A body will float in a liquid, if the weight of the body is equal to the weight of the liquid displaced by the immersed part of the body.

If W is the weight of the body and w is the buoyant force, then

(a) If $W>w$, then body will sink to the bottom of the liquid.

(b) If $W<w$, then body will float partially submerged in the liquid.

(c) If $W=w$, then body will float in liquid if its whole volume is just immersed in the liquid.

The floating body will be in stable equilibrium, if meta-centre lies vertically above the centre of gravity of the body.

The floating body will be in unstable equilibrium, if meta-centre lies vertically below the centre of gravity of the body. The floating body will be in neutral equilibrium, if meta-centre coincides with the centre of gravity of the body.

Fraction of volume of a floating body outside the liquid

$$\left(\frac{V_{out}}{V}\right)=\left[1-\frac{\rho}{\sigma}\right]$$

where, ρ = density of body and σ = density of liquid

If two different bodies A and B are floating in the same liquid, then

$\frac{\rho_A}{\rho_B}=\frac{(V_{in})_A}{(V_{in})_B}$, where $(V_{min})_A$ = fraction of volume of body A inside liquid and $(V_{in})_B$ = fraction of volume of body B inside liquid.

If the same body is made to float in different liquids of densities σ_A and σ_B respectively, then

$$\frac{\sigma_A}{\sigma_B}=\frac{(V_{in})_B}{(V_{in})_A}$$

Density and Relative Density

Density of a substance is defined as the ratio of its mass to its volume.

$$\text{Density of a liquid}=\frac{\text{Mass}}{\text{Volume}}$$

$$\text{Density of water}=1\text{ g/cm}^3\text{ or }10^3\text{ kg/m}^3$$

In case of homogneous (isotropic) substance it has no directional properties, so it is scalar quantity and its dimensional formula is $[ML^{-3}]$.

Relative Density

Relative density of a substance is defined as the ratio of its density to the density of water at 4°C.

$$\text{Relative density}=\frac{\text{Density of substance}}{\text{Density of water at }4^\circ\text{ C}}=\frac{\text{Weight of substance in air}}{\text{Loss of weight in water}}$$

Relative density also known as specific gravity has no unit, no dimensions.

For a solid body, density of body = density of substance.

While for a hollow body, density of body is lesser than that of substance.

When immiscible liquids of different densities are poured in a container, the liquid of highest density will be at the bottom while that of lowest density at the top and interfaces will be plane.

Knowledge Booster

- When two liquids of masses m_1 and m_2 having densities ρ_1 and ρ_2 are mixed together, then density of mixture is

$$\rho = \frac{m_1 + m_2}{\left(\frac{m_1}{\rho_1}\right) + \left(\frac{m_2}{\rho_2}\right)} = \frac{\rho_1\rho_2 (m_1 + m_2)}{(m_1 \rho_2 + m_2 \rho_1)}$$

- When two liquids of same mass m but of different densities ρ_1 and ρ_2 are mixed together, then density of mixture is $\rho = \frac{2\rho_1\rho_2}{\rho_1 + \rho_2}$.
- When two liquids of same volume V but of different densities ρ_1 and ρ_2 are mixed together, then density of mixture is $\rho = \frac{\rho_1 + \rho_2}{2}$.

  Density of a liquid varies with pressure, $\rho = \rho_0 \left[1 + \frac{\Delta p}{K}\right]$

  where, ρ_0 = initial density of the liquid, K = bulk modulus of elasticity of the liquid and Δp = change in pressure.
- With rise in temperature (ΔT) due to thermal expansion of a given body, volume will increase while mass will remain constant, so density will decrease $\rho = \frac{\rho_0}{(1 + \gamma \cdot \Delta T)} \simeq \rho_0 (1 - \gamma \cdot \Delta T)$;

  where γ is volumetric expansion.

Chapter 11

Hydrodynamics

Flow of Liquid

(i) **Streamline Flow** The flow of liquid in which each of its particle follows the same path as followed by the preceding particles is called streamline flow.

Two streamlines cannot cross each other and the greater the crowding of streamlines at a place, the greater is the velocity of liquid at that place and *vice-versa*.

(ii) **Laminar Flow** The steady flow of liquid over a horizontal surface in the form of layers of different velocities is called laminar flow.

The laminar flow is generally used synonymously with streamline flow of liquid.

(iii) **Turbulent Flow** The flow of liquid with a velocity greater than its critical velocity is disordered and called turbulent flow.

In case of turbulent flow, maximum part of external energy is spent for producing eddies in the liquid and small part of external energy is available for forward flow.

Critical Velocity

The critical velocity is the velocity of liquid flow, below which its flow is streamlined and above which it becomes turbulent.

$$\text{Critical velocity, } v_c = \frac{K\eta}{r\rho}$$

where, K = Reynold's number,

η = coefficient of viscosity of liquid
r = radius of capillary tube
and ρ = density of the liquid.

Competition Insight

Reynold's Number

Reynold's number is a pure number. It is equal to the ratio of the inertial force per unit area to the viscous force per unit area for a flowing fluid.

or Reynold number,

$$K = \frac{\text{Inertial force}}{\text{Force of viscosity}} = \frac{v_c \rho d}{\eta}$$

where, v_c = critical velocity.

For pure water flowing in a cylindrical pipe, K is about 1000. When $0 < K < 1000$, the flow of liquid is streamlined.

When $1000 < K < 2000$, the flow of liquid is variable between streamlined and turbulent.

When $K > 2000$, the flow of liquid is turbulent.

It has no unit and dimension.

Equation of Continuity

If a liquid is flowing in streamline flow in a pipe of non-uniform cross-sectional area, then rate of flow of liquid across any cross-section remains constant.

i.e. $$a_1 v_1 = a_2 v_2$$

$\Rightarrow$ $$av = \text{constant}$$

or $$a \propto \frac{1}{v}$$

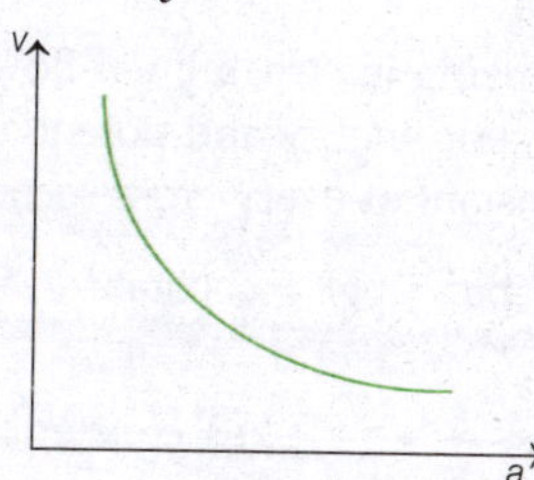

The velocity of liquid is slower where area of cross-section is larger and faster where area of cross-section is smaller.

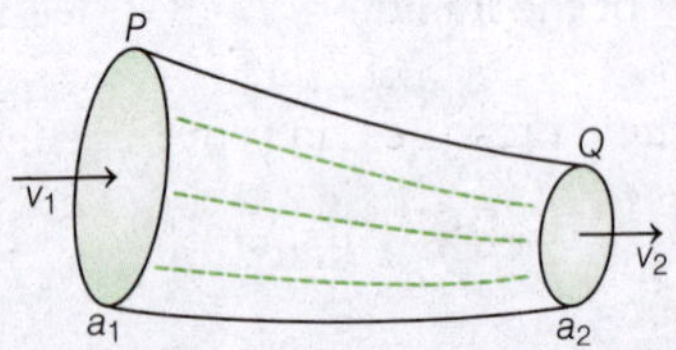

The falling stream of water becomes narrower, as the velocity of falling stream of water increases and therefore its area of cross-section decreases. Deep water appears still because it has large cross-sectional area.

Energy of a Liquid

A liquid in motion possess three types of energy

(i) **Pressure Energy**

Pressure energy per unit mass $= \frac{p}{\rho}$

where, $p =$ pressure of the liquid and $\rho =$ density of the liquid.
Pressure energy per unit volume $= p$

(ii) **Kinetic Energy**

Kinetic energy per unit mass $= \frac{1}{2} v^2$

Kinetic energy per unit volume $= \frac{1}{2} \rho v^2$

(iii) **Potential Energy**

Potential energy per unit mass $= gh$

Potential energy per unit volume $= \rho gh$

Bernoulli's Theorem

If an ideal liquid is flowing in streamlined flow, then total energy, *i.e.* sum of pressure energy, kinetic energy and potential energy per unit volume of the liquid remains constant at every cross-section of the tube.

Mathematically, $p + \frac{1}{2} \rho v^2 + \rho gh =$ constant

It can be expressed as, $\frac{p}{\rho g} + \frac{v^2}{2g} + h =$ constant

where, $\frac{p}{\rho g} =$ pressure head, $\frac{v^2}{2g} =$ velocity head and $\quad h$ = gravitational head or potential head.

For horizontal flow of liquid, $p + \frac{1}{2}\rho v^2$ = constant

where, p is called static pressure and $\frac{1}{2}\rho v^2$ is called dynamic pressure.

Therefore in horizontal flow of liquid, if p increases, v decreases and *vice-versa*.

Value Points

Bernoulli's theorem is applicable to ideal liquid, *i.e.* a liquid which is non-viscous incompressible and irrotational.

Applications of Bernoulli's Theorem

(i) The action of carburetor, paintgun, scent sprayer, atomiser and insect sprayer is based on Bernoulli's theorem.

(ii) The action of Bunsen's burner, gas burner, oil stove and exhaust pump is also based on Bernoulli's theorem.

(iii) Motion of a spinning ball (Magnus effect) is based on Bernoulli's theorem.

(iv) Blowing of roofs by wind storms, attraction between two closely parallel moving boats, fluttering of a flag etc are also based on Bernoulli's theorem.

(v) Bernoulli's theorem helps in explaining blood flow in artery.

(vi) Working of an aeroplane is based on Bernoulli's theorem.

Knowledge Booster

Venturimeter

It is a device used for measuring the rate of flow of liquid through pipes. Its working is based on Bernoulli's theorem.

Rate of flow of liquid, $v_1 = \sqrt{\dfrac{2gh}{\left(\dfrac{a_1}{a_2}\right)^2 - 1}}$

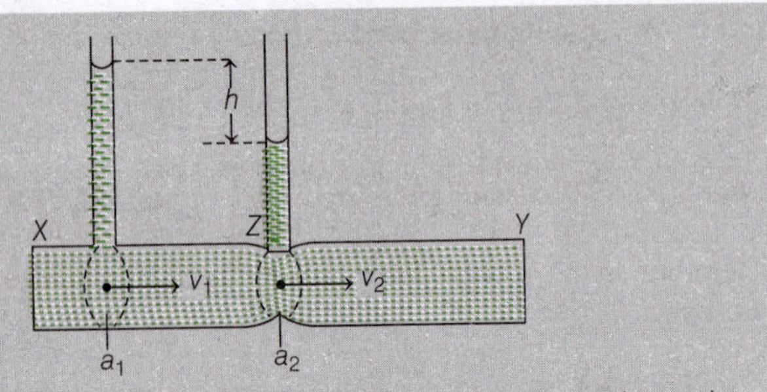

where, a_1 and a_2 are area of cross-sections of tube at broader and narrower part and h is difference of liquid columns in vertical tubes.

Torricelli's Theorem

Velocity of efflux (the velocity with which the liquid flows out of an orifice or a narrow hole) is equal to the velocity acquired by a freely falling body through the same vertical distance equal to the depth of orifice below the free surface of liquid.

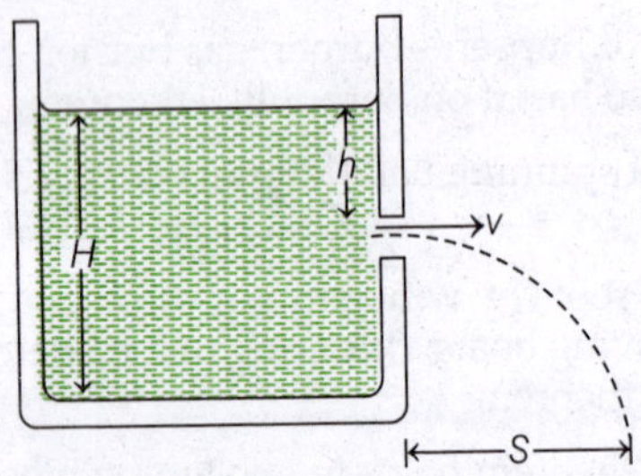

Velocity of efflux, $v = \sqrt{2gh}$

where, h = depth of orifice below the free surface of liquid.

For closed tank $p_2 >> p_1$

$$v_1 = \sqrt{\frac{2(p_2 - p_1)}{\rho}}$$

Time taken by the liquid to reach the base-level $t = \sqrt{\frac{2(H-h)}{g}}$

Horizontal range, $S = \sqrt{4h(H-h)}$
where, H = height of liquid column.

Horizontal range is maximum, equal to height of the liquid column H, when orifice is at half of the height of liquid column.

If the hole is at the bottom of the tank, then time required to make the tank empty is

$$t = \frac{A}{A_0}\sqrt{\frac{2H}{g}}$$

where, A is area of the container and A_0 is area of orifice.

Volume of liquid coming out from the orifice per second = $VA_0 = A_0\sqrt{2gh}$

Viscosity

The property of a fluid by virtue of which an internal frictional force acts between its different layers which opposes their relative motion is called **viscosity.**

These internal frictional force is called **viscous force.**

Viscous forces are intermolecular forces acting between the molecules of different layers of liquid moving with different velocities.

$$\text{Viscous force } (F) = -\eta A\frac{dv}{dx} \quad \text{or} \quad \eta = -\frac{F}{A\left(\frac{dv}{dx}\right)}$$

where, $\frac{dv}{dx}$ = rate of change of velocity with distance called velocity gradient, A = area of cross-section and η = coefficient of viscosity.

SI unit of η is Nsm^{-2} or pascal-second or decapoise. Its dimensional formula is $[ML^{-1}T^{-1}]$.

The knowledge of the coefficient of viscosity of different oils and its variation with temperature helps us to select a suitable lubricant for a given machine.

The cause of viscosity in liquid is due to cohesive force between liquid molecules, while in gases, it is due to diffusion.

Viscosity is due to transport of momentum. The value of viscosity (and compressibility) for ideal liquid is zero.

The viscosity of air and of some liquids is utilised for damping the moving parts of some instruments.

The knowledge of viscosity of some organic liquids is used in determining the molecular weight and shape of large organic moleculars like proteins and cellulose.

In any layer of liquid, the pulling of lower layers backwards while upper layers forward direction is known as laminar flow.

EXPERT Scale Up

Always remember that the velocity of viscous fluid flowing within a pipe is maximum along its axis.

Variation of Viscosity

The viscosity of liquids decreases with increase in temperature

$$\eta_t = \frac{\eta_0}{(1 + \alpha t + \beta t^2)}$$

where, η_0 and η_t are coefficient of viscosities at 0°C and t°C, α and β are constants.

The viscosity of gases increases with increase in temperatures as

$$\eta \propto \sqrt{T}$$

The viscosity of liquids increases with increase in pressure but the viscosity of water decreases with increase in pressure.

The viscosity of gases increases with increase of temperature because when temperature of gas increases, then rate of diffusion increases.

Stoke's Law and Terminal Velocity

When a small spherical body falls in a long liquid column, then after sometime it falls with a constant velocity, called **terminal velocity.**

When a small spherical body falls in a liquid column with terminal velocity, then viscous force acting on it is

$$F = 6\pi\eta\, rv$$

where, r = radius of the body, v = terminal velocity and η = coefficient of viscosity.

This is called **Stoke's law.**

Terminal velocity, $v = \dfrac{2}{9} \dfrac{r^2 (\rho - \sigma) g}{\eta}$

where, ρ = density of body,

σ = density of liquid,

η = coefficient of viscosity of liquid

and g = acceleration due to gravity.

(i) If $\rho > \sigma$, the body falls downwards.

(ii) If $\rho < \sigma$, the body moves upwards with the constant velocity.

(iii) If $\sigma << \rho, v = \frac{2r^2\rho g}{9\eta}$.

- Terminal velocity depends on the radius of the sphere in such a way that, if radius becomes n times, then terminal velocity will become n^2 times.
- Terminal velocity-time/distance graph

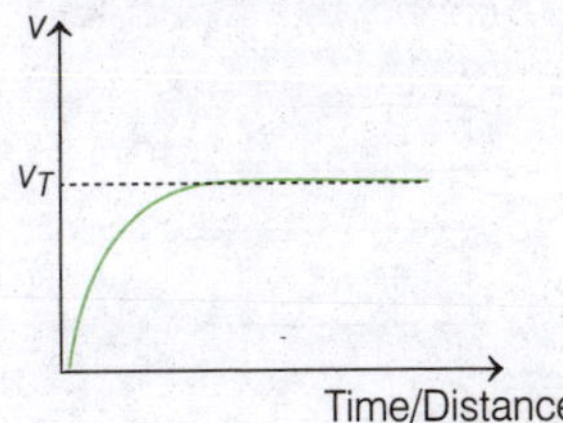

Importance of Stoke's Law

(i) This law is used in the determination of electronic charge by Millikan in his oil drop experiment.

(ii) This law helps a man coming down with the help of parachute.

(iii) This law accounts for the formation of clouds.

Knowledge Booster

Poiseuille's Formula

The rate of flow (v) of liquid through a horizontal pipe (for steady flow) is given by

$$v = \frac{\pi}{8}\frac{pr^4}{\eta l}$$

where, p = pressure difference across the two ends of the tube, r = radius of the tube, η = coefficient of viscosity and l = length of the tube.

Rate of Flow of Liquid

Rate of flow of liquid through a tube is given by

$$v = \frac{p}{R}$$

where, $R = \frac{8\eta l}{\pi r^4}$ called liquid resistance and p = liquid pressure difference.

(i) **When two tubes are connected in series**

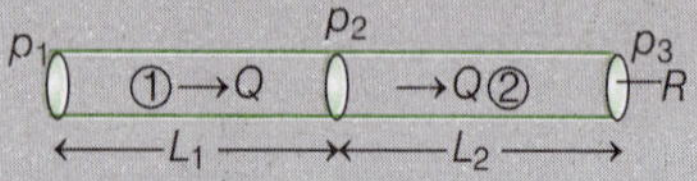

(a) Resultant pressure difference, $p = p_1 + p_2$.

(b) Rate of flow of liquid (v) is same through both tubes.

(c) Equivalent liquid resistance, $R = R_1 + R_2$.

(ii) **When two tubes are connected in parallel**

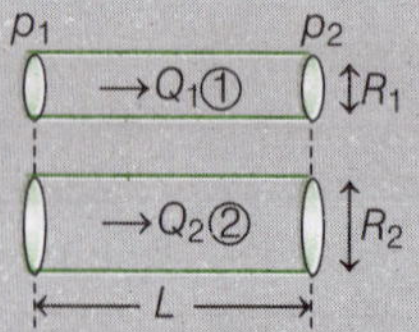

(a) Pressure difference (p) is same across both tubes.

(b) Rate of flow of liquid, $v = v_1 + v_2$.

(c) Equivalent liquid resistance $\frac{1}{R} = \frac{1}{R_1} + \frac{1}{R_2}$.

Chapter 12

Surface Tension

Surface tension is the property of any liquid by virtue of which it tries to minimise its free surface area.

Surface tension of a liquid is measured as the force acting per unit length on an imaginary line drawn tangentially on the free surface of the liquid.

$$\text{Surface tension, } S = \frac{\text{Force}}{\text{Length}} = \frac{F}{l} = \frac{\text{Work done}}{\text{Change in area}}$$

Its SI unit is Nm^{-1} or Jm^{-2} and its dimensional formula is $[MT^{-2}]$.

It is a scalar quantity. Surface tension is a molecular phenomenon which is due to cohesive force.

Surface tension of a liquid depends only on the nature of liquid and is independent of the surface area of film or length of the line considered.

Small liquid drops are spherical due to the property of surface tension.

Adhesive Force

The force of attraction acting between the molecules of different substances is called adhesive force, *e.g.* the force of attraction acting between the molecules of paper and ink, water and glass etc.

Cohesive Force

The force of attraction acting between the molecules of same substance is called cohesive force, *e.g.* the force of attraction acting between the molecules of water, glass, etc.

Value Points

- Cohesive forces and adhesive forces are van der Waals' forces.
- These forces vary inversely as the eighth power of distance between the molecules.

Force of Surface Tension on Different Shape

S.No.	Shape	Figure	Force of Surface tension
1.	Thin ring of radius r	F, O, r	$F = 2\pi (r + r) \cdot S + W$ $= 4\pi\, r \cdot S + W$ where, S = surface Tension W = Weight
2.	Circular plate or disc of radius r	F, O, r	$F = 2\pi r \cdot S + W$
3.	Square frame of side a	F	$F = 8a \cdot S + W$
4.	Square plate of side a	F	$F = 4aS + W$
5.	Hollow disc of inner radius r_1 and outer radius r_2	F	$F = 2\pi\, (r_1 + r_2) \cdot S + W$
6.	Wire of length l	F	$F = 2 \cdot l \cdot S + W$

Molecular Range

The maximum distance upto which a molecule can exert a force of attraction on other molecules is called molecular range.

Molecular range is different for different substances.

In solids and liquids, it is of the order of 10^{-9} m.

If the distance between the molecules is greater than 10^{-9} m, the force of attraction between them is negligible.

Factors Affecting Surface Tension

(i) Surface tension of a liquid decreases with increase in temperature and becomes zero at critical temperature.

(ii) At boiling point, surface tension of a liquid becomes zero and becomes maximum at freezing point.

(iii) Surface tension decreases when partially soluble impurities such as soap, detergent, dettol, phenol etc are added in water.

(iv) Surface tension increases when highly soluble impurities such as salt is added in water.

(v) When dust particles or oil spreads over the surface of water, its surface tension decreases.

When charge is given to a soap bubble, its size increases because surface tension of the liquid decreases due to electrification.

Surface Energy

If we increase the free surface area of a liquid, then work has to be done against the force of surface tension. This work done is stored in liquid surface as potential energy.

This additional potential energy per unit area of free surface of liquid is called surface energy.

$$\text{Surface energy } (E) = S \times \Delta A$$

where, S = surface tension and ΔA = increase in surface area.

(i) **Work Done in Blowing a Liquid Drop** If a liquid drop is blown up from a radius r_1 to r_2, then work done for that is

$$W = S \cdot 4\pi(r_2^2 - r_1^2)$$

(ii) **Work Done in Blowing a Soap Bubble** As a soap bubble has two free surfaces, hence work done in blowing a soap bubble so as to increase its radius from r_1 to r_2 is given by

$$W = S \cdot 8\pi(r_2^2 - r_1^2)$$

(iii) **Work Done in Splitting a Bigger Drop into *n* Smaller Droplets**

If a liquid drop of radius R is split up into n smaller droplets, all of same size, then radius of each droplet

$$r = R \cdot (n)^{-1/3}$$

$$\text{Work done, } W = 4\pi S(nr^2 - R^2) = 4\pi SR^2\,(n^{1/3} - 1)$$

(iv) **Coalescance of Drops** If n small liquid drops of radius r each combine together so as to form a single bigger drop of radius $R = n^{1/3} \cdot r$, then in the process energy is released. Release of energy is given by $\Delta U = S \cdot 4\pi(nr^2 - R^2) = 4\pi Sr^2 n(1 - n^{-1/3})$

Excess Pressure due to Surface Tension

(i) Excess pressure inside a liquid drop $= \dfrac{2S}{R}$

(ii) Excess pressure inside an air bubble in a liquid $= \dfrac{2S}{R}$

(iii) Excess pressure inside a soap bubble $= \dfrac{4S}{R}$.

where, S = surface tension and R = radius of drop/bubble.

Excess Pressure in Different Cases

S.No.	Nature of Surface	Excess Pressure
1.	Plane surface 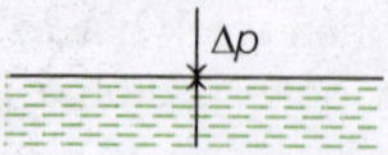 (Δp)	$\Delta p = 0$
2.	Convex surface of radius R 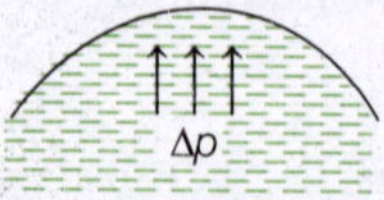 (Δp)	$\Delta p = \dfrac{2S}{R}$
3.	Concave surface of radius R 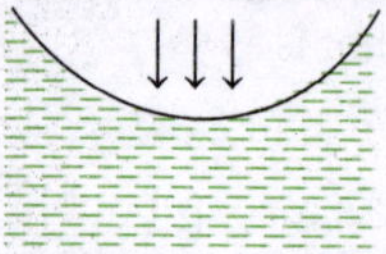	$\Delta p = \dfrac{2S}{R}$
4.	Cylindrical liquid surface of radius R 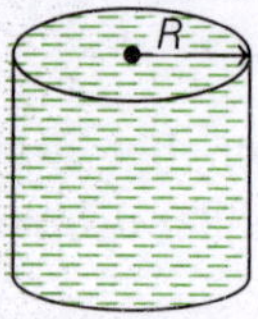 (R)	$\Delta p = \dfrac{S}{R}$
5.	Liquid surface of unequal radii 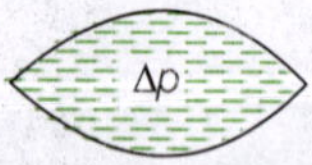 (Δp)	$\Delta p = S\left[\dfrac{1}{R_1} + \dfrac{1}{R_2}\right]$
6.	Liquid film of unequal radii 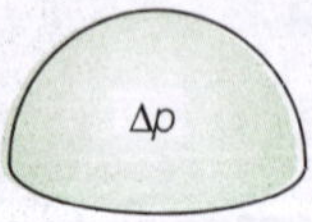 (Δp)	$\Delta p = 2S\left[\dfrac{1}{R_1} + \dfrac{1}{R_2}\right]$

Competition Insight

- Work done in spraying a liquid drop of radius R into n droplets of radius $r = S \times$ Increase in surface area

$$= 4\pi S R^3 \left(\frac{1}{r} - \frac{1}{R}\right)$$

Fall in temperature, $\Delta\theta = \frac{3S}{J}\left(\frac{1}{r} - \frac{1}{R}\right)$

where, $J = 4.2$ J/cal.

- When n small drops are combined into a bigger drop, then work done is given by

$$W = 4\pi R^2 S\,(n^{1/3} - 1)$$

Temperature increase, $\Delta\theta = \frac{3S}{J}\left(\frac{1}{r} - \frac{1}{R}\right)$

- When two bubbles of radii r_1 and r_2 coalesce into a bubble of radius r isothermally, then

$$r^2 = r_1^2 + r_2^2$$

- When two soap bubbles of radii r_1 and r_2 are in contact with each other, then radius r of common interface

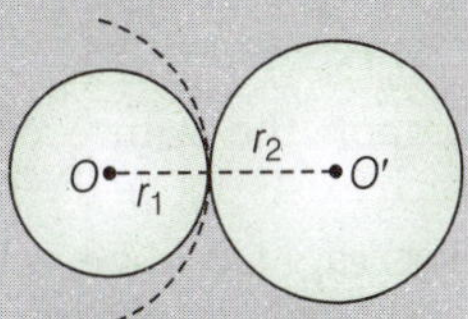

Common interface

$$\frac{1}{r} = \frac{1}{r_1} - \frac{1}{r_2} \quad \text{or} \quad r = \frac{r_1 r_2}{r_2 - r_1}$$

Formation of a Single Bubble

- If two bubbles of radius r_1 and r_2 coalesce isothermally to form a single bubble of radius r under external pressure p_0, then surface tension of the liquid

$$S = \frac{p_0[r^3 - r_1^3 - r_2^3]}{4\,[r_1^2 + r_2^2 - r^2]}$$

- Pressure inside bubbles are

$$p_1 = \left(p_0 + \frac{4S}{r_1}\right), p_2 = \left(p_0 + \frac{4S}{r_2}\right), p_3 = \left(p_0 + \frac{4S}{r}\right)$$

Also, $p_1V_1 + p_2V_2 = p_3V_3$

where, p_1, V_1 are pressure and volume of first bubble,

p_2, V_2 are pressure and volume of second bubble

and p_3, V_3 are pressure and volume of new bubble.

Angle of Contact

The angle subtended between the tangents drawn at liquid surface and at solid surface inside the liquid at the point of contact is called angle of contact (θ).

If liquid molecules is in contact with solid (*i.e.* wall of capillary tube), then forces acting on liquid molecules are

(i) Force of cohesion F_c (acts at an angle 45° to the vertical)

(ii) Force of adhesion F_a (acts outwards at right angle to the wall of the tube)

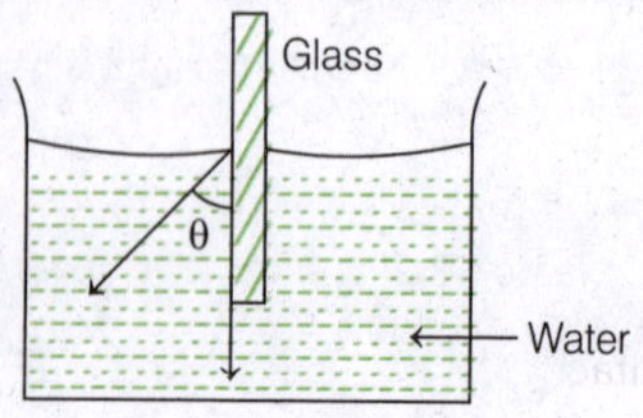

Angle of contact depends upon the nature of the liquid and solid in contact and the medium which exists above the free surface of the liquid.

When wax is coated on a glass capillary tube, it becomes water-proof. The angle of contact increases and becomes obtuse. Water does not rise in it. Rather it falls in the tube by virtue of obtuse angle of contact.

Angle of contact increases with increase in temperature of liquid. Angle of contact decreases on adding soluble impurity to a liquid.

Angle of contact for pure water and glass is zero.

For ordinary water and glass, it is 8°.

For alcohol and clean glass $\theta = 0°$.

Angle of Contact, Meniscus and Shape of liquid surface

Property	Angle of Contact $< 90°$	Angle of Contact $= 90°$	Angle of Contact $> 90°$
Substances	Water and glass	Water and silver	Mercury and glass
Angle of contact	Almost zero, acute angle	Right angle = 90°	Obtuse angle = 138°
Meniscus shape	Concave	Plane	Convex
Capillary action	Liquid rises	No effect	Liquid falls

Property	Angle of Contact <90°	Angle of Contact =90°	Angle of Contact >90°
Sticking to solid	Stick/wets	Does not wet	Does not wet
Relation between cohesive force (F_c) and adhesive force (F_a)	$F_a > \frac{F_c}{\sqrt{2}}$ $F_a > F_c$	$F_a = \frac{F_c}{\sqrt{2}}$	$F_a < \frac{F_c}{\sqrt{2}}$ $F_c > F_a$
Shape of liquid surface	Almost round	Spreads on surface	Flat on interface

Capillarity

The phenomenon of rise or fall of liquid column in a capillary tube is called capillarity.

Ascent of a liquid column in a capillary tube is given by

$$h = \frac{2S\cos\theta}{r\rho g} - \frac{r}{3}$$

If capillary is very narrow, then $h = \frac{2S\cos\theta}{r\rho g}$

where, r = radius of capillary tube, ρ = density of the liquid,

θ = angle of contact and S = surface tension of liquid.

- If $\theta < 90°$, $\cos\theta$ is positive, so h is positive, *i.e.* liquid rises in a capillary tube.
- If $\theta > 90°$, $\cos\theta$ is negative, so h is negative, *i.e.* liquid falls in a capillary tube.
- Rise of liquid in a capillary tube does not violate law of conservation of energy.

EXPERT Scale Up

In weightlessness condition, liquid does not rise in capillary tube.

Some Practical Examples of Capillarity

(i) The kerosene oil in a lantern and the melted wax in a candle, rise in the capillaries formed in the cotton wick and burns.

(ii) Coffee powder is easily soluble in water because water immediately wets the fine granules of coffee by the action of capillarity.

(iii) The water given to the fields rises in the innumerable capillaries formed in the stems of plants and trees and reaches the leaves.

Zurin's Law

If a capillary tube of insufficient length is placed vertically in a liquid, then liquid never come out from the tube on its own, as

$$Rh = \text{constant} \Rightarrow R_1h_1 = R_2h_2$$

where, R = radius of curvature of liquid meniscus

and h = height of liquid column.

When a tube is kept in inclined position in a liquid and the vertical height h remains unchanged, then length of liquid column

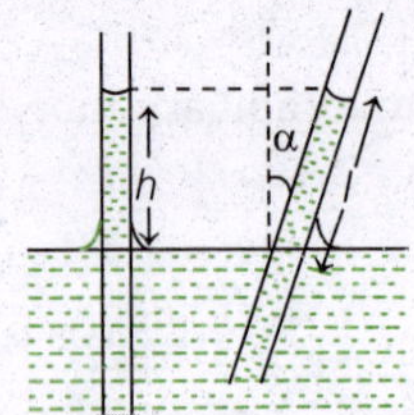

$$\cos\alpha = \frac{h}{l}$$

or

$$l = \frac{h}{\cos\alpha}$$

Liquid rises (water in glass capillary) or falls (mercury in glass capillary) due to property of surface tension

$$S = \frac{R\rho g h}{2\cos\theta}$$

where, R = radius of capillary tube, h = height of liquid,
ρ = density of liquid, θ = angle of contact,
S = surface tension of liquid
and g = acceleration due to gravity.

Value Points

Some Phenomena Based on Surface Tension

- Medicines used for washing wounds, as dettol, have a surface tension lower than water.
- Hot soup is more tasteful than the cold one because the surface tension of the hot soup is less than that of the cold and so it spreads over a larger area of the tongue.
- Insects and mosquitoes swim on the surface of water in ponds and lakes due to surface tension. If kerosene oil is sprayed on the water surface, the surface tension of water is lowered and the insects and mosquitoes sink in water and are dead.
- If we deform a liquid drop by pushing it slightly, then due to surface tension it again becomes spherical.
- The detergents are used for cleaning the dirty clothes. The molecule of detergent can attached with water and dirt molecules and they take away the dirt with them, when we wash the clothes with detergent.

Chapter 13

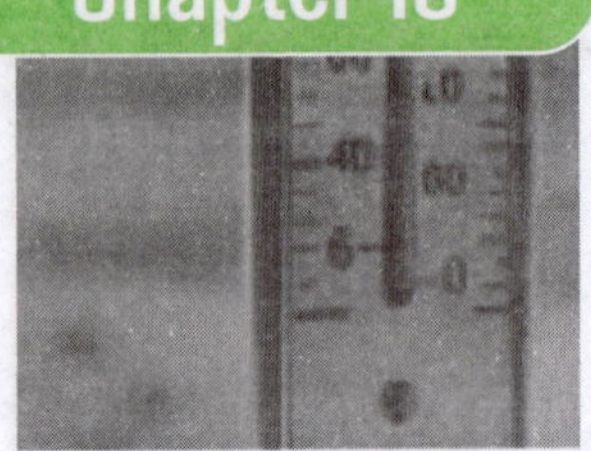

Thermometry and Calorimetry

The branch dealing with measurement of temperature is called **thermometry** and the devices used to measure temperature are called **thermometers.**

Heat

Heat is a form of energy called thermal energy which flows from a (hotter) higher temperature body to a lower temperature body (colder) when they are placed in contact.

Heat or thermal energy of a body is the sum of kinetic energies of all its constituent particles, on account of translational, vibrational and rotational motion.

The SI unit of heat energy is joule (J).

The practical unit of heat energy is calorie.

$$1 \text{ cal} = 4.18 \text{ J}$$

1 calorie is the quantity of heat required to raise the temperature of 1 g of water by 1°C (from 14.5°C to 15.5°C).

Mechanical energy or work (W) can be converted into heat (Q) by

$$W = JQ$$

where, J = Joule's mechanical equivalent of heat.

J is a conversion factor (not a physical quantity) and its value is 4.186 J/cal.

Temperature and its Measurement

Temperature of a body is the degree of hotness or coldness of the body.

Highest possible temperature achieved in laboratory is about 10^8 K, while lowest possible temperature attained is 10^{-8} K.

 Knowledge Booster

Branch of Physics dealing with production and measurement of temperature close to 0 K is known as **cryogenics**, while that dealing with the measurement of very high temperature is called **pyrometry**.

Temperature of the core of the sun is 10^7 K while that of its surface is 6000 K.

NTP or STP implies 273.15 K (0°C = 32°F).

Different Scale of Temperature

(i) Celsius Scale

In this scale of temperature, the melting point of ice is taken as 0°C and the boiling point of water as 100°C and the space between these two points is divided into 100 equal parts.

(ii) Fahrenheit Scale

In this scale of temperature, the melting point of ice is taken as 32°F and the boiling point of water as 212°F and the space between these two points is divided into 180 equal parts.

(iii) Kelvin Scale

In this scale of temperature, the melting point of ice is taken as 273 K and the boiling point of water as 373 K and the space between these two points is divided into 100 equal parts.

(iv) Reaumer Scale

In this scale of temperature, the melting point of ice is taken as 0° R and the boiling point of water as 80° R and the space between these two points is divided into 80 equal parts.

Relation between Different Scales of Temperatures

$$\frac{C}{100} = \frac{F-32}{180} = \frac{K-273}{100} = \frac{R}{80}$$

Absolute Temperature

There is no limit for maximum temperature but there is a sharp point for minimum temperature that nobody can have the temperature lower than this minimum value of temperature, which is known as absolute temperature. On absolute scale temperature, −273.15°C is taken as the zero point that is 0K.

Thermometric Property

The property of an object which changes with temperature is called a thermometric property. Different thermometric properties and thermometers have been given below

(i) Pressure of a Gas at Constant Volume

$$\frac{p_1}{T_1} = \frac{p_2}{T_2} \text{ and } p_t = p_0\left(1 + \frac{t}{273}\right)$$

$$t = \left(\frac{p_t - p_0}{p_{100} - p_0} \times 100\right)°\text{C}$$

where, p_0, p_{100} and p_t are pressure of a gas at constant volume at 0°C, 100°C and t°C.

A constant volume gas thermometer can measure temperature from −200°C to 500°C.

(ii) Electrical Resistance of Metals

$$R_t = R_0\,(1 + \alpha t + \beta t^2)$$

where, α and β are constants for a metal.

As β is too small therefore, we can take

$$R_t = R_0\,(1 + \alpha t)$$

where, α = temperature coefficient of resistance and

R_0 and R_t are electrical resistances at 0°C and t°C.

$$\alpha = \frac{R_2 - R_1}{R_1 t_2 - R_2 t_1}$$

where, R_1 and R_2 are electrical resistances at temperatures t_1 and t_2.

or
$$t = \frac{R_t - R_0}{R_{100} - R_0} \times 100°\text{C}$$

where, R_{100} is the resistance at 100°C.

Platinum resistance thermometer can measure temperature from −200°C to 1200°C.

(iii) **Length of Mercury Column in a Capillary Tube**

$$l_t = l_0 (1 + \alpha t)$$

where α = coefficient of linear expansion and l_0, l_t are lengths of mercury column at 0°C and t°C.

Thermometers

The thermometers work on the thermometric property, *i.e.*, the property which changes with temperature like any physical quantity such as length, volume, pressure and resistance etc., which varies linearly with a certain range of temperature.

Different Types of Thermometers

Some different types of thermometers are given below

(i) **Mercury thermometer** In this thermometer, the length of a mercury column from some fixed point is taken as thermometric property.

If length of mercury column at 0° and 100° are l_0 and l_{100} respectively and at t° the length of mercury is l_t. Then

$$t = \left(\frac{l_t - l_0}{l_{100} - l_0} \right) \times 100°C$$

(ii) **Constant volume gas thermometer** It works on the principle of change in pressure with temperature when the volume is kept constant. If p_0, p_{100} and p_t are the pressures of gas at temperatures 0° C, 100°C, and unknown temperature (t°C) respectively keeping the volume constant, then

$$t = \left(\frac{p_t - p_0}{p_{100} - p_0} \times 100 \right) °C$$

For constant pressure gas thermometers, $t = \frac{V_t - V_0}{V_{100} - V_0} \times 100°C$

(iii) **Platinum resistance thermometer** It works on the principle of variation of resistance of metals with temperature.

If R_0, R_{100} and R_t are the resistances of a platinum wire at temperature 0°C, 100°C and unknown temperature (t°C) respectively.

Then, $$t = \left(\frac{R_t - R_0}{R_{100} - R_0} \times 100 \right) °C = \left(\frac{R_t}{R_{tr}} \times 273.16 \right) K$$

Here, temperature coefficient of resistance (α) is given by

$$\alpha = \frac{R_{100} - R_0}{R_0 \times 100}$$

(iv) **Pyrometers** Pyrometers are the devices used to measure the temperature by measuring the intensity of radiations received from the body.

Thermal Expansion

When matter is heated without any change in its state, it usually expand. This phenomena of expansion of matter on heating, is called thermal expansion. There are three types of thermal expansion

1. Expansion of Solids

Three types of expansion takes place in solid

(i) **Linear Expansion** Expansion in length on heating is called linear expansion.

Increase in length, $\Delta l = l_0 (1 + \alpha \Delta t)$

Coefficient of linear expansion, $\alpha = \dfrac{\Delta l}{l_0 \times \Delta t}$

where, l_0 = initial length and Δl = change in length

and Δt = change in temperature.

(ii) **Superficial Expansion** Expansion in area on heating is called superficial expansion.

Increase in area, $\Delta A = A_0 (1 + \beta \Delta t)$

Coefficient of superficial expansion, $\beta = \dfrac{\Delta A}{A_0 \times \Delta t}$

where, A_0 = initial surface area, ΔA = change in area and Δt = change in temperature.

(iii) **Cubical Expansion** Expansion in volume on heating is called cubical expansion.

Increase in volume, $\Delta V = V_0 (1 + \gamma \Delta t)$

Coefficient of cubical expansion, $\gamma = \dfrac{\Delta V}{V_0 \times \Delta t}$

where, V_0 = initial volume,

ΔV = change in volume

and Δt = change in temperature.

Dimension of α, β and γ are same $[\theta^{-1}]$ and units are K^{-1} or $(°C)^{-1}$.

Value Points

- Relation between coefficients of linear, superficial and cubical expansions $\beta = 2\alpha$ and $\gamma = 3\alpha$

  or $\alpha : \beta : \gamma = 1 : 2 : 3$
- The value of α, β and γ depend on the nature of the materials.

2. Expansion of Liquids

In liquids only expansion in volume takes place on heating.

(i) **Apparent Expansion of Liquids** When expansion of the container containing liquid on heating is not taken into account, then observed expansion is called apparent expansion of liquids.

Coefficient of apparent expansion of a liquid

$$(\gamma_a) = \frac{\text{apparent (or observed) increase in volume}}{\text{original volume} \times \text{change in temperature}}$$

(ii) **Real Expansion of Liquids** When expansion of the container containing liquid on heating is also taken into account, then observed expansion is called real expansion of liquids.

Coefficient of real expansion of a liquid

$$(\gamma_r) = \frac{\text{real increase in volume}}{\text{original volume} \times \text{change in temperature}}$$

Both γ_r and γ_a are measured in $^\circ C^{-1}$.

We can show that

$$\gamma_r = \gamma_a + \gamma_g$$

where, γ_r and γ_a are coefficient of real and apparent expansion of liquids and γ_g is coefficient of cubical expansion of the container (vessel).

EXPERT Scale Up

- All substance does not expand with rising temperature.
- Some substances contract with rising temperature because transverse vibration of atoms of such substances dominate on the longitudinal vibration which is responsible for their contraction, e.g. Ruthenate ceramic material.

Anomalous Expansion of Water

When temperature of water is increased from 0°C, then its volume decreases upto 4°C, becomes minimum at 4°C and then increases. This behaviour of water around 4°C is called anomalous expansion of water.

3. Thermal Expansion of Gases

There are two types of coefficient of expansion in gases

(i) **Volume Coefficient (γ_V)** At constant pressure, the change in volume per unit volume per degree celsius is called volume coefficient.

$$\gamma_V = \frac{V_2 - V_1}{V_0 (t_2 - t_1)}$$

where V_0, V_1 and V_2 are volumes of the gas at 0°C, t_1 °C and t_2 °C.

(ii) **Pressure Coefficient (γ_p)** At constant volume, the change in pressure per unit pressure per degree celsius is called pressure coefficient.

$$\gamma_p = \frac{p_2 - p_1}{p_0 (t_2 - t_1)}$$

where p_0, p_1 and p_2 are pressure of the gas at 0°C, t_1 °C and t_2 °C.

Variation of Density with Temperature

Most substances expand when they are heated *i.e.* volume of a given mass of a substance increases on heating, so density decreases. Hence $\rho \propto \frac{1}{V}$,

$$\rho' = \rho(1 + \gamma\Delta T)^{-1}, \text{ as } \gamma \text{ is small } (1 + \gamma\Delta T)^{-1} \approx 1 - \gamma\Delta T$$

$$\rho' \approx \rho(1 - \gamma\Delta T)$$

Practical Applications of Thermal Expansion

(i) When rails are laid down on the ground, space is left between the end of two rails.

(ii) The transmission cables are not tightly fixed to the poles.

(iii) The iron rim to be put on a cart wheel is always of slightly smaller diameter than that of wheel.

(iv) A glass stopper jammed in the neck of a glass bottle can be taken out by heating the neck of the bottle.

Thermal Equilibrium

When there is no transfer of heat between two bodies in contact, then the bodies are called in thermal equilibrium.

Triple Point of Water

The values of pressure and temperature at which water coexists in equilibrium in all three states of matter, *i.e.* ice, water and vapour is called triple point of water.

Triple point of water is 273.16 K temperature and 0.46 cm of mercury pressure.

Specific Heat

The amount of heat required to raise the temperature of unit mass of the substance through 1°C is called its specific heat.

It is denoted by *c* or *s*.

Its SI unit is 'joule/kilogram-°C' (J/kg-°C) or $\text{Jkg}^{-1}\text{K}^{-1}$ and its dimensional formula is $[L^2T^{-2}\theta^{-1}]$.

The specific heat of water is 4200 J $\text{kg}^{-1}\text{°C}^{-1}$ or 1 cal g^{-1} °C^{-1} which is high as compared with most other substances.

Gases have two types of specific heat

(i) The specific heat capacity at constant volume (C_V).

(ii) The specific heat capacity at constant pressure (C_p).

Specific heat at constant pressure (C_p) is greater than specific heat at constant volume (C_V), *i.e.* $C_p > C_V$.

For molar specific heats, $C_p - C_V = R$

where, R = gas constant and this relation is called **Mayer's formula.**

The ratio of two principal sepecific heats of a gas is represented by γ, *i.e.*

$$\gamma = \frac{C_p}{C_V}$$

The value of γ depends on atomicity of the gas.

Amount of heat energy required to change the temperature of any substance is given by $Q = mc\Delta t$

where, m = mass of the substance,

c = specific heat of the substance

and Δt = change in temperature.

Thermal (Heat) Capacity

Heat capacity of any body is equal to the amount of heat energy required to increase its temperature through 1°C.

Heat capacity = mc

where, c = specific heat of the body and m = mass of the body.

Its SI unit is joule/kelvin (J/K) and dimensional formula $[ML^2T^{-2}K^{-1}]$.

Molar specific heat capacity, $c = \frac{s}{\mu} = \frac{\Delta Q}{\mu \Delta T}$

where, μ = number of moles of substances (gas).

Relation between c and M are

$$c = MS$$

where, M = molecular mass of substance

and S = specific heat capacity.

Water Equivalent

It is the quantity of water whose thermal capacity is same as the heat capacity of the body. It is denoted by W.

$$W = ms = \text{heat capacity of the body.}$$

The water equivalent of a body is expressed in grams.

Calorimetry

This is the branch of heat transfer that deals with the measurement of heat. The heat is usually measured in calories or kilo calories.

Principle of Calorimetry

When a hot body is mixed with a cold body, then heat lost by hot body is equal to the heat gained by cold body.

$$\text{Heat lost} = \text{Heat gain}$$

i.e. principle of calorimetry follows the law of conservation of heat energy.

If two substances having masses m_1 and m_2, specific heats c_1 and c_2 kept at temperatures T_1 and T_2 $(T_1 > T_2)$ are mixed, such that temperature of mixture at equilibrium is T_{mix}.

Then, $m_1 . c_1 (T_1 - T_{mix}) = m_2 c_2 (T_{mix} - T_2)$

or $$T_{mix} = \frac{m_1 c_1 T_1 + m_2 c_2 T_2}{m_1 c_1 + m_2 c_2}$$

Competition Insight

Temperature of Mixture in Different Cases

Condition	Temperture of mixture
If bodies are of same material, *i.e.* $c_1 = c_2$	$T_{mix} = \frac{m_1T_1 + m_2T_2}{m_1 + m_2}$
If bodies are of same mass, *i.e.* $m_1 = m_2$	$T_{mix} = \frac{c_1T_1 + c_2T_2}{c_1 + c_2}$
If bodies are of same mass and same material, *i.e.* $m_1 = m_2$ and $c_1 = c_2$	$T_{mix} = \frac{T_1 + T_2}{2}$
If water at T_w°C is mixed with ice at 0°C. First, ice will melt and then its temperature rises to attain thermal equilibrium (say final temperature is T_{mix})	$T_{mix} = \frac{m_wT_w - \frac{m_iL_i}{c_W}}{m_w + m_i}$
If $m_w = m_i$	$T_{mix} = \frac{T_w - \frac{L_i}{c_W}}{2}$

Change of State

Physical process in which a matter change from one state to another, e.g., solid to liquid, liquid to vapour, etc.

Melting

Conversion of solid into liquid state at constant temperature is called melting.

Fusion and Freezing Point

The process of change of state from liquid to solid is called fusion. The temperature at which liquid starts to freeze is known as the freezing point of the liquid.

Evaporation

Conversion of liquid into vapour at all temperatures (even below its boiling point) is called evaporation.

Boiling

When a liquid is heated gradually, at a particular temperature the saturated vapour pressure of the liquid becomes equal to the atmospheric pressure, now bubbles of vapour rise to the surface of the liquid. This process is called boiling of the liquid.

The temperature at which liquid boils is called **boiling point**.

The boiling point of water increases with increase in pressure and decreases with decrease in pressure.

Sublimation

The conversion of a solid into vapour state is called sublimation.

Hoar Frost

The conversion of vapours into solid state is called hoar frost.

Knowledge Booster

Joule's Law

According to Joule, whenever heat is converted into work or work is converted into heat, then the ratio of work and heat is constant.

$\frac{W}{Q} = J$, where J is mechanical equivalent of heat.

When water falls from height h, then increase in temperature dT at the bottom is

$$dT = \left(\frac{gh}{J \cdot C}\right)°C$$

- When m kg of ice-block falls from height h and its some part m' is melt down, then

$$h = \frac{m'}{m}\left(\frac{JL}{g}\right) \text{ meter}$$

- If ice-block melts completely, then $m = m'$ and hence $h = \frac{JL}{g}$.

Latent Heat

The heat energy absorbed or released at constant temperature per unit mass for change of state is called latent heat.

Heat energy absorbed or released during change of state is given by

$$Q = mL$$

where, $m =$ mass of the substance and $L =$ latent heat.

Its unit is cal/g or J/kg and its dimensional formula is $[L^2 T^{-2}]$.

Latent heat of vapourisation

For water at its normal boiling point or condensation temperature (100°C), the latent heat of vaporisation is

$$L = 540 \text{ cal/g} = 40.8 \text{ kJ / mol}$$
$$= 2260 \text{ kJ/kg}$$

Latent heat of fusion

For water at its normal freezing temperature or melting point (0°C), the latent heat of fusion is

$$L = 80 \text{ cal / g} = 60 \text{ kJ/mol}$$
$$= 336 \text{ kJ/kg}$$

Value Points

- It is more painful to get burnt by steam rather than by boiling water at 100°C. Steam converted to water at 100°C, then it gives out 536 cal of heat, so, it is clear that steam at 100°C has more heat than water at 100°C (*i.e.* boiling of water).
- After snow falls, the temperature of the atmosphere becomes very low. This is because the snow absorbs the heat from the atmosphere to melt down. So, in the mountains, when snow falls, one does not feel too cold but when ice melts, he feels too cold.
- There is more shivering effect of icecream on teeth as compared to that of water (obtained from ice). This is because when icecream melts down, it absorbs large amount of heat from teeth.

Chapter 14

Kinetic Theory of Gases

Kinetic Theory of Ideal gases

Kinetic theory of gases explains the behavior of gases, it correlates the macroscopic properties of gases *e.g.*, Pressure, temperature etc., to the microscopic properties like speed, momentum, kinetic energy etc.

Assumptions of Kinetic Theory of Gases

(i) Every gas consists of extremely small particles known as molecules. The molecules of a given gas are all identical but are different from those of another gas.

(ii) The molecules of a gas are identical spherical, rigid and perfectly elastic point masses.

(iii) Their molecular size is negligible in comparison to intermolecular distance (10^{-9} m).

(iv) The speed of gas molecules lies between zero and infinity (very high speed).

(v) The distance covered by the molecules between two successive collisions is known as **free path** and mean of all free path is known as **mean free path**.

(vi) The number of collisions per unit volume in a gas remains constant.

(vii) No attractive or repulsive force acts between gas molecules.

(viii) Gravitational attraction among the molecules is ineffective due to extremely small masses and very high speed of molecules.

(ix) The density of gas is constant at all points of the vessel.

(x) The molecules of a gas keep on moving randomly in all possible directions with all possible velocities.

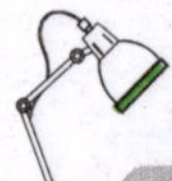

EXPERT Scale Up

At low temperature and high pressure, molecules of gases come closer to each other and the volume of gas is compressed. In this case, kinetic theory is not applicable to gases.

Gas Laws

Through experiments, it was established that gases irrespective of their nature obey the following laws

Boyle's Law

At constant temperature, the volume (V) of given mass of a gas is inversely proportional to its pressure (p), *i.e.*

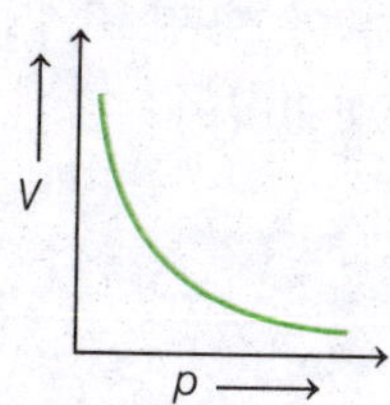

$$V \propto \frac{1}{p} \Rightarrow pV = \text{constant}$$

For a given gas, $p_1V_1 = p_2V_2$

Charles' Law

At constant pressure, the volume (V) of a given mass of gas is directly proportional to its absolute temperature (T), *i.e.*

$$V \propto T$$

$$\Rightarrow \quad \frac{V}{T} = \text{constant}$$

For a given gas, $$\frac{V_1}{T_1} = \frac{V_2}{T_2}$$

At constant pressure, the volume (V) of a given mass of a gas increases or decreases by $\frac{1}{273.15}$ of its volume at 0°C for each 1°C rise or fall in temperature.

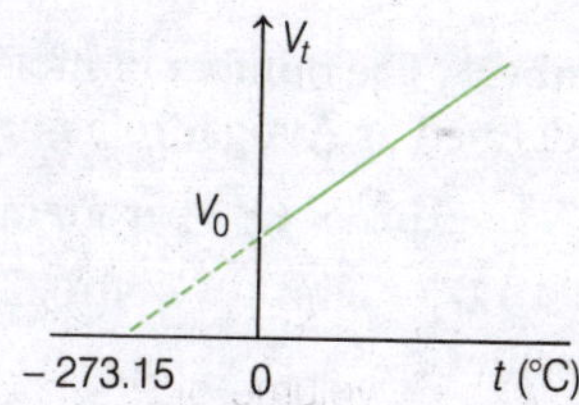

Volume of the gas at t°C,

$$V_t = V_0\left(1 + \frac{t}{273.15}\right)$$

where, V_0 is the volume of gas at 0°C.

Gay Lussac's or Regnault's Law

At constant volume, the pressure p of a given mass of gas is directly proportional to its absolute temperature T, *i.e.*

$$p \propto T \quad \Rightarrow \quad \frac{p}{T} = \text{constant}$$

For a given gas, $\frac{p_1}{T_1} = \frac{p_2}{T_2}$

At constant volume, the pressure p of a given mass of a gas increases or decreases by $\frac{1}{273.15}$ of its pressure at 0°C for each 1°C rise or fall in temperature.

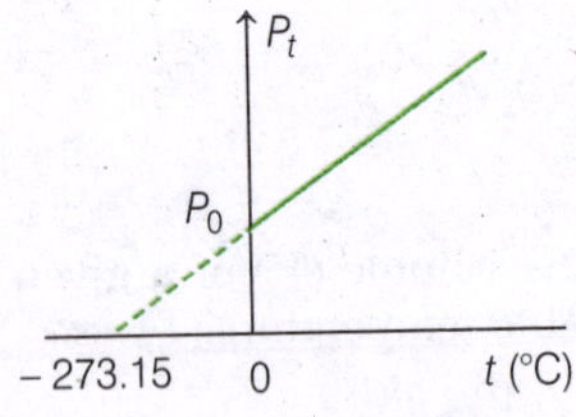

Volume of the gas at t°C, $p_t = p_0\left(1 + \frac{t}{273.15}\right)$

where, p_0 is the pressure of gas at 0°C.

Avogadro's Law

Avogadro stated that equal volume of all the gases under similar conditions of temperature and pressure contain equal number of molecules. This statement is called Avogadro's hypothesis. According to Avogadro's law $N_1 = N_2$, where N_1 and N_2 are number of molecules in two gases respectively.

(i) **Avogadro's number** The number of molecules present in 1g mole of a gas is defined as **Avogadro's number.**

$$N_A = 6.023 \times 10^{23} \text{ per gram mole}$$

(ii) At STP or NTP ($T = 273$ K and $p = 1$ atm), 22.4 L of each gas has 6.023×10^{23} molecules.

(iii) One mole of any gas at STP occupies 22.4 L of volume.

Dalton's Law of Partial Pressure

It states that the total pressure of a mixture of non-interacting ideal gases is the sum of partial pressures exerted by individual gases in the mixture. i.e. $p = p_1 + p_2 + p_3 + \ldots\ldots$.

 **Knowledge Booster**

Grahm's Law of Diffusion

The rate at which a gas diffuses is inversely proportional to the square root of its molar mass.

$$D_A \propto \frac{1}{\sqrt{M_A}}$$

or, at constant P and T, Rate of diffusion $\propto \frac{1}{\sqrt{\rho}}$

where, ρ = density of gas

Ideal or Perfect Gas Equation

Gases which obey all gas laws in all conditions of pressure and temperature are called perfect gases.

Equation of perfect gas

$$pV = nRT$$

where, p = pressure, V = volume, T = absolute temperature, R = universal gas constant and n = number of moles of a gas.

Universal gas constant, $R = 8.31 \text{ J mol}^{-1}\text{K}^{-1}$.

Real Gases

Real gases deviate slightly from ideal gas laws because

(i) Real gas molecules attract one another.

(ii) Real gas molecules occupy a finite volume.

Real or van der Waals' Gas Equation

$$\left(p + \frac{a}{V^2}\right)(V - b) = RT \qquad \text{[For 1 mole of gas]}$$

where, a and b are called van der Waals' constants.

Dimension $[a] = [ML^5T^{-2}]$ and $[b] = [L^3]$

Units $a = \text{N-m}^4$ and $b = \text{m}^3$.

Real gases obey this equation at high pressure and low temperature.

Pressure of a gas

Pressure due to an ideal gas is given by

$$p = \frac{1}{3}\frac{mn}{V}\bar{v}^2 = \frac{1}{3}\rho\bar{v}^2$$

For one mole of an ideal gas, $p = \frac{1}{3}\frac{M}{V}\bar{v}^2$

where, m = mass of one molecule, n = number of molecules,

V = volume of gas, $\bar{v} = \sqrt{\frac{\bar{v}_1^2 + \bar{v}_2^2 + \ldots + \bar{v}_n^2}{n}}$,

$\bar{v}$ is called root mean square (rms) velocity of the gas molecules and M = molecular weight of the gas.

If p is the pressure of the gas and E is the kinetic energy per unit volume is E, then

$$p = \frac{2}{3}E$$

 **Value Points**

Effect of mass, volume and temperature on pressure

- when volume and temperature of a gas are constant, then pressure $\propto$ mass of gas.
- when mass and temperature of a gas are constant, then

$$\text{pressure} \propto \frac{1}{\text{volume}}$$

- when mass and volume of gas are constant, then pressure $\propto$ temperature $\propto c^2$.

Kinetic Energy of a Gas and Speed of Gas Molecules

(i) Average kinetic energy of translation per molecule of a gas is given by

$$E = \frac{3}{2}kT$$

where, k = Boltzmann's constant.

(ii) Average kinetic energy of translation per mole of a gas is given by

$$E = \frac{3}{2}RT$$

where, R = universal gas constant.

(iii) Kinetic energy per unit volume,

$$E_V = \frac{3}{2}p$$

(iv) For a given gas kinetic energy

$$E \propto T$$

$$\Rightarrow \qquad \frac{E_1}{E_2} = \frac{T_1}{T_2}$$

(v) Root mean square (rms) velocity of the gas molecules is given by

$$v_{\text{rms}} = \sqrt{\frac{3RT}{M}} = \sqrt{\frac{3p}{\rho}} = \sqrt{\frac{3kT}{m}}$$

(vi) Boltzmann's constant, $k = \frac{R}{N}$

where, R is an ideal gas constant and N = Avogadro number. Value of Boltzmann's constant is 1.38×10^{-23} J/K.

(vii) The average speed of molecules of a gas is given by

$$\bar{v} = \sqrt{\frac{8kT}{\pi m}} = \sqrt{\frac{8RT}{\pi M}}$$

(viii) The most probable speed of molecules v_{mp} of a gas is given by

$$v_{\text{mp}} = \sqrt{\frac{2kT}{m}} = \sqrt{\frac{2RT}{M}} \Rightarrow v_{\text{rms}} > \bar{v} > v_{\text{mp}}$$

(ix) With rise in temperature rms speed of gas molecules increases as

$$v_{\text{rms}} \propto \sqrt{T}$$

(x) With the increase in molecular weight rms speed of gas molecule decrease as

$$v_{\text{rms}} \propto \frac{1}{\sqrt{M}}$$

(xi) Rms speed of gas molecules is of the order of km/s, *e.g.* at NTP for hydrogen gas

$$v_{\text{rms}} = \sqrt{\frac{3RT}{M}} = \sqrt{\frac{3 \times 8.31 \times 273}{2 \times 10^3}} = 1.84 \text{ km/s}$$

(xii) Rms speed of gas molecules does not depend on the pressure of gas (if temperature remains constant) because $p \propto \rho$ (Boyle's law). If pressure is increased n times, then density will also increase by n times but v_{rms} remains constant.

Degree of Freedom

The degree of freedom for a dynamic system is the number of directions in which a particle can move freely or the total number of coordinates required to describe completely the position and configuration of the system.

It is denoted by f or N.

Degree of freedom of a system is given by

$$f \text{ or } N = 3A - R$$

where, A = number of particles in the system and R = number of independent relations between the particles.

Degree of freedom for different atomic particles are given below.

(i) For monoatomic gas = 3 (all translational).
(ii) For diatomic gas = 5 (3 translational, 2 rotational)
(iii) For non-linear triatomic gas = 6 (3 translational, 3 rotational)
(iv) For linear triatomic gas = 7 (3 translational,3 rotational and 1 vibrational)

Specific heat of a gas

(a) At constant volume, $C_V = \frac{f}{2} R$.

(b) At constant pressure, $C_p = \left(\frac{f}{2} + 1\right) R$.

(c) Ratio of specific heat of a gas at constant pressure and at constant volume is given by $\gamma = 1 + \frac{2}{f}$.

Specific heat of solids, $C = 3R \Rightarrow C = 24 \cdot 93 \text{ Jmol}^{-1} \text{ K}^{-1}$.

Specific heat of water, $C = 9R \Rightarrow C = 74 \cdot 97 \text{ Jmol}^{-1} \text{ K}^{-1}$.

Nature of gas	$U = \frac{f}{2} RT$	$C_V = \frac{dU}{dT} = \frac{f}{2} R$	$C_p = C_V + R$	$\gamma = \frac{C_p}{C_V} = 1 + \frac{2}{f}$
Monoatomic	$\frac{3}{2} RT$	$\frac{3}{2} R$	$\frac{5}{2} R$	1.67
Dia and linear polyatomic	$\frac{5}{2} RT$	$\frac{5}{2} R$	$\frac{7}{2} R$	1.4
Non-linear polyatomic	$3RT$	$3R$	$4R$	1.33

Competition Insight

Maxwell's Law or the Distribution of Molecular Speeds

It derives an equation giving the distribution of molecules at different speeds

$$dN = 4\pi N\left(\frac{m}{2\pi kT}\right)^{3/2} v^2 e^{-\left(\frac{mv^2}{2kT}\right)} .dv$$

where, dN is number of molecules with speed between v and $v + dv$.

The $\frac{dN}{dv}$ *versus* v curve is shown below

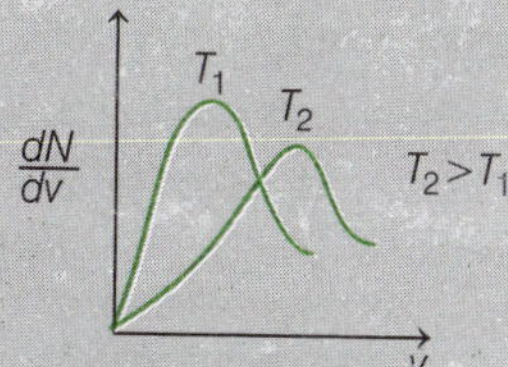

According to Maxwell's distribution of molecules, $v_{rms} > v_{av} > v_{mp}$

Law of Equipartition of Energy

This law states that, for a dynamic system in thermal equilibrium, the total energy is distributed equally amongst all the degree of freedom and the energy associated with each molecule per degree of freedom is $\frac{1}{2} k_B T$.

where, $k_B = 1.38 \times 10^{-23}$ JK^{-1} is Boltzmann constant and T is absolute temperature of system on the kelvin scale.

Mean Free Path

The average distance travelled by a molecule between two successive collisions is called mean free path (λ).

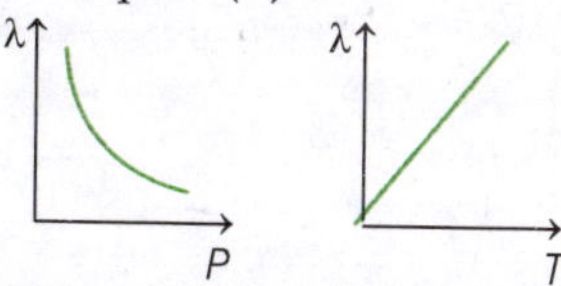

Mean free path is given by $\lambda = \frac{kT}{\sqrt{2}\,\pi d^2 p}$

where, d = diameter of the molecule, p = pressure of the gas,
T = temperature and k = Botlzmann's constant.

Mean free path, $\lambda \propto T$ and $\lambda \propto \frac{1}{p}$

Knowledge Booster

Brownian Motion

The continuous random motion of the particles of microscopic size suspended in air or any liquid is called Brownian motion.

Brownian motion is observed with many kind of small particles suspended in both liquids and gases.

Brownian motion is due to the unequal bombardment of the suspended particles by the molecules of the surrounding medium.

Critical Temperature, Pressure and Volume

Gases can't be liquified above a temperature called critical temperature (T_C) however large the pressure may be.

The pressure required to liquify the gas at critical temperature is called critical pressure (p_C) and the volume of the gas at critical temperature and pressure is called critical volume (V_C). Value of critical constants in terms of van der Waals' constants a and b are as under

$$V_C = 3b, \; p_C = \frac{a}{27b^2} \quad \text{and} \quad T_C = \frac{8a}{27Rb}$$

Further, $\frac{RT_C}{p_C V_C} = \frac{8}{3}$ is called critical coefficient and is same for all gases.

Chapter 15

Thermodynamics

The branch of physics which deals with the study of transformation of heat energy into other forms of energy and *vice-versa* is called thermodynamics.

Thermodynamic Terms

In order to understand these transformation we need to understand the terms given below.

Thermodynamical System

An assembly of an extremely large number of particles which is capable of exchange of energy with its surroundings is called thermodynamic system.

Thermodynamic system is classified into the following three systems

(i) **Open System** It exchanges both energy and matter with surroundings.

(ii) **Closed System** It exchanges only energy (not matter) with surroundings.

(iii) **Isolated System** It exchanges neither energy nor matter with the surroundings.

Thermodynamic Parameters or Coordinates or Variables

The state of thermodynamic system can be described by specifying pressure, volume, temperature, internal energy and number of moles, etc. These are called thermodynamic parameters or coordinates or variables.

The state variables can be extensive or intensive in nature.

Extensive State Variables

Extensive state variables depend on the size of the system, *e.g.* volume, total mass, internal energy etc.

Intensive State Variables

These are state variables that do not depend on the size of the system, *e.g.* pressure, temperature and density.

Thermal Equilibrium

Thermodynamical systems are said to be in thermal equilibrium, if there is no net flow of heat between them when they are brought into thermal contact.

Adiabatic Wall

It is an insulating wall (can be movable) between two thermodynamic systems that does not allow flow of energy (or heat) from one system to another system.

Diathermic Wall

It is a conducting wall between two thermodynamic systems that allows energy flow (or heat) from one system to another system.

Work Done

Work done by a thermodynamic system is given by

$$W = p \times \Delta V$$

where, p = pressure and ΔV = change in volume.

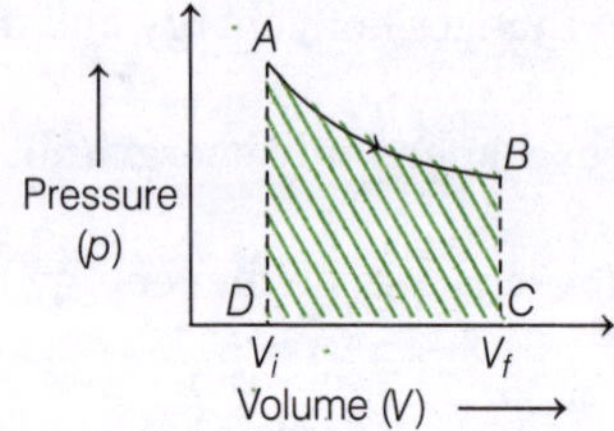

Value Points

- Work done by a thermodynamic system is equal to the area enclosed between the p-V curve and the volume axis.
- Work done in process A-$B = \int_{V_i}^{V_f} p\,dV$ = Area $ABCDA$
- Work done by a thermodynamic system depends not only upon the initial and final states of the system but also depend upon the path followed in the process.

Work done by the thermodynamic system is taken as

Positive → as volume increases.

Negative → as volume decreases.

Internal Energy (U)

The total energy possessed by any system due to molecular motion and molecular configuration is called its internal energy.

Internal energy of a thermodynamic system depends on temperature.

It is the characteristic property of the state of the system.

Zeroth Law of Thermodynamics

According to this law, two systems in thermal equilibrium with a third system separately, are also in thermal equilibrium with each other. Thus, if A and B are separately in equilibrium with C, *i.e.* if $T_A = T_C$ and $T_B = T_C$, then this implies that $T_A = T_B$, *i.e.* the systems A and B are also in thermal equilibrium.

First Law of Thermodynamics

Heat given to a thermodynamic system (ΔQ) is partially utilised in doing work (ΔW) against the surrounding and the remaining part increases the internal energy (ΔU) of the system.

Therefore,
$$\Delta Q = \Delta U + \Delta W$$

In differential form,
$$dQ = dU + dW$$

First law of thermodynamics is a restatement of the principle of conservation of energy.

Thermodynamic Processes

A thermodynamical process is said to take place when some changes occur in the state of a thermodynamic system *i.e.* the thermodynamic parameters of the system change with time.

(i) **Quasi-static Process** Quasi-static is a thermodynamic process which proceeds extremely slowly such that at every instant of time, the temperature and pressure are the same in all parts of the system.

(ii) **Isothermal Process** A process taking place in a thermodynamic system at constant temperature is called an isothermal process.

Isothermal processes are very slow processes.

This process follows **Boyle's law**, according to which

$$pV = \text{constant}$$

From $dU = nC_V dT$ as $dT = 0$ so $dU = 0$, *i.e.* internal energy is constant.

From first law of thermodynamic $dQ = dW$, *i.e.* heat given to the system is equal to the work done by the system on surroundings.

$$\text{Work done } W = 2.3026\,\mu RT \log_{10}\left(\frac{V_f}{V_i}\right)$$

$$= 2.3026\,\mu RT \log_{10}\left(\frac{p_i}{p_f}\right)$$

where, μ = number of moles, R = ideal gas constant, T = absolute temperature and V_i, V_f and p_i, p_f are initial and final volumes and pressures, respectively.

After differentiating pV = constant, we have

$$\frac{dp}{dV} = -\frac{p}{V} \text{ and } -\frac{dp}{\frac{dV}{V}} = p$$

i.e. bulk modulus of gas in isothermal process, $K = p$.

p-V Diagram

p-V curve for this process is a rectangular hyperbola as shown below

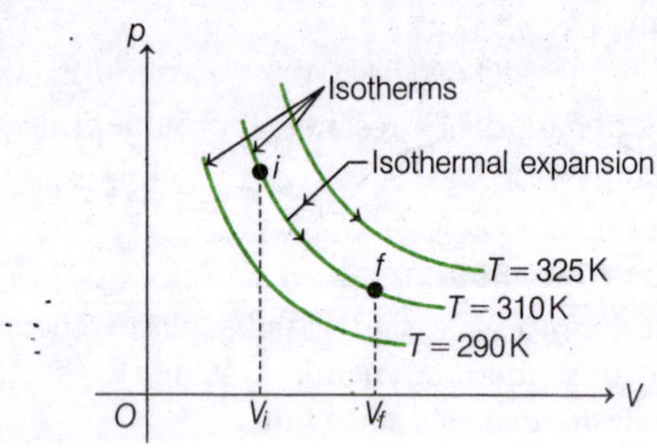

Examples

(a) Melting process is an isothermal process, because temperature of a substance remains constant during melting.

(b) Boiling process is also an isothermal process.

(iii) **Adiabatic Process** A process taking place in a thermo- dynamic system for which there is no exchange of heat between the system and its surroundings.

Adiabatic processes are very fast processes.

This process follows **Poisson's law,** according to which

$$pV^{\gamma} = TV^{\gamma-1} = \frac{T^{\gamma}}{p^{\gamma-1}} = \text{Constant}$$

where, $\gamma = \frac{C_p}{C_V}$

From $dQ = nCdT$, $C_{adi} = 0$ as $dQ = 0$, *i.e.* molar heat capacity for adiabatic process is zero.

From first law, $dU = -dW$, *i.e.* work done by the system is equal to decrease in internal energy. When a system expands adiabatically, work done is positive and hence internal energy decreases, *i.e.* the system cools down and *vice-versa.*

Work done in an adiabatic process is

$$W = \frac{nR(T_i - T_f)}{\gamma - 1} = \frac{p_i V_i - p_f V_f}{\gamma - 1}$$

where, T_i and T_f are initial and final temperatures.

p-V Diagram

In *p-V* curve of this process, pressure decreases exponentially with increase in volume as shown below

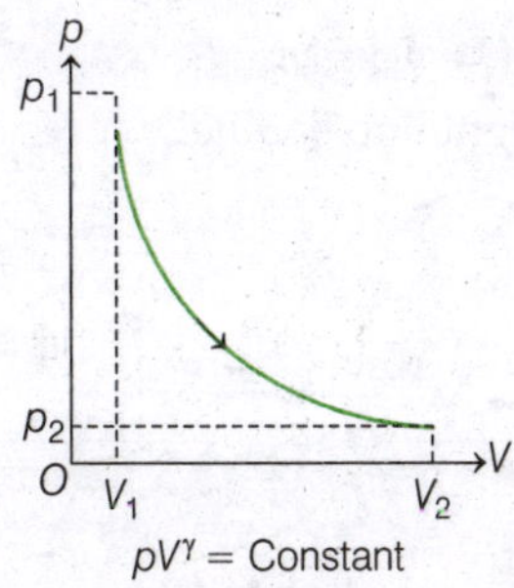

pV^{γ} = Constant

Examples

(a) Sudden compression or expansion of a gas in a container with perfectly non-conducting wall.

(b) Sudden bursting of the tube of a bicycle tyre.

(c) Propagation of sound waves in air and other gases.

(iv) **Isobaric Process** A process taking place in a thermodynamic system at constant pressure is called an **isobaric process**.

Process equation is $\frac{V}{T}$ = Constant.

Molar heat capacity of the process is C_p and $dQ = nC_p dT$.

Internal energy $\quad dU = nC_V\, dT$

From the first law of thermodynamics,

$$dQ = dU + dW$$

$$dW = pdV = nRdT$$

p-V curve is a straight line parallel to volume axis as shown below

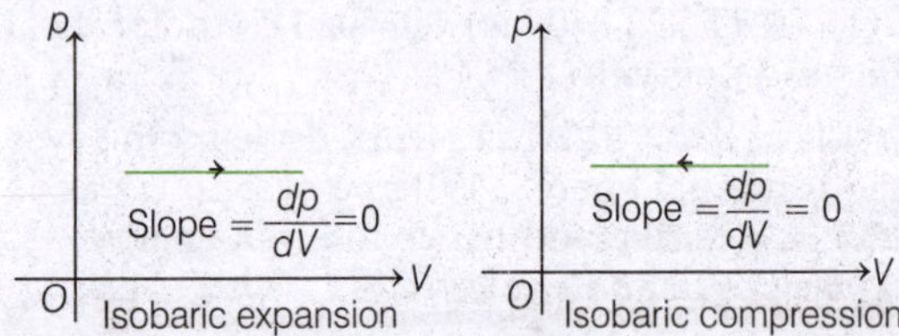

(v) **Isochoric Process** A process taking place in a thermodynamic system at constant volume is called an **isochoric process.**

Process equation is $\frac{p}{T}$ = Constant.

$dQ = nC_V dT$, molar heat capacity for isochoric process is C_V.

Volume is constant, so $dW = 0$.

From the first law of thermodynamics,

$$dQ = dU = nC_V dT$$

p-V curve is a straight line parallel to pressure axis as shown below.

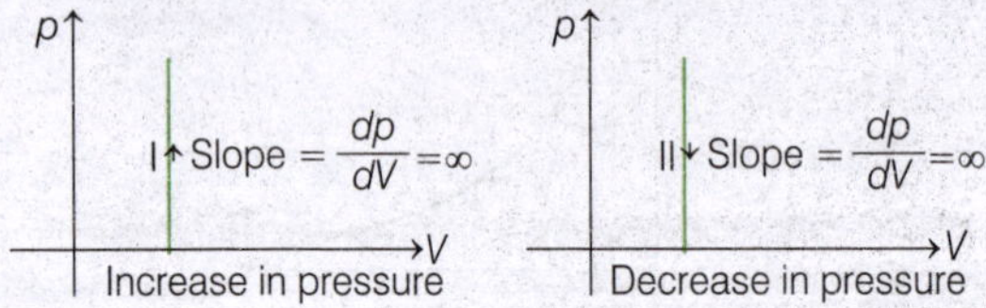

(vi) **Cyclic Process** When a thermodynamic system returns to its initial state after passing through several states, then it is called a cyclic process.

For cyclic process, $\quad dU = 0$

or $\quad dQ = dW$

Efficiency of the cycle is given by

$$\eta = \frac{\text{Work done}}{\text{Heat supplied}}$$

Work done by the cycle can be computed from area enclosed by cycle on p-V curve.

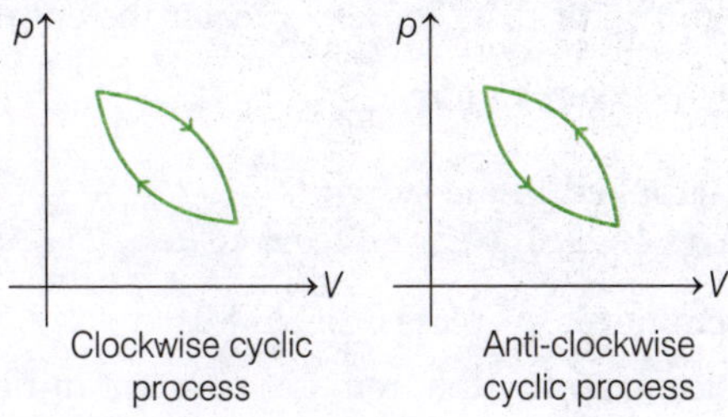

Clockwise cyclic process

Anti-clockwise cyclic process

Second Law of Thermodynamics

The second law of thermodynamics gives a fundamental limitation to the efficiency of a heat engine and the coefficient of performance of a refrigerator. It says that efficiency of a heat engine can never be unity (or 100%). This implies that heat released to the cold reservoir can never be made zero.

Kelvin-Planck Statement

No process is possible whose sole result is the absorption of heat from a reservoir and the complete conversion of the heat into work.

Clausius' Statement

It is impossible to transfer heat from a lower temperature body to a higher temperature body without use of an external agency.

Reversible and Irreversible Processes

Reversible Process A process which could be reserved in such a way that the system and its surrounding returns exactly to their initial states with no other changes in the universe is known as reversible process.

Irreversible Process Any process which is not reversible exactly is an irreversible process.

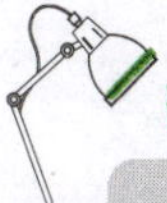

EXPERT Scale Up

Always remember that all isothermal process are not reversible but an isothermal expansion is always reversible.

Entropy

Entropy is related to the disorderness of molecular motion of the system. Greater the randomness or disorderness, greater the entropy.

Change in entropy is given by $dS = \frac{dQ}{T}$

where, dQ = heat supplied to the system

and T = absolute temperature.

Entropy of a system never decreases, *i.e.* $dS \geq 0$.

Entropy is a physical quantity that remains constant during a reversible adiabatic change.

Entropy of a system increases in an irreversible process.

Competition Insight

Change in Entropy for Solids and Liquids

(i) When heat is supplied to a solid and its state changes such that temperature remains constant, then

Change in entropy, $\Delta S = \frac{\Delta Q}{T}$

$$\Rightarrow \quad dS = \frac{dQ}{T} = \frac{\pm |mL|}{T}$$

Positive sign is used for heat absorption and negative sign is used for heat rejection.

(ii) When temperature of a substance changes from T_1 to T_2, then

$$dS = \int \frac{dQ}{T} = mS \int_{T_1}^{T_2} \frac{dT}{T} = mS \ln\left(\frac{T_2}{T_1}\right)$$

$$= 2.303\, mS \log_{10}\left(\frac{T_2}{T_1}\right)$$

where, m = mass of the substance

and S = specific heat of the substance.

Heat Engine

A heat engine is a device which converts heat energy into mechanical energy. A heat engine consists of three parts

(i) Source of heat at higher temperature

(ii) Working substance

(iii) Sink of heat at lower temperature.

Thermal efficiency of a heat engine is given by

$$\eta = \frac{\text{Work done / cycle}}{\text{Total amount of heat absorbed / cycle}}$$

$$\eta = 1 - \frac{Q_2}{Q_1} = 1 - \frac{T_2}{T_1}$$

where, Q_1 is heat absorbed from the source, Q_2 is heat rejected to the sink and T_1 and T_2 are temperatures of source and sink.

Knowledge Booster

Heat engine are of two types

(i) **External Combustion Engine** In this engine, fuel is burnt in a chamber outside the main body of the engine, *e.g.* steam engine. In practical life, thermal efficiency of a steam engine varies from 12% to 16%.

(ii) **Internal Combustion Engine** In this engine, fuel is burnt in inside the main body of the engine, *e.g.* petrol and diesel engine.
In practical life, thermal efficiency of a petrol engine is 26% and for a diesel engine is 40%.

Carnot's Cycle

Carnot devised an ideal cycle of operation for a heat engine called Carnot's cycle.

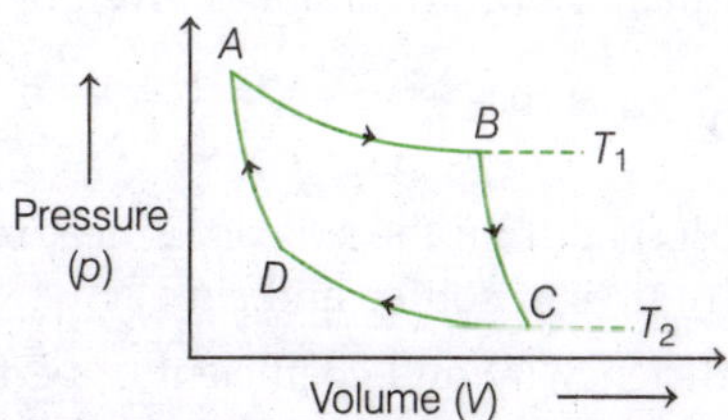

A Carnot's cycle contains the following four processes

(i) Isothermal expansion (AB)

(ii) Adiabatic expansion (BC)

(iii) Isothermal compression (CD)

(iv) Adiabatic compression (DA)

The net work done per cycle by the engine is numerically equal to the area of the loop representing the Carnot's cycle.

After doing the calculations for different processes, we can show that

$$\frac{Q_2}{Q_1} = \frac{T_2}{T_1}$$

Therefore, efficiency of the cycle is

$$\eta = 1 - \frac{T_2}{T_1}$$

Efficiency of Carnot engine is maximum (not 100%) for given temperatures T_1 and T_2. But still Carnot engine is not a practical engine because many ideal situations have been assumed while designing this engine which can practically not be obtained.

Carnot Theorem

According to Carnot theorem,

(i) Any heat engine working between the two given temperatures T_1 of hot reservoir *i.e.*, source and T_2 of cold reservoir can never have more efficiency than the carnot engine operating between the same reservoirs.

(ii) The efficiency of the Carnot engine is independent of the nature of working substance.

Refrigerator

A refrigerator is a device used for cooling things. It absorbs heat from sink at lower temperature and rejects a large amount of heat to source at higher temperature.

Coefficient of performance of refrigerator is given by

$$\beta = \frac{Q_2}{W} = \frac{Q_2}{Q_1 - Q_2} = \frac{T_2}{T_1 - T_2}$$

where, Q_2 is heat absorbed from the sink, Q_1 is heat rejected to source and T_1 and T_2 are temperatures of source and sink.

Relation between efficiency (η) and coefficient of performance (β)

$$\beta = \frac{1 - \eta}{\eta}$$

Chapter 16

Transmission of Heat

Heat Transfer

Heat can be transferred from one part of system to another. It is called heat transfer.

There are three methods of heat transmission :

(i) **Conduction** In solids, heat is transmitted from higher temperature to lower temperature without actual movements of the particles. This mode of transmission of heat is called conduction.

(ii) **Convection** The process of heat transmission in which the particles of the fluid (liquid or gas) move is called convection.

Land breeze, see-breeze and trade wind are formed due to convection.

(iii) **Radiation** The process of heat transmission in the form of electromagnetic waves, is called radiation.

Radiation do not require any medium for propagation.

It propagates without heating the intervening medium.

The heat energy transferred by radiation is called radiant energy.

Heat from the sun reaches the earth by radiation.

Conduction of Heat in a Conducting Rod

Heat conduction in a conducting rod is the process of transfer to heat from one end of the rod to the other through the vibration of particles.

Steady State

The state of a conducting rod in which no part of the rod absorbs heat is called the steady state.

Isothermal Surface

A surface of a material whose all points are at the same temperature is called an isothermal surface.

Temperature Gradient

The rate of change of temperature with distance between any two isothermal surfaces is called temperature gradient.

$$\text{Temperature gradient} = \frac{\text{Change in temperature}}{\text{Perpendicular distance}} = \frac{\Delta\theta}{\Delta x}$$

Its SI unit is °C per metre and dimensional formula is $[L^{-1}K]$.

Thermal Conductivity

It measures the ability of a material to conduct heat.

The amount of heat flow in a conducting rod,

$$Q = \frac{KA\,\Delta\theta t}{l}$$

where, K = coefficient of thermal conductivity,
A = area of cross - section,
l = length of rod,
$\Delta\theta$ = temperature difference between the ends of the rod
and t = time.

The SI unit of K is $Wm^{-1}\,K^{-1}$ and its dimensional formula is $[MLT^{-3}K^{-1}]$.

The value of K is large for good conductors and very small for insulators.

Thermal Current and Thermal Resistance

The rate of flow of heat is known as thermal or heat current. It is denoted by H.

$$H = \frac{KA\Delta\theta}{l}$$

Thermal resistance is given by

$$R = \frac{\Delta\theta}{H} = \frac{l}{KA}$$

where, $\Delta\theta$ is temperature difference at the ends of the rod and H is rate of flow of heat.

SI unit of thermal resistance is K/W and its dimensional formula is $[M^{-1}L^{-2}\,T^{3}K^{-1}]$.

When Two Conducting Rods are Connected in Series

Rate of heat flow, $H = \dfrac{Q}{t} = \dfrac{K_1 A(\theta_1 - \theta)}{l_1} = \dfrac{K_2 A(\theta - \theta_2)}{l_2}$

Temperature of contact surface, $\theta = \dfrac{\dfrac{K_1\theta_1}{l_1} + \dfrac{K_2\theta_2}{l_2}}{\dfrac{K_1}{l_1} + \dfrac{K_2}{l_2}} = \dfrac{K_1\theta_1 l_2 + K_2\theta_2 l_1}{K_1 l_2 + K_2 l_1}$

Equivalent thermal conductivity, $K = \dfrac{l_1 + l_2}{\dfrac{l_1}{K_1} + \dfrac{l_2}{K_2}}$

When two Conducting Rods are Connected in Parallel

Rate of heat flow,

$$H = \frac{Q}{t} = \left(\frac{K_1 A_1}{l} + \frac{K_2 A_2}{l}\right)(\theta_1 - \theta_2)$$

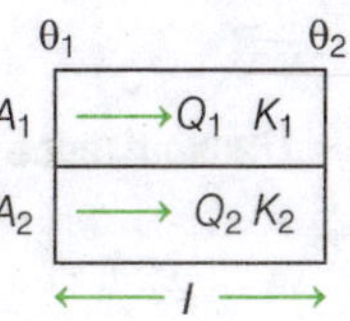

Temperature gradient $= \dfrac{\theta_1 - \theta_2}{l}$

Equivalent thermal conductivity, $K = \dfrac{K_1 A_1 + K_2 A_2}{A_1 + A_2}$

Knowledge Booster

Ingen-Hausz Experiment

The thermal conductivities of different materials are proportional to the square of the lengths of the melted wax on the rods of these materials in the steady state.

If $l_1, l_2, l_3, \ldots$ are the lengths of the melted wax on the rods of different materials having coefficient of thermal conductivities $K_1, K_2, K_3, \ldots$, respectively, then $K_1 : K_2 : K_3 : \ldots = l_1^2 : l_2^2 : l_3^2 : \ldots$ or $\dfrac{K_1}{K_2} = \dfrac{l_1^2}{l_2^2}$

Formation of Ice on Lakes

Time taken to from x thickness of ice on lake, $t = \dfrac{\rho L}{2K\theta} x^2$

where, ρ = density of ice, L = latent heat of freezing of ice,

K = coefficient of thermal conductivity of ice

and θ = temperature above lake.

Time taken to increase the thickness of ice from x_1 to x_2,

$$t = \frac{\rho L}{2K\theta}(x_2^2 - x_1^2)$$

Reflectance or Reflecting Power

The ratio of the amount of thermal radiations reflected by a body in a given time to the total amount of thermal radiations incident on the body in that time is called reflectance or reflecting power of the body.

It is denoted by r.

Absorptance or Absorbing Power

The ratio of the amount of thermal radiations absorbed by a body in a given time to the total amount of thermal radiations incident on the body in that time is called absorptance or absorbing power of the body.

It is denoted by a.

Transmittance or Transmitting Power

The ratio of the amount of thermal radiations transmitted by the body in a given time to the total amount of thermal radiations incident on the body in that time is called transmittance or transmitting power of the body. It is denoted by t.

Relation among reflecting power, absorbing power and transmitting power

$$r + a + t = 1$$

If body does not transmit any heat radiations, then $t = 0$

$$\therefore \quad r + a = 1$$

(i) r, a and t all are the pure ratio, so they have no unit and dimensions.
(ii) For perfect reflector, $r = 1$, $a = 0$ and $t = 0$.
(iii) For perfect absorber, $a = 1$, $r = 0$ and $t = 0$ (perfect black body).
(iv) For perfect transmitter, $t = 1$, $a = 0$ and $r = 0$.

Emissive Power

Emissive power of a body at a particular temperature is the total amount of thermal energy emitted per unit time per unit area of the body for all possible wavelengths.

It is denoted by e_λ.

$$e_\lambda = \frac{1}{A} \cdot \frac{d\theta}{dt}$$

Its SI unit is $Js^{-1}m^{-2}$ or Wm^{-2} and its dimensional formula is $[MT^{-3}]$.

Emissivity

Emissivity of a body at a given temperature is equal to the ratio of the total emissive power of the body (e_λ) to the total emissive power of a perfectly black body (E_λ) at that temperature.

Emissivity, $\varepsilon = \frac{e_\lambda}{E_\lambda}$

Perfectly Black Body

A body which absorbs completely the radiations of all wavelengths incident on it, is called a perfectly black body.

For a perfectly black body, emissivity $(\varepsilon) = 1$.

An ideal black body need not be black in colour.

The radiation from a black body depend upon its temperature only. These heat radiations do not depend on density mass, size or the nature of the body.

Lamp black is 96% black and platinum black is about 98% black.

A perfectly black body cannot be realised in practice. The nearest example of an ideal black body is the **Ferry's black body**.

Kirchhoff's Law

The ratio of emissive power (e_λ) to the absorptive power (a_λ) corresponding to a particular wavelength and at any given temperature is always a constant for all bodies and it is equal to the emissive power (E_λ) of a perfectly black body at the same temperature and corresponding to the same wavelength.

Mathematically, $\left(\frac{e_\lambda}{a_\lambda}\right)_{\text{for any body}} = \text{constant } (E_\lambda)$

Value Points

A body can absorb only those wavelengths which it is capable of emitting.

Stefan's Law

Heat energy emitted per second per unit area of a perfectly black body

$$E \propto T^4 \quad \Rightarrow \quad E = \sigma T^4$$

If T_0 is the temperature of the surroundings, then $E = \sigma (T^4 - T_0^4)$
If ε is the emissivity of the body, then $E = \varepsilon \sigma T^4$
Energy radiated by whole body in t time, $E = \sigma A \varepsilon t T^4$

Newton's Law of Cooling

The rate of loss of heat of a liquid is directly proportional to the difference in temperature of the liquid and its surroundings, *i.e.* $-\frac{dQ}{dt} \propto (T - T_0)$

where, T and T_0 are the temperatures of the liquid and its surroundings.

Wien's Displacement Law

Wavelength corresponding to maximum emission of radiation decreases with increasing temperature.

$$\lambda_m T = \text{constant } (b)$$

where, λ_m = Wavelength corresponding to which maximum energy is radiated,
T = Absolute temperature
and b = Wien's constant $= 2.898 \times 10^{-3} \approx 3 \times 10^{-3}$ mK

When temperature of a black body increases, colour changes towards higher frequency, *i.e.* from red → orange → yellow → green → blue → violet.

Competition Insight

Solar Constant

The amount of heat received from the sun by one square centimetre area of a surface placed normally to the sun rays at mean distance of the earth from the sun is known as solar constant. It is denoted by S.

$$S = \left(\frac{r}{R}\right)^2 \sigma T^4$$

where, r is the radius of sun and R is the mean distance of earth from the centre of sun. Value of solar constant is 1.937 cal cm^{-2} min^{-1}.

Solar Insolation

Solar radiation received at a certain point on the surface of the earth.

$$I = S \cos \theta$$

S is solar constant
θ is zenith angle
SI unit of solar insolation is watt per square metre.

Chapter 17

Oscillations

Periodic Motion

A motion which repeats itself identically after a fixed interval of time is called periodic motion, *e.g.* orbital motion of the earth around the sun, motion of arms of a clock etc.

Oscillatory Motion

A periodic motion taking place to and fro or back and forth about a fixed point is called oscillatory motion, *e.g.* motion of a simple pendulum, motion of a loaded spring etc.

Every oscillatory motion is periodic motion but every periodic motion is not oscillatory motion. e.g. Circular motion is a periodic motion, but it is not oscillatory.

Harmonic Oscillation

The oscillation which can be expressed in terms of single harmonic function, *i.e.* sine or cosine function is called harmonic oscillation.

Simple Harmonic Motion

A harmonic oscillation of constant amplitude and of single frequency under a restoring force whose magnitude is proportional to the displacement and always acts towards mean position is called Simple Harmonic Motion (SHM).

A simple harmonic oscillation can be expressed as

$$y = a \sin \omega t$$

or

$$y = a \cos \omega t$$

where, a = amplitude of oscillation.

Some Terms Related to SHM

(i) **Time Period** Time taken by the body to complete one oscillation is known as time period. It is denoted by T.

(ii) **Frequency** The number of oscillations completed by the body in one second is called frequency. It is denoted by ν.

$$\text{Frequency} = \frac{1}{\text{Time period}}$$

Its SI unit is hertz or second^{-1}.

(iii) **Angular Frequency** The product of frequency with factor 2π, is called angular frequency. It is denoted by ω.

$$\text{Angular frequency } (\omega) = 2\pi\nu$$

Its SI unit is radian per second.

(iv) **Displacement** A physical quantity which represents change in position with respect to mean position or equilibrium position is called displacement. It is denoted by y.

(v) **Amplitude** The maximum displacement in any direction from mean position is called amplitude. It is denoted by a.

(vi) **Phase** A physical quantity which express the position and direction of motion of an oscillating particle is called phase. It is denoted by $\omega t + \phi$. The value of phase at $t = 0$ is ϕ and is called phase constant (or phase angle).

Some Important Formulae of SHM

(i) Displacement in SHM at any instant is given by

$$y = A \sin \omega t$$

or

$$y = A \cos \omega t$$

where, a = amplitude

and ω = angular frequency.

(ii) Velocity of a particle executing SHM at any instant is given by

$$v = \omega\sqrt{(A^2 - y^2)}$$

At mean position, $y = 0$ and v is maximum

$$v_{\max} = a\omega$$

At extreme position, $y = a$ and v is zero.

(iii) Acceleration of a particle executing SHM at any instant is given by $a = -\omega^2 y$

Negative sign indicates that the direction of acceleration is opposite to the direction in which displacement increases, *i.e.* towards mean position.

At mean position, $y = 0$ and acceleration is also zero.

At extreme position, $y = A$ and acceleration is maximum

$$a_{max} = -A\omega^2$$

(iv) Time period in SHM is given by

$$T = 2\pi\sqrt{\frac{\text{Inertia factor}}{\text{Spring factor}}}$$

In general, inertia factor $= m$, (mass of the particle)

spring factor $= k$ (force constant)

Graphical Representation of SHM

(i) **Displacement-Time Graph**

When $y(t) = A\sin\omega t$

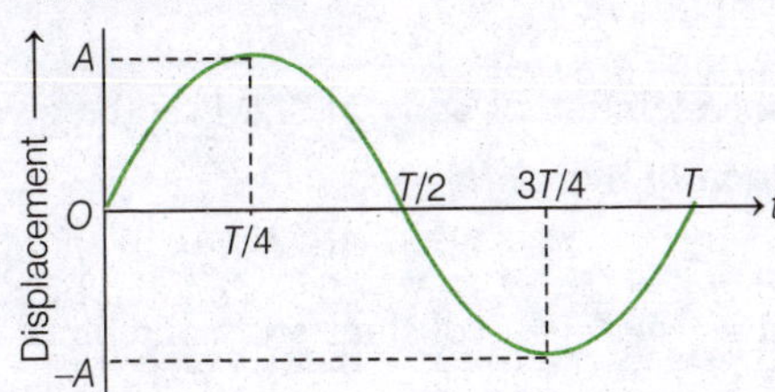

(ii) **Velocity-Time Graph**

When $v(t) = +\omega A\cos\omega t$

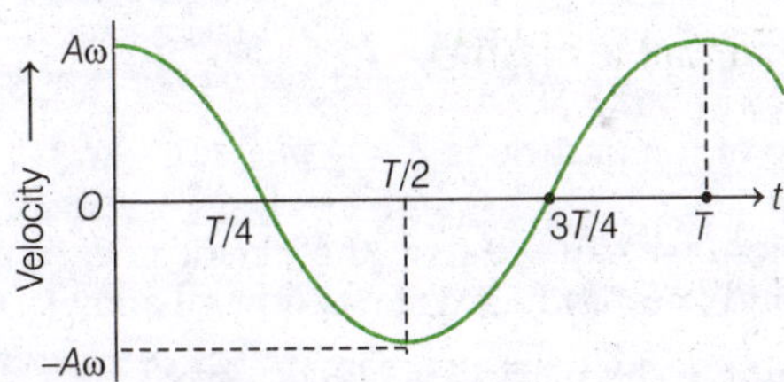

(iii) **Acceleration-Time Graph**

When $a(t) = -\omega^2 A\sin\omega t$

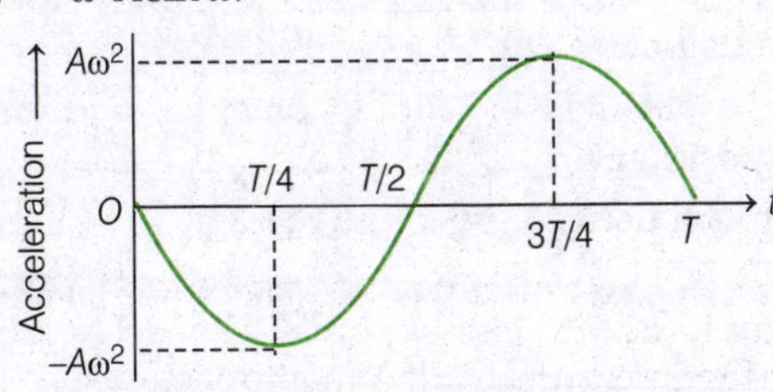

From the above mentioned graphs, it can be concluded that for a particle executing SHM, the phase difference between

(i) Instantaneous displacement and instantaneous velocity $= \left(\frac{\pi}{2}\right)$ rad

(ii) Instantaneous velocity and instantaneous acceleration $= \left(\frac{\pi}{2}\right)$ rad

(iii) Instantaneous acceleration and instantaneous displacement $= \pi$ rad

Value Points

- The acceleration is maximum at a place, where the velocity is minimum and *vice-versa*.
- The graph between velocity and displacement for a particle executing SHM is elliptical.

Force in SHM

We know that, the acceleration of body in SHM can be given as $a = -\omega^2 x$.
Applying the equation of motion $\mathbf{F} = m\mathbf{a}$,
We have,

$$F = -m\omega^2 x = -kx$$

where, $\omega = \sqrt{\frac{k}{m}}$ and $k = m\omega^2$ is a constant and sometimes it is called the elastic constant.

Thus, in SHM, the force is directly proportional and opposite to the displacement and is always directed towards the mean position.

Energy in SHM

The kinetic energy of the particle is $K = \frac{1}{2} m\omega^2 (A^2 - x^2)$

From this expression, we can see that, the kinetic energy is maximum at the centre ($x = 0$) and zero at the extremes of oscillation ($x = \pm A$).

The potential energy of the particle is $U = \frac{1}{2} m\omega^2 x^2$.

From this expression, we can see that, the potential energy has a minimum value at the centre ($x = 0$) and increases as the particle approaches either extreme of the oscillation ($x \pm a$).

Total energy can be obtained by adding potential and kinetic energies. Therefore,

$$E = K + U$$

$$= \frac{1}{2} m(A^2 - x^2)\,\omega^2 + \frac{1}{2} m\omega^2 x^2 = \frac{1}{2} m\omega^2 A^2$$

where, A = amplitude,

m = mass of particle executing SHM

and ω = angular frequency.

Changes in kinetic and potential energies during oscillations is represented in the graph given below.

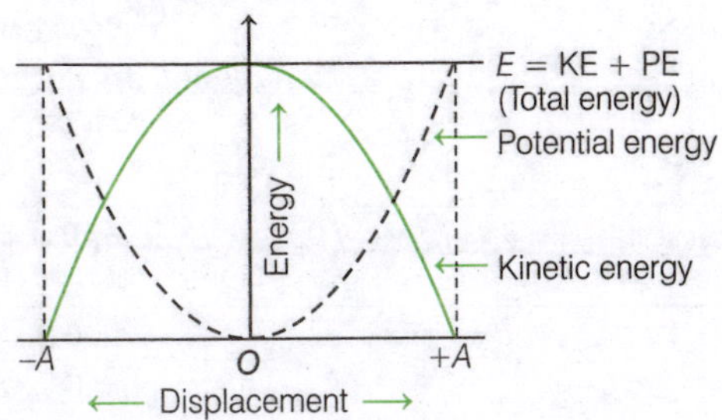

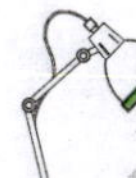

EXPERT Scale Up

- **Tips to find frequency of KE, PE and TE from frequency of SHM**
- The frequency of kinetic energy or potential energy of a particle executing SHM is double than that of the frequency of SHM.
- The frequency of total energy of particles executing SHM is zero as total energy in SHM remains constant at all positions.

Variation of different physical quantities (*e.g.* displacement, velocity, acceleration, kinetic energy etc) with time or displacement are listed ahead in tabular form.

S.No.	Name of the equation	Expression of the equation	Remarks
1.	Displacement-time	$x = A\cos(\omega t + \phi)$	x varies between $+A$ and $-A$
2.	Velocity-time $\left(v = \frac{dx}{dt}\right)$	$v = -A\omega\sin(\omega t + \phi)$	v varies between $+A\omega$ and $-A\omega$
3.	Acceleration-time $\left(a = \frac{dv}{dt}\right)$	$a = -A\omega^2\cos(\omega t + \phi)$	a varies between $+A\omega^2$ and $-A\omega^2$
4.	Kinetic energy-time $\left(K = \frac{1}{2}mv^2\right)$	$K = \frac{1}{2}mA^2\omega^2\sin^2(\omega t + \phi)$	K varies between 0 and $\frac{1}{2}mA^2\omega^2$

S.No.	Name of the equation	Expression of the equation	Remarks
5.	Potential energy-time $\left(U = \frac{1}{2} m\omega^2 x^2\right)$	$U = \frac{1}{2} m\omega^2 A^2 \cos^2(\omega t + \phi)$	U varies between $0 \frac{1}{2} mA^2\omega^2$ and 0
6.	Total energy-time $(E = K + U)$	$E = \frac{1}{2} m\omega^2 A^2$	E is constant
7.	Velocity-displacement	$v = \omega\sqrt{A^2 - x^2}$	$v = 0$ at $x = \pm A$ and at $x = 0$, $v = \pm A\omega$
8.	Acceleration-displacement	$a = -\omega^2 x$	$a = 0$ at $x = o$ and $a = \pm \omega^2 A$ at $x = \pm A$
9.	Kinetic energy-displacement	$K = \frac{1}{2} m\omega^2 (A^2 - x^2)$	$K = 0$ at $x = \pm A$ and $K = \frac{1}{2} m\omega^2 A^2$ at $x = 0$
10.	Potential energy-displacement	$U = \frac{1}{2} m\omega^2 x^2$	$U = 0$ at $x = 0$ and $U = \frac{1}{2} m\omega^2 A^2$ at $x = \pm A$
11.	Total energy- displacement	$E = \frac{1}{2} m\omega^2 A^2$	E is constant

Simple Pendulum

A simple pendulum consists of a heavy point mass suspended from a rigid support by means of an elastic inextensible string.

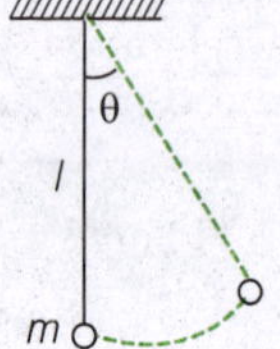

The time period of the simple pendulum is given by

$$T = 2\pi\sqrt{\frac{l}{g}}$$

where, l = effective length of the pendulum and g = acceleration due to gravity.

If the effective length l of simple pendulum is very large and comparable with the radius of earth (R), then its time period is given by

$$T = 2\pi\sqrt{\frac{Rl}{(l + R)g}}$$

For a simple pendulum of length equal to radius of earth,

$$T = 2\pi\sqrt{\frac{R}{2g}} = 60 \text{ min}$$

For a simple pendulum of infinite length ($l >> R$),

$$T = 2\pi\sqrt{\frac{R}{g}} = 84.6 \text{ min}$$

Competition Insight

- If the bob of the simple pendulum is suspended by a metallic wire of length l, having coefficient of linear expansion α, then due to increase in temperature by $d\theta$, then

  Effective length, $l' = l\,(1 + \alpha\, d\theta)$

  and $$T' = 2\pi\sqrt{\frac{l(1 + \alpha d\theta)}{g}}$$

- When a bob of simple pendulum of density ρ oscillates in a fluid of density ρ_0 ($\rho_0 < \rho$), then time period get increased.

  Increased time period, $$T' = 2\pi\sqrt{\frac{\rho l}{(\rho - \rho_0)g}}$$

- When simple pendulum is in a horizontally accelerated vehicle, then its time period is given by

  $$T = 2\pi\sqrt{\frac{l}{\sqrt{(a^2 + g^2)}}}$$

  where, a = horizontal acceleration of the vehicle.

- When simple pendulum is in a vehicle sliding down an inclined plane, then its time period is given by $T = 2\pi\sqrt{\frac{l}{g\cos\theta}}$

  where, θ = inclination of plane.

- When a bob of simple pendulum has positive q charge and made to oscillate in uniform electric field acting in upward direction, then $$T = 2\pi\sqrt{\frac{l}{g - \frac{qE}{m}}}$$

Second's Pendulum

A simple pendulum having time period of 2 seconds is called second's pendulum.

The effective length of a second's pendulum is 99.992 cm of approximately 1 m on earth.

Spring Pendulum

A point mass suspended from a massless (or light) spring constitutes a spring pendulum. If the mass is once pulled downwards so as to stretch the spring and then released, the system oscillated up and down about its mean position simple harmonically. Time period and frequency of oscillations are given by

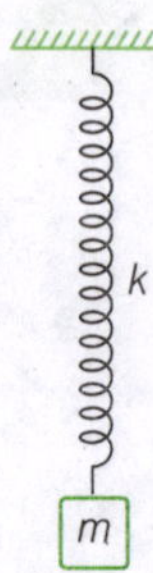

$$T=2\pi\sqrt{\frac{m}{k}} \text{ or } v=\frac{1}{2\pi}\sqrt{\frac{k}{m}}$$

Knowledge Booster

If the spring is not light but has a definite mass m_s, then time period of oscillation will be $T=2\pi\sqrt{\frac{m+\frac{m_s}{3}}{k}}$

When two springs of force constants k_1 and k_2 are connected in parallel to mass m as shown in figure, then

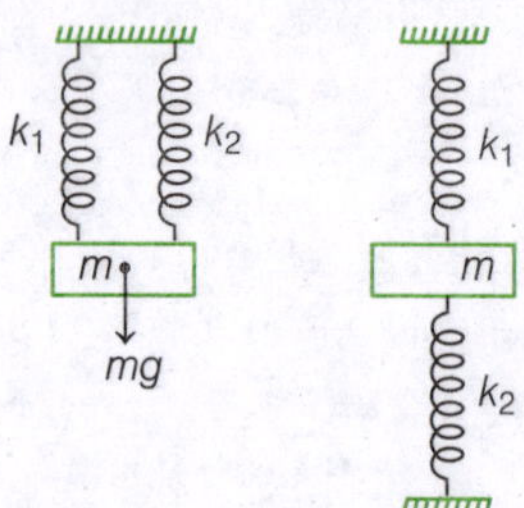

(i) Effective force constant of the spring combination

$$k = k_1 + k_2$$

(ii) Time period, $T = 2\pi\sqrt{\frac{m}{(k_1 + k_2)}}$

When two springs of force constant k_1 and k_2 are connected in series to mass m as shown in figure, then

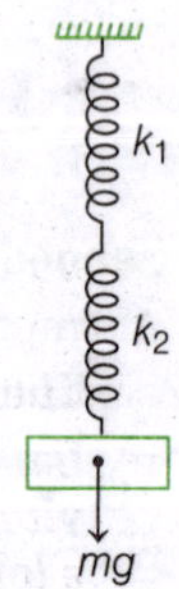

(i) Effective force constant of the spring combination,

$$\frac{1}{k} = \frac{1}{k_1} + \frac{1}{k_2}$$

(ii) Time period, $T = 2\pi\sqrt{\frac{m(k_1 + k_2)}{k_1 k_2}}$

Chapter 18

Waves and Sound

Wave

A wave is a vibratory disturbance in a medium which carries energy from one point to another point without any actual movement of the medium. There are three types of waves

(i) **Mechanical Waves** Those waves which require a material medium for their propagation, are called mechanical waves, e.g. sound waves, water waves etc.

(ii) **Electromagnetic Waves** Those waves which do not require a material medium for their propagation, are called electromagnetic waves, e.g. light waves, radio waves etc.

(iii) **Matter Waves** These waves are associated with electrons, protons and other fundamental particles.

Nature of Waves

(i) **Transverse Waves** A wave in which the particles of the medium vibrate at right angles to the direction of propagation of wave, is called a transverse wave.

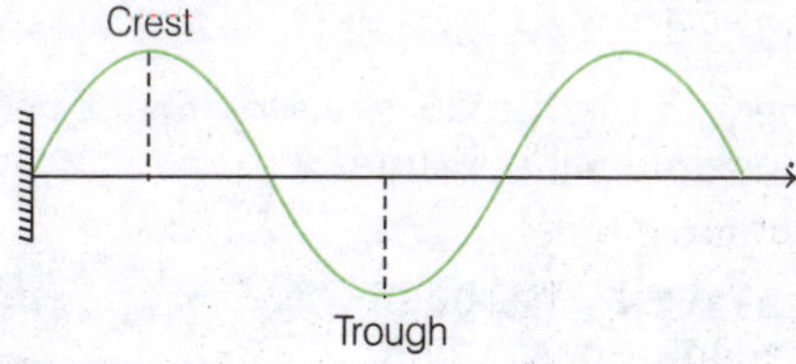

These waves travel in the form of crests and troughs.

(ii) **Longitudinal Waves** A wave in which the particles of the medium vibrate in the same direction in which wave is propagating, is called a longitudinal wave.

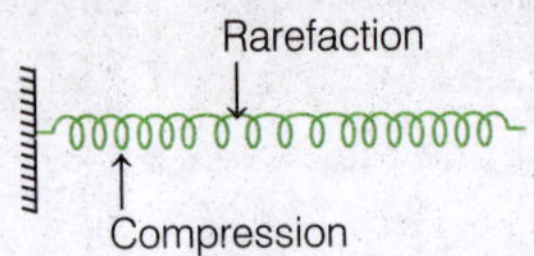

These waves travel in the form of compressions and rarefactions.

Some Important Terms Related to Wave Motion

(i) **Amplitude** The amplitude of a wave is the magnitude of maximum displacement of the particles from their equilibrium position, as the wave passes through them.

(ii) **Wavelength** The distance between two nearest points in a wave which are in the same phase of vibration is called the wavelength (λ).

(iii) **Time Period** Time taken to complete one vibration is called time period (T).

(iv) **Frequency** The number of vibrations completed in one second is called frequency of the wave.

$$\text{Frequency, } f = \frac{1}{\text{Time period } (T)}$$

Its SI unit is hertz.

Angular frequency, $\omega = \frac{2\pi}{T}$

Its SI unit is rad s^{-1}.

(v) **Velocity of Wave or Wave Velocity** The distance travelled by a wave in one second is called velocity of the wave (v).

Relation among velocity, frequency and wavelength of a wave is given by

$$v = f\lambda$$

Sound Waves

Sound is a form energy which produces a sensation of hearing in our ears. Sound waves are longitudinal in nature.

Sound waves are of three types

(i) **Infrasonic Waves** The sound waves of frequency range 0 to 20 Hz are called infrasonic waves.

(ii) **Audible Waves** The sound waves of frequency range 20 Hz to 20000 Hz are called audible waves.

(iii) **Ultrasonic Waves** The sound waves of frequency greater than 20000 Hz are called ultrasonic waves.

Sound waves require medium for their propagation. Sound waves can travel through any material medium (i.e. solids, liquid and gases) with speed that depends on the properties of the medium.

Value Points

Sound waves cannot propagate through vacuum.

- If v_s, v_l and v_g are speed of sound waves in solid, liquid and gases, then $v_s > v_l > v_g$
- Sound waves (longitudinal waves) can reflect, refract, interfere and diffract but cannot be polarised as only transverse waves can polarised.

Velocity of Longitudinal (Sound) Waves

Velocity of longitudinal (sound) wave in any medium is given by

$$v = \sqrt{\frac{E}{\rho}}$$

where, E is coefficient of elasticity of the medium and ρ is density of the medium.

Newton's Formula

According to Newton, the propagation of longitudinal waves in a gas is an **isothermal process**. Therefore, velocity of longitudinal (sound) waves in gas

$$v = \sqrt{\frac{E_T}{\rho}} = \sqrt{\frac{p}{\rho}}$$

where, E_T is the isothermal coefficient of volume elasticity and it is equal to the pressure of the gas.

Laplace's Correction

According to Laplace, the propagation of longitudinal wave is an **adiabatic process**. Therefore, velocity of longitudinal (sound) wave in gas should be

$$v = \sqrt{\frac{E_s}{\rho}} = \sqrt{\frac{\gamma p}{\rho}}$$

where, E_s is the adiabatic coefficient of volume elasticity and it is equal to γp.

Factors Affecting Velocity of Longitudinal (Sound) Wave

(i) **Effect of Pressure** The formula for velocity of sound in a gas.

$$v = \sqrt{\frac{\gamma p}{\rho}} = \sqrt{\frac{\gamma RT}{M}}$$

Therefore, $\left(\frac{p}{\rho}\right)$ remains constant at constant temperature. Hence, there is no effect of pressure on velocity of longitudinal wave.

(ii) **Effect of Temperature** Velocity of longitudinal wave in a gas

$$v = \sqrt{\frac{\gamma p}{\rho}} = \sqrt{\frac{\gamma RT}{M}}$$

$$\therefore \qquad v \propto \sqrt{T}$$

$$\Rightarrow \qquad \frac{v_1}{v_2} = \sqrt{\frac{T_1}{T_2}}$$

Velocity of sound in a gas is directly proportional to the square root of its absolute temperature.

If v_0 and v_t are velocities of sound in air at 0°C and t°C, then

$$v_t = v_0\left(1 + \frac{t}{273}\right)^{1/2}$$

or

$$v_t = v_0 + 0.61\, t$$

(iii) **Effect of Density** The velocity of sound in gaseous medium

$$v \propto \frac{1}{\sqrt{\rho}} \quad \Rightarrow \quad \frac{v_1}{v_2} = \sqrt{\frac{\rho_2}{\rho_1}}$$

The velocity of sound in a gas is inversely proportional to the square root of density of the gas.

(iv) **Effect of Humidity** The velocity of sound increases with increase in humidity in air. Thus, speed of sound in moist air is slightly greater than in dry air.

EXPERT Scale Up

Keep this caution point in mind while solving the questions.

Speed of sound in air is independent of its frequency, so sound waves of different frequency travels at the same speed, however their wavelengths in air are different.

Shock Waves

If speed of a body in air is greater than the speed of sound, then it is called **supersonic speed**. Such a body leaves behind a conical region of disturbance which spreads continuously. Such a disturbance is called a shock wave.

Characteristics of Musical Sound

Musical sound has three characteristics

(i) **Intensity or Loudness** Intensity of sound is energy transmitted per second per unit area by sound waves. Its SI unit is watt/metre^2. Intensity is measured in decibel (dB).

(ii) **Pitch or Frequency** Pitch of sound directly depends on frequency.

A shrill and sharp sound has higher pitch and a grave and dull sound has lower pitch.

(iii) **Quality or Timbre** Quality is the characteristic of sound that differentiates between two sounds of same intensity and same frequency.

Quality depends on harmonics and their relative order and intensity.

Speed of Transverse Wave

On a stretched string $v = \sqrt{\dfrac{T}{m}}$

where, T = tension in the string and m = mass per unit length of the string.

Speed of transverse wave in a solid $v = \sqrt{\dfrac{\eta}{\rho}}$

where, η is modulus of rigidity and ρ is density of solid.

Plane Progressive Simple Harmonic Wave

Equation of a plane progressive simple harmonic wave travelling along positive direction of X-axis

$$y = A\sin(\omega t - kx)$$

or
$$y = A\sin 2\pi\left(\frac{t}{T} - \frac{x}{\lambda}\right)$$

or
$$y = A\sin\frac{2\pi}{\lambda}(vt - x)$$

where, y = displacement, A = amplitude of vibration of particle,

λ = wavelength of wave, T = time period of wave,

x = distance of particle from the origin

and v = velocity of wave.

k = propagation constant of wave.

Important Relation Related to Equation of Progressive Wave

Some important relation related to equation of progressive wave are given as

Wave velocity, $v = \dfrac{\text{Coefficient of } t}{\text{Coefficient of } x} = \dfrac{\omega}{k}$

where, $k = \frac{2\pi}{\lambda}$ is called propagation constant of wave motion. It is also called angular wave number.

Wavelength, $\lambda = \frac{2\pi}{\text{Coefficient of } x} = \frac{2\pi}{k}$

Angular wave number, $k = \frac{2\pi}{\lambda}$ rad m^{-1}

Time period $T = \frac{2\pi}{\text{Coefficient of } t} = \frac{2\pi}{\omega}$

Frequency $f = \frac{\text{Coefficient of } t}{2\pi} = \frac{\omega}{2\pi}$

Particle velocity $v_p = \frac{dy}{dt} = a\cos\frac{2\pi}{T}\left(\frac{t}{T} - \frac{x}{\lambda}\right)$

$$(v_p)_{\max} = a\left(\frac{2\pi}{T}\right) = a\omega$$

Also, $v_p = -v \times$ slope of wave at that point.

Phase of the vibration is the angle of sine in equation of plane progressive wave. It is denoted by ϕ.

$$\phi = 2\pi\left(\frac{t}{T} - \frac{x}{\lambda}\right)$$

Relation between phase difference, path difference and time difference

$$\Delta\phi = \frac{2\pi}{\lambda}\Delta x \quad \text{or} \quad \Delta\phi = \frac{2\pi}{T}\Delta t$$

Energy in a Wave

Regarding the energy in wave motion, we come across three terms namely, energy density (u), power (P) and intensity (I).

1. Energy Density (u)

The energy density is defined as the total mechanical energy (kinetic + potential) per unit volume of the medium through which the wave is passing.

So, kinetic energy per unit volume,

$$\Delta K = \frac{1}{2}\rho\omega^2 A^2 \cos^2(kx - \omega t)$$

Potential energy per unit volume,

$$\Delta U = \frac{1}{2}\rho\omega^2 A^2 \cos^2(kx - \omega t)$$

Total energy per unit volume,

$$\Delta E = \Delta K + \Delta U = \rho\omega^2 A^2 \cos^2(kx - \omega t)$$

Thus, energy density $u = \Delta E = (\Delta K + \Delta U)$

$$= \rho\omega^2 A^2 \cos^2(kx - \omega t) = \frac{1}{2}\rho\omega^2 A^2$$

$$[\because \text{Average value of } \cos^2(kx - \omega t) = \frac{1}{2}]$$

$$u = \frac{1}{2}\rho\omega^2 A^2$$

2. Power (P)

The instantaneous rate at which energy is transferred along the string if we consider a transverse wave on a string, is called power.

In unit time, the wave will travel a distance v. If S be the area of cross-section of the string, then volume of this length would be Sv.

Thus,
$$P = \text{Energy density} \times \text{Volume}$$
$$= \frac{1}{2}\rho\omega^2 A^2 \times Sv = \frac{1}{2}\rho\omega^2 A^2 Sv$$

3. Intensity (I)

Flow of energy per unit area of cross-section of the string in unit time is known as intensity of the wave.

Thus,
$$I = \frac{\text{Power}}{\text{Area of cross-section}} = \frac{P}{S}$$

or
$$I = \frac{1}{2}\rho\omega^2 A^2 v$$

Superposition of Waves

Two or more progressive waves can travel simultaneously in the medium without effecting the motion of one another. Therefore, resultant displacement of each particle of the medium at any instant is equal to vector sum of the displacements produced by two waves separately. This principle is called principle of superposition.

Interference

When two waves of same frequency travel in a medium simultaneously in the same direction, then due to their superposition, the resultant intensity at any point of the medium is different from the sum intensities of the two waves. At some points the intensity of the resultant wave is very large while at some other points it is very small or zero. This phenomenon is called **interference of waves.**

Constructive Interference

Phase difference between two waves $= 0, 2\pi, 4\pi$

$$\text{Maximum amplitude} = (A_1 + A_2)$$

$$\text{Intensity} \propto (\text{Amplitude})^2 \propto (A_1 + A_2)^2$$

In general, $$\text{amplitude} = \sqrt{A_1^2 + A_2^2 + 2A_1A_2\cos\phi}$$

Destructive Interference

Phase difference between two waves $= \pi, 3\pi, 5\pi$

Minimum amplitude $= (A_1 - A_2)$ = Difference of component amplitudes.

$$\text{Intensity} \propto (\text{Amplitude})^2$$
$$\propto (A_1 - A_2)^2$$

A vibrating tunning fork, when rotated near an ear produced loud sound and silence due to constructive and destructive interference.

Beats

When two sound waves of nearly equal frequencies are produced simultaneously, then intensity of the resultant sound produced by their superposition increases and decreases alternately with time. This rise and fall intensity of sound is called beats.

The number of maxima or minima heard in one second is called beats frequency.

 **Value Points**

- The difference of sound wave frequencies should not be more than 10. Sound persists on human ear drums for 0.1 second. Hence, beats will not be heard if the frequency difference exceeds 10.
- Number of beats heard per second $= n_1 - n_2$
  = difference of frequencies of two waves.
- Beat period = reciprocal of beat frequency
- For loudness, time intervals are $\frac{1}{n_1 - n_2}, \frac{2}{n_1 - n_2}, \ldots$

Reflection of Wave

The rebouncing back of waves when it strikes a hard surface is called reflection of wave.

If equation of incident travelling wave is $y(x, t) = A\sin(kx - \omega t)$

A travelling wave or pulse suffers a phase change of π on reflection at a rigid boundary.

Equation of reflected wave, $y(x, t) = A \sin (kx + \omega t + \pi)$

If the reflecting end is free to move transversely, then there is no phase change between the incident and the reflected wave.

Equation of incident wave,

$$y(x,t) = A\sin(-\omega t)$$

Equation of reflected wave,

$$y(x,t) = A\sin(kx + \omega t)$$

If a wave is incident obliquely on the boundary between two different media, the transmitted wave is called the refracted wave.

Echo

The repetition of sound caused by the reflection of sound waves at a distant surface, *e.g.* a cliff, a row of building etc is called an echo.

Sound persists in ear for 0.1 s.

The minimum distance from a sound reflecting surface to hear an echo is 16.5 m.

If first echo be heard after t_1 second, second echo after t_2 second, then third echo will be heard after $(t_1 + t_2)$ s.

Stationary or Standing Waves

When two similar waves propagate in a bounded medium in opposite directions, then due to their superposition a new type of wave is obtained, which appears stationary in the medium. This wave is called stationary or standing waves.

Equation of a stationary wave, $y = 2a \sin \dfrac{2\pi t}{T} \cos \dfrac{2\pi x}{\lambda}$

Nodes (N) and antinodes (A) are obtained alternatively in a stationary waves.

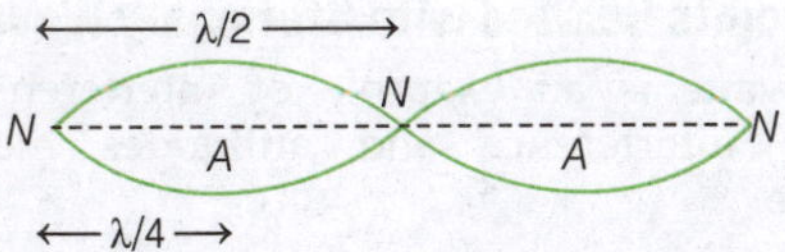

At nodes, the displacement of the particles remains minimum, strain is maximum, pressure and density variations are maximum.

At antinodes, the displacement of the particles remains maximum, strain is minimum, pressure and density variations are minimum.

The distance between two consecutive nodes or two consecutive antinodes $= \dfrac{\lambda}{2}$.

The distance between a node and adjoining antinode $= \frac{\lambda}{4}$.

All the particles between two nodes vibrate in same phase.

Particles on two sides of a node vibrate in opposite phase.

n consecutive nodes are separated by $\frac{(n-1)\lambda}{2}$.

Position of Nodes

Nodes are the points on the string where the amplitude of oscillation of constituents is zero.

i.e., $\sin kx = 0$

$$kx = n\pi \qquad \text{where, } n = 0, 1, \ldots$$

$$\frac{2\pi}{\lambda}x = n\pi$$

$$x = \frac{n\lambda}{2}$$

Position of Antinodes

Antinodes are the points where the amplitude of oscillation of the constituents is maximum.

for maximum amplitude $\sin kx = \pm 1$

$$\Rightarrow \quad kx = (2n+1)\frac{\pi}{2} \qquad \text{where, } n = 0, 1, 2, \ldots$$

$$\frac{2\pi}{\lambda}x = (2n+1)\frac{\pi}{2}$$

or $$x = (2n+1)\frac{\lambda}{4}$$

For $n = 0, 1, 2, \ldots$

Some Important Points Related with Stationary Waves

(i) Standing wave is an example of interference. Nodes means destructive interference and antinodes means constructive interference.

(ii) Two identical waves moving in opposite directions along the string will still produce standing waves even, if their amplitudes are unequal. This is the case when an incident travelling wave is only partially reflected from a boundary, the resulting superposition of two waves having different amplitudes and travelling in opposite directions gives a standing wave pattern of waves whose envelope is shown in figure.

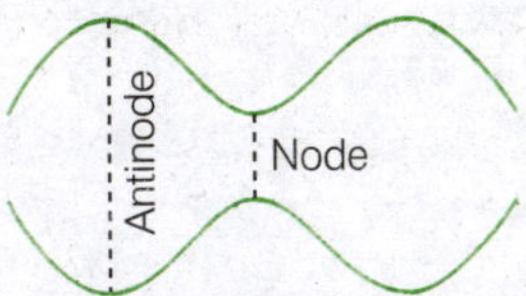

The standing wave ratio (SWR) is defined as

$$\frac{A_{\text{max}}}{A_{\text{min}}} = \frac{A_i + A_r}{A_i - A_r}$$

where, A_i and A_r are the amplitude of incident and reflected wave respectively.

For 100% reflection, SWR $= \infty$ and for no reflection, SWR $= 1$.

(iii) In this pattern, at antinode position, displacement is maximum and hence velocity is maximum, but strain is minimum.

Strain = slope of stationary wave pattern $\left(\frac{dy}{dx}\right)$

At nodal position, displacement and velocity is minimum but strain is maximum.

(iv) When a wave is reflected off a real surface, part of energy is absorbed by the surface. As a result, energy, intensity and amplitude of reflected wave is always less than that of incident wave. Two waves differ in their amplitude having same frequency and wavelength and propagate in reverse or opposite direction always give stationary wave pattern by their superposition.

(v) In standing wave nodes are permanently at rest, so no energy can be transmitted across them *i.e.*, energy of one region is confined in that region. However, this energy oscillates between elastic PE and KE of the particles of the medium. When particles are at mean position, KE is maximum while elastic PE is minimum. When particles are at their extreme positions KE is minimum while elastic PE is maximum.

Competition Insight

- The intensity of a travelling wave is given by

$$I = \frac{1}{2}\rho A^2 \omega^3 v \quad i.e., \quad I \propto A^2$$

So, we can write, $\frac{I_1}{I_2} = \left(\frac{A_1}{A_2}\right)^2$ if ρ, ω and v are same for two waves.

- For example, when an incident travelling wave is partly reflected and partly transmitted from a boundary, we can write

$$\frac{I_i}{I_r} = \left(\frac{A_i}{A_r}\right)^2$$

- As incident and reflected waves are in the same medium hence, they have same values of ρ and v. But we cannot write

$$\frac{I_i}{I_t} = \left(\frac{A_i}{A_t}\right)^2$$

where, A_t is the amplitude of transmitted wave.

as they have different value of ρ and v.

Vibrations in a Stretched String

When a string of definite length l, rigidly held at both ends. If this string is plucked and released, then a stationary transverse wave is set up in it. If n is the frequency of vibrating string, then

(i) $n \propto \frac{1}{l}$, where l is length of string or $nl =$ constant

(ii) $n \propto \sqrt{T}$, where T is tension in string or $\frac{n}{\sqrt{T}} =$ constant

(iii) $n \propto \frac{1}{\sqrt{\mu}}$, where μ is mass per unit length of a string.

From this we have, $n \propto \frac{1}{r}$, where r is radius of string

and $n \propto \frac{1}{\sqrt{\rho}}$, where ρ is density of string.

Vibrations of a String Fixed at One End

Fundamental frequency of vibration or first harmonic is

$$n_0 = \frac{v}{4l} = \frac{2n+1}{4l}\sqrt{\frac{T}{m}}$$

Frequency of third harmonic, $n_1 = \frac{3v}{4l} = 3n_0$

Frequency of fifth harmonic, $n_2 = \frac{5v}{4l} = 5n_0$

$$n_0 : n_1 : n_2 .... = 1:3:5 : .....$$

For mth overtone, frequency is $(2m+1)n_0$

Standing Waves in a String Fixed at Both Ends

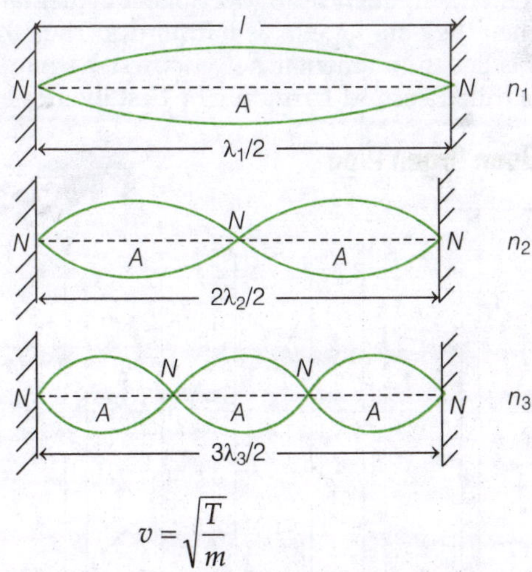

$$v = \sqrt{\frac{T}{m}}$$

Fundamental frequency or frequency of first harmonic

$$n_1 = \frac{v}{2l} = \frac{1}{2l}\sqrt{\frac{T}{m}}$$

Frequency of first overtone or second harmonic

$$n_2 = 2 \cdot \frac{v}{2l} = 2n_1$$

Frequency of second overtone or third harmonic

$$n_3 = 3 \cdot \frac{v}{2l} = 3n_1$$

$\therefore \quad n_1 : n_2 : n_3 : ... = 1 : 2 : 3 : ...$

Organ Pipes

Organ pipes are those cylindrical pipes which are used for producing musical (longitudial) sounds. Organ pipes are of two types

(i) **Open Organ Pipe** Cylindrical pipes open at both ends.

(ii) **Closed Organ Pipe** Cylindrical pipes open at one end and closed at other end.

Terms Related to Vibrating Air Columns/Strings

Fundamental Note It is the sound of lowest frequency produced in fundamental note of vibration of a system.

Overtones Tones having frequencies greater than the fundamental note are called overtones.

Harmonics When the frequencies of overtone are integral multiples of the fundamental, then they are known as **harmonics**. Thus the note of lowest frequency n is called fundamental note or **first harmonics.** The note of frequency $2n$ is called **second harmonic** or **first overtone.**

Vibrations in Open Organ Pipe

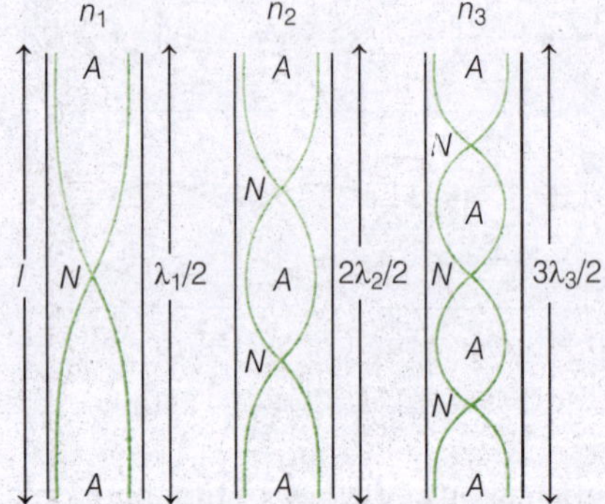

Fundamental frequency or frequency of first harmonic $n_1 = \frac{v}{2l}$

Frequency of first overtone or second harmonic $n_2 = 2\frac{v}{2l} = 2n_1$

Frequency of second overtone or third harmonic $n_3 = 3\frac{v}{2l} = 3n_1$

$\therefore \qquad n_1 : n_2 : n_3 : \ldots = 1 : 2 : 3 : \ldots$

Therefore, even and odd harmonics are produced by an open organ pipe.

Vibrations in Closed Organ Pipe

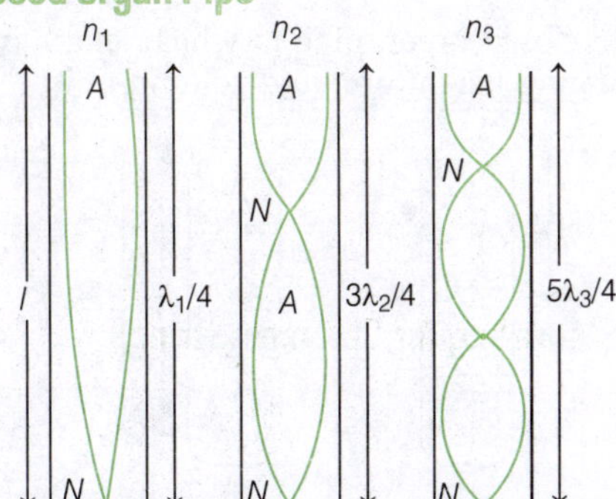

Fundamental frequency or frequency of first harmonic, $n_1 = \dfrac{v}{4l}$

Frequency of first overtone or third harmonic, $n_2 = \dfrac{3v}{4l} = 3n_1$

Frequency of second overtone or fifth harmonic, $n_3 = 5 \cdot \dfrac{v}{4l} = 5n_1$

$\therefore \qquad n_1 : n_2 : n_3 : \ldots = 1:3:5: \ldots$

Therefore only odd harmonics are produced by a closed organ pipe.

End Correction

Antinode is not obtained at exact open end of the organ pipe but slightly above it. The distance between open end and antinode is called end correction.

It is denoted by e.

Effective length of an open organ pipe $= (l + 2e)$

Effective length of a closed organ pipe $= (l + e)$

If r is the radius of closed organ pipe, then $e = 0.6\, r$

If r is the radius of an open organ pipe, then $e = 1.2\, r$

Factors Affecting Frequency of Wave in a Pipe

(i) Length of air column, $n \propto 1/l$

(ii) Radius of air column, $n \propto 1/r$

(iii) Temperature of air column, $n \propto \sqrt{T}$

(iv) Pressure of air inside air column, $n \propto \sqrt{p}$

(v) Density of air, $n \propto \dfrac{1}{\sqrt{\rho}}$

(vi) Velocity of sound in air column, $n \propto v$

Resonance Tube

Resonance tube is a closed organ pipe in which length of air column can be changed by changing height of liquid column in it.

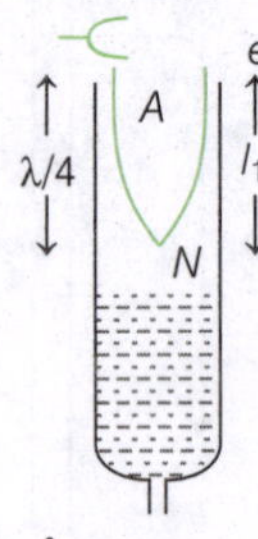

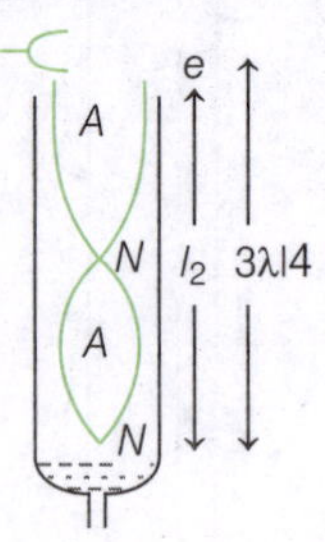

For first resonance, $\dfrac{\lambda}{4} = l_1 + e$

For second resonance, $\dfrac{3\lambda}{4} = l_2 + e$

Velocity of sound $v = n\lambda = 2n(l_2 - l_1)$

End correction, $e = \dfrac{l_2 - 3l_1}{2}$

 **Knowledge Booster**

Melde's Experiment

In longitudinal mode, vibrations of the prongs of tuning fork are along the length of the string.

Frequency of vibration of string = $\dfrac{\text{Frequency of tuning fork}}{2}$

$$n_L = \frac{p}{l}\sqrt{\frac{T}{m}}$$

In transverse mode, vibrations of tuning fork are at 90° to the length of string.

Frequency of vibration of string = Frequency of tuning fork.

$$n_T = \frac{p}{2l}\sqrt{\frac{T}{m}} = \frac{n_L}{2}$$

In both modes of vibrations, Melde's law

p^2T = constant, is obeyed.

Chapter 19

Electrostatics

Charge

Charge is that property of an object by virtue of which it apply electrostatic force of interaction on other objects.

Charges are of two types

(i) Positive charge

(ii) Negative charge

Like charges repel and unlike charges attract each other.

Conductors

Conductors are those substances which can be used to carry or conduct electric charge from one point to other, e.g. silver, copper, aluminium etc.

Insulators

Insulators are those substances which cannot conduct electric charge, e.g. glass, rubber, plastic etc.

 **Knowledge Booster**

Earthing When we bring a charged body in contact with the earth, all the excess charge on the body disappears by causing a momentary current to pass to the ground through the connecting conductor. This process is called grounding or earthing.

Charging by Induction The process of charging a neutral body by bringing a charged body nearby it without making contact between the two bodies is known as charging by induction.

Basic Properties of Electric Charges

Basic properties of electric charges are given as

Additivity of Charge

If a system consists of n charges q_1, q_2, q_3 .... q_n, then the total charge of the system will be $q_1 + q_2 + q_3 + q_4 + ... + q_n$.

Quantisation of Charge

Charge on any object can be an integer multiple of a smallest charge (e).

$$Q = \pm ne$$

where, $n = 1, 2, 3, \ldots$ and $e = 1.6 \times 10^{-19}$ C.

Value Points

The protons and neutrons are combination of other entities called quarks, which have charges $\frac{1}{3}e$. However, isolated quarks have not been observed, so, quantum of charge is still e.

Conservation of Charge

Charge can neither be created nor be destroyed, but can be transferred from one object to another object.

Coulomb's Law of Electrostatics

Coulomb's law is a quantitative statement about the force between two point charges. It states that "the force of interaction between any two point charges is directly proportional to the product of the charges and inversely proportional to the square of the distance between them".

Suppose two point charges q_1 and q_2 are separated in vacuum by a distance r, then force between two charges is given by $F_e = \frac{K|q_1 q_2|}{r^2}$

The constant K is usually put as $K = \frac{1}{4\pi\varepsilon_0}$, where ε_0 is called the permittivity of free space and has the value $\varepsilon_0 = 8.854 \times 10^{-12} \text{C}^2/\text{N-m}^2$. For all practical purposes we will take $\frac{1}{4\pi\varepsilon_0} \simeq 9 \times 10^9 \text{N-m}^2/\text{C}^2$.

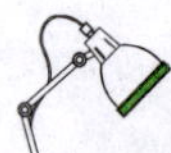

EXPERT Scale Up

If there is another medium between the point charges except air or vacuum, then ε_0 is replaced by $\varepsilon_0 K$ or ε. Here K or ε_r is called dielectric constant or relative permittivity of the medium.

$$\varepsilon_0 k = \varepsilon = \varepsilon_r$$

or

$$K = \varepsilon_r = \frac{\varepsilon}{\varepsilon_0}$$

where, ε = permittivity of the medium.

For air or **vacuum**, $K = 1$, **For water**, $K = 81$, **For metals**, $K = \infty$

Coulomb's Law in Vector Form

Let q_1 and q_2 both are positive.

Force on q_2 due to q_1,

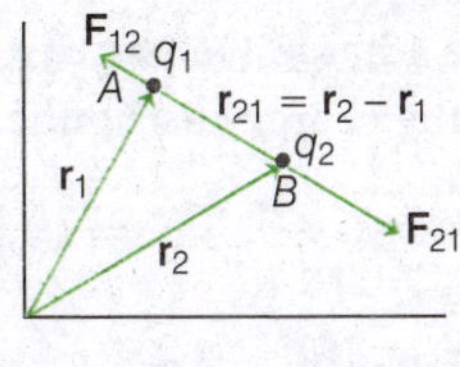

$$\mathbf{F}_{21} = \frac{1}{4\pi\varepsilon_0} \cdot \frac{q_1 q_2}{r^2} \hat{\mathbf{r}}_{21}$$

$$\mathbf{F}_{21} = \frac{1}{4\pi\varepsilon_0} \cdot \frac{q_1 q_2}{r^3} \mathbf{r}_{21}$$

$$\mathbf{F}_{21} = \frac{q_1 q_2}{4\pi\varepsilon_0} \cdot \frac{\mathbf{r}_2 - \mathbf{r}_1}{|\mathbf{r}_2 - \mathbf{r}_1|^3}$$

The above equations give the Coulomb's law in vector form.

Also, force on q_1 due to q_2 is

$$\mathbf{F}_{12} = \frac{q_1 q_2}{4\pi\varepsilon_0} \cdot \frac{\mathbf{r}_1 - \mathbf{r}_2}{|\mathbf{r}_1 - \mathbf{r}_2|^3}$$

$\therefore$ Force on q_1 due to q_2 = – Force on q_2 due to q_1

or $\mathbf{F}_{12} = -\mathbf{F}_{21}$

The forces due to two point charges are parallel to the line joining the point charges; such forces are called **central forces** and so electrostatic forces are **conservative forces**.

Forces between Multiple Charges : Superposition Principle

According to the principle of superposition, "total force on a given charge due to number of charges is the vector sum of individual forces acting on that charge due to the presence of other charges".

Consider a system of n point charges $q_1, q_2, q_3 \ldots q_n$ distributed in space. Let the charges be $q_2, q_3 \ldots q_n$, exert forces $\mathbf{F}_{12}, \mathbf{F}_{13}, \ldots \mathbf{F}_{1n}$ on charge q_1. The total force on charge q_1 is given by

$$\mathbf{F}_1 = \frac{1}{4\pi\varepsilon_0}\left(\frac{q_1 q_2}{r_{12}^2}\hat{\mathbf{r}}_{12} + \frac{q_1 q_3}{r_{13}^2}\hat{\mathbf{r}}_{13} + \ldots + \frac{q_1 q_n}{r_{1n}^2}\hat{\mathbf{r}}_{1n}\right)$$

Contiuous Charge Distribution

The region in which charges are closely spaced is said to have continuous distribution of charge. It is of three types; linear charge distribution, surface charge distribution and volume charge distribution.

Linear Charge Density (λ) It is defined as the charge per unit length of linear charge distribution. Its unit is coulomb/metre.

$$\lambda = \frac{dq}{dL}$$

Surface Charge Density (σ) It is defined as the charge per unit surface area of surface charge distribution. Its unit is coulomb/metre^2.

$$\sigma = \frac{dq}{dS}$$

Volume Charge Density (ρ) It is defined as the charge per unit volume of volume charge distribution. Its unit is coulomb/metre^3.

$$\rho = \frac{dq}{dV}$$

Electric Field

The space in the surrounding of any charge in which its influence can be experienced by other charges is called electric field.

Electric Field Intensity (E)

The electrostatic force acting per unit positive charge at a point in electric field is called electric field intensity at that point.

Electric field intensity $\mathbf{E} = \lim_{q_0 \to 0} \frac{\mathbf{F}}{q_0}$

where $\mathbf{F}$ = force experienced by the test charge q_0.

Its SI unit is NC^{-1} or V/m and its dimensions are $[MLT^{-3}A^{-1}]$.

It is a vector quantity and its direction is in the direction of electrostatic force acting on positive charge.

Electric Field due to a Point Charge

Electric field intensity due to a point charge q at a distance r is given by

$$E = \frac{1}{4\pi\varepsilon_0} \frac{q}{r^2}$$

Electric Field due to System of Charges

Electric field $\mathbf{E}$ at point P due to the systems of charges is given by

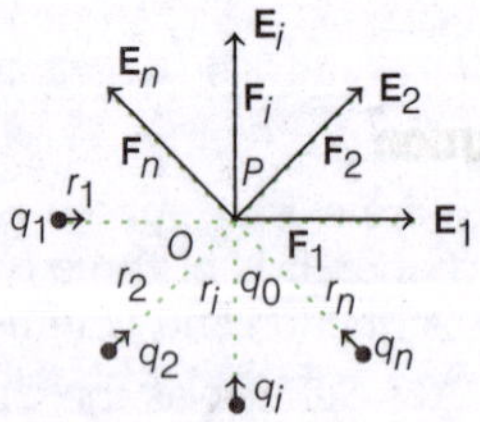

$$\mathbf{E}(r) = \frac{1}{4\pi\varepsilon_0} \sum_{i=1}^{n} \frac{q_i}{r_i^2} \hat{\mathbf{r}}_i$$

Electric Field Lines

"An electric field line is an imaginary line or curve drawn through a region of space so that its tangent at any point is in the direction of the electric field vector at that point.

The relative closeness of the lines at some place gives an idea about the intensity of electric field at that point."

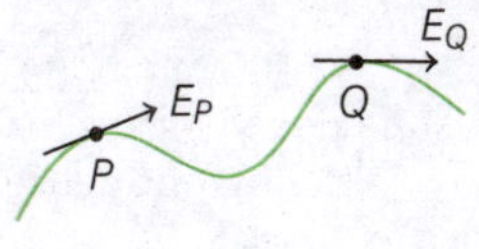

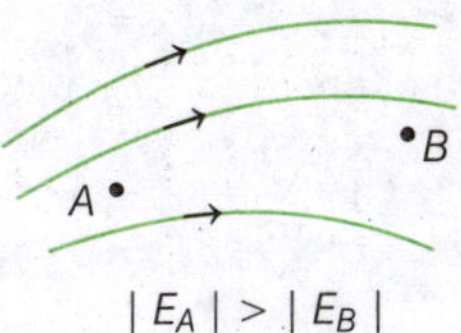

Properties of Electric Field Lines

(i) Electric field lines (lines of force) start from positive charge and terminate on negative charge.

(ii) Two electric lines of force never intersect each other.

(iii) Electric field lines do not form any closed loops.

(iv) In a charge-free region, electric field lines can be taken to be continuous curves without breaks.

Electric Field Due to Continuous Charge Distribution

(i) Electric field due to the line charge distribution at the location of charge q_0 is

$$\mathbf{E}_L = \frac{1}{4\pi\varepsilon_0}\int_L \frac{\lambda}{r^2}\, dL\hat{\mathbf{r}}$$

(ii) Electric field due to the surface charge distribution at the location of charge q_0 is

$$\mathbf{E}_S = \frac{1}{4\pi\varepsilon_0}\int_S \frac{\sigma}{r^2}\, dS\hat{\mathbf{r}}$$

(iii) Electric field due to the volume charge distribution at the location of charge q_0 is

$$\mathbf{E}_V = \frac{1}{4\pi\varepsilon_0}\int \frac{\rho}{r^2}\, dV\hat{\mathbf{r}}$$

Competition Insight

Electric Field of a Charged Ring

- Electric field at distance x from the centre of uniformly charged ring of total charge q on its axis is given by $E_x = \left(\frac{1}{4\pi\varepsilon_0}\right)\frac{qx}{(x^2 + R^2)^{3/2}}$
- Direction of this electric field is along the axis and away from the ring in case of positively charged ring and towards the ring in case of negatively charged ring.

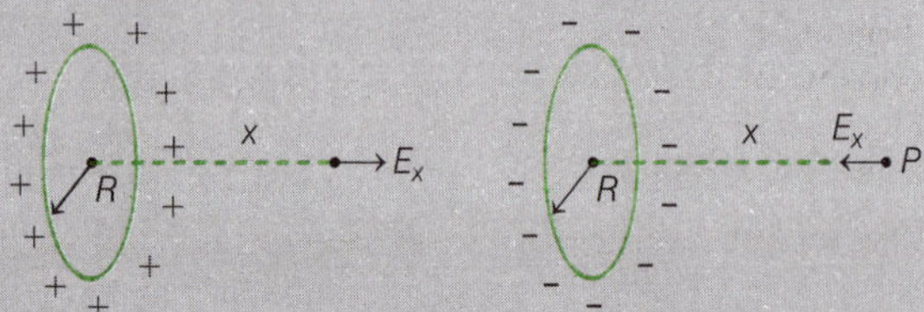

Special cases

From the above expression, we can see that

(i) $E_x = 0$ at $x = 0$ *i.e.*, **field is zero at the centre of the ring.** This would occur because charges on opposite sides of the ring would push in opposite directions on a test charge at the centre, and the forces would add to zero.

(ii) $E_x = \frac{1}{4\pi\varepsilon_0}\cdot\frac{q}{x^2}$ for $x \gg R$, *i.e.*, when the point P is much farther from the ring, its field is the same as that of a point charge.

To an observer far from the ring, the ring would appear like a point, and the electric field reflects this.

(iii) E_x will be maximum where $\frac{dE_x}{dx} = 0$. Differentiating E_x w.r.t. x and putting it equal to zero, we get $x = \frac{R}{\sqrt{2}}$ and E_{max} comes out to be, $\frac{2}{\sqrt[3]{3}}\left(\frac{1}{4\pi\varepsilon_0}\cdot\frac{q}{R^2}\right)$.

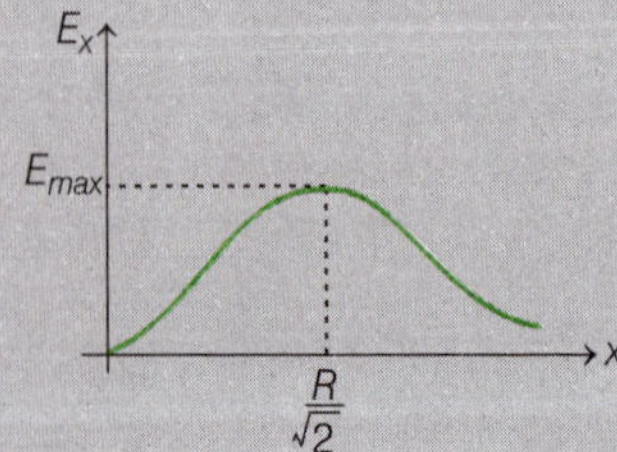

Electric Potential (V)

Electric potential at any point is equal to the work done per unit positive charge in carrying it from infinity to that point in electric field.

Electric potential, $V = \frac{W}{q}$

Its SI unit is J/C or volt and its dimensions are $[ML^2T^{-3}A^{-1}]$.

It is a scalar quantity.

Electric Potential Difference

The electric potential difference between two points A and B is equal to the work done by the external force in moving a unit positive charge against the electrostatic force from point B to A along any path between these two points.

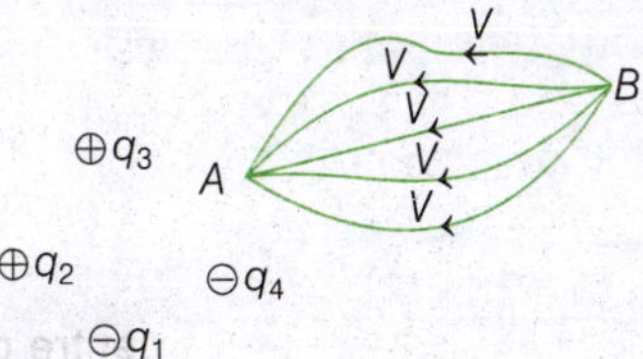

If V_A and V_B be the electric potential at point A and B respectively, then $\Delta V = V_A - V_B$

or $$\Delta V = \frac{W_{AB}}{q}$$

The SI unit of potential difference is volt (V).

The dimensional formula for electric potential difference is given by $[ML^2T^{-3}A^{-1}]$.

Electric Potential due to a Point Charge

Electric potential due to a point charge at a distance r is given by

$$V = \frac{1}{4\pi\varepsilon_0}\frac{q}{r}$$

Potential due to System of Charges

Let there be n number of point charges $q_1, q_2, q_3, \ldots, q_n$ at distances $r_1, r_2, r_3, \ldots, r_n$ respectively from the point P, where electric potential is given by

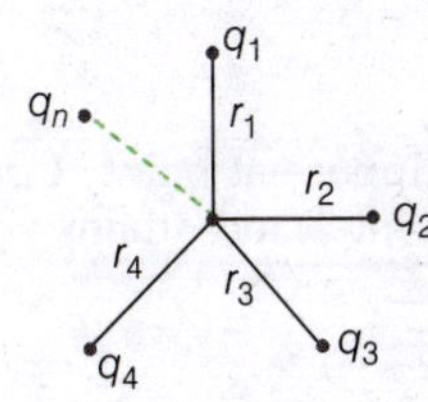

$$V = \frac{1}{4\pi\varepsilon_0}\sum_{i=1}^{n}\frac{q_i}{r_i}$$

Potential Gradient

The rate of change of potential with distance in electric field is called potential gradient.

Potential gradient $= \frac{dV}{dr}$. Its unit is V/m.

Relation between potential gradient and electric field intensity is given by

$$E = -\left(\frac{dV}{dr}\right)$$

Equipotential Surface

Equipotential surface is an imaginary surface joining the points of same potential in an electric field. So, we can say that the potential difference between any two points on an equipotential surface is zero. The electric lines of force at each point of an equipotential surface are normal to the surface.

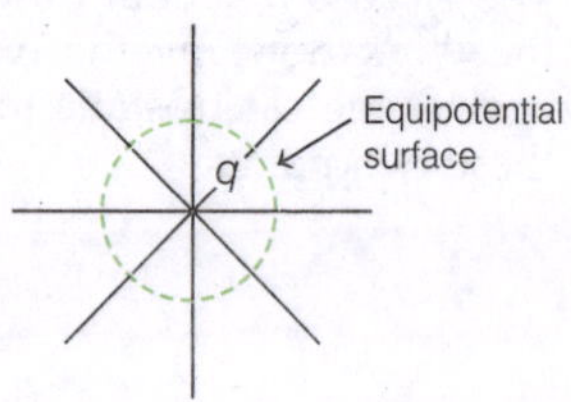

Properties of equipotential surfaces are as follows

(i) Equipotential surface may be planer, solid etc. But equipotential surface can never be of point size.

(ii) Electric field is always perpendicular to equipotential surface.

(iii) Equipotential surface due to an isolated point charge is spherical.

(iv) Equipotential surface are planer in an uniform electric field.

(v) Equipotential suface due to a line charge is cylindrical.

Motion of Charged Particle in Electric Field

Consider a charged particle having charge q and mass m is initially at rest in an electric field of strength E. The particle will experience an electric force which causes its motion.

The force experienced by the charged particle is F, where $F = qE$

$\therefore$ Acceleration produced by this force is

$$a = \frac{F}{m} = \frac{qE}{m} \quad \text{...(i)}$$

Suppose at point A particle is at rest and after some time, t it reaches the point B and attains velocity v.

$\therefore \quad v = at$

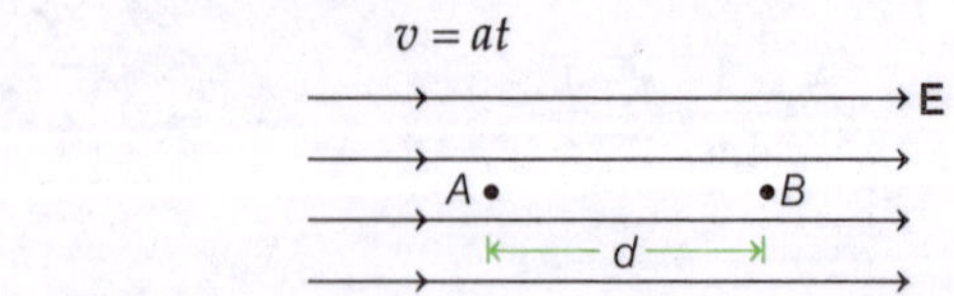

If potential difference between A and B be ΔV and the distance between them is d, then

$$v = \frac{qEt}{m} = \sqrt{\frac{2q\Delta V}{m}} \quad \text{... (ii)}$$

As momentum, $p = mv$

$\therefore$ $p = m\left(\frac{qEt}{m}\right)$ [from Eq. (ii)]

$$p = qEt$$

$$= m \times \sqrt{\frac{2q\Delta V}{m}} = \sqrt{2mq\Delta V}$$

Kinetic Energy of a Charged Particle

Kinetic energy gained by the particle in time t is

$$K = \frac{1}{2}mv^2 = \frac{1}{2}m\left(\frac{qEt}{m}\right)^2 \quad \text{[from Eq. (ii)]}$$

$$= \frac{q^2E^2t^2}{2m}$$

or $K = \frac{1}{2}m \times \frac{2q\Delta V}{m} = q\Delta V$

Electric Flux (ϕ_E)

Electric flux over an area is equal to the total number of electric field lines crossing this area.

Electric flux through a small area element dS is given by $\phi_E = \mathbf{E} \cdot d\mathbf{S}$

where, $\mathbf{E}$ = electric field intensity and $d\mathbf{S}$ = area vector.

Its SI unit is N-m^{2}C^{-1}.

Gauss' Theorem

The electric flux over any closed surface is $\frac{1}{\varepsilon_0}$ times the total charge enclosed by that surface, i.e. $\phi_E = \oint_s \mathbf{E} \cdot d\mathbf{S} = \frac{1}{\varepsilon_0} \Sigma q$

If a charge q is placed at the centre of a cube, then

total electric flux linked with the whole cube $= \frac{q}{\varepsilon_0}$

and electric flux linked with one face of the cube $= \frac{q}{6\varepsilon_0}$

Applications of Gauss' Theorem

(i) **Electric Field Intensity due to an Infinite Line Charge**

$$E = \frac{1}{2\pi\varepsilon_0}\frac{\lambda}{r}$$

where, λ is linear charge density and r is distance from the line charge.

(ii) **Electric Field Near an Infinite Plane Sheet of Charge**

$$E = \frac{\sigma}{2\,\varepsilon_0}$$

where, σ = surface charge density.

If there are two uniformly charged parallel sheets with surface charge densities σ and $-\sigma$, then $E = \frac{\sigma}{\varepsilon_0}$

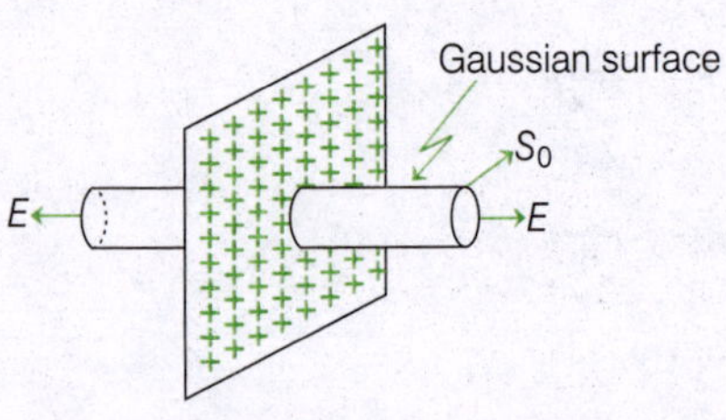

(iii) **Electric Field and Potential due to a Charged Spherical Shell**

At an extreme point ($r > R$)

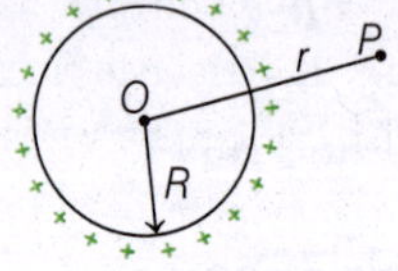

(a) Electric field intensity, $E = \frac{1}{4\pi\varepsilon_0}\frac{q}{r^2}$

(b) Electric potential, $V = \frac{1}{4\pi\varepsilon_0}\frac{q}{r}$

At the surface of a shell ($r = R$)

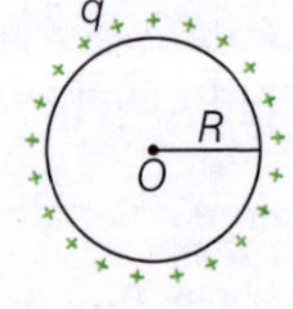

(a) Electric field intensity, $E = \frac{1}{4\pi\varepsilon_0}\frac{q}{R^2}$

(b) Electric potential, $V = \frac{1}{4\pi\varepsilon_0}\frac{q}{R}$

At an internal point $(r < R)$

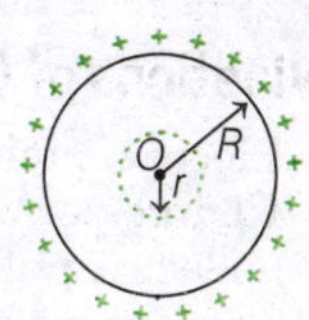

(a) Electric field intensity, $E = 0$

(b) Electric potential, $V = \frac{1}{4\pi\varepsilon_0}\frac{q}{R}$

Therefore, potential inside a charged conducting spherical shell is equal to the potential at its surface.

(iv) **Electric Field and Potential due to a Charged Non-Conducting Sphere**

At an extreme point, ($r > R$)

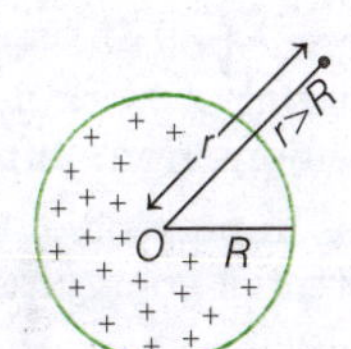

(a) Electric field intensity $E = \frac{1}{4\pi\varepsilon_0}\frac{q}{r^2}$

(b) Electric potential $V = \frac{1}{4\pi\varepsilon_0}\frac{q}{r}$

On the surface, $(r = R)$

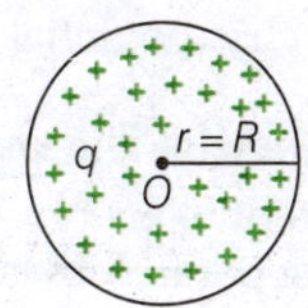

(a) Electric field intensity $E = \frac{1}{4\pi\varepsilon_0}\frac{q}{R^2}$

(b) Electric potential $V = \frac{1}{4\pi\varepsilon_0}\frac{q}{R}$

Inside the sphere, $(r < R)$

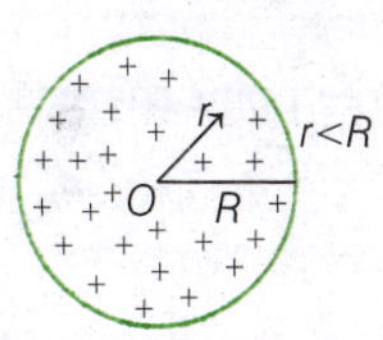

(a) Electric field intensity $E = \frac{1}{4\pi\varepsilon_0}\frac{qr}{R^3}$

(b) Electric potential $V = \frac{1}{4\pi\varepsilon_0}\frac{q(3R^2 - r^2)}{2R^3}$

At the centre of the sphere, $(r = 0)$

(a) Electric field intensity $E = 0$

(b) Electric potential $V = \frac{3}{2} \times \frac{1}{4\pi\varepsilon_0}\frac{q}{R}$

(v) **Potential due to a Spherical Shell**

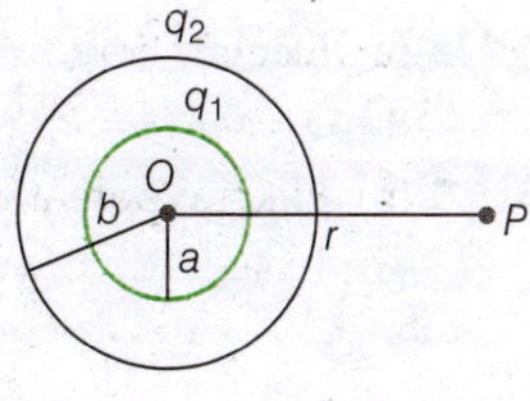

(a) **At point** P, where $OP = r$

$$V = \frac{q_1 + q_2}{4\pi\varepsilon_0 r}$$

(b) **At a point**, where $a < r < b$

$$V = \frac{q_1}{4\pi\varepsilon_0 r} + \frac{q_2}{4\pi\varepsilon_0 b}$$

(c) **At a point**, where $r < a$

$$V = \frac{q_1}{4\pi\varepsilon_0 a} + \frac{q_2}{4\pi\varepsilon_0 b}$$

(vi) Electric potential at any point on the axis of a uniformly charged ring at a distance x from its centre is given as

$$V = \frac{1}{4\pi\varepsilon_0} \frac{a}{(x^2 + a^2)^{1/2}},$$ where a is radius of ring.

Electric Potential Energy

Electric potential energy of a system of point charges is defined as the total amount of work done in bringing the different charges to their respective positions from infinitely large mutual separations.

It is represented by U. Thus, electric potential can also be written as potential energy per unit charge, *i.e.*,

$$V = \frac{W}{q} = \frac{U}{q}$$

Electric potential energy is defined only in a conservative field.

Potential Energy of Charge System

Potential energy of two point charges system, that contains charges q_1 and q_2 separated by a distance r is given by

$$U = \frac{1}{4\pi\varepsilon_0} \frac{q_1 q_2}{r}$$

Three point charges system

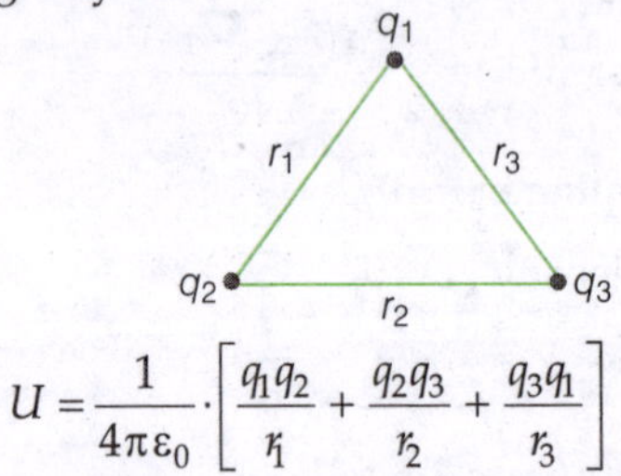

$$U = \frac{1}{4\pi\varepsilon_0} \cdot \left[\frac{q_1 q_2}{r_1} + \frac{q_2 q_3}{r_2} + \frac{q_3 q_1}{r_3}\right]$$

Value Points

- The potential energy of two unlike charges is negative.
- This negative potential energy indicates that an external agency will have to do work to seperate the charges infinite distance apart.

Potential Energy in an External Field

Potential energy of a single charge q at a point with position vector $\mathbf{r}$ in an external field $= q \cdot V(\mathbf{r})$, where $V(\mathbf{r})$ is the potential at the point due to external electric field $\mathbf{E}$.

For a system of two charges q_1 and q_2, the potential energy is given as

$$U = q_1 \cdot V(\mathbf{r}_1) + q_2 \cdot V(\mathbf{r}_2) + \frac{q_1 q_2}{4\pi\varepsilon_0 r_{12}}$$

where, q_1, q_2 = two point charges at position vectors $\mathbf{r}_1$ and $\mathbf{r}_2$, respectively

$V(\mathbf{r}_1)$ = potential at $\mathbf{r}_1$ due to the external field

and $V(\mathbf{r}_2)$ = potential at $\mathbf{r}_2$ due to the external field.

Potential Energy for a Collection of More than Two Charges

The potential energy of a system of n charges is given by

$$U = \frac{K}{2} \sum_{\substack{i,j \\ i \neq j}}^{n} \frac{q_i q_j}{r_{ij}} \qquad \left(\text{here, } K = \frac{1}{4\pi\varepsilon_0}\right)$$

The factor of 1/2 is applied only with the summation sign because on expanding the summation, each pair is counted twice. It is reqresented by U.

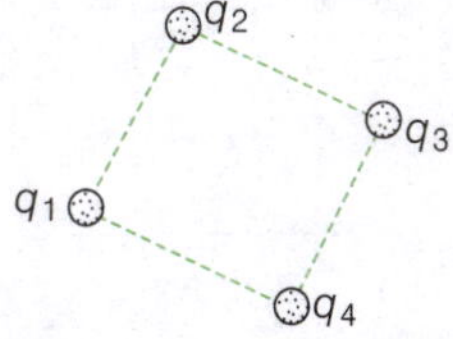

For example electric potential energy of four point charges q_1, q_2, q_3 and q_4 would be given by

$$U = \frac{1}{4\pi\varepsilon_0}\left[\frac{q_4 q_3}{r_{43}} + \frac{q_4 q_2}{r_{42}} + \frac{q_4 q_1}{r_{41}} + \frac{q_3 q_2}{r_{32}} + \frac{q_3 q_1}{r_{31}} + \frac{q_2 q_1}{r_{21}}\right]$$

Electric Dipole

An electric dipole consists of two equal and opposite point charges separated by a very small distance. e.g. a molecule of HCl, a molecule of water etc.

2a

$-q$ $+q$

Electric Dipole Moment, $p = q \times 2a$

Its SI unit is 'coulomb-metre' and its dimensions are [LTA].

It is a vector quantity and its direction is from negative charge towards positive charge.

Electric Field Intensity and Potential due to an Electric Dipole

(i) **On Axial Line**

Electric field intensity, $E = \frac{1}{4\pi\varepsilon_0} \frac{2pr}{(r^2 - a^2)^2}$

If $r >> 2a$, then $E = \frac{1}{4\pi\varepsilon_0} \frac{2p}{r^3}$

Electric potential, $V = \frac{1}{4\pi\varepsilon_0} \frac{p}{(r^2 - a^2)}$

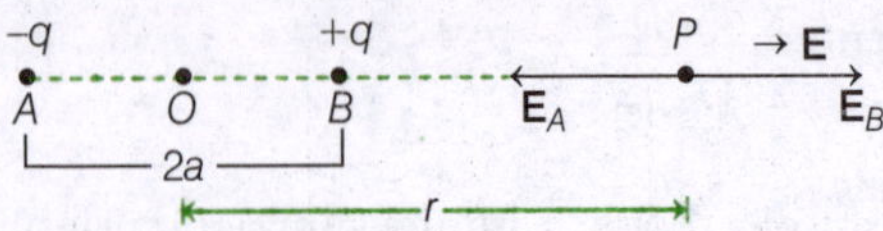

If $r >> 2a$, then $V = \frac{1}{4\pi\varepsilon_0} \frac{p}{r^2}$

(ii) **On Equatorial Line**

Electric field intensity

$$E = \frac{1}{4\pi\varepsilon_0} \frac{p}{(r^2 + a^2)^{3/2}}$$

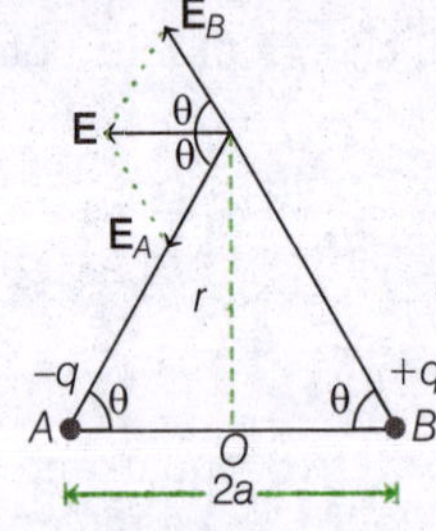

If $r >> 2a$, then

$$E = \frac{1}{4\pi\varepsilon_0} \frac{p}{r^3}$$

Electric potential, $V = 0$

(iii) **At any Point along a Line Making θ Angle with Dipole Axis**

Electric field intensity $E = \frac{1}{4\pi\varepsilon_0}\frac{p\sqrt{(1+3\cos^2\theta)}}{r^3}$

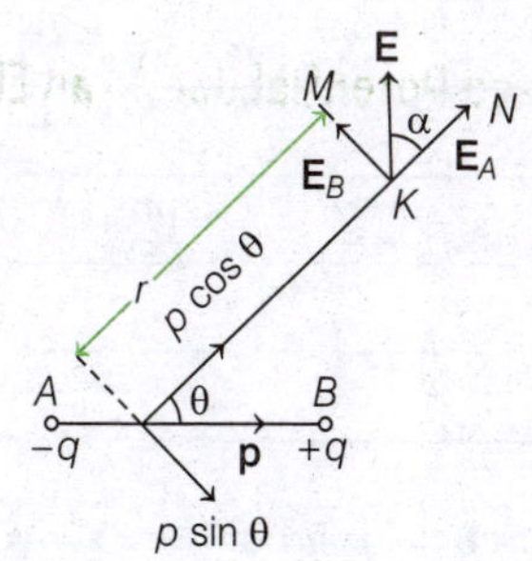

Electric potential $V = \frac{1}{4\pi\varepsilon_0}\frac{p\cos\theta}{(r^2 - a^2\cos^2\theta)}$

If $r >> 2a$, then $V = \frac{1}{4\pi\varepsilon_0}\frac{p\cos\theta}{r^2}$

Potential Energy of a Dipole in a Uniform Electric Field

The work done in rotating the dipole through small angle $d\theta$, then $dW = \tau d\theta$.

$$dW = pE\sin\theta d\theta$$

Suppose initially dipole is kept in a uniform electric field at angle θ_1. Now, to turn it through an angle θ_2 (with the field). Then, work done

$$W = \int_{\theta_1}^{\theta_2} pE\sin\theta d\theta$$

$$W = -pE[\cos\theta_2 - \cos\theta_1]$$

If $\theta_1 = 0°$ and $\theta_2 = \theta$, *i.e.*, Initially dipole is kept along the field then it turns through θ so work done,

$$W = pE(1 - \cos\theta)$$

Potential energy of dipole is defined as work done in rotating a dipole from a direction perpendicular to the field to the given direction.

If the dipole is rotated by an angle $\theta_1 = 90°$ to $\theta_2 = \theta$, then potential energy is given by

$$W = U = pE(\cos 90° - \cos\theta)$$

$$= -pE\cos\theta$$

$$= -\mathbf{p}\cdot\mathbf{E}$$

Torque on Dipole in a Uniform External Field

Torque acting on an electric dipole placed in uniform electric field is given by

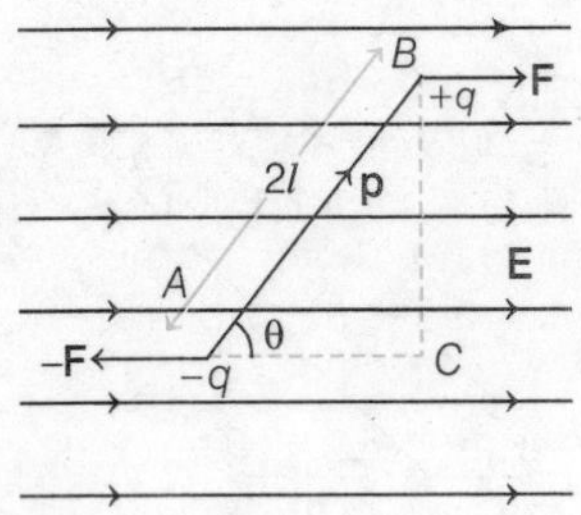

$$\tau = (q \times 2l)E \sin \theta = Ep \sin \theta \quad \text{or} \quad \tau = \mathbf{p} \times \mathbf{E}$$

When $\theta = 90°$, then $\tau_{max} = Ep$

When electric dipole is parallel to electric field, it is in stable equilibrium and when it is anti-parallel to electric field, it is in unstable equilibrium.

Dipole in Non-uniform Electric Field

When an electric dipole is placed in a non-uniform electric field, then a resultant force as well as a torque act on it.

Net force on electric dipole $= (qE_1 - qE_2)$, along the direction of greater electric field intensity.

Therefore, electric dipole undergoes rotational as well as linear motion.

Behaviour of a Conductor in an Electrostatic Field

(i) Electric field at any point inside the conductor is zero.

(ii) Electric field at any point on the surface of charged conductor is directly proportional to the surface density of charge at that point, but electric potential does not depend upon the surface density of charge.

(iii) Electric potential at any point inside the conductor is constant and equal to potential on its surface.

Electrostatic Shielding

The process of protecting certain region from external electric field is called electrostatic shielding.

Electrostatic shielding is achieved by enclosing that region in a closed hollow metallic chamber.

Value Points

When a charged cloud passes by a tall building, the charge on the cloud passes to the earth through the building. This causes huge damage to the building. Thus to protect the tall building from lightning, the **lightning conductors**, (which are pointed metal rods) are installed at the top of these buildings. They help in passing over the charge on the clouds to earth, thus protecting the building.

Dielectric

Dielectrics are insulating (non-conducting) materials that can produce electric effect without conduction.

Dielectrics are of two types

Non-polar Dielectric

The non-polar dielectrics (like N_2, O_2, benzene, methane etc.) are made up of non-polar atoms/molecules, in which the centre of positive charge coincides with the centre of negative charge of the atom/molecule.

Polar Dielectric

The polar dielectric (like H_2O, CO_2, NH_3 etc) are made up of polar atoms/molecules, in which the centre of positive charge does not coincide with the centre of negative charge of the atom.

Dielectric Constant (K)

The ratio of the strength of the applied electric field to the strength of the reduced value of electric field on placing the dielectric between the plates of a capacitor is the dielectric constant. It is denoted by K (or ε_r). $K = \frac{E_0}{E}$

Polarisation (P) and Electric Susceptibility (χ_e)

The induced dipole moment developed per unit volume in a dielectric slab on placing it in an electric field is called polarisation. It is denoted by P.

$$P = \chi_e E$$

where, χ_e is known as electric susceptibility of the dielectric medium.

It is a dimensionless constant.It describes the electrical behaviour of a dielectric. It has different values for different dielectrics.

For vacuum, $\chi = 0$. Relation between dielectric constant and electric susceptibility can be given as

$$\boxed{K = 1 + \chi_e}$$

Capacitor

A capacitor is a device which is used to store huge charge over it, without changing its dimensions.

It is a pair of two conductors of any shape, close to each other and have equal and opposite charges.

Capacitance of a conductor, $C = \frac{q}{V}$

Its SI unit is coulomb/volt or farad.

Its other units are $1\,\mu F = 10^{-6}$ F

$$1\,\mu\mu F = 1\,pF = 10^{-12}\,F$$

Its dimensional formula is $[M^{-1}L^{-2}T^4A^2]$.

When an earthed conductor is placed near a charged conductor, then it decreases its potential and therefore more charge can be stored over it.

Capacitance of an Isolated Spherical Conductor

$$C = 4\pi\varepsilon_0 K R$$

For air $K = 1$

$$\therefore \quad C = 4\pi\varepsilon_0 R = \frac{R}{9 \times 10^9}$$

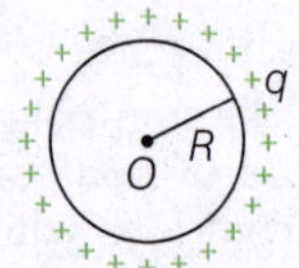

Capacity of a Spherical Conductor Enclosed by an Earthed Concentric Spherical Shell

It consists of two concentric conducting spheres of radii a and b $(a < b)$. Inner sphere is given charge q while outer sphere is earthed. Potential difference between the spheres is given by

$$V = \frac{q}{4\pi\varepsilon_0}\left(\frac{1}{a} - \frac{1}{b}\right) \quad \ldots(i)$$

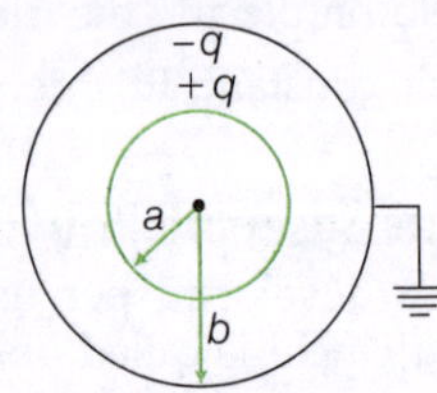

Hence, the capacitance of this system will be

$$C = \frac{q}{V}$$

or $$C = 4\pi\varepsilon_0\left(\frac{ab}{b-a}\right) \quad \text{[From Eq. (i)]}$$

Parallel Plate Capacitor

The parallel plate capacitor consists of two metal plates parallel to each other and separated by a distance *d*.

Capacitance $C = \dfrac{KA\varepsilon_0}{d}$

For air $C_0 = \dfrac{A\varepsilon_0}{d}$

When a dielectric slab is inserted between the plates partially, then its capacitance

$$C = \frac{A\varepsilon_0}{\left(d - t + \dfrac{t}{K}\right)}$$

If a conducting (metal) slab is inserted between the plates, then

$$C = \frac{A\varepsilon_0}{(d - t)}$$

When more than one dielectric slabs are placed fully between the plates, then

$$C = \frac{A\varepsilon_0}{\left(\dfrac{t_1}{K_1} + \dfrac{t_2}{K_2} + \dfrac{t_3}{K_3} + \ldots + \dfrac{t_n}{K_n}\right)}$$

The plates of a parallel plate capacitor attract each other with a force,

$$F = \frac{Q^2}{2A\varepsilon_0}$$

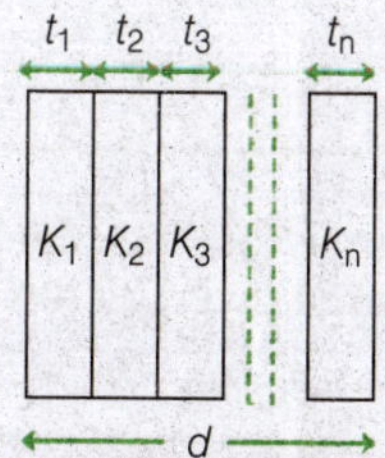

When a dielectric slab is placed between the plates of a capacitor than charge induced on its side due to polarization of dielectric is

$$q' = q\left(1 - \frac{1}{K}\right)$$

Capacitors Combinations

(i) **In Series**

Resultant capacitance, $\frac{1}{C} = \frac{1}{C_1} + \frac{1}{C_2} + \frac{1}{C_3} + \dots$

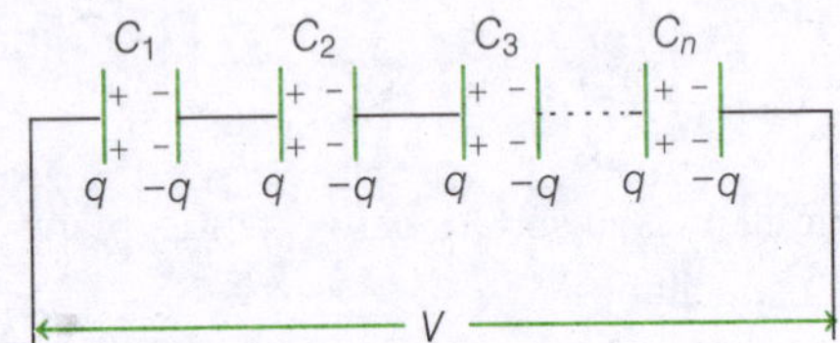

In series, charge is same on each capacitor, which is equal to the charge supplied by the source.

If $V_1, V_2, V_3, \dots$ are potential differences across the plates of the capacitors then total voltage applied by the source

$$V = V_1 + V_2 + V_3 + \dots$$

(ii) **In Parallel**

Resultant capacitance

$$C = C_1 + C_2 + C_3 + \dots$$

In parallel, potential differences across the plates of each capacitor is same.

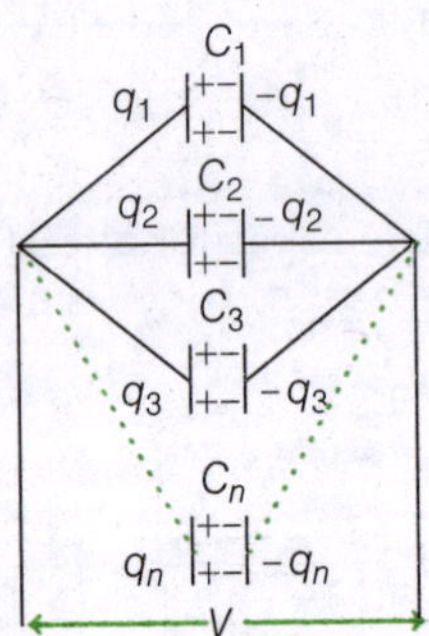

If $q_1, q_2, q_3, \dots$ are charges on the plate of capacitors connected in parallel, then total charge given by the source

$$q = q_1 + q_2 + q_3 + \dots$$

Potential Energy Stored in a Capacitor

Electric potential energy of a charged conductor or a capacitor is given by

$$U = \frac{1}{2} Vq = \frac{1}{2} CV^2 = \frac{1}{2} \frac{q^2}{C}$$

Energy density between the plates

The energy stored per unit volume of space in a capacitor is called energy density. Charge on either plate of capacitor is

$$Q = \sigma A = \varepsilon_0 EA$$

Energy stored in the capaitor is

$$U = \frac{Q^2}{2C} = \frac{(\varepsilon_0 EA)^2}{2 \cdot \varepsilon_0 A/d} = \frac{1}{2}\varepsilon_0 E^2 \cdot Ad$$

Energy density , $u = \dfrac{\text{Energy stored}}{\text{Volume of capacitor}} = \dfrac{U}{Ad}$

$\therefore \quad u = \dfrac{1}{2}\varepsilon_0 E^2$

Redistribution of Charge

When two isolated charged conductors are connected to each other then charge is redistributed in the ratio of their capacitances.

$$\text{Common potential } V = \frac{q_1 + q_2}{C_1 + C_2} = \frac{C_1 V_1 + C_2 V_2}{C_1 + C_2}$$

$$\text{Energy loss } = \frac{1}{2}\frac{C_1 C_2 (V_1 - V_2)^2}{(C_1 + C_2)}$$

This energy is lost in the form of heat in connecting wires.

When n small drops, each of capacitance C, charged to potential V with charge q, surface charge density σ and potential energy U coalesce to form a single drop.

Then for new drop,

Total charge $= nq$

Total capacitance $= n^{1/3}C$

Total potential $= n^{2/3}\ V$

Surface charge density $= n^{1/3}\ \sigma$

Total potential energy $= n^{5/3}\ U$

Competition Insight

Van-de-Graaff Generator

- It is a device used to build up very high potential difference of the order of few million volt.

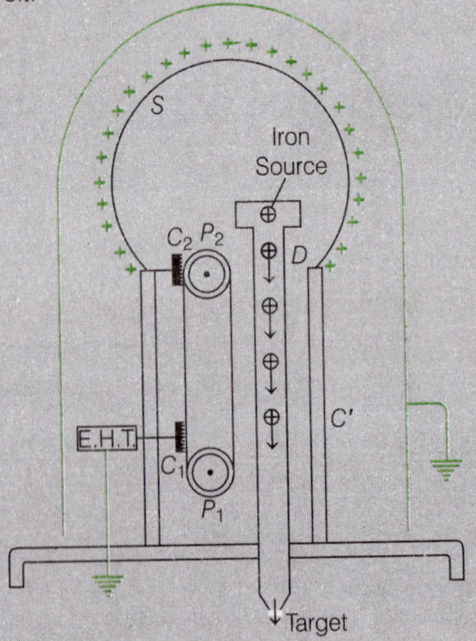

- Its working is based on two points
  (i) The action of sharp points (corona discharge)
  (ii) Total charge given to a spherical shell resides on its outer surface.

Chapter 20

Current Electricity

Electric Current (I)

The rate of flow of charge through any cross-section of a wire w.r.t. time is called electric current flowing through it.

Electric current $(I) = \frac{q}{t}$. Its SI unit is ampere (A).

The conventional direction of electric current is the direction of motion of positive charge.

The current is the same for all cross-sections of a conductor of non-uniform cross-section. Similar to the water flow, charge flows faster where the conductor is smaller in cross-section and slower where the conductor is larger in cross-section, so that charge rate remains unchanged.

If a charge q revolves in a circle with frequency f, the equivalent current,

$$i = qf$$

In a metallic conductor current flows due to motion of free electrons while in electrolytes and ionised gases current flows due to electrons and positive ions.

According to its magnitude and direction electric current is of two types

(i) **Direct Current (DC)** Its magnitude and direction do not change with time. A cell, battery or DC dynamo are the sources of direct current.

(ii) **Alternating Current (AC)** An electric current whose magnitude changes continuously and direction changes periodically is called an alternating current. AC dynamo is the source of an alternating current.

Thermal Velocity of Free Electrons

Free electrons in a metal move randomly with a very high speed of the order of 10^5 ms^{-1}. This speed is called thermal velocity of free electrons. Average thermal velocity of free electrons in any direction remains zero.

Relaxation Time (τ)

The time interval between two successive collisions of electrons with the positive ions in the metallic lattice is defined as relaxation time.

$$\tau = \frac{\text{mean free path}}{\text{rms velocity of electrons}} = \frac{\lambda}{v_{rms}}$$

Drift Velocity of Free Electrons

When a potential difference is applied across the ends of a conductor, the free electrons in it move with an average velocity opposite to the direction of electric field, which is called drift velocity of free electrons.

Drift velocity $v_d = -\frac{eE\tau}{m} = -\frac{eV\tau}{ml}$

where, τ = relaxation time,
e = charge on electron,
E = electric field intensity,
l = length of the conductor,
V = potential difference across the ends of the conductor
and m = mass of the electron.

Relation between electric current and drift velocity is given by

$$v_d = \frac{I}{Ane}$$

Current Density

The electric current flowing per unit area of cross-section of a conductor is called current density.

Current density $(J) = \frac{I}{A} = nev_d$

Its SI unit is ampere metre^{-2} (Am^{-2}) and dimensional formula is [AL^{-2}]. It is a vector quantity and its direction is in the direction of motion of positive charge or in the direction of flow of current.

Mobility

The drift velocity of electron per unit electric field applied is called mobility of electron.

Mobility of electron $(\mu) = \frac{v_d}{E} = \frac{e\tau}{m}$

Its SI unit is $m^2s^{-1}V^{-1}$ and its dimensional formula is $[M^{-1}T^2A]$.

Ohm's Law

If physical conditions of a conductor such as temperature remains unchanged, then the electric current (I) flowing through the conductor is directly proportional to the potential difference (V) applied across its ends.

$$I \propto V \text{ or } V = IR$$

where, R is the electrical resistance of the conductor and $R = \frac{ml}{Ane^2\tau}$.

Ohmic Conductors

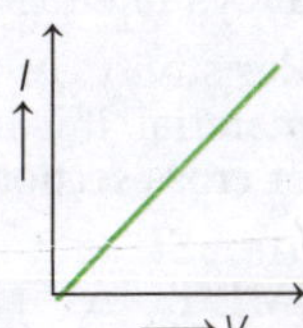

Those conductors which obey Ohm's law, are called ohmic conductors, *e.g.* all metallic conductors are ohmic conductor.

For ohmic conductors *V-I* graph is a straight line.

Non-ohmic Conductors

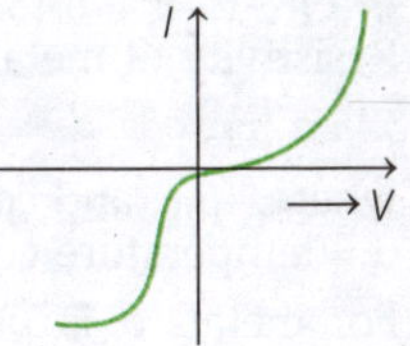

Those conductors which do not obey Ohm's law, are called non-ohmic conductors, *e.g.* diode valve, triode valve, transistor, vacuum tubes etc.

For non-ohmic conductors *V-I* graph is not a straight line.

Electrical Resistance

The obstruction offered by any conductor in the path of flow of current is called its electrical resistance.

Electrical resistance, $R = \frac{V}{I}$

Its SI unit is ohm (Ω) and its dimensional formula is $[ML^2 T^{-3} A^{-2}]$.

Electrical resistance of a conductor, $R = \frac{\rho l}{A}$

where, l = length of the conductor,
A = cross-sectional area
and ρ = resistivity of the material of the conductor.

If a resistance wire is stretched to a greater length, keeping volume constant, then

$$R \propto l^2 \Rightarrow \frac{R_1}{R_2} = \left(\frac{l_1}{l_2}\right)^2$$

and

$$R \propto \frac{1}{r^4} \Rightarrow \frac{R_1}{R_2} = \left(\frac{r_2}{r_1}\right)^4$$

where, l is the length of wire and r is the radius of cross-section area of wire.

Resistivity

Resistivity of a material of a conductor is given by

$$\rho = \frac{m}{ne^2\tau}$$

where, n = number of free electrons per unit volume.

Resistivity is low for metals, more for semiconductors and very high for alloys like nichrome, constantan etc.

Resistivity of a material depend on temperature and nature of the material. It is independent of dimensions of the conductor, *i.e.* length, area of cross-section etc.

The SI unit of resistivity is Ω m and its dimensional formula is $[ML^3T^{-3}A^{-2}]$.

Temperature Dependence of Resistivity

Resistivity of metals increases with increase in temperature as

$$\rho_t = \rho_0 (1 + \alpha t)$$

where, ρ_0 and ρ_t are resistivity of metals at 0°C and t°C and α = temperature coefficient of resistivity of the material.

For metals α is positive, for some alloys like nichrome, manganin and constantan, α is positive but very low.

For semiconductors and insulators, α is negative.

Therefore, resistivity of metal increases with increase in temperature. However, for semiconductors, it decreases with increase in temperature. But in the case of alloy, dependence on temperature is weak.

Value Points

In magnetic field, the resistivity of metals increases. But resistivity of ferromagnetic materials such as iron, nickel, cobalt etc decreases in magnetic field.

Electrical Conductivity

The reciprocal of resistivity is called electrical conductivity.

Electrical conductivity $(\sigma) = \frac{1}{\rho} = \frac{l}{RA} = \frac{ne^2\tau}{m}$

Its SI units is $ohm^{-1}m^{-1}$ or mho m^{-1} or siemen m^{-1}.

Relation between current density (J) and electrical conductivity (σ) is given by $J = \sigma E$

where, E = electric field intensity.

Superconductors

When few metals are cooled, then below a certain critical temperature their electrical resistance suddenly becomes zero. In this state, these substances are called **superconductors** and this phenomena is called **superconductivity.**

Mercury become superconductor at 4.2 K, lead at 7.25 K and niobium at 9.2 K.

Colour Coding of Carbon Resistors

The resistance of a carbon resistor can be calculated by the code given on it in the form of coloured strips.

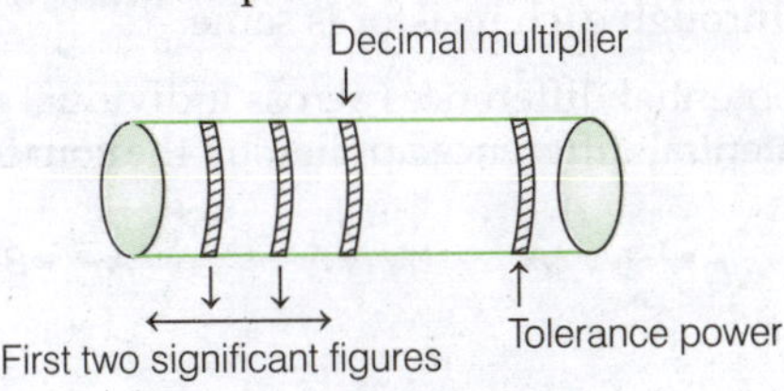

Colour coding

Colour	Figure	Multiplier
Black	0	1
Brown	1	10^1
Red	2	10^2
Orange	3	10^3
Yellow	4	10^4
Green	5	10^5
Blue	6	10^6
Violet	7	10^7
Grey	8	10^8
White	9	10^9

EXPERT Scale Up

To remember the colour code sequence for carbon resistor, the following sentence should be kept in memory.

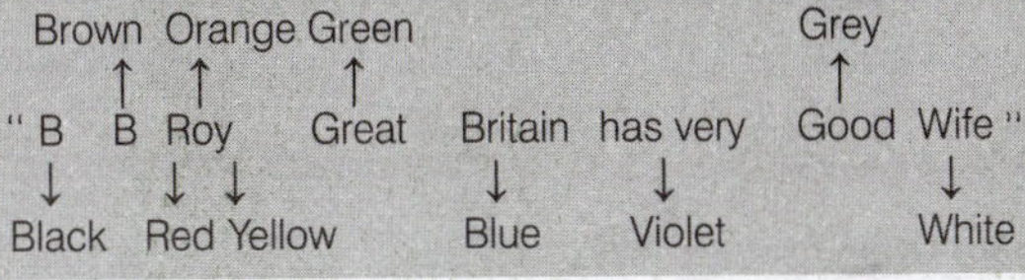

Tolerance power

Colour	Tolerance
Gold	5%
Silver	10%
No colour	20%

Combination of Resistors

1. In Series

(i) Equivalent resistance, $R = R_1 + R_2 + R_3$

(ii) Current through each resistor is same.

(iii) Sum of potential differences across individual resistors is equal to the potential difference applied by the source.

2. In Parallel

(i) Equivalent resistance, $\frac{1}{R} = \frac{1}{R_1} + \frac{1}{R_2} + \frac{1}{R_3}$

(ii) Potential difference across each resistor is same.

(iii) Sum of electric currents flowing through individual resistors is equal to the electric current drawn from the source.

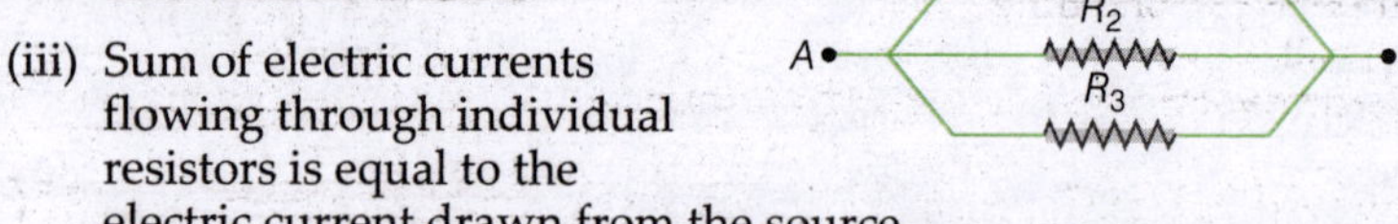

If n identical resistances are first connected in series and then in parallel, the ratio of the equivalent resistance

$$\frac{R_s}{R_p} = \frac{n^2}{1}$$

If a skeleton cube is made with 12 equal resistors, each having a resistance R, then the net resistance across

(a) the diagonal of cube $= \frac{5}{6} R$

(b) the diagonal of a face $= \frac{3}{4} R$

(c) along a side $= \frac{7}{12} R$

Electric Cell

An electric cell is a device which converts chemical energy into electrical energy.

Electric cells are of two types

(i) Primary Cells

Primary cells cannot be charged again. Voltaic, Daniel and Leclanche cells are primary cells.

(ii) Secondary Cells

Secondary cells can be charged again and again. Acid and alkali accumulators are secondary cells.

Electromotive Force (emf) of a Cell

The energy given by a cell in flowing unit positive charge throughout the circuit completely one time is equal to the emf of a cell.

Emf of a cell $(e) = \frac{W}{q}$. Its SI unit is volt.

Terminal Potential Difference of a Cell

The energy given by a cell in flowing unit positive charge through the outer circuit one time from one terminal of the cell to the other terminal of the cell.

Its SI unit is also volt. It is always less than the emf of a cell.

Internal Resistance of a Cell

The obstruction offered by the electrolyte of a cell in the path of electric current is called internal resistance (r) of the cell. Internal resistance of a cell

(i) increases with increase in concentration of the electrolyte.

(ii) increases with increase in distance between the electrodes.

(iii) decreases with increase in area of electrodes dipped in electrolyte.

Relation between e, V and r

$$e = V + Ir, \quad r = \left(\frac{e}{V} - 1\right) R$$

If cell is in charging state, then $e = V - Ir$

Maximum Power Theorem

It states that the output power of a source of emf is maximum, when external resistance in the circuit is equal to the internal resistance of the source.

Grouping of Cells

(i) **In Series** If n cells, each of emf e and internal resistance r are connected in series to a resistance R, then equivalent emf

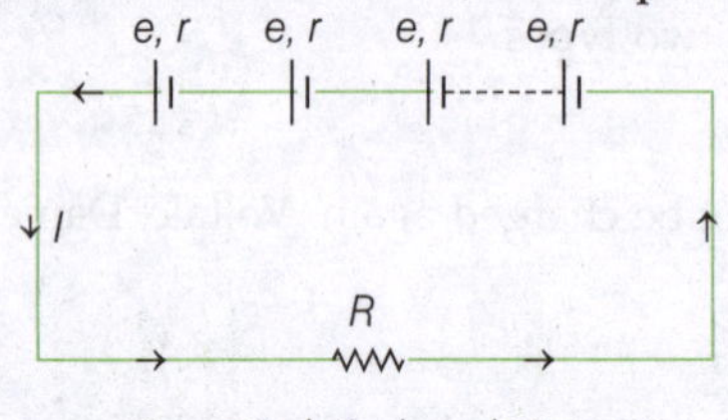

$$e_{eq} = e_1 + e_2 + \ldots + e_n = ne$$

Equivalent internal resistance, $r_{eq} = r_1 + r_2 + \ldots + r_n = nr$

Current in the circuit $I = \dfrac{e_{eq}}{(R + r_{eq})} = \dfrac{ne}{(R + nr)}$

(ii) **In Parallel** If n cells, each of emf e and internal resistance r are connected in parallel to a resistance R, then equivalent emf, $e_{eq} = e$

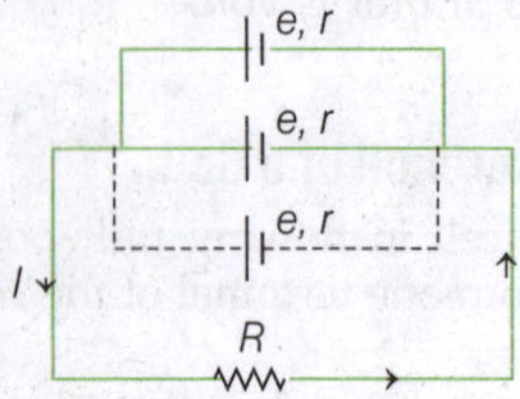

Equivalent internal resistance,

$$\frac{1}{r_{eq}} = \frac{1}{r_1} + \frac{1}{r_1} + \ldots + \frac{1}{r_n} = \frac{n}{r} \quad \text{or} \quad r_{eq} = \frac{r}{n}$$

Current in the circuit, $I = \dfrac{e}{(R + r/n)}$

(iii) **Mixed Grouping of Cells** If n cells, each of emf e and internal resistance r are connected in series and such m rows are connected in parallel, then

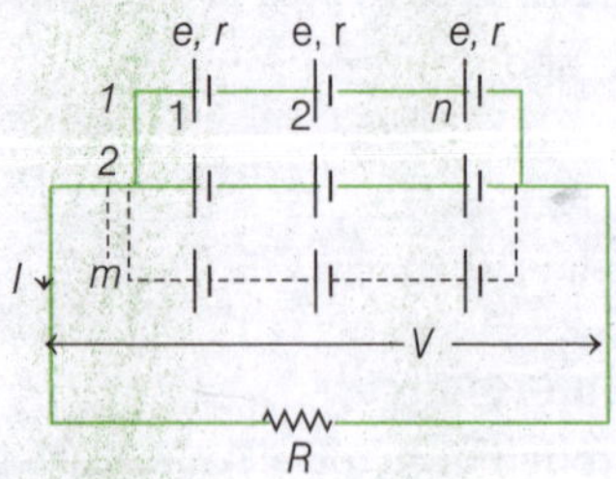

Equivalent emf, $e_{eq} = ne$

Equivalent internal resistance, $r_{eq} = \dfrac{nr}{m}$

Current in the circuit, $I = \dfrac{ne}{\left(R + \dfrac{nr}{m}\right)}$ or $I = \dfrac{mne}{mR + nr}$

If two non-identical cells are connected in parallel, then

$$E_{net} = \frac{E_1 r_2 + E_2 r_1}{r_1 + r_2}$$

Current in the circuit will be maximum when external resistance is equal to the equivalent internal resistance, i.e., $R = \dfrac{nr}{m} \Rightarrow mR = nr$

Kirchhoff's Laws

There are two Kirchhoff's laws for solving complicated electrical circuits

(i) **Junction Rule** The algebraic sum of all currents meeting at a junction in a closed circuit is zero, *i.e.* $\Sigma I = 0$.

This law follows law of conservation of charge.

(ii) **Loop Rule** The algebraic sum of all the potential differences in any closed circuit is zero, *i.e.* $\Sigma \Delta V = 0$

This law follows law of conservation of energy.

Wheatstone Bridge

Wheatstone bridge is also known as a **meter bridge** or **slide wire bridge.**

This is an arrangement of four resistances in which one resistance is unknown but rest are known. The Wheatstone bridge is as shown in figure

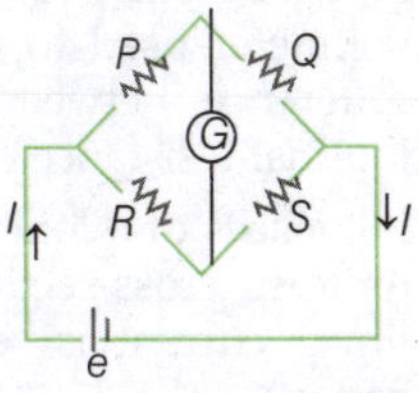

Principle of Wheatstone Bridge

The bridge is said to be balanced when deflection in galvanometer is zero, *i.e.* $I_G = 0$.

Thus, we have the balance condition as $\dfrac{P}{Q} = \dfrac{R}{S}$

The value of unknown resistance S can found, as we know the value of P, Q and R. It may be remembered that the bridge is most sensitive, when all the four resistances are of the same order.

Competition Insight

Meter Bridge

- This is the simplest form of Wheatstone bridge. It is specially useful for comparing resistances more accurately and for measuring an unknown resistance.

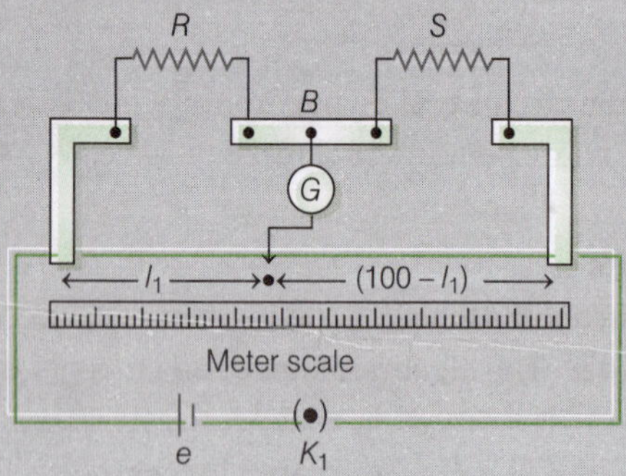

- At balancing situation of bridge, $\frac{R}{S} = \frac{l_1}{(100 - l_1)}$
- where, l_1 is the length of wire from one end where null point is obtained.

Potentiometer

Potentiometer is an ideal device voltmeter used to measure the potential difference between two points or the internal resistance of an unknown source.

It consists of a long resistance wire AB of uniform cross-section in which a steady direct current is set up by means of a battery.

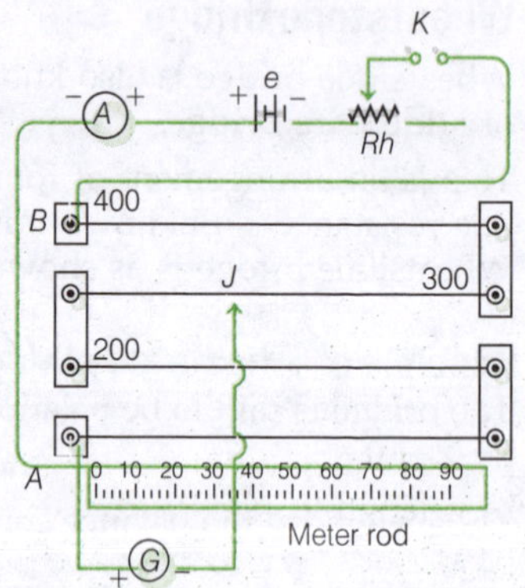

The principle of potentiometer states that, when a constant amount of current flows through a wire of uniform cross-section, then the potential drop across the wire is directly proportional to its length,

i.e. $V \propto l \Rightarrow V = kl$

where, k is known as potential gradient.

SI unit of k is Vm^{-1}.

Sensitivity of potentiometer is increased by increasing length of potentiometer wire.

To Compare the emf's of two Cells using Potentiometer

The arrangement of two cells of emfs e_1 and e_2 which are to be compared is shown in the figure below.

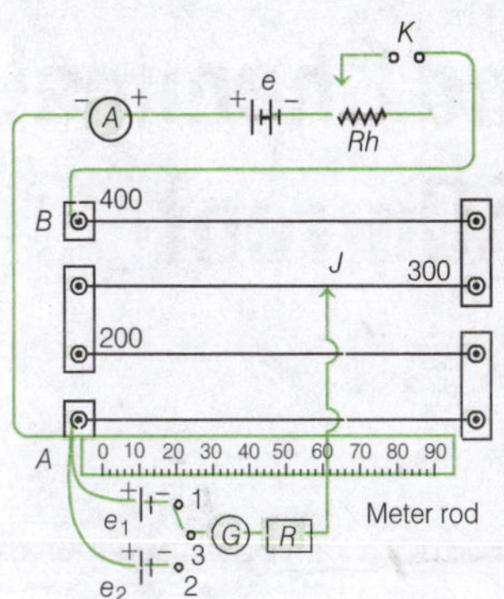

If the plug is put in the gap between 1 and 3, we get

$$e_1 = (x\,l_1)\,I \qquad \ldots\text{(i)}$$

where, x = resistance per unit length

Similarly, when the plug is put in the gap between 2 and 3, we get

$$e_2 = (x\,l_2)\,I \qquad \ldots\text{(ii)}$$

From Eqs. (i) and (ii), we get

or $$\frac{e_1}{e_2} = \frac{l_1}{l_2}$$

Determination of Internal Resistance of a Cell using Potentiometer

The arrangement is shown in figure.

When K_2 is kept out, $e = xl_1 I$

But if by inserting key K_2 and introducing some resistance S (say), then potential difference V is balanced by a length l_2, where

$$V = kl_2$$

Internal resistance of cell,

$$r = \frac{e - V}{V}\,R$$

$$= \frac{l_1 - l_2}{l_2}\,R$$

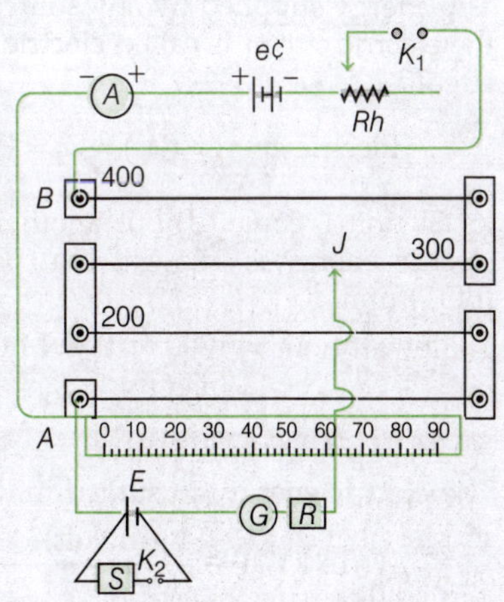

Chapter 21

Heating and Chemical Effects of Current

Electric Power

The electrical energy produced or consumed per unit time is called electric power.

$$\text{Electric power, } P = VI = I^2R = \frac{V^2}{R}$$

where, V is the potential difference across the conductor, I is current flowing through the conductor and R is the resistance.

Its SI unit is watt (W).

The other units of electric power are kilowatt and horse power.

$$1 \text{ kW} = 1000 \text{ W}$$

$$1 \text{ HP} = 746 \text{ W}$$

Electric Energy

The energy supplied by any source in maintaining the current in the electric circuit is called electric energy consumed by the electric circuit.

$$\text{Electric energy } (W) = Vq = VIt = I^2Rt = \frac{V^2}{R}t$$

Its SI unit is joule (J) but another unit is watt-hour. The bigger unit of electric energy is kilowatt hour (kWh). It is known as Board of Trade (BOT) unit.

$$\begin{aligned} 1 \text{ kilowatt hour} &= 1000 \text{ watt} \times 1 \text{ hour} \\ &= 1000 \text{ J/s} \times 3600 \text{ s} \\ &= 3.6 \times 10^6 \text{ J} \end{aligned}$$

The electric energy consumed in kWh is given by

$$W \text{ (in kWh)} = \frac{V \text{ (in volt)} \times I \text{ (in ampere)} \times t \text{ (in hour)}}{1000}$$

Heating Effects of Current (Joule's Law)

When current I flows through a conductor of resistance R for a time t, then heat generated in it is given by

$$H = I^2 Rt \text{ joule}$$

$$= \frac{I^2 Rt}{4.18} \text{ cal}$$

or

$$H = \frac{V^2}{R} t \text{ joule}$$

$$= \frac{V^2 t}{4.18\, R} \text{ cal}$$

where, V = potential difference applied across the ends of the conductor.

The electrical resistance of the wires supplying current is very small, therefore these wire do not heat up when current passes through them.

The electrical resistance of filament of a lamp is very high, therefore it shows more heating effect, when electric current passes through it.

A heater wire must be of high resistivity and of high melting point

Competition Insight

Electric Fuse

- An electric fuse is a safety device used for protecting electric circuits from damaging it due to excess flow of current. It is made up of tin-lead alloy (63% tin + 37% lead).
- It should have high resistance and low melting point and should be connected in series with the live wire.
- Maximum safe current which can be passed through a fuse wire is independent of its length. However, it depends on the radius r of wire as $I \propto r^{3/2}$

Short Circuiting

- When accidently the live wire comes in contact with neutral wire, then resistance of the circuit decreases and a high current flows through the circuit. This phenomena is called short circuiting.

Overloading

- When a high current flows through the wire which is beyond the rating of wire, then heating of wire takes place. This phenomena is called overloading.

Rating of Electrical Appliances

The values of power and voltage taken together for an electrical appliance is called rating of the appliance.

- When a 40 W and a 100 W bulbs are connected in series, then 40 W bulb will glow brighter than 100 W bulb.
- When a 40 W and a 100 W bulbs are connected in parallel, then 100 W bulb will glow brighter than 40 W bulb.
- In series, if any bulb gets fused, then others will not glow.
- In parallel, if any one bulb get fused, then others will continue to glow.
- All switches should be connected in series with a live wire.

Fusing of Bulb When it is Switched ON

Usually filament bulbs get fused when they are switched ON. This is because with rise in temperature the resistance of the bulb increases and becomes constant in steady state.

So, the power consumed by the bulb $\left(\frac{V^2}{R}\right)$ initially is more than that in steady state and hence the bulb glows more brightly in beginning and may get fused.

Chapter 22

Magnetic Effect of Current

Oersted's Experiment

HC Oersted by his experiment concluded that a current carrying conductor deflects magnetic compass needle placed near it. It means a magnetic field is produced due to current carrying conductor which deflects magnetic compass.

Magnetic Field

The space in the surrounding of a magnet or any current carrying conductor in which its magnetic influence can be experienced is called magnetic field.

SI unit of magnetic field is Wb/m^2 or T (tesla).

The strength of magnetic field is called one tesla, if a charge of one coulomb, when moving with a velocity of $1\ ms^{-1}$ along a direction perpendicular to the direction of the magnetic field experiences a force of one newton.

$$1 \text{ tesla (T)} = 1 \text{ weber metre}^{-2} \ (Wbm^{-2})$$
$$= 1 \text{ newton ampere}^{-1} \text{ metre}^{-1} \ (NA^{-1}\ m^{-1})$$

CGS units of magnetic field are called gauss or oersted.

$$1 \text{ gauss} = 10^{-4} \text{ tesla.}$$

Rules to Find Direction of Magnetic Field

Following are the few rules that can be used to find out the direction of magnetic field

Maxwell's Cork Screw Rule

If a right handed cork screw is imagined to be rotated in such a direction that tip of the screw points in the direction of the current, then direction of rotation of cork screw gives the direction of magnetic line of force.

The conventional sign for a magnetic field coming out of the plane and normal to it is denoted by ⊙.

The magnetic field perpendicular to the plane in the downward direction is denoted by ⊗.

Ampere's Swimming Rule

If a man is swimming along the wire in the direction of current with his face turned towards the magnetic needle, so that the current enters through his feet, then North pole of the magnetic needle will be deflected towards his left hand.

Biot Savart's Law

The magnetic field produced by a current carrying element of length dl, carrying current I at a point separated by a distance r is given by

$$d\mathbf{B} = \frac{\mu_0}{4\pi} \frac{I(d\mathbf{l} \times \mathbf{r})}{r^3} \quad \text{or} \quad d\mathbf{B} = \frac{\mu_0}{4\pi} \frac{Idl \sin \theta}{r^2}$$

where, θ is the angle between length of the current element and line joining the element to point (**p**) and μ_0 is absolute permeability of the free space.

The direction of magnetic field $d\mathbf{B}$ is that of $d\mathbf{l} \times \mathbf{r}$.

In a medium, $$\mathrm{d}\mathbf{B} = \frac{\mu}{4\pi} \cdot \frac{I(d\mathbf{l} \times \mathbf{r})}{|\mathbf{r}|^3} = \frac{\mu_0 \mu_r}{4\pi} \cdot \frac{I(d\mathbf{l} \times \mathbf{r})}{r^3}$$

Also, $$\mathrm{d}\mathbf{B} = \frac{\mu_0}{4\pi} \frac{(\mathbf{J} \times \mathbf{r})}{r^3} dv = \frac{\mu_0}{4\pi} \frac{q(\mathbf{v} \times \mathbf{r})}{r^3}$$

Magnetic Field Due to a Straight Current Carrying Conductor

Consider a straight conductor carrying current I in upward direction, then magnetic field at a point P at r distance from it, is given by

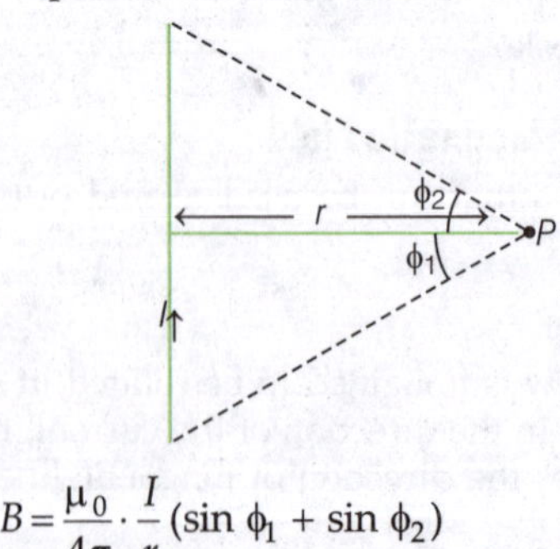

$$B = \frac{\mu_0}{4\pi} \cdot \frac{I}{r} (\sin \phi_1 + \sin \phi_2)$$

where ϕ_1 and ϕ_2 are angles, which the lines joining the two ends of the conductor to the observation point make with the perpendicular from the observation point to the conductor.

For infinite length conductor and observation point is near the centre of the conductor, $B = \frac{\mu_0}{4\pi} \cdot \frac{2I}{r}$

For infinite length conductor and observation point is near one end of the conductor, $B = \frac{\mu_0}{4\pi} \frac{I}{r}$

Value Points

- The magnetic field lines due to a straight current carrying conductor are concentric circles having centre at conductor and in a plane perpendicular to the conductor.

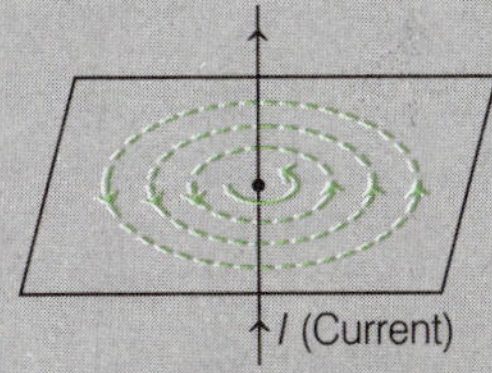

- The direction of magnetic field lines can be obtained by Right Hand Thumb Rule.

Right Hand Thumb Rule

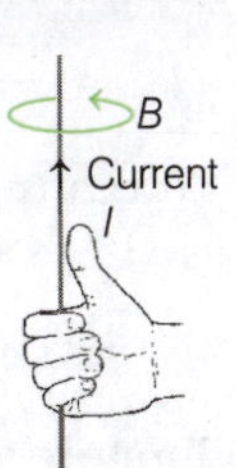

If we hold a current carrying conductor in the grip of the right hand in such a way that thumb points in the direction of current, then curling of fingers represents the direction of magnetic field lines.

Magnetic Field at the Centre of a Circular Current Carrying Coil

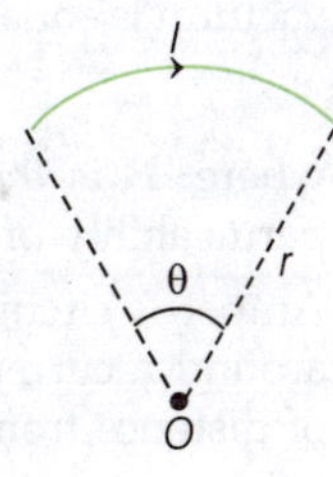

- The magnetic field at the centre due to the whole circular loop is

$$B = \frac{\mu_0 i}{2r}$$

- Magnetic field at the centre of a current carrying coil. Magnetic field due to an arc of circular current carrying coil at the centre is

$$B = \left(\frac{\mu_0}{4\pi}\right)\left(\frac{I}{r}\right)\theta$$

If we look at one face of the coil and the direction of current flowing through the coil is **clockwise**, then that face has South polarity and if direction of current is **anti-clockwise**, then that face has North polarity.

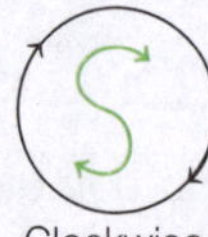

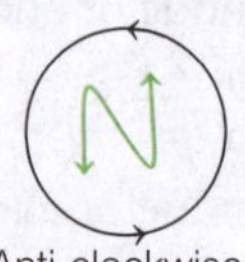

Clockwise Anti-clockwise

Magnetic Field on the Axis of a Current Carrying Circular Coil

Magnetic field at axis at a distance x from centre O.

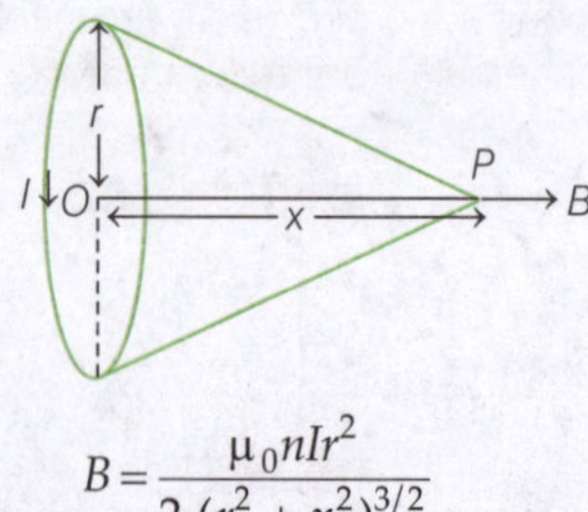

$$B = \frac{\mu_0 n I r^2}{2\,(r^2 + x^2)^{3/2}}$$

where, r = radius of the coil,

n = number of turns in the coil and

I = current.

At centre of the coil $(x = 0)$

$$B = \frac{\mu_0\, n I}{2\, r}$$

Ampere's Circuital Law

The line integral of magnetic field induction **B** around any closed path in vacuum is equal to μ_0 times the total current threading the closed path, *i.e.*

$$\oint \mathbf{B} \cdot d\mathbf{l} = \mu_0 I$$

where, **B** is the magnetic field, $d\mathbf{l}$ is small element, μ_0 is the absolute permeability of free space and I is the current.

Ampere's circuital law holds good for a closed path of any size and shape around a current carrying conductor because the relation is independent of distance from conductor.

Magnetic Field Due to a Current Carrying Long Circular Cylindrical Wire

- Outside the cylinder $(r > R)$

$$B = \frac{\mu_0}{2\pi} \frac{I}{r}$$

- Inside the cylinder when it is made of a thin metal sheet,

$$B = 0$$

- Inside the cylinder when current is uniformly distributed throughout the cross-section of the cylinder $(r < R)$

$$B = \frac{\mu_0 \mu_r}{2\pi} \frac{Ir}{R^2}$$

where, μ_0 and μ_r are permeabilities of free space and material of the cylinder, I is current flowing through the cylinder and r is radius of the cylinder.

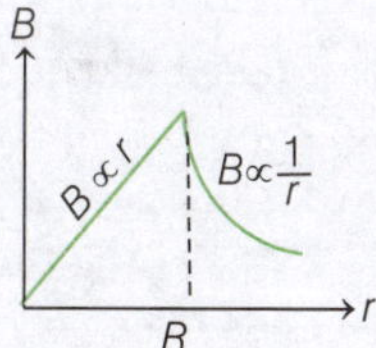

Variation in magnetic field with radius

Solenoid

A solenoid is a closely wound helix of insulated copper wire.

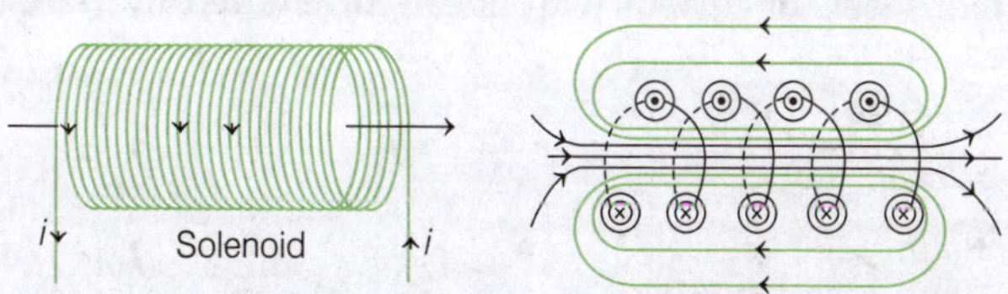

Magnetic field at a point well inside a long solenoid is given by

$$B = \mu_0 nI$$

or $$B = \mu \cdot \left(\frac{N}{l}\right) I$$

where, n = number of turns per unit length

N = number of turns

and I = current flowing through the solenoid.

Magnetic field at a point on one end of a long solenoid is given by

$$B = \frac{\mu_0 nI}{2}$$

Competition Insight

Toroid

- A toroidal solenoid is an anchor ring around which a large number of turns of a copper wire are wrapped.

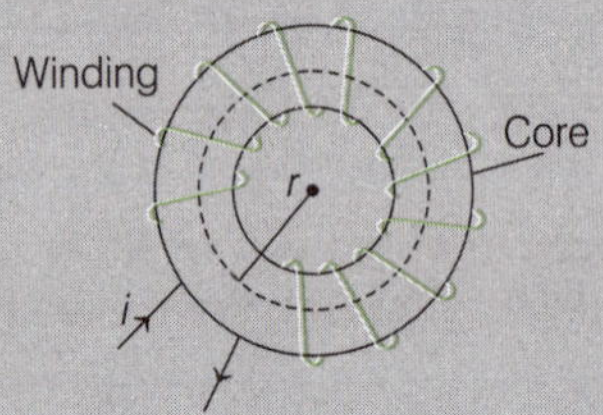

- A toroid is an endless solenoid in the form of a ring. Magnetic field inside the turns of toroid is given by $B = \mu_0 nI$
- Magnetic field inside a toroid is constant and is always tangential to the circular closed path.
- Magnetic field at any point inside the empty space surrounded by the toroid and outside the toroid is zero, because net current enclosed by these space is zero.

Magnetic Field due to an Infinitely Large Current Carrying Sheet

Both infinite sheets of current with linear current density J are shown in the figure

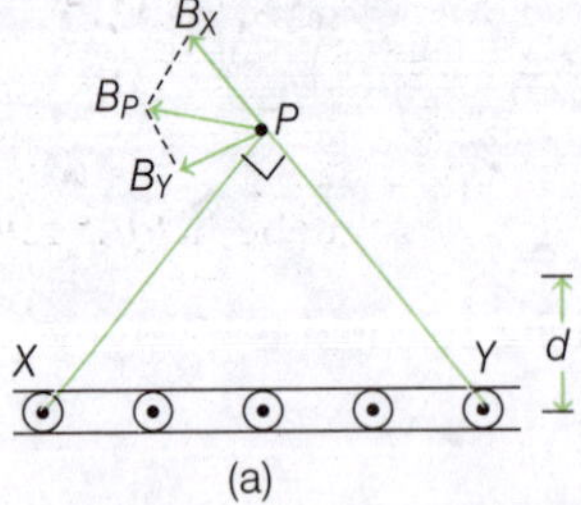

(a)

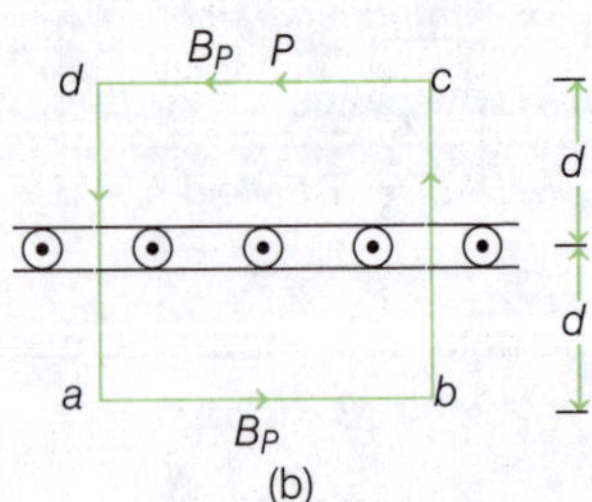

(b)

Magnetic field due to an infinitely large current carrying sheet is given by

$$B = \frac{\mu_0 J}{2}$$

Force Acting on a Charge Particle Moving in a Uniform Magnetic Field

$$\mathbf{F} = q(\mathbf{v} \times \mathbf{B})$$

or $$F = |\mathbf{F}| = Bqv \sin \theta$$

where, B = magnetic field intensity,
q = charge on particle,
v = speed of the particle
and θ = angle between magnetic field and direction of motion.

This force is perpendicular to **B** as well as **v**.

Its direction can be obtained from **Fleming's left hand rule.**

Fleming's Left Hand Rule

If we stretch the thumb, the forefinger and the central finger of left hand in such a way that all three are perpendicular to each other, then if forefinger represents the direction of magnetic field, central finger represents the direction of current flowing through the conductor, then thumb will represent the direction of magnetic force.

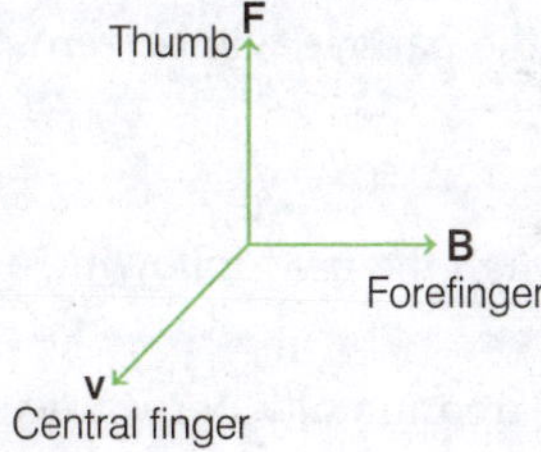

Motion of a Charged Particle in a Uniform Magnetic Field

When the charged particle enters parallel or anti-parallel to the magnetic field, then its follows a straight line path.

When charged particle enters normally to the magnetic field it follows a circular path.

The radius of the path, $r = \dfrac{mv}{Bq}$

$$\therefore \quad r \propto mv \text{ and } r \propto \frac{1}{(q/m)}$$

Time period, $T = \dfrac{2\pi m}{Bq}$

When charged particle enters magnetic field at any angle except $0°, 180°$ or $90°$, then it follows helical path.

The radius of the path, $r = \dfrac{mv \sin\theta}{Bq}$

$$\text{Time period, } T = \frac{2\pi m}{Bq}$$

The distance travelled by the charged particle in one time period due to component of velocity $v \cos\theta$ is called pitch of the path.

$$\text{Pitch} = T \times v \cos\theta = \frac{2\pi m v \cos\theta}{Bq}$$

Motion of Charged Particle in Combined Electric and Magnetic Field : Lorentz Force

The total force experienced by a charge moving inside the electric and magnetic fields is called Lorentz force. It is given by

$$\mathbf{F} = q(\mathbf{E} + \mathbf{v} \times \mathbf{B})$$

Case I When **vE** and **B** are all collinear

In this magnetic force on the particle will be zero. So,

$$\mathbf{a} = \frac{q\mathbf{E}}{m}$$

The particle will pass through the field following a straight line path with change in it's speed.

Case II When **v**, **E** and **B** are mutually perpendicular

In this, $\mathbf{F} = \mathbf{F}_e + \mathbf{F}_m = 0$

or $\mathbf{a} = 0$

The particle will pass through the field with same velocity without any deviation in it's path.

Thus, $F_e = F_m$

or $v = \dfrac{E}{B}$

This principle is used in '**velocity selector**' to get a charged beam having a specific velocity.

Competition Insight

Cyclotron

Cyclotron is a device used to accelerate positively charged particles such as proton, deuteron etc.

Principle of Cyclotron

- A positively charged particle can be accelerated through a moderate electric field by crossing it again and again by use of strong magnetic field.

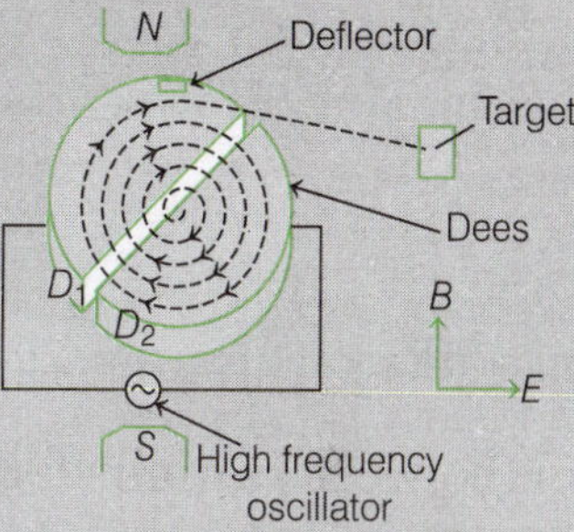

- Radius of circular path, $r = \frac{mv}{Bq}$
- Cyclotron frequency, $\nu = \frac{Bq}{2\pi m}$

  where, m and q are mass and charge of the positive ion and B is strength of the magnetic field.

- Maximum kinetic energy gained by the particle, $E_{max} = \frac{B^2 q^2 r_0^2}{2m}$

  where, r_0 = maximum radius of circular path.

- When a positive ion is accelerated by the cyclotron, it moves with greater and greater speed.

Limitations of the Cyclotron

(i) Cyclotron cannot accelerated uncharged particle like neutron.

(ii) The positively charged particles having large mass, *i.e.* ions cannot move at limitless speed in a cyclotron.

(iii) As the speed of ion becomes comparable with that of light, the mass of the ion increases according to the relation.

$$m = \frac{m_0}{\sqrt{1 - \frac{v^2}{c^2}}}$$

where, m = mass of the ion,

m_0 = rest mass of the ion,

v = speed of ion and c = speed of light.

At high velocities, the cyclotron frequency will decrease due to increase in mass. This will throw the particles out of resonance with the oscillating field. That is, as the ions reach the gap between the dees, the polarity of the dees is not reversed at that instant. Consequently the ions are not accelerated further.

Force on a Current Carrying Conductor in a Magnetic Field

Magnetic force acting on a current carrying conductor in a uniform magnetic field is given by, $\mathbf{F} = I(\mathbf{l} \times \mathbf{B})$

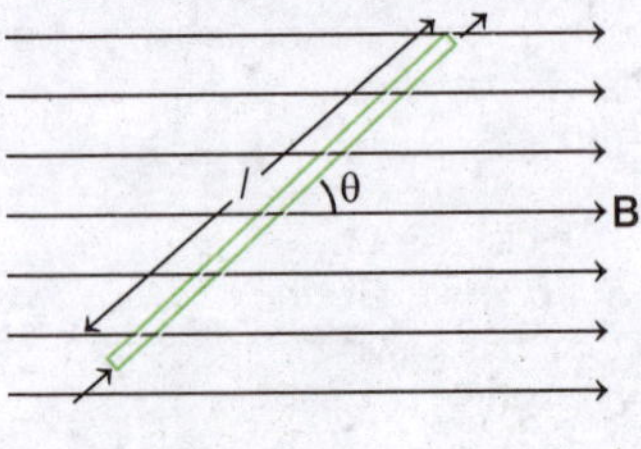

or $$F = BIl \sin \theta$$

Direction of force on a current carrying conductor can be found out by Fleming's left hand rule.

Force between Two Infinitely Long Parallel Current Carrying Conductors

Force between two long parallel current carrying conductors is given by

$$F = \frac{\mu_0}{2\pi} \cdot \frac{I_1 I_2}{r} l$$

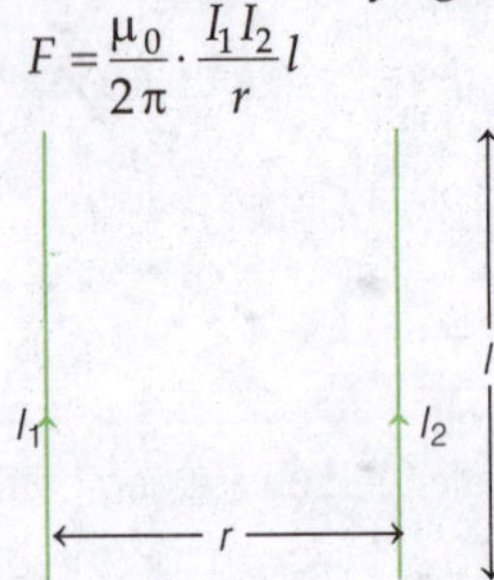

The force is attractive if current in both conductors is in same direction and repulsive if current in both conductors is in opposite direction.

EXPERT Scale Up

If the currents in both parallel wires are equal and in same direction, then magnetic field at a point exactly half way between the wire is always zero.

Definition of Ampere

1 ampere is that steady current which when flowing in each of two infinitely long parallel conductors placed 1 m apart in vacuum, from each other produces between them a force of exactly 2×10^{-7} newton per metre of their length.

Magnetic Force between two Moving Charges

Consider two charges q_1 and q_2 are moving with velocities v_1 and v_2 respectively and at any instant the distance between them is r.

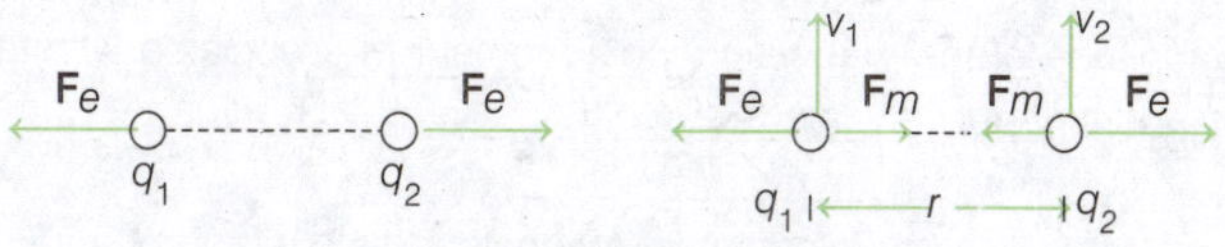

Two moving charges

A magnetic force F_m will appear between them alongwith the electric force.

i.e.,

$$F_m = \frac{\mu_0}{4\pi} \frac{q_1 q_2 \, v_1 v_2}{r^2}$$

Magnetic Dipole

Every current carrying loop is a magnetic dipole. It has two poles South (S) and North (N). This is similar to a bar magnet.

Each magnetic dipole has some magnetic moment (M).

The magnitude of M is $|M| = NiA$

where, N = number of turns in the loop,

i = current in the loop

and A = area of cross-section of the loop.

The current carrying loop behaves as a small magnetic dipole placed along the axis, one face of the loop behaves as North pole while the other face of loop behaves as South pole.

Competition Insight

Magnetic Moment of an Atom

Magnetic moment of an atom, $M = \frac{1}{2} e\omega r^2$

where, e = charge on an electron,

ω = angular velocity of electron

and r = radius of orbit.

or

$$M = n \frac{eh}{4\pi m}$$

where, h = Planck's constant and m = mass of an electron

and $\frac{eh}{4\pi m} = \mu_B$ called Bohr's magneton and its value is 9.27×10^{-24} A-m^2.

Magnetic Dipole Moment of a Revolving Electron in an Atom

The circular motion of an electron around the positively charged nucleus of an atom can be treated as a current loop producing a magnetic field. Hence, it behaves like a magnetic dipole.

The magnitude of the magnetic dipole moment **M** associated with the revolving electron,

$$M = \frac{neh}{4\pi m_e} \quad \text{...(i)}$$

When $n = 1$, $M = \mu_B$ (the elementary magnetic dipole moment), thus

$$\therefore \quad \mu_B = \frac{eh}{4\pi m_e} \quad \text{...(ii)}$$

The elementary magnetic moment of a revolving electron is also known as **Bohr magneton** (μ_B).

Now, substituting $e = 1.6 \times 10^{-19}$ C, $h = 6.626 \times 10^{-34}$ J-s, $\pi = 3.14$ and $m_e = 9.01 \times 10^{-31}$ kg in Eq. (ii), we get

$$\mu = \frac{1.6 \times 10^{-19} \times 6.626 \times 10^{-34}}{4 \times 3.14 \times 9.01 \times 10^{-31}} = 9.27 \times 10^{-24} \text{ A - m}^2$$

$\therefore$ 1 Bohr magneton = 9.27×10^{-24} A-m^2

Torque acting on a Current Carrying Coil Placed Inside a Uniform Magnetic Field

Torque acting on a current carrying coil placed inside a uniform magnetic field is given by

$$\tau = NBIA \sin \theta$$

where, N = number of turns in the coil,
B = magnetic field intensity,
I = current in the coil,
A = area of cross-section of the coil
and θ = angle between magnetic field and normal to the plane of the coil.

Moving Coil Galvanometer

It is a device used for the detection and measurement of the small currents. In equilibrium, deflecting torque = restoring torque

$$NBIA = k\theta \quad \text{or} \quad I = \frac{k}{NBA}\theta$$

where, k = restoring torque per unit twist,
N = number of turns in the coil,
B = magnetic field intensity,

A = area of cross-section of the coil and θ = angle of twist.

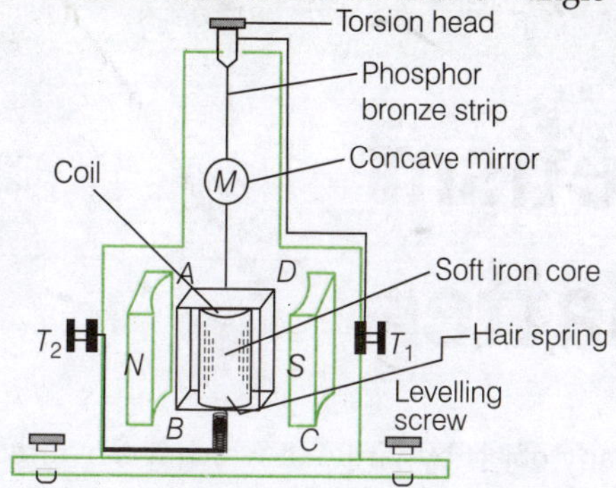

Current Sensitivity

The deflection produced per unit current in galvanometer is called its current sensitivity.

Current sensitivity, $I_S = \frac{\theta}{I} = \frac{NBA}{k}$

Voltage Sensitivity

The deflection produced per unit voltage applied across the ends of the galvanometer is called its voltage sensitivity.

Voltage sensitivity, $V_s = \frac{\theta}{V} = \frac{NBA}{kR}$

where, R is the resistance of the galvanometer.

Therefore for a sensitive galvanometer

(i) N should be large (ii) B should be large

(iii) A should be large (iv) k should be small.

Advantage of Moving Coil galvanometer

- It is not affected by a strong magnetic field.
- It is very accurate
- Its scales are uniform.
- It has a high torque to weight ratio.

Disadvantage of Moving Coil Galvanometer

- Temperature change can cause a change in restoring torque.
- The phosphor-bronze fibre or hair spring may be damage due to severe stress.
- Such type of instrument can be used only for DC current but not used for AC current.

Chapter 23

Magnetism and Matter

The property of any object by virtue of which it can attract a piece of iron or steel is called **magnetism.**

Natural Magnet

A natural magnet is an ore of iron (Fe_3O_4), which attracts small pieces of iron, cobalt and nickel towards it.

Magnetite or lodestone is a natural magnet.

Artificial Magnet

A magnet which is prepared artificially is called an artificial magnet, *e.g.* a bar magnet, an electromagnet, a magnetic needle, a horse-shoe magnet etc.

According to molecular theory, every molecule of magnetic substance (whether magnetised or not) is a complete magnet itself.

The poles of a magnet are the two points near but within the ends of the magnet, at which the entire magnetism can be assumed to be concentrated.

Properties of Magnet

(i) A freely suspended magnet always aligns itself into North-South direction.

(ii) Like magnetic poles repel and unlike magnetic poles attract each other.

(iii) Magnetic poles exist in pair and they are of equal strength.

(iv) Magnetic length $= \frac{5}{6} \times$ Geometric length of magnet.

Magnetic Field Lines

These are the imaginary lines which continuously represent the direction of the magnetic field.

Following are the properties of magnetic field lines

(i) These lines forms closed continuous loops.

(ii) The tangent at any point of a field line represents the direction of net magnetic field.

(iii) These lines do not intersect each other.

(iv) Direction of field lines is from *N* to *S*, if they are outside the magnet and from *S* to *N*, if they are inside the magnet.

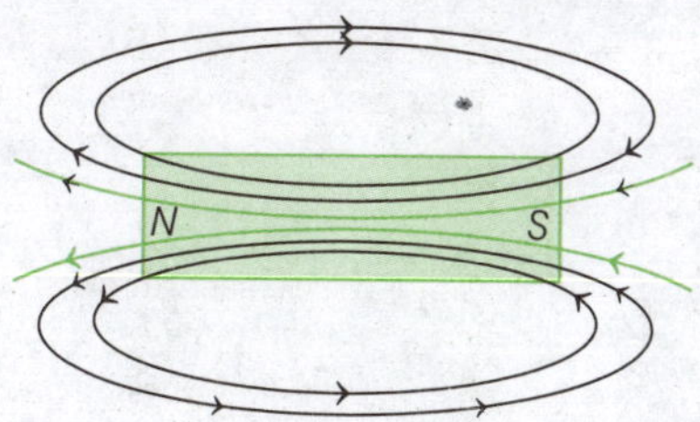

Magnetic Dipole

Magnetic dipole is an arrangement of two unlike magnetic poles of equal pole strength separated by a very small distance, *e.g.* a small bar magnet, a magnetic needle, a current carrying loop etc.

Pole Strength

It can be defined as the strength of magnetic pole to attract magnetic material towards itself. It is a scalar quantity and its SI unit is ampere-metre (A-m).

Magnetic Dipole Moment

The product of the distance ($2l$) between the two poles and the pole strength of either pole is called magnetic dipole moment.

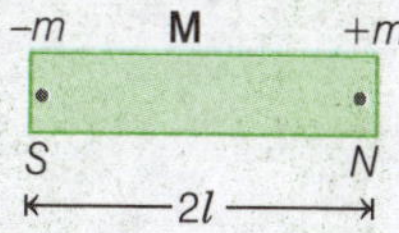

Magnetic dipole moment, $\mathbf{M} = \mathbf{m}(2l)$

Its SI unit is joule/tesla (J/T) or ampere-metre^2 (A-m^2).

Its direction is from South pole towards North pole.

About 90% of magnetic moment is due to spin motion of electrons and remaining 10% of magnetic moment is due to the orbital motion of electrons.

Competition Insight

Pole Strength and Magnetic Dipole Moment in Special Cases

Special Cases	Figure	Effect on Pole strength	Formula for new magnetic dipole moment
If bar magnet is cut into two equal pieces such that the length of each piece becomes half	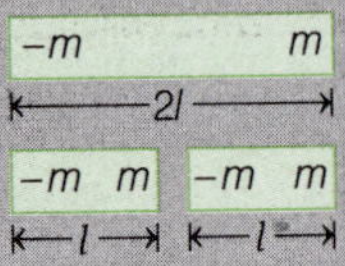 $-m$ m ; $2l$; $-m$ m $-m$ m ; l l	Remains unchanged	$M' = m \cdot \frac{2l}{2} = \frac{M}{2}$ (becomes half)
If bar magnet is cut into two equal pieces such that the width of each piece becomes half	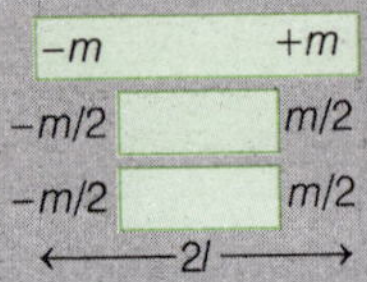 $-m$ $+m$; $-m/2$ $m/2$; $-m/2$ $m/2$; $2l$	Pole strength of each piece becomes half	$M' = \left(\frac{m}{2}\right)(2l) = \frac{M}{2}$ (becomes half)
If bar magnet is bent in the form of semi-circle	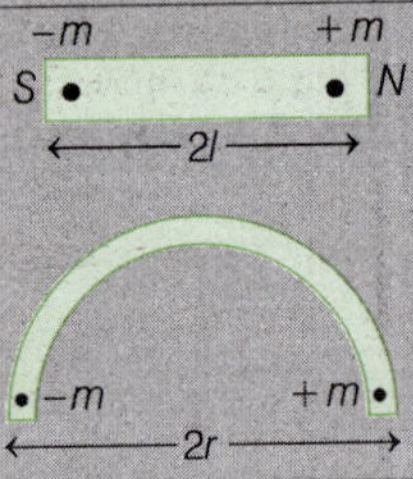 $-m$ $+m$; S N ; $2l$; $-m$ $+m$; $2r$	Remains unchanged	$M' = m(2r) [\because 2l = \pi r]$ $M' = m \times 2\left(\frac{2l}{\pi}\right) = \frac{2M}{\pi}$ $\left(\text{becomes } \frac{2}{\pi} \text{ times}\right)$
When two identical bar magnets are joined perpendicular to each other	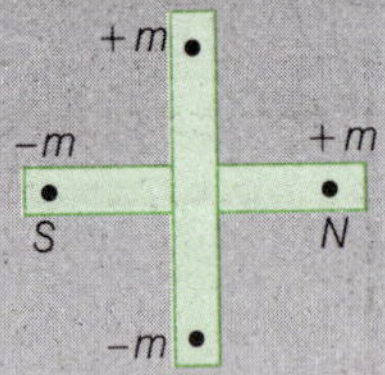 $+m$; $-m$ $+m$; S N ; $-m$	Remains unchanged	$M = \sqrt{M_1^2 + M_2^2} = \sqrt{2}M$
When two bar magnets are inclined at an angle θ.	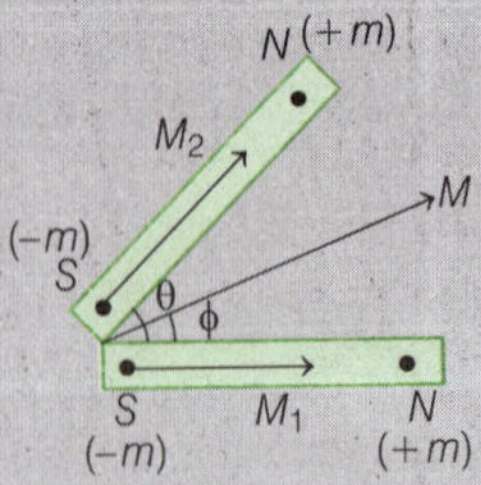 $N(+m)$; M_2 ; M ; $(-m)$ S ; θ ϕ ; S M_1 N ; $(-m)$ $(+m)$	Remains unchanged	Resultant magnetic moment, $M' = \sqrt{M_1^2 + M_2^2 + 2M_1 M_2 \cos\theta}$ Angle made by resultant magnetic moment (M) with M_1 is given by, $\tan\phi = \frac{M_2 \sin\theta}{M_1 + M_2 \cos\theta}$

Magnetic Field Due to a Magnetic Dipole

(i) **On Axial Line**

$$B = \frac{\mu_0}{4\pi} \frac{2Mr}{(r^2 - l^2)^2}$$

If $r >> l$, then $$B = \frac{\mu_0}{4\pi} \frac{2M}{r^3}$$

(ii) **On Equatorial Line**

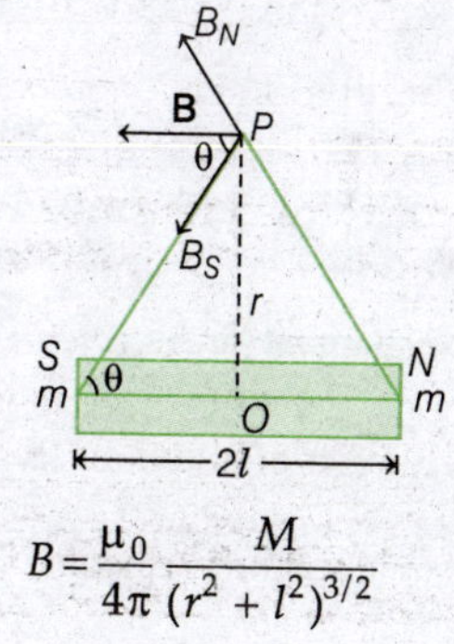

$$B = \frac{\mu_0}{4\pi} \frac{M}{(r^2 + l^2)^{3/2}}$$

If $r >> l$, then $$B = \frac{\mu_0}{4\pi} \frac{M}{r^3}$$

(iii) On a line making an angle θ with axis of dipole

$$B = \frac{\mu_0}{4\pi} \cdot \frac{M}{r^3} \sqrt{1 + 3\cos^2\theta}$$

Torque Acting on a Magnetic Dipole

When a magnetic dipole (**M**) is placed in a uniform magnetic field (**B**), then a torque acts on it, which is given by

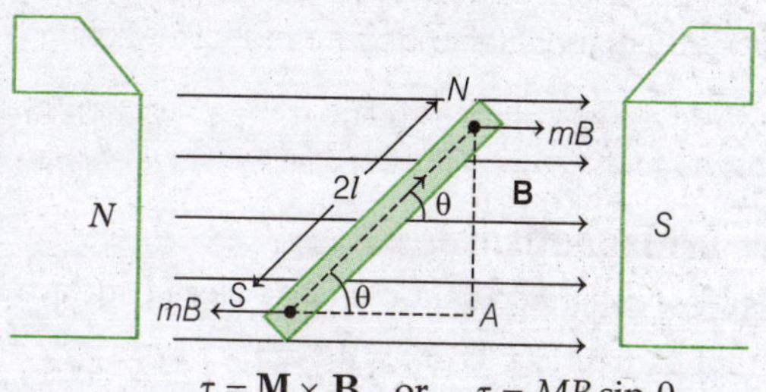

$$\tau = \mathbf{M} \times \mathbf{B} \quad \text{or} \quad \tau = MB\sin\theta$$

where, θ is the angle between the dipole axis and magnetic field.

Potential Energy of a Magnetic Dipole in a Uniform Magnetic Field

The work done in rotating the dipole against the action of the torque is stored as potential energy of the dipole.

Potential energy, $U = W = -MB\cos\theta = -\mathbf{M}\cdot\mathbf{B}$

 Knowledge Booster

Coulomb's Law

The force of interaction acting between two magnetic poles is directly proportional to the product of their pole strengths and inversely proportional to the square of the distance between them.

$$F = \frac{\mu_0}{4\pi}\cdot\frac{m_1 m_2}{r^2}$$

where, m_1, m_2 = pole strengths, r = distance between poles and μ_0 = permeability of free space.

Oscillations of a Freely Suspended Magnet

When a small bar magnet of magnetic moment **M** is placed in a uniform magnetic field **B** such as it is free to vibrate in a horizontal plane of magnetic field **B** about a vertical axis passing through its centre of mass. This bar magnet oscillates. The restoring torque in this case will be,

$$\tau = -MB\theta \qquad (\because \text{For small oscillation, } \sin\theta \simeq \theta)$$

The deflecting torque on the magnet is $\tau = I\alpha = I\dfrac{d^2\theta}{dt^2}$

In equilibrium, deflecting torque = Restoring torque

or $$\frac{d^2\theta}{dt^2} = \frac{-MB\theta}{I} = -\omega^2\theta, \text{ where } \omega = \sqrt{\frac{MB}{I}}$$

The period of vibration is given by $T = \dfrac{2\pi}{\omega} = 2\pi\sqrt{\dfrac{I}{MB}}$

Magnetic field B can be calculated from above equation and is given as

$$B = \frac{4\pi^2 I}{MT^2}$$

Gauss's Law in Magnetism

Surface integral of magnetic field over any closed surface is always zero.

$$\oint_S \mathbf{B}\cdot d\mathbf{S} = 0$$

This law tells that the net magnetic flux through any closed surface is always zero.

Earth's Magnetism

Earth behaves like a huge magnet. The value of magnetic field on the surface of earth is a few of tenths of a gauss.

Its strength varies from place to place on the earth's surface.

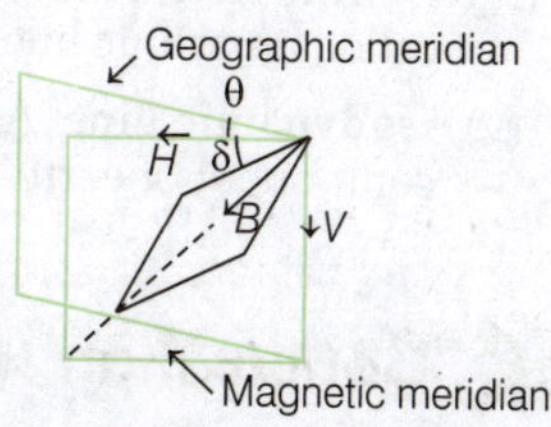

Magnetic Meridian

A vertical plane passing through the magnetic axis is called magnetic meridian.

Geographic Meridian

A vertical plane passing through the geographic axis is called geographic meridian.

Elements of Earth's Magnetism

(i) **Magnetic Declination (θ)** The smaller angle subtended between the magnetic meridian and geographic meridian is called magnetic declination.

(ii) **Magnetic Inclination or Magnetic Dip** (δ) The smaller angle subtended between the magnetic axis and horizontal line is called magnetic inclination or magnetic dip.

Angle of dip is zero at magnetic equator and 90° at poles.

(iii) **Horizontal and Vertical Component of Earth's Magnetic Field** If B is the intensity of earth's magnetic field, then horizontal component of earth's magnetic field $H = B\cos\delta$

It acts from South to North direction.

Vertical component of earth's magnetic field, $V = B\sin\delta$

$$\therefore \qquad B = \sqrt{H^2 + V^2} \quad \text{and} \quad \tan\delta = \frac{V}{H}$$

Magnetic Map

Magnetic map is obtained by drawing lines on the surface of earth, which passes through different places having same magnetic elements.

The main lines drawn on earth's surface are given below

(i) **Isogonic Line** A line joining places of equal declination is called an isogonic line.

(ii) **Agonic Line** A line joining places of zero declination is called an agonic line.

(iii) **Isoclinic Line** A line joining places of equal inclination or dip is called an isoclinic line.

(iv) **Aclinic Line** A line joining places of zero inclination or dip is called an aclinic line.

(v) **Isodynamic Line** A line joining places of equal horizontal component of earth's magnetic field (H) is called an isodynamic line.

Competition Insight

Magnetic Latitude

(i) If at any place, the angle of dip is δ and magnetic latitude is λ, then $\tan \delta = 2 \tan \lambda$.

(ii) The total intensity of earth's magnetic field

$$I = I_0 \sqrt{1 + 3\sin^2 \lambda} \quad \text{where,} \quad I_0 = \frac{M}{R^3}$$

It is assumed that a bar magnet of earth has magnetic moment M and radius of earth is R.

Neutral Points

- Neutral point of a bar magnet is a point at which the resultant magnetic field of a bar magnet and horizontal component of earth's magnetic field are zero.
- When North pole of a bar magnet is placed towards South pole of the earth, then neutral point is obtained on axial line.

$$B = \frac{\mu_0}{4\pi} \frac{2Mr}{(r^2 - l^2)^2} = H$$

- If $r >> l$, then $\quad B = \frac{\mu_0}{4\pi} \frac{2M}{r^3} = H$
- When North pole of a bar magnet is placed towards North pole of the earth, then neutral point is obtained on equitorial line.

$$B = \frac{\mu_0}{4\pi} \frac{M}{(r^2 + l^2)^{3/2}} = H$$

If $r >> l$, then $\quad B = \frac{\mu_0}{4\pi} \frac{M}{r^3} = H$

Tangent Law

- It states that, if a magnet is placed in two magnetic fields right angle to each other, then it will be acted upon by two couples tending to rotate it in opposite directions. It will be deflected through an angle θ, such that two couples balance each other.
- Also, $\quad \tan \theta = \frac{B_1}{B_2}$

where, θ is the angle between magnet and magnetic field B_2

Important Terms used to Describe the Properties of Magnetic Materials

To describe the magnetic properties of materials, following terms are required

(i) **Magnetic Permeability** It is the ability of a material to permit the passage of magnetic lines of force through it.

Magnetic permeability $(\mu) = \frac{B}{H}$

where, B is magnetic induction and H is magnetising force or magnetic intensity.

(ii) **Magnetising Force or Magnetic Intensity** The degree up to which a magnetic field can magnetise a material is defined in terms of magnetic intensity.

$$\text{Magnetic intensity } (H) = \frac{B}{\mu}$$

(iii) **Intensity of Magnetisation** The magnetic dipole moment developed per unit volume of the material is called intensity of magnetisation.

Intensity of magnetisation $(\mathbf{I}) = \frac{\mathbf{M}}{V} = \frac{m}{A}$

where, V = volume and A = area of cross-section of the specimen.

Magnetic induction, $B = \mu_0 (H + I)$.

(iv) **Magnetic Susceptibility (χ_m)** The ratio of the intensity of magnetisation (I) induced in the material to the magnetising force (H) applied is called magnetic susceptibility.

$$\text{Magnetic susceptibility } (\chi_m) = \frac{I}{H}$$

Value Points

Relation between magnetic permeability and susceptibility is given by $\mu = \mu_0 (1 + \chi_m)$

Classification of Magnetic Materials

On the basis of their magnetic properties, magnetic materials are divided into three categories

(i) Diamagnetic substances

(ii) Paramagnetic substances

(iii) Ferromagnetic substances

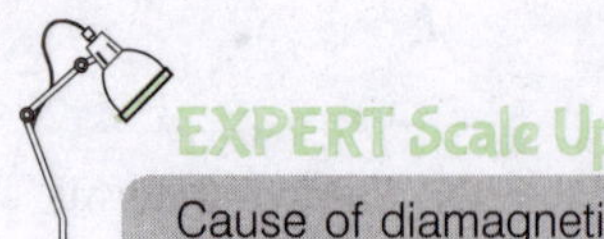

Cause of diamagnetism is orbital motion and cause of paramagnetism is spin motion of electrons. Cause of ferromagnetism lies in formation of domains.

S. No.	Diamagnetic substances	Paramagnetic substances	Ferromagnetic substances
1.	These substances when placed in a magnetic field, acquire feeble magnetism opposite to the direction of the magnetic field.	These substances when placed in a magnetic field, acquire feeble magnetism in the direction of the magnetic field.	These substances when placed in a magnetic fields are strongly magnetised in the direction of the field.
2.	These substances are repelled by a magnet.	These substances are feebly attracted by a magnet.	These substances are strongly attracted by a magnet.
3.	When a diamagnetic solution is poured into a U- tube and one arm is placed between the poles of strong magnet, the level of solution in that arm is lowered.	The level of the paramagnetic solution in that arm rises.	No liquid is ferromagnetic.

S. No.	Diamagnetic substances	Paramagnetic substances	Ferromagnetic substances
4.	If a rod of diamagnetic material is suspended freely between two magnetic poles, its axis becomes perpendicular to the magnetic field. 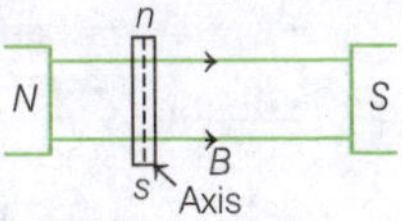	Paramagnetic rod becomes parallel to the magnetic field. 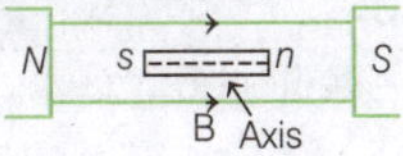	Ferromagnetic rod also becomes parallel to the magnetic field. 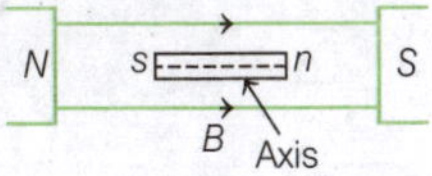
5.	In non-uniform magnetic field, the diamagnetic substances are attracted towards the weaker fields, *i.e.* they move from stronger to weaker magnetic field.	In non-uniform magnetic field, they move from weaker to stronger part of the magnetic field slowly.	In non-uniform magnetic field, they move from weaker to stronger magnetic field rapidly.
6.	Their permeability is less than one ($\mu < 1$).	Their permeability is slightly greater than one ($\mu > 1$).	Their permeability is much greater than one ($\mu >> 1$).
7.	Their susceptibility is small and negative. Their susceptibility is independent of temperature.	Their susceptibility is small and positive. Their susceptibility is inversely proportional to absolute temperature.	Their susceptibility is large and postitve. They also follow Curie's law.
8.	Shape of diamagnetic liquid in a glass crucible and kept over two magnetic poles. 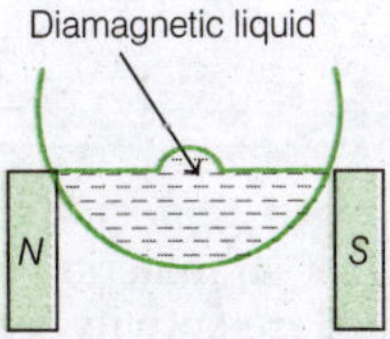 Diamagnetic liquid N S	Shape of paramagnetic liquid in a glass crucible and kept over two magnetic poles. 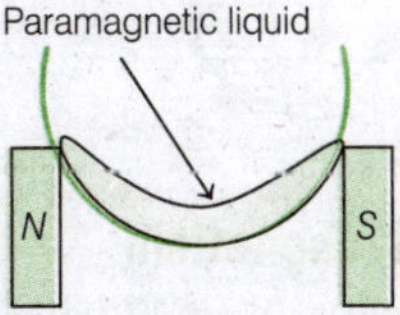 Paramagnetic liquid N S	No liquid is ferromagnetic.
9.	In these substances, the magnetic lines of force are farther than in air.	In these substances, the magnetic lines of force are closer than in air.	In these substances, magnetic lines of force are much closer than in air.
10.	The resultant magnetic moment of these substances is zero.	These substances have a permanent magnetic moment.	These substances also have a permanent magnetic moment.

Value Points

- In a ferromagnetic substance, there are several tiny regions called **domains**. Each domain contain approximately 10^{10} atoms.
- Each domain is a strong magnet as all atoms or molecules in a domain have same direction of magnetic moment.

Curie Law in Magnetism

The magnetic susceptibility of a paramagnetic substance is inversely proportional to its absolute temperature.

$$\chi_m \propto \frac{1}{T} \quad \Rightarrow \quad \chi_m T = \text{constant}$$

where, χ_m = magnetic susceptibility of a paramagnetic substance and
T = absolute temperature.

At Curie temperature, ferromagnetic substances changes into paramagnetic substances.

Hysteresis

The lagging of intensity of magnetisation (I) or magnetic induction (B) behind magnetising field (H), when a specimen of a magnetic substance is taken through a complete cycle of magnetisation is called hysteresis.

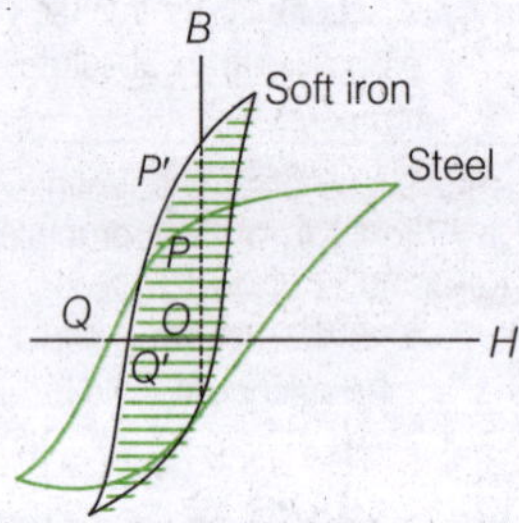

Retentivity or Residual Magnetism

The value of the intensity of magnetisation of a material, when the magnetising field is reduced to zero is called retentivity or residual magnetism of the material.

Coercivity

The value of the reverse magnetising field that should be applied to a given sample in order to reduce its intensity of magnetisation or magnetic induction to zero is called coercivity.

Permanent Magnets and Electromagnets

Substances which retain their ferromagnetic property for a long period of time at room temperature are called permanent magnets.

Characteristics of permanent magnets

(i) High retentivity

(ii) High coercivity

(iii) High permeability

An electromagnet is a type of magnet whose magnetic field is produced by the flow of electric current.

Characteristics of electromagnets

(i) High initial permeability, so that magnetisation is large even for a small magnetising field.

(ii) Low retentivity

(iii) Low coercivity

Factors affecting strength of electromagnets

(i) The strength of magnetic field increases on increasing the number of turns of the winding and *vice-versa.*

(ii) The strength of magnetic field increases on increasing the current through the coil and *vice-versa.*

Value Points

- For steel coercivity is large and retentivity is comparatively small, so steel is used to make permanent magnets.
- For soft iron, coercivity and area of hysteresis loop are very small. So, soft iron is an ideal material for making electromagnets.

Chapter 24

Electromagnetic Induction

Whenever the magnetic flux linked with an electric circuit changes, an emf is induced in the circuit. This phenomenon is called **electromagnetic induction.**

Magnetic Flux

The total number of magnetic field lines crossing through any surface normally, when it is placed in a magnetic field is known as magnetic flux of that surface.

$$\phi = \mathbf{B} \cdot d\mathbf{s} = Bds \cos \theta$$

Its SI unit is tesla-metre^2 (or weber)

$$\text{CGS unit of } \phi = \text{maxwell}, 1 \text{ weber} = 10^8 \text{ maxwell},$$

Dimensional formula of magnetic flux

$$[\phi] = [ML^2 T^{-2} A^{-1}]$$

Faraday's Laws of Electromagnetic Induction

(i) Whenever the magnetic flux linked with a circuit changes, an induced emf is produced in it.

(ii) The induced emf lasts, so long as the change in magnetic flux continues.

(iii) The magnitude of induced emf is directly proportional to the rate of change in magnetic flux, *i.e.*

$$e \propto \frac{d\phi}{dt} \Rightarrow e = -\frac{d\phi}{dt}$$

where, constant of proportionality is one and negative sign indicates that the induced emf in the circuit due to the changing flux always opposes the change in magnetic flux.

Induced current is given as

$$I = \frac{1}{R} \cdot \left(\frac{-d\phi}{dt} \right)$$

If induced current is produced in a coil rotating in uniform magnetic field, then

$$I = \frac{NBA\,\omega \sin \omega t}{R} = I_0 \sin \omega t$$

where, $I_0 = \frac{NBA\omega}{R}$ = peak value of induced current,

N = number of turns in the coil ,
B = magnetic induction,
ω = angular velocity of rotation,
A = area of cross-section of the coil and
R = resistance of the coil.

Induced charge is given as $q = -\frac{1}{R}(d\phi)$.

Lenz's Law

The direction of induced emf or induced current is always in such a way, that it opposes the cause due to which it is produced.

Lenz's law is in accordance with the conservation of energy.

Direction of the induced current can be determined as

(i) if flux is decreasing, the magnetic field due to induced current will be along the existing magnetic field.

(ii) if flux is increasing, the magnetic field due to induced current will be opposite to existing magnetic field.

EXPERT Scale Up

You can remember RIN or ⊗ In (when the loop lies on the plane of paper), to apply Lenz's law where

(i) **RIN** In RIN, R stands for right, I stands for increasing and N for north pole (anti-clockwise). It means, if a loop is placed on the right side of a straight current-carrying conductor and the current in the conductor is increasing, then induced current in the loop is anti-clockwise (Ⓝ).

(ii) ⊗ **IN** In ⊗ IN, suppose the magnetic field in the loop is perpendicular to paper inwards ⊗ and this field is increasing, then induced current in the loop is anti-clockwise (Ⓝ).

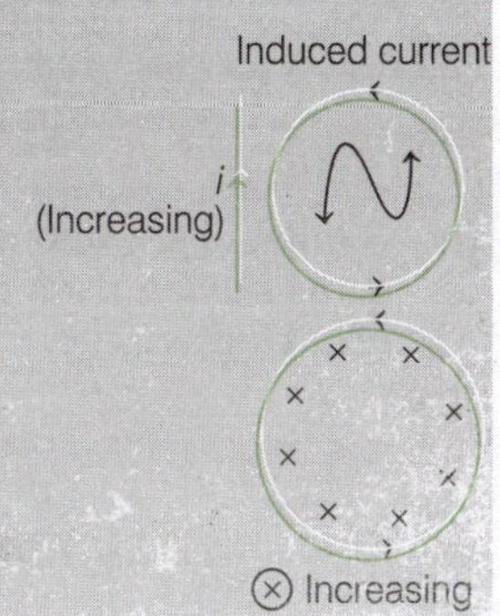

Direction of Induced Current in Coil or Ring by Moving Bar Magnet

The following are some important points that will explain the direction of induced current according to Lenz's law.

(i) When north pole moves towards ring, then flux will increase, induced current will oppose this, so north pole will be formed in loop as seen by observer.

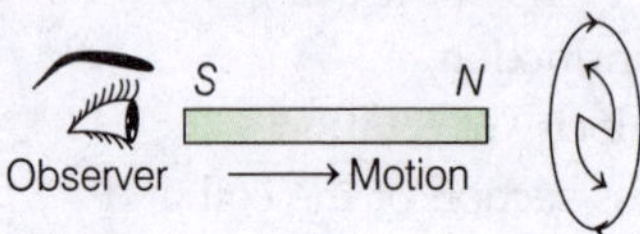

Induced current will be anti-clockwise.

(ii) When north pole moves away from ring, then flux will decrease, induced current will oppose this, so south pole will be formed in loop as seen by observer.

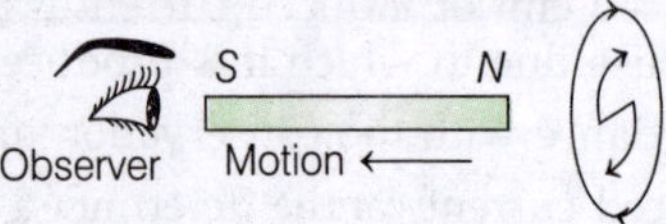

Induced current will be clockwise.

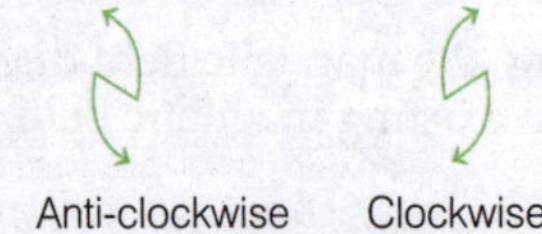

(iii) Similar observations (as in case (i) can be observed when south pole moves towards ring. So, induced current will be clockwise here.

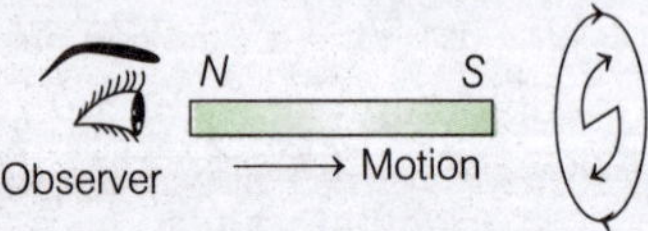

(iv) Similar observations (as in case (ii) can be observed when south pole moves away from the ring. So, induced current in this case will be anti-clockwise.

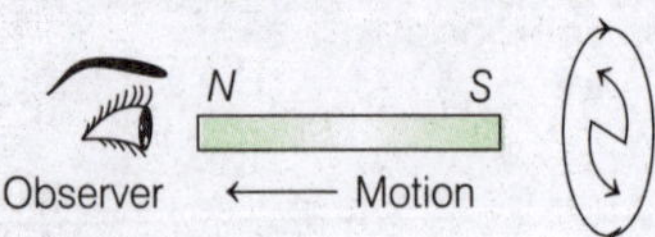

Motional Emf

If a conducting rod of length l moves perpendicular to a magnetic field B, with a velocity v, then induced emf produced in it is given by $e = Bvl$

> Motional emf is produced by moving a conductor instead of varying the magnetic field.

If a rectangular coil moves linearly in a field, when coil moves with constant velocity in an uniform magnetic field, flux and induced emf will be zero.

A rod moves at an angle θ with the direction of magnetic field, with velocity v, then

$$e = Blv \sin \theta$$

If a metallic rod of length l rotates about one of its ends in a plane perpendicular to the magnetic field, then the induced emf produced across, its ends is given by

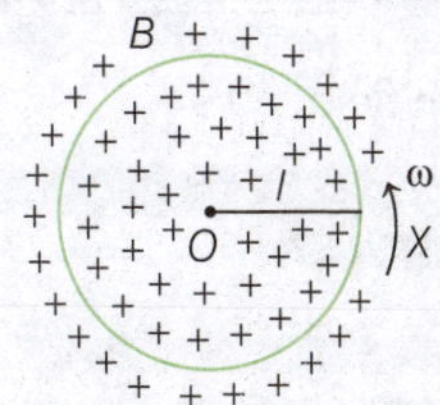

$$e = \frac{1}{2} B\omega l^2 = BAf$$

where, ω = angular frequency of rotation,

$A = \pi l^2$ = area of circle

and f = frequency of rotation.

If a metallic disc of radius r rotates about its own centre in a plane perpendicular to the magnetic field B, then the induced emf produced between the centre and the edge is given by $e = \frac{1}{2} B\omega r^2 = BAf$

where, ω = angular velocity of rotation,

f = frequency of rotation and $A = \pi r^2$ = area of disc.

The direction of induced current in any conductor can be obtained from Fleming's right hand rule.

Fleming's Right Hand Rule

If we stretch the thumb, the forefinger and the central finger of right hand in such a way that all three are perpendicular to each other, then if thumb represent the direction of motion, the forefinger represent the direction of magnetic field, then central finger will represent the direction of induced current.

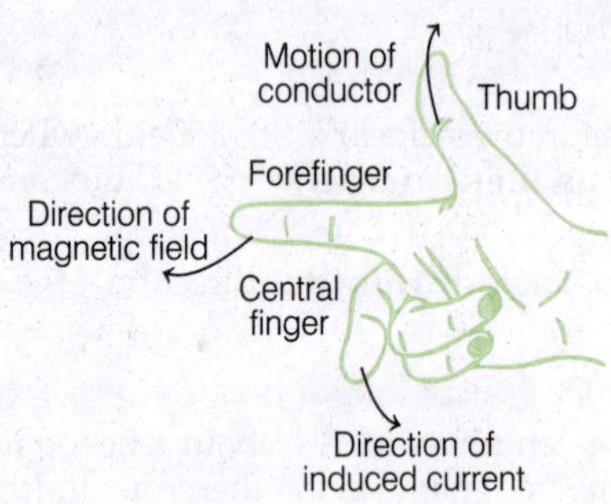

Integral form of Faraday's law of electromagnetic induction is $\oint \mathbf{E} \cdot d\mathbf{l} = \frac{-d\phi}{dt}$

where, E is induced electric field.

Competition Insight

Eddy Currents

- If a piece of metal is placed in a varying magnetic field or rotating with high speed in an uniform magnetic field, then induced currents set up in the piece are like whirlpool of air, called eddy currents.
- The magnitude of eddy currents is given by $I = -\frac{e}{R} = \frac{d\phi / dt}{R}$

  where, R is the resistance.
- Eddy currents are also known as Foucault's currents.
- Eddy currents causes unnecessary heating and wastage of power. The heat, thus produced may even damage the insulation of coils of dynamos and generators.
- Eddy currents can be reduced by laminations of metal to make a metal core.
- Application of Eddy current
  - Magnetic braking in a train.
  - Induction furnace.
  - Coating thickness measurement.

Inductance

It is the property of electric circuit that generates emf by changing the current flowing in the circuit. It is a scalar quantity.

(i) Self-Induction

The phenomena of production of induced emf in a circuit due to change in current flowing in its own, is called self-induction.

The magnetic flux linked with a coil, $\phi = LI$

where, L = coefficient of self-induction.

The induced emf in the coil, $e = -L\dfrac{dI}{dt}$

SI unit of self-induction is henry (H) and its dimensional formula is $[ML^2T^{-2}A^{-2}]$.

- Self-inductance of a **long solenoid** is given by normal text,

$$L = \frac{\mu_0 N^2 A}{l} = \mu_0 n^2 Al$$

where, N = total number of turns in the solenoid,

l = length of the coil, n = number of turns per unit length

and A = area of cross-section of the coil.

- If core of the solenoid is of any other magnetic material, then

$$L = \frac{\mu_0 \mu_r N^2 A}{l}$$

- Self-inductance of a **toroid**, $L = \dfrac{\mu_0 N^2 A}{2\pi r}$

where, r = radius of the toroid.

- Energy stored in an inductor, $E = \dfrac{1}{2}LI^2$.

(ii) Mutual Induction

The phenomena of production of induced emf in a circuit due to the change in magnetic flux in its neighbouring circuit, is called mutual induction.

If two coils are coupled with each other, then magnetic flux linked with a coil (secondary coil)

$$\phi = MI$$

where, M is coefficient of mutual induction and I is current flowing through primary coil.

The induced emf in the secondary coil, $e = -M\dfrac{dI}{dt}$

where, $\frac{dI}{dt}$ is the rate of change of current through primary coil.

The unit of coefficient of mutual induction is henry (H) and its dimensional formula is $[ML^2T^{-2}A^{-2}]$.

The coefficient of mutual induction depends on geometry of two coils, distance between them and orientation of the two coils.

Mutual inductance of **two long co-axial solenoids** is given by,

$$M = \frac{\mu_0 N_1 N_2 A}{l} = \mu_0 n_1 n_2 A l$$

where, N_1 and N_2 are total number of turns in both coils, n_1 and n_2 are number of turns per unit length in coils, A is area of cross-section of coils and l is length of the coils.

Knowledge Booster

Coefficient of Coupling

Coefficient of coupling of two coils gives a measure of the manner in which the two coils are coupled together.

$$K = \frac{M}{\sqrt{L_1 L_2}}, \; M_{12} = M_{21} = M = K\sqrt{L_1 L_2}$$

where, L_1 and L_2 are coefficients of self-induction of the two coils and M is coefficient of mutual induction of the two coils.

Co-efficient of coupling is maximum ($K = 1$) in case (a), when coils are co-axial or for tight coupling and minimum in case (b), when coils are placed a right angles.

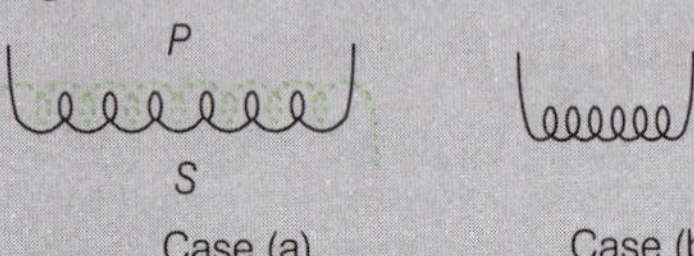

Grouping of Coils

(a) When three coils of inductances L_1, L_2 and L_3 are connected in series and the coefficient of coupling $K = 0$ as in series, then

$$L = L_1 + L_2 + L_3$$

(a) (b)

(b) When three coils of inductances L_1, L_2 and L_3 are connected in parallel and the coefficient of coupling $K = 0$ as in parallel, then

$$\frac{1}{L} = \frac{1}{L_1} + \frac{1}{L_2} + \frac{1}{L_3}$$

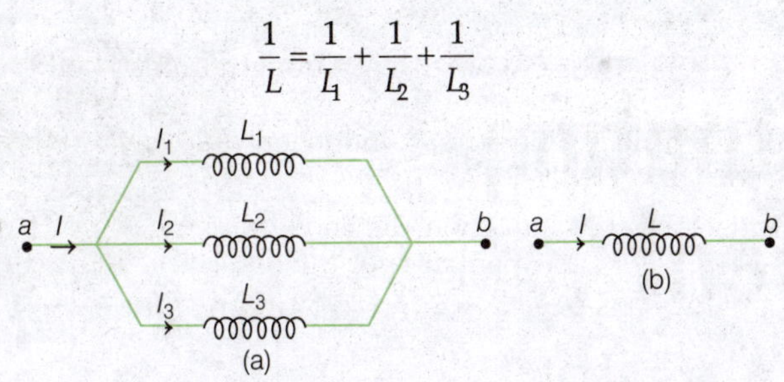

EXPERT Scale Up

Following description can help you to find inductance in grouping of coils, if coefficient of coupling $k = 1$

- **In series**
  (a) If current in two coils are in the same direction, then
  $$L = L_1 + L_2 + 2M$$
  (b) If current in two coils are in opposite directions, then
  $$L = L_1 + L_2 - 2M$$
- **In parallel**
  (a) If current in two coils are in same direction, then
  $$L = \frac{L_1L_2 - M^2}{L_1 + L_2 - 2M}$$
  (b) If current in two coils are in opposite directions, then
  $$L = \frac{L_1 L_2 - M^2}{L_1 + L_2 + 2M}$$

Chapter 25

Alternating Current

Alternating Current

An electric current whose magnitude and direction changes continuously (periodically) with time is called an alternating current.

The instantaneous value of alternating current at any instant of time t is given by

$$I = I_0 \sin \omega t$$

where, I_0 = peak value of alternating current.

The variation of alternating current with time is shown in graph given below

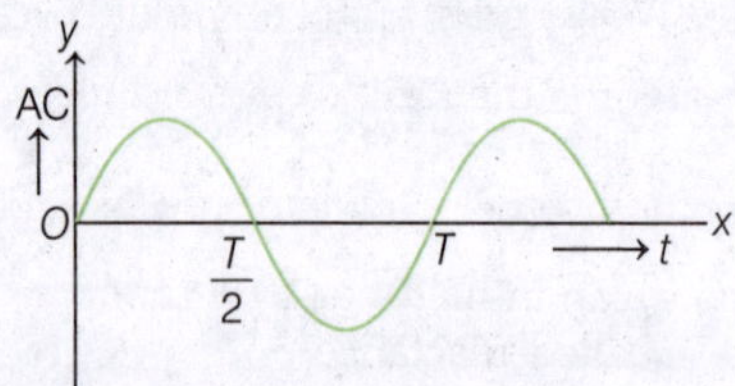

Mean Value and Root-Mean-Square Value of Alternating Current

(i) **Mean Value** The mean value of alternating current over half-a cycle is a finite quantity and infact, it is this quantity which is defined as the mean value of alternating current.

It is given by $\quad I_{\text{mean}} = \dfrac{1}{T/2}\displaystyle\int_0^{T/2} I dt$

Mean or average value of alternating current for first half cycle

$$I_m = \frac{2 I_0}{\pi} = 0.637\ I_0$$

Mean or average value of alternating current for next half cycle

$$I'_m = -\frac{2 I_0}{\pi} = -0.637\ I_0$$

Mean or average value of alternating current for one complete cycle = 0.

In the same way, mean value of alternating voltage,

$$V_m = 0.637\, V_0$$

(iii) **Root-Mean-Square Value** The root-mean-square value of an alternating current is defined as the square root of the average of I^2 during a complete cycle.

The average value of I^2 over a complete cycle is given by

$$I^2 = \frac{1}{T}\int_0^T I^2 dt$$

Root-mean-square value of alternating current

$$I_{\text{rms}} = \frac{I_0}{\sqrt{2}} = 0.707\ I_0$$

In the same way, root-mean-square value of alternating voltage

$$V_{\text{rms}} = \frac{V_0}{\sqrt{2}} = 0.707\ V_0$$

Form factor is defined as the ratio of rms value of AC to its average value during half-cycle.

However, peak factor is the ratio of peak value to the rms value.

Reactance

The opposition offered by an inductor or by a capacitor in the path of flow of alternating current is called reactance.

Reactance is of two types

(i) **Inductive Reactance** (X_L) Inductive reactance is the resistance offered by an inductor.

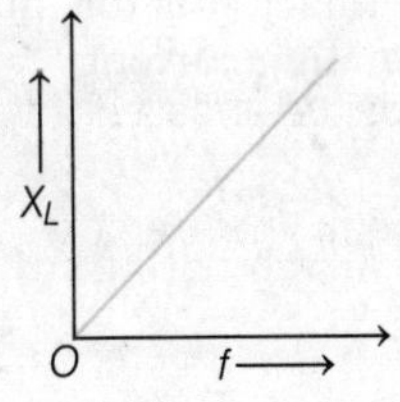

Inductive reactance $(X_L) = L\omega = L2\pi f = \dfrac{L2\pi}{T}$

$$X_L \propto f$$

For direct current, $X_L = 0$ $(\because f = 0)$

Its unit is ohm.

Knowledge Booster

Susceptance

$$\text{Susceptance} = \frac{1}{\text{Reactance}} = S_L = \frac{1}{X_L} = \frac{1}{\omega L}$$

It is measured in siemen or ohm^{-1}.

(ii) **Capacitive Reactance** (X_C) Capacitive reactance is the resistance offered by a capacitor.

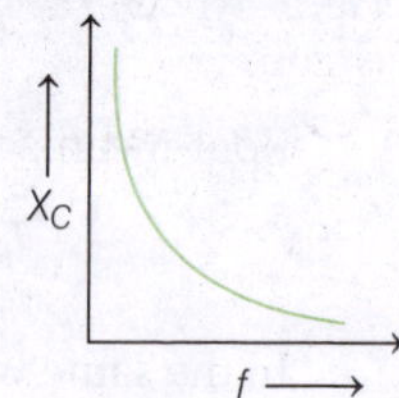

Capacitive reactance,

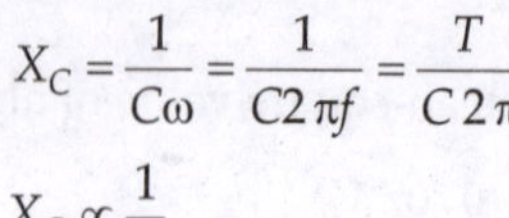

$$X_C = \frac{1}{C\omega} = \frac{1}{C 2\pi f} = \frac{T}{C 2\pi}$$

$$X_C \propto \frac{1}{f}$$

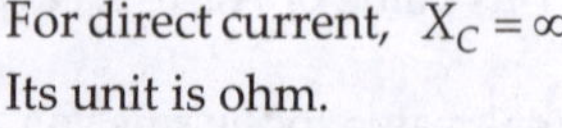

For direct current, $X_C = \infty$ $(\because f = 0)$

Its unit is ohm.

Impedance

The opposition offered by an AC circuit containing more than one out of three components L, C and R is called impedance (Z) of the circuit.

Impedance of an AC circuit, $Z = \sqrt{R^2 + (X_L - X_C)^2}$

Its SI unit is ohm.

Value Points

- Reciprocal of impedance is called admittance, $k = \frac{1}{Z}$
- It is measured in $(\text{ohm})^{-1}$ or siemen.

Power in an AC Circuit

The power is defined as the rate at which work is being done in the circuit. The average power in an AC circuit,

$$P_{av} = V_{rms} I_{rms} \cos\theta$$

$$= \frac{V}{\sqrt{2}} \frac{I}{\sqrt{2}} \cos\theta = \frac{VI}{2} \cos\theta$$

where, $\cos\theta = \dfrac{\text{Resistance}(R)}{\text{Impedance}(Z)}$ is called the power factor of AC circuit.

or, Power factor of an AC circuit $= \dfrac{\text{True power}}{\text{Apparent power}}$

Its value lies between 0 and 1.

Current and Potential Relations for Different AC Circuits

Here, we will discuss current and potential relations for different AC circuits.

(i) **Pure Resistive Circuit** (R Circuit)

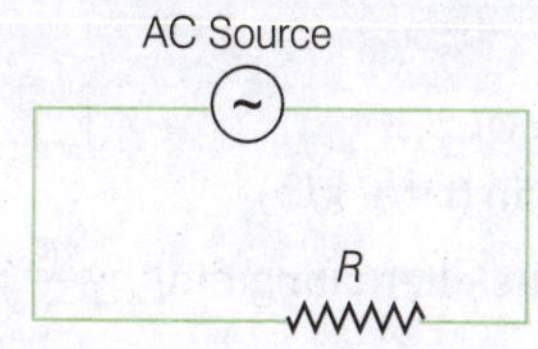

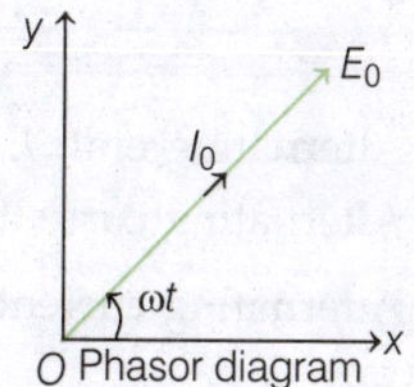

Phasor diagram

(a) Alternating emf, $E = E_0 \sin \omega t$

(b) Alternating current, $I = I_0 \sin \omega t$

(c) Alternating emf and alternating current both are in the same phase.

(d) Average power decay, $(\overline{P}) = E_{\text{rms}} \cdot I_{\text{rms}}$

(e) Power factor, $\cos\theta = 1$

(ii) **Pure Inductive Circuit** (L Circuit)

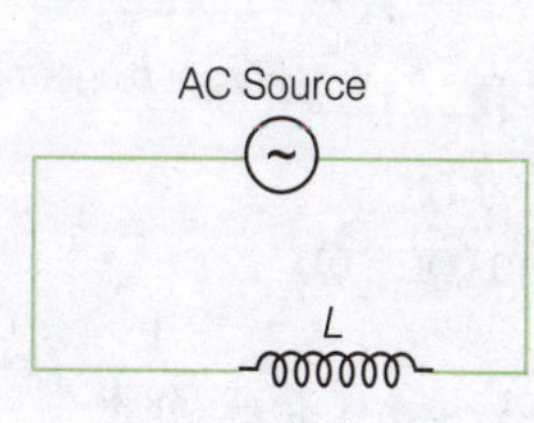

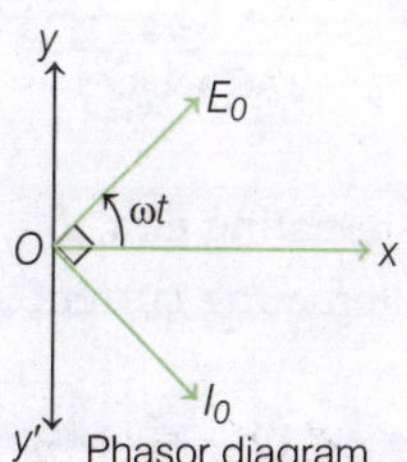

Phasor diagram

y

(a) Alternating emf, $E = E_0 \sin \omega t$

(b) Alternating current, $I = I_0 \sin (\omega t - \pi/2)$

(c) Alternating current lags behind alternating emf by $\frac{\pi}{2}$.

(d) Average power decay, $(\overline{P}) = 0$

(e) Power factor, $\cos\theta = \cos 90° = 0$

(iii) **Pure Capacitive Circuit**

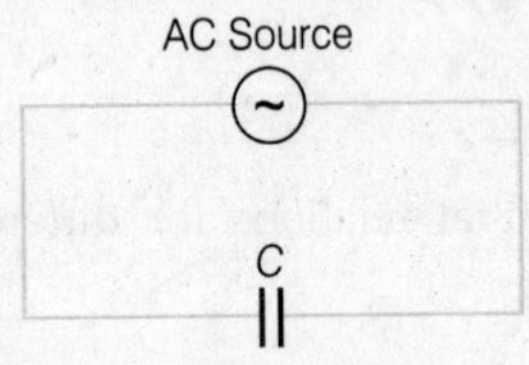

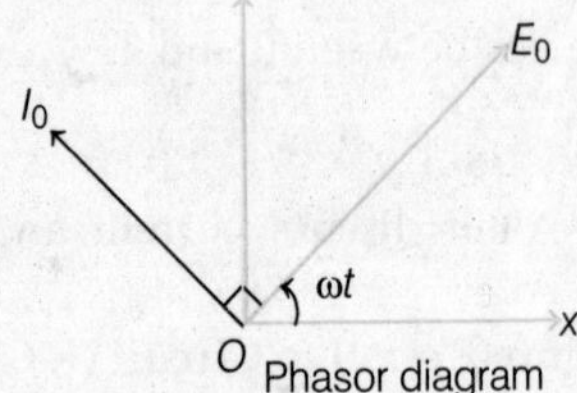

Phasor diagram

(a) Alternating emf, $E = E_0 \sin \omega t$

(b) Alternating current, $I = I_0 \sin(\omega t + \pi/2)$

(c) Alternating current leads the alternating emf by $\frac{\pi}{2}$.

(d) Capacitive reactance, $X_C = C\omega = C2\pi f$

(e) Avearge power decay, $(\overline{P}) = 0$

(f) Power factor, $\cos\theta = \cos 90° = 0$

(iv) ***R-C* Circuit**

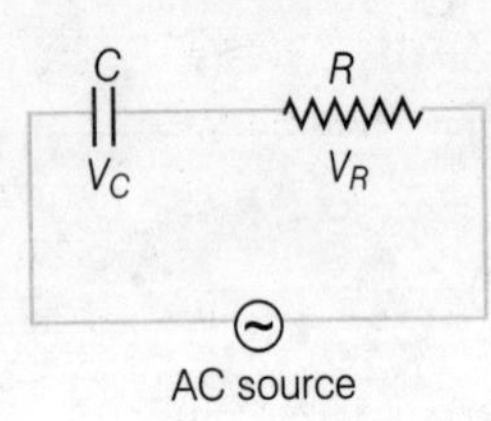

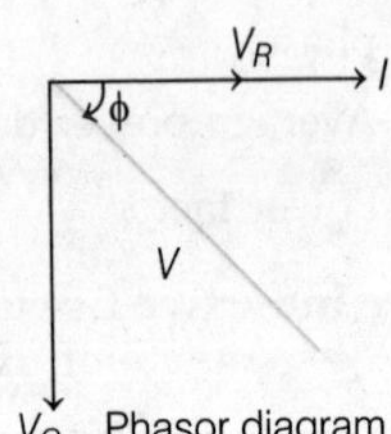

Phasor diagram

(a) Alternating emf, $E = E_0 \sin \omega t$

(b) Alternating current, $I = I_0 \sin(\omega t + \phi)$

(c) Impedance, $Z = \sqrt{R^2 + \left(\frac{1}{\omega C}\right)^2}$ and $\tan\phi = \frac{\frac{1}{\omega C}}{R}$

(d) Current leads the voltage by ϕ, where

$$V^2 = V_R^2 + V_C^2$$

(v) ***L-C* Circuit**

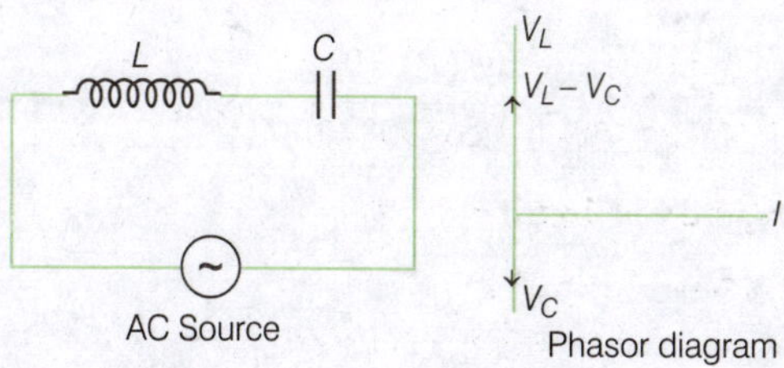

(a) Alternating emf, $E = E_0 \sin \omega t$,

(b) Alternating current, $I = I_0 \sin (\omega t - \phi)$

(c) Impedance, $Z = X_L \sim X_C$ and $\tan \phi = \dfrac{X_L - X_C}{0}$

- For $X_L > X_C, \phi = \dfrac{\pi}{2}$ and for $X_L < X_C, \phi = -\dfrac{\pi}{2}$.
- If $X_L = X_C$ at $\omega = \dfrac{1}{\sqrt{LC}}, Z = 0$.

(vi) ***L-C-R* Circuit**

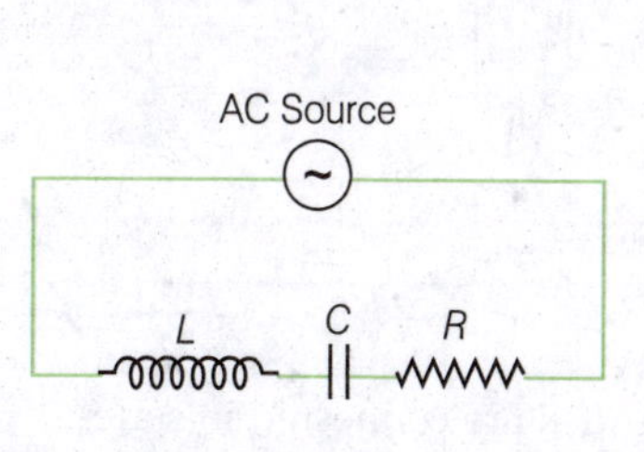

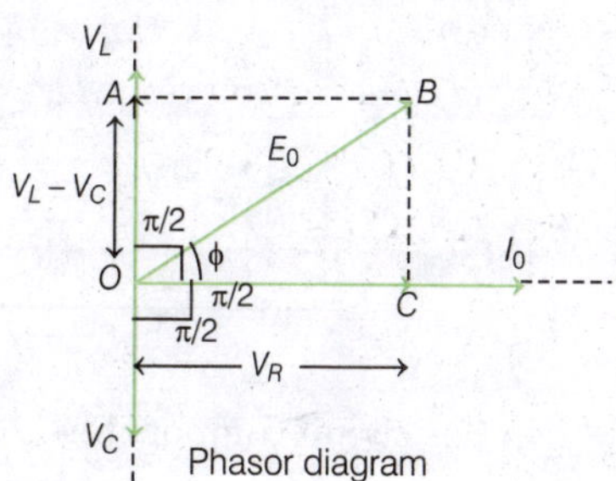

(a) Alternating emf, $E = E_0 \sin \omega t$

(b) Alternating current, $I = I_0 \sin (\omega t \pm \phi)$

(c) Alternating current either lags or leads by alternating emf by ϕ.

(d) Resultant voltage, $V = \sqrt{V_R^2 + (V_L - V_C)^2}$

(e) Impedance, $Z = \sqrt{R^2 + (X_L - X_C)^2}$

EXPERT Scale Up

Power factor of L-C-R series circuit is easily determined by the impedance triangle.

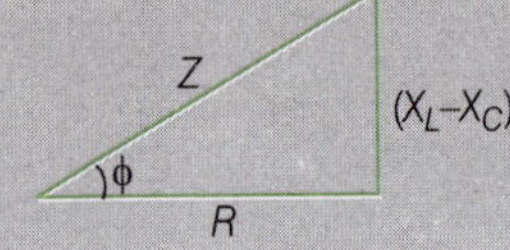

(f) Power factor, $\cos\phi = \frac{R}{Z} = \frac{R}{\sqrt{R^2 + (X_L - X_C)^2}}$

(g) Average power decay, $(\overline{P}) = E_{rms} I_{rms} \cos\theta$

Resonance in an AC Circuit

The condition in which current is maximum or impedance is minimum or *vice-versa* in an AC circuit is called resonance.

(i) **Series Resonance Circuit**

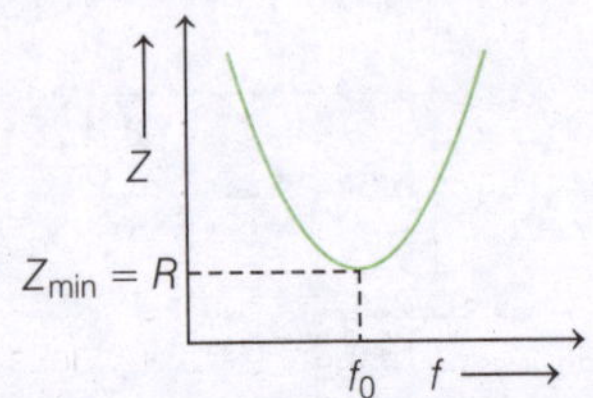

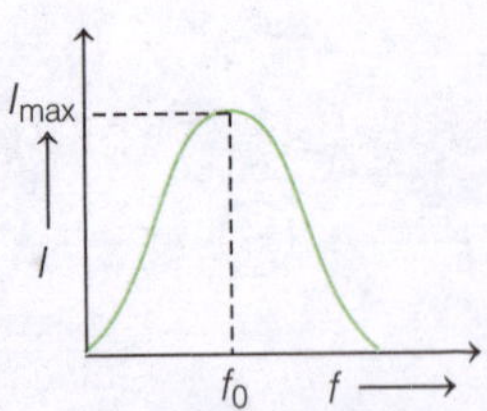

In this circuit components L, C and R are connected in series.

At resonance, $X_L = X_C$

Resonance frequency, $f = \frac{1}{2\pi\sqrt{LC}}$

At resonance impedance is minimum and equal to the resistance, *i.e.* $Z = R$.

Also, maximum current flows through the circuit.

Q-factor or sharpness at resonance, $Q = \frac{1}{R}\sqrt{\frac{L}{C}}$

A series resonance circuit is also known as acception circuit.

(ii) **Parallel Resonance Circuit**

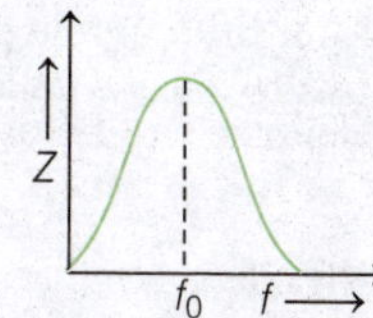

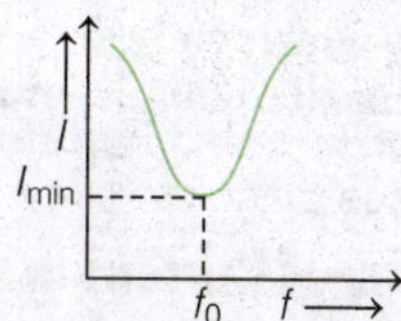

In this circuit, L and C are connected in parallel with each other.

At resonance, $X_L = X_C$

Impedance (Z) of the circuit is maximum.

Current in the circuit is minimum.

Wattless Current

The current which consumes no power for its maintainance in the circuit is called wattless current.

So, for an AC circuit if resistance is zero, its power factor will be zero. Although the current flows in the circuit, yet the average power remains zero. Such a circuit is called wattless circuit.

Competition Insight

L-C Oscillations

- When a charged capacitor is allowed to discharge through a non-resistive inductor, electrical oscillations of constant amplitude and frequency are produced. These oscillations are called L-C oscillations.
- The equation of L-C oscillations is given by $\frac{d^2q}{dt^2} + \frac{1}{LC}q = 0$

  and the charge oscillates with a frequency, $\nu = \frac{\omega}{2\pi} = \frac{1}{2\pi\sqrt{LC}}$

Choke Coil

Choke coil is a device having high inductance and negligible resistance. It is used in AC circuits for the purpose of adjusting current to any required value in such a way that power loss in a circuit can be minimised. It is used in fluorescent tubes.

It is based on the principle of wattless current.

Impedance of choke coil, $Z = \sqrt{\omega^2 L^2 + R^2}$

Power factor of choke coil, $\cos\phi = \frac{R}{\sqrt{R^2 + \omega^2 L^2}} = \frac{R}{\omega L} \; (R << \omega L)$

Transient Current

An electric current which vary for a small finite time, while growing from zero to maximum or decaying from maximum to zero is called a transient current.

Growth and Decay of Current in an Inductor

Growth of current in an inductor at any instant of time t is given by

$$I = I_0(1 - e^{-Rt/L})$$

where, I_0 = maximum current, L = self-inductance of the inductor and R = resistance of the circuit.

Here $\frac{R}{L} = \tau$ is called time constant of a L-R circuit.

Time constant of a L-R circuit is the time in which current in the circuit grows to 63.2% of the maximum value of current.

Decay of current in an inductor at any time t is given by

$$I = I_0 \, e^{-Rt/L}$$

Time constant of a L-R circuit is the time in which current decays to 36.8% of the maximum value of current.

Charging and Discharging of a Capacitor

The instantaneous charge on a capacitor on charging at any instant of time t is given by

$$q = q_0 \, [1 - e^{-t/RC}]$$

where $RC = \tau$, is called time constant of a R-C circuit.

The instantaneous charge on a capacitor in discharging at any instant of time t is given by $q = q_0 e^{-t/RC}$.

Time constant of a R-C circuit is the time in which charge in the capacitor grows to 63.8% or decay to 36.8% of the maximum charge on capacitor.

AC Generator or Dynamo

It is a device which converts mechanical energy into alternating current energy. Its working is based on electromagnetic induction.

The induced emf produced by the AC generator is given by

$$e = NBA\omega \sin \omega t = e_0 \sin \omega t$$

There are four main parts of an AC generator

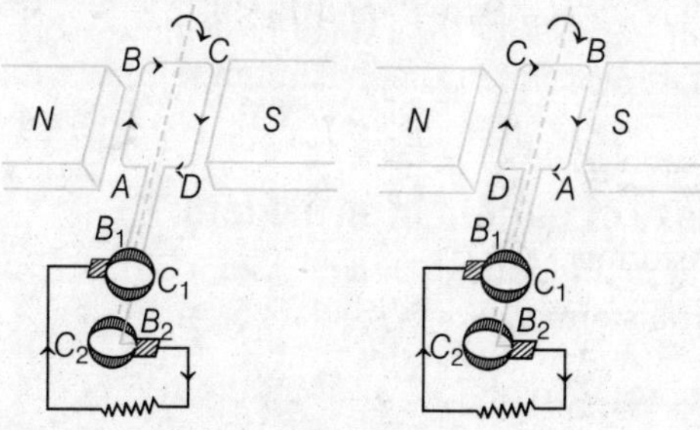

Working of AC dynamo

(i) **Armature** It is rectangular coil of insulated copper wire having a large number of turns.

(ii) **Field Magnets** These are two pole pieces of a strong electromagnet.

(iii) **Slip Rings** These are two hollow metallic rings.

(iv) **Brushes** These are two flexible metals or carbon rods, which remains slightly in contact with slip rings.

Transformer

It is a device which can change a low voltage of high current into a high voltage of low current and *vice-versa.*

Its working is based on mutual induction.

There are two types of transformers

(i) **Step-up Transformers** It converts a low voltage of high current into a high voltage of low current.

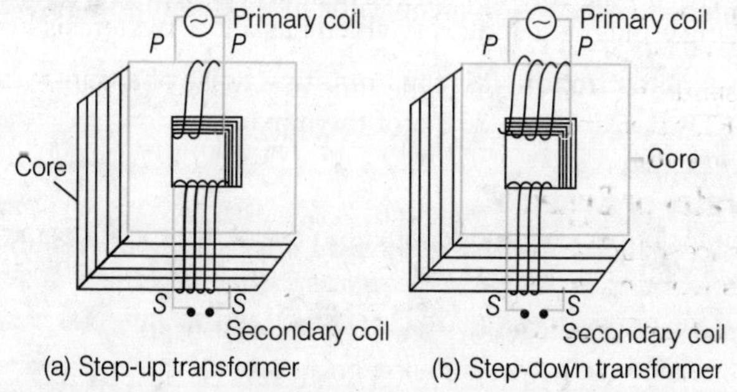

(a) Step-up transformer (b) Step-down transformer

In this transformer, $N_S > N_P, E_S > E_P$

and $I_P > I_S$

(ii) **Step-down Transformer** It converts a high voltage of low current into a low voltage of high current.

In this transformer,

$$N_P > N_S,\ E_P > E_S \text{ and } I_P < I_S$$

Transformation Ratio

Transformation ratio, $K = \dfrac{N_S}{N_P} = \dfrac{E_S}{E_P} = \dfrac{I_P}{I_S}$

For step-up transformer, $K > 1$

For step-down transformer, $K < 1$

Energy Losses in Transformers

In actual transformers, small energy losses occurs due to the following reasons.

(i) **Flux leakage** There is always some leakage of flux *i.e.*, not all of the flux due to primary passes through the secondary due to poor design of the core or the air gaps in the core. It can be reduced by winding the primary and secondary coils one over the other.

(ii) **Resistance of the windings** The wire used for the windings has some resistance and so, energy is lost due to heat produced in the wire ($I^2 R$). In high current, low voltage windings, these are minimised by using thick wire.

(iii) **Eddy currents** The alternating magnetic flux induces eddy currents in the iron core and causes heating. The effect can be reduced by using a laminated core.

(iv) **Hysteresis** The magnetisation of the core is repeatedly reversed by an alternating magnetic field. The resulting expenditure of energy in the core appears as heat and is kept to a minimum by using a magnetic material which has a low hysteresis loss.

(v) **Magnetostriction** It is the humming noise of a transformer.

Value Points

- Transformer does not operate on direct current. It operates only on alternating voltages at input as well as at output.
- Transformer does not amplify power as vacuum tube.
- Transformer, a device based on mutual induction converts magnetic energy into electrical energy.
- Efficiency, $\eta = \dfrac{\text{Output power}}{\text{Input power}}$

  Generally, its efficiency ranges from 70% to 90%.

Chapter 26

Electromagnetic Waves

Displacement Current

It is a current which produces in the region in which the electric field changes and hence the electric flux changes with time.

Displacement current, $I_D = \varepsilon_0 \cdot \frac{d\phi_E}{dt}$

where, ϕ_E is the electric flux.

Maxwell's Equations

(i) $\oint_S \mathbf{E} \cdot d\mathbf{S} = \frac{q}{\varepsilon_0}$

This equation is Gauss's law in electrostatics.

(ii) $\oint_S \mathbf{B} \cdot d\mathbf{S} = 0$

This equation is Gauss's law in magnetostatics.

(iii) $\oint_S \mathbf{E} \cdot d\mathbf{l} = -\frac{d\phi_{\mathbf{B}}}{dt}$

This equation is Faraday's law of electromagnetic induction.

(iv) $\oint \mathbf{B} \cdot d\mathbf{l} = \mu_0 (I_C + I_D) = \mu_0 \left(I_C + \varepsilon_0 \frac{d\phi_E}{dt} \right)$

This equation is Ampere-Maxwell law.

Electromagnetic Waves

Electromagentic waves are those waves in which electric and magnetic field vectors change sinusoidally and are perpendicular to each other as well as at right angles to the direction of propagation of wave.

Electromagnetic waves are produced by accelerated charge particles.

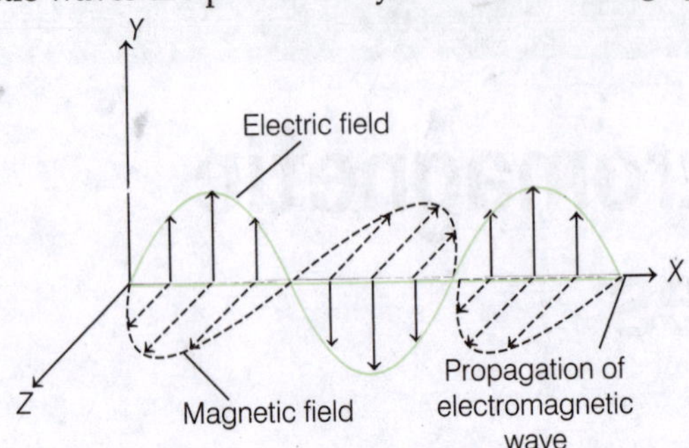

The equation of plane progressive electromagnetic wave can be written as

$$E = E_0 \sin \omega\left(t - \frac{x}{c}\right) \text{ and } B = B_0 \sin \omega\left(t - \frac{x}{c}\right),$$

where $\omega = 2\pi\nu$

Properties of EM Waves

(i) These waves are transverse in nature.

(ii) These waves propagate through space with speed of light, *i.e.*, 3×10^8 m/s

(iii) The speed of electromagnetic wave, $c = \dfrac{1}{\sqrt{\mu_0 \varepsilon_0}}$

where, μ_0 is permeability of free space and ε_0 is permittivity of free space,

$\therefore$ $$c = \frac{E_0}{B_0}$$

where, E_0 and B_0 are maximum values of electric and magnetic field vectors.

Knowledge Booster

- The rate of flow of energy in an electromagnetic wave is described by the vector **S** called the poynting vector, which is defined by the expression, $\mathbf{S} = \dfrac{1}{\mu_0}(\mathbf{E} \times \mathbf{B})$

  SI unit of **S** is watt/m^2 or joules/second.
- Magnitude of **S** is related to the rate at which energy is transported by a wave across a unit area at any instant.

(iv) The energy in electromagnetic waves is divided equally between electric field and magnetic field vectors.

(v) The average electric energy density.

$$U_E = \frac{1}{2}\varepsilon_0 E^2 = \frac{1}{4}\varepsilon_0 E_0^2$$

(vi) The average magnetic energy density,

$$U_B = \frac{1}{2}\frac{B^2}{\mu_0} = \frac{1}{4}\frac{B_0^2}{\mu_0}$$

(vii) The electric vector is responsible for the optical effects of an electromagnetic wave.

(viii) Intensity of electromagnetic wave is defined as energy crossing per unit area per unit time perpendicular to the directions of propagation of electromagnetic wave.

(ix) The intensity I is given by the relation, $I = \langle u \rangle c = \frac{1}{2}\varepsilon_0 E_0^2 c$

(x) Linear momentum of an EM wave is, $p = \frac{U}{c}$

If wave is incident on a completely absorbing surface, then

$$p = \frac{U}{c}$$

If wave is incident on a totally reflecting surface, then $p = \frac{2U}{c}$

(xi) The existence of electromagnetic waves was confirmed by Hertz experimentally in 1888.

Value Points

The ratio of contribution made by the electric field and magnetic field components to the intensity of an electromagnetic wave is 1:1.

Electromagnetic Spectrum

The arranged array of electromagnetic radiations in the sequence of their wavelength or frequency is called electromagnetic spectrum.

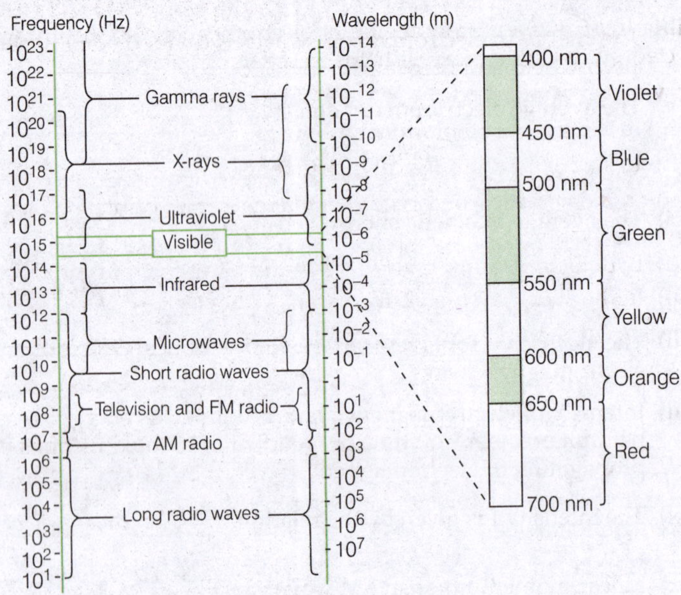

Electromagnetic spectrum with common names for various parts of it

Uses of the EM waves are as given below

Radio waves are used in radio and TV communication.

Microwaves are used

(i) In RADAR systems for aircraft navigation.

(ii) In microwave oven for cooking purpose.

(iii) To measure the speed of vehicle, speed of cricket ball, etc.

Infrared rays are used

(i) To treat muscular strain.

(ii) For taking photographs in fog or smoke.

(iii) In green house to keep plants warm.

(iv) In weather forecasting through infrared photography.

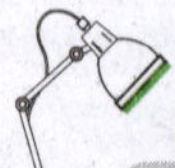

EXPERT Scale Up

Infrared waves are also known as heat waves because when infrared waves fall on a material, the atoms and molecules of material start to vibrate and these vibrations increased the thermal motion of molecules, which heats up the material.

Visible light is the narrow region of electromagnetic spectrum, which is detected by the human eye. It helps to see things around us.

Ultraviolet rays are used

(i) In the study of molecular structure.

(ii) In sterilizing the surgical instruments.

(iii) In the detection of forged documents, finger prints.

X-rays are used

(i) In detecting faults, cracks, flaws and holes in metal products.

(ii) In the study of crystal structure.

(iii) For the detection of pearls in oysters.

γ-rays are used

(i) For the study of nuclear structure.

(ii) In cancer therapy to destroy cancer cells.

(iii) To preserve food items for long time by exposing them in gamma rays.

Chapter 27

Ray Optics

Light

Light is a form of energy which produces the sensation of sight on our eyes. Sources of light are of three types-thermal sources, gas discharge sources and luminescent sources.

Photometry is a branch of ray optics which deals with the measurement of light energy.

Characteristics of Light

Light waves are electromagnetic waves, whose nature is transverse.

The speed of light in vacuum is 3×10^8 m/s but it is different in different media. The speed and wavelength of light change when it travels from one medium to another but its frequency remains unchanged.

Important Terms

(i) **Luminous Objects** The objects which emits its own light are called luminous objects, *e.g.* sun, other stars, an oil lamp etc.

(ii) **Non-Luminous Objects** The objects which do not emit its own light but become visible due to the reflection of light falling on them are called non-luminous objects, *e.g.* moon, table, chair, trees etc.

(iii) **Ray of Light** A straight line drawn in the direction of propagation of light is called a ray of light.

(iv) **Beam of Light** A bundle of the adjacent light rays is called a beam of light.

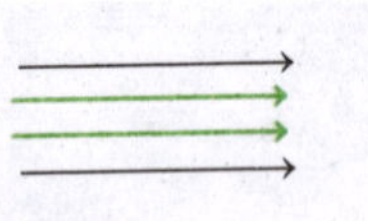

Parallel beam of light

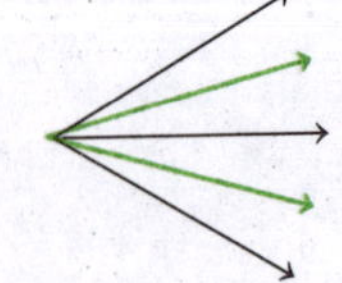

Divergent beam of light

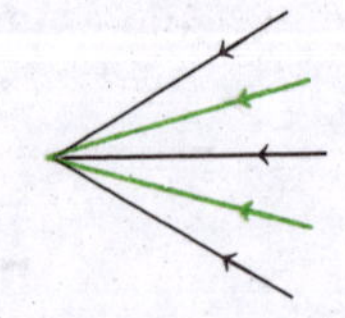

Convergent beam of light

(v) **Image** If light ray coming from an object meets or appear to meet at a point after reflection or refraction, then this point is called image of the object.

(vi) **Real Image** The image obtained by the real meeting of light rays is called a real image.

Real image can be obtained on a screen.

Real image is inverted.

(vii) **Virtual Image** The image obtained when light rays are not really meeting but appears to meet only, is called a virtual image.

Reflection of Light

The rebouncing back of light rays into the same medium on striking a highly polished surface such as a mirror is called reflection of light.

Laws of Reflection

There are two laws of reflection

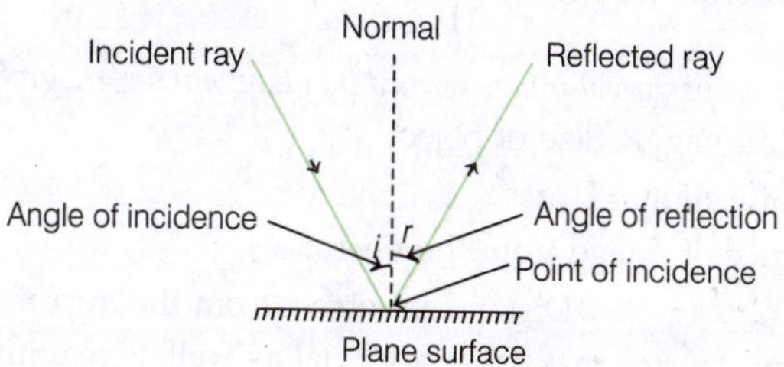

(i) The incident ray, the reflected ray and the normal at the point of incidence all three lie in the same plane.

(ii) The angle of incidence (i) is always equal to the angle of reflection (r).

Types of Reflection

(i) **Regular Reflection** When a parallel beam of reflected light rays is obtained from a parallel beam of incident light rays after reflection from a plane reflecting surface, then such type of reflection is called regular reflection.

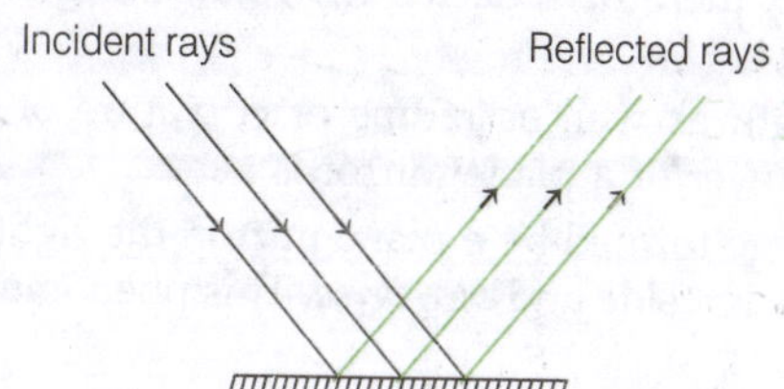

(ii) **Irregular or Diffused Reflection** When a non-parallel beam of reflected light rays is obtained from a parallel beam of incident light rays after reflection from a surface, then such type of reflection is called irregular or diffused reflection.

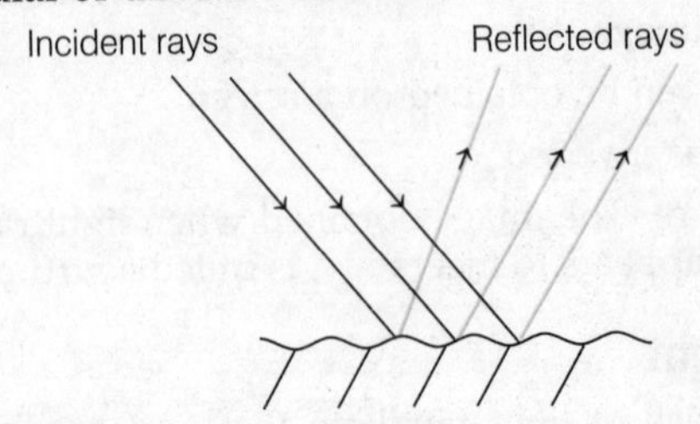

Mirror

A smooth and highly polished reflecting surface is called a mirror.

(i) **Plane Mirror** A highly polished plane surface is called a plane mirror.

Different properties of image formed by plane mirror are given below

- Size of image = Size of object

  Magnification = Unity
- Distance of image from the mirror

  = Distance of object from the mirror
- A plane mirror may form a virtual as well as real image.
- A man may see his full image in a mirror of half height of man.
- When two plane mirror are held at an angle θ, the number of images of an object placed between them is given as below

  (a) $n = \left(\frac{360°}{\theta} - 1\right)$, if $\frac{360°}{\theta}$ is an even integer.

  (b) n = integral part of $\frac{360°}{\theta}$, when $\frac{360°}{\theta}$ is an odd integer.
- If keeping an object fixed, a plane mirror is rotated in its plane by an angle θ, then the reflected ray rotates in the same direction by an angle 2θ.
- Focal length as well as radius of curvature of a plane mirror is infinity. Power of a plane mirror is zero.
- In the image formed by a plane mirror, the right side of the object appears as left side and *vice-versa*. This phenomena is called **lateral inversion**.

(ii) **Spherical Mirror** A highly polished curved surface whose reflecting surface is a cut part of a hollow glass sphere is called a spherical mirror. Spherical mirrors are of two types

(a) **Concave Mirror** A spherical mirror whose bent in surface is reflecting surface, is called a concave mirror.

(b) **Convex Mirror** A spherical mirror whose buldging out surface is reflecting surface, is called a convex mirror.

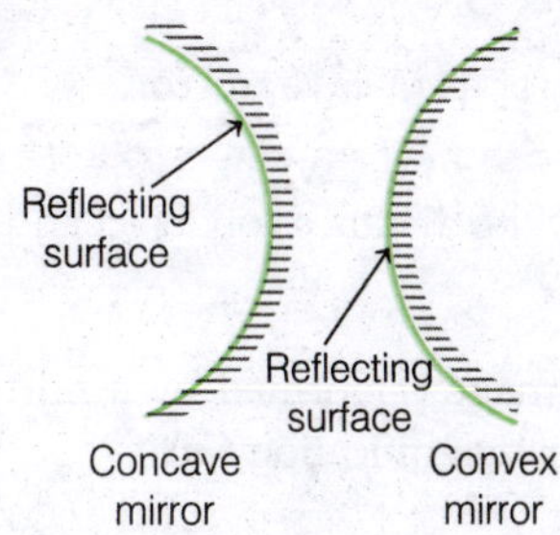

Some Terms Related to Spherical Mirrors are Given Below

(i) **Centre of Curvature** (C) It is the centre of the sphere of which the mirror is a part.

(ii) **Radius of Curvature** (R) The radius of the hollow sphere of which the mirror is a part is called radius of curvature.

(iii) **Pole** (P) The central point of the spherical mirror is called its pole (P).

(iv) **Focus** (F) When a parallel beam of light rays is incident on a spherical mirror, then after reflection it meets or appears to meet at a point on principal axis which is called focus of the spherical mirror.

(v) **Focal Length** (f) The distance between the pole and focus is called focal length (f).

Relation between focal length and radius of curvature is given by

$$f = \frac{R}{2}$$

The power of a mirror is given as $P = \frac{1}{f}$ (metre)

(vi) **Mirror formula** $$\frac{1}{f} = \frac{1}{v} + \frac{1}{u}$$

where, f = focal length of the mirror, u = distance of the object and v = distance of the image.

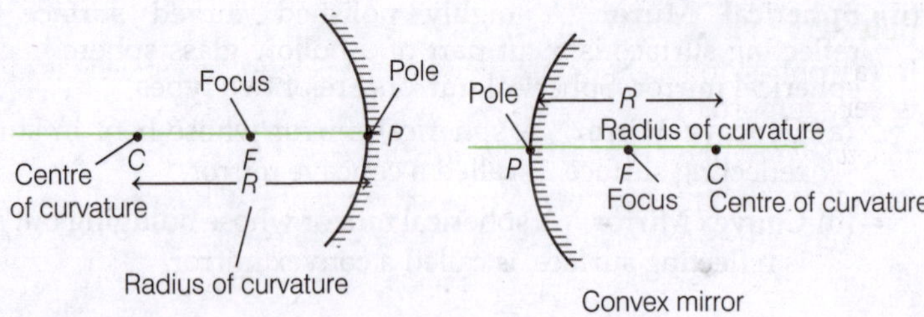

Newton's formula for a concave mirror,

$$f = \sqrt{x_1 x_2} \Rightarrow f^2 = x_1 x_2$$

where, x_1 and x_2 are the distances of object and image from the focus.

Linear Magnification

The ratio of height of image (I) formed by a mirror to the height of the object (O) is called linear magnification (m).

Linear magnification $(m) = \dfrac{I}{O} = -\dfrac{v}{u}$

Areal and Axial Magnification

The ratio of area of image to the area of object is called areal magnification.

$$\text{Areal magnification} = m^2 = \frac{\text{Area of image}}{\text{Area of object}} = \frac{v^2}{u^2}$$

When a small sized object is placed linearly along the principle axis, then its longitudinal or axial magnification is given by

$$\text{Axial magnification} = -\frac{dv}{du} = \left(\frac{v}{u}\right)^2 = \left(\frac{f}{f-u}\right)^2 = \left(\frac{f-v}{f}\right)^2$$

Sign Convention for Spherical Mirrors

(i) All distances are measured from the pole of the mirror.

(ii) Distances measured in the direction of incident light rays are taken as positive.

(iii) Distances measured in opposite direction to the incident light rays are taken as negative.

(iv) Distances measured above the principal axis are positive.

(v) Distances measured below the principal axis are negative.

Value Points

The focal length of concave mirror is taken negative and for a convex mirror taken as positive.

Rules for Image Formation in Spherical Mirrors

In ray optics, to locate the image of an object, tracing of a ray as it reflects is very important.

Following four types of rays are used for image formation

Ray 1. A ray through the centre of curvature which strikes the mirror normally and is reflected back along the same path.

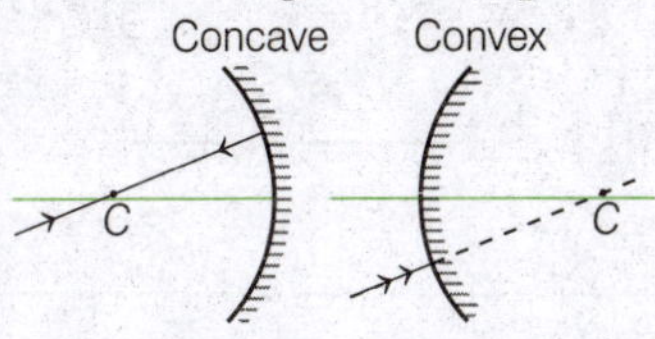

Ray 2. A ray parallel to principal axis after reflection either actually passes through the principal focus F or appears to diverge from it.

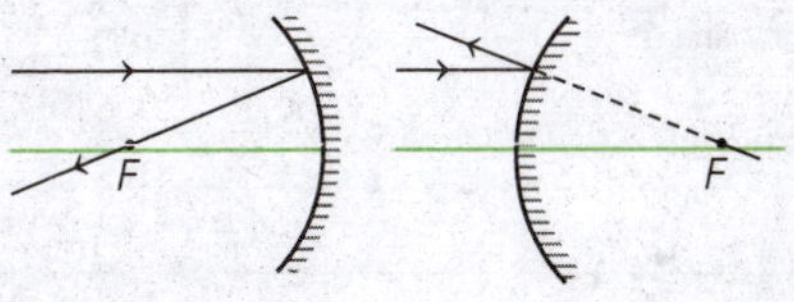

Ray 3. A ray passing through the principal focus F or a ray which appears to converge at F is reflected parallel to the principal axis.

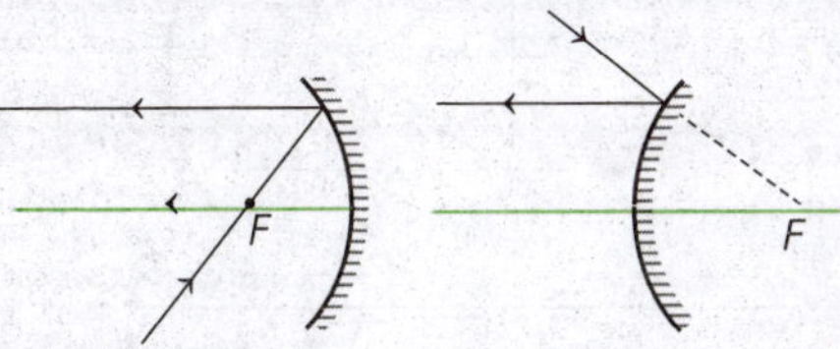

Ray 4. A ray striking at pole P is reflected symmetrically back in the opposite side.

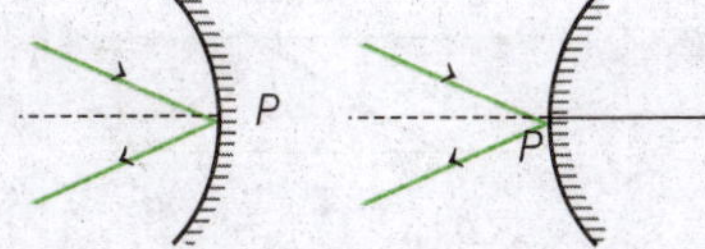

Image Formation by Spherical Mirrors

1. Image formation by concave mirror

In case of a concave mirror, the image is erect and virtual when the object is placed between F and P. In all other positions of object, the image is real and inverted as shown in the table given below.

Image Formation by Concave Mirror

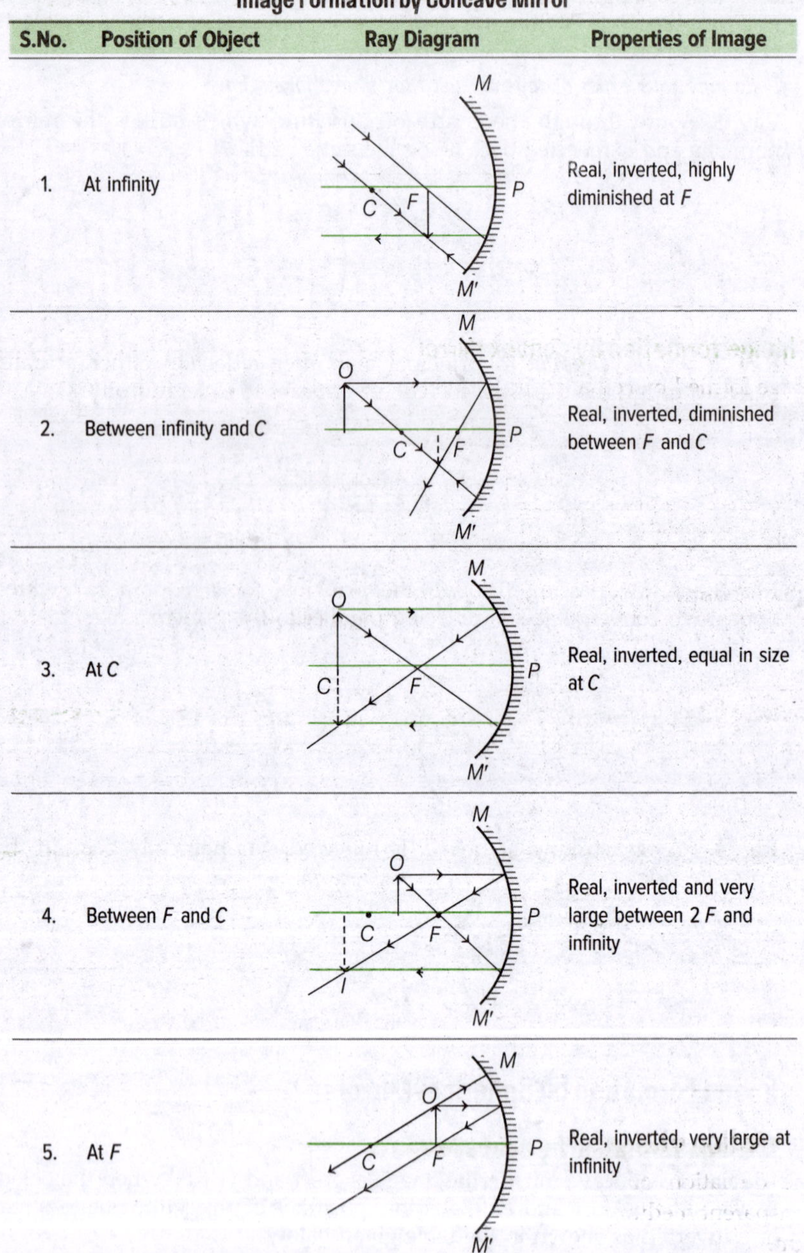

S.No.	Position of Object	Ray Diagram	Properties of Image
1.	At infinity		Real, inverted, highly diminished at *F*
2.	Between infinity and *C*		Real, inverted, diminished between *F* and *C*
3.	At *C*		Real, inverted, equal in size at *C*
4.	Between *F* and *C*		Real, inverted and very large between 2 *F* and infinity
5.	At *F*		Real, inverted, very large at infinity

S.No.	Position of Object	Ray Diagram	Properties of Image
6.	Between F and P	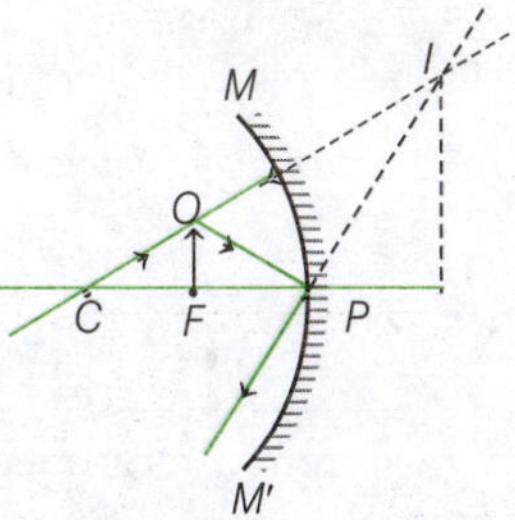 M, I, O, C, F, P, M′	Virtual, erect, large in size behind the mirror

2. Image formation by convex mirror

Image formed by convex mirror is always virtual, erect and diminished no matter where the object is. All the images formed by this mirror will be between pole and focus as shown in the table given below.

Image Formation by Convex Mirror

S.No.	Position of Object	Ray Diagram	Details of Image
1.	At infinity	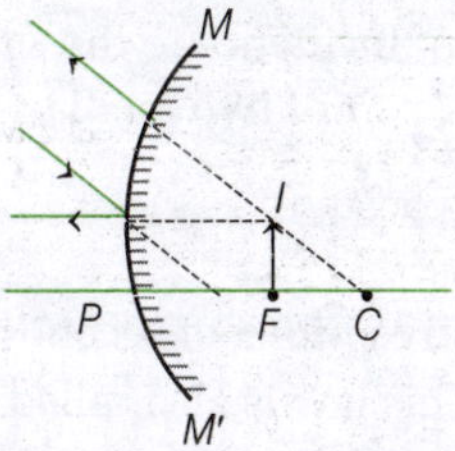 M, I, P, F, C, M′	Virtual, erect, very small in size at F, behind the mirror
2.	In front of mirror	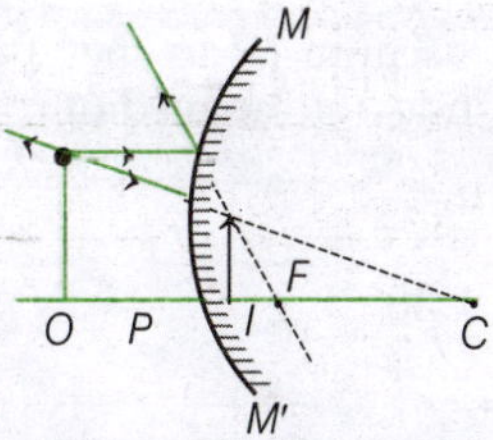 M, F, O, P, I, C, M′	Virtual, erect, diminished between P and F, behind the mirror

Refraction of Light

The deviation of light rays from its path when it travels from one transparent medium to another transparent medium is called refraction of light.

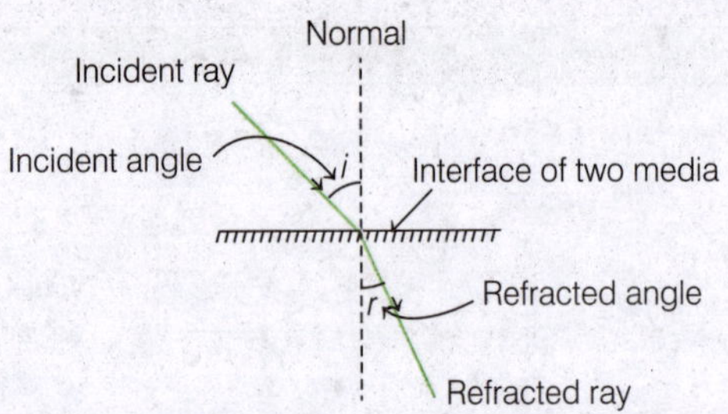

- When a ray of light goes from a rarer medium to a denser medium, it bends towards the normal.
- When a ray of light goes from a denser medium to a rarer medium, it bends away from the normal.

Cause of Refraction

The speed of light is different in different media.

Laws of Refraction

(i) The incident ray, the refracted ray and the normal at the point of incidence, all three lies in the same plane.

(ii) The ratio of sine of angle of incidence to the sine of angle of refraction is constant for a pair of two media,

i.e. $$\frac{\sin i}{\sin r} = \text{constant } ({}_1\mu_2)$$

where ${}_1\mu_2$ is called **refractive index** of second medium with respect to first medium. This law is also called **Snell's law.**

Refractive Index

The ratio of speed of light in vacuum (c) to the speed of light in any medium (v) is called refractive index of the medium.

Refractive index of a medium, $\mu = \frac{c}{v}$

Refractive index of water $= \frac{4}{3} = 1.33$

Refractive index of glass $= \frac{3}{2} = 1.50$

When light is reflected by a denser medium, phase difference of π radian or path difference of $\frac{\lambda}{2}$ or time difference $\frac{T}{2}$ is produced. This is known as Stoke's law. Distance x travelled by light in a medium of refractive index μ is equal to distance (μx) travelled in vacuum.

Time taken by light to transverse a thickness $x = \frac{\mu x}{c}$
where c = velocity of light in vacuum.

Relative Refractive Index

The refractive index of second medium with respect to first medium

$$_1\mu_2 = \frac{v_1}{v_2}$$

where, v_1 is the speed of light in medium 1 and v_2 is the speed of light in medium 2.

Competition Insight

Cauchy's Formula

Refractive index of a medium, $\mu = A + \frac{B}{\lambda^2} + \frac{C}{\lambda^4} + ...$

where, λ = wavelength of light and A, B, C ..... are constants.

$\therefore$ Refractive index, $\mu \propto \frac{1}{\lambda^2}$

Refraction through a Glass Slab

When a glass slab is placed in the path of a light ray it produces a shift in the position of object when viewed through it, which is $= \left(1 - \frac{1}{n}\right)t$.

When object is in denser medium and seen from rarer medium normally through the plane surface, then apparent depth of object $= \left(\frac{1}{n}\right) \times$ actual depth of object in denser medium.

Critical Angle

The angle of incidence in a denser medium for which the angle of refraction in rarer medium becomes 90° is called critical angle (C).

Critical angle for diamond = 24°

Critical angle for glass = 42°

Critical angle for water = 48°

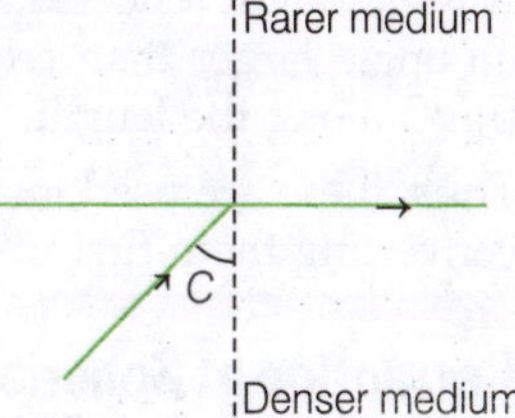

Refractive index of denser medium,

$$\mu = \frac{1}{\sin C}$$

Critical angle increases with temperature.

The refractive index is maximum for violet colour of light and minimum for red colour of light, *i.e.* $\mu_V > \mu_R$, therefore critical angle is maximum for red colour of light and minimum for violet colour of light, *i.e.* $C_V < C_R$.

Total Internal Reflection (TIR)

When a light ray travelling from a denser medium towards a rarer medium and it incident at the interface at an angle of incidence greater than critical angle, then light rays are totally reflected back in to the denser medium. This phenomena is called TIR.

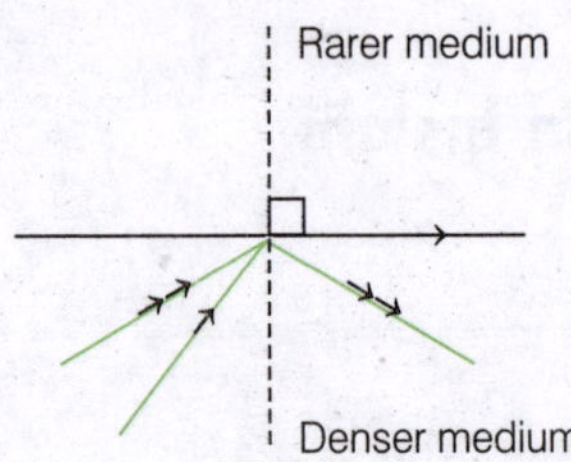

For total internal reflection to take place following set of conditions must be obeyed

(i) The ray must travel from denser medium to rarer medium.

(ii) The angle of incidence ($\angle i$) must be greater than critical angle ($\angle C$).

Mirage is an optical illusion observed in deserts and roads on a hot day which is an application of TIR.

Optical Fibres

Optical fibres are also based on the phenomenon of total internal reflection. Optical fibres consist of several thousands of very long fine quality fibres of glass or quartz.

The diameter of each fibre is of the order of 10^{-4} cm with refractive index of material being of the order of 1.5. These fibres are fabricated in such a way that light reflected at one side of the inner surface strikes the other at an angle larger than critical angle. Even, if fibre is bent, light can easily travel along the length.

Thus, these are used in transmission and reception of electrical signals by converting them first into light signals.

Refraction at Spherical surfaces

When two transparent media are separated by a spherical surface, light incident on the surface from one side get refracted into the medium on the other side.

Spherical surfaces are of two types as shown in figure.

Spherical surface (i) convex (ii) concave

For both surfaces refraction formula is given by

$$\frac{\mu_2}{v} - \frac{\mu_1}{u} = \frac{\mu_2 - \mu_1}{R}$$

or

$$\frac{\mu}{v} - \frac{1}{u} = \frac{(\mu - 1)}{R}$$

$$\mu_1 = 1 \text{ (for air)}$$

$$\mu_2 = \mu \text{ (for medium)}$$

where, μ = refractive index, u = distance of object, v = distance of image and R = radius of curvature of the spherical surface.

Lens

A lens is a uniform transparent medium bounded between two spherical or one spherical and one plane surface.

Convex Lens

A lens which is thinner at edges and thicker at middle is called a convex or converging lens.

Convex Lens

Concave Lens

A lens which is thicker at edges and thinner at middle is called a concave or diverging lens.

Concave Lens

Some definitions related to lenses

(i) **Optical centre** The optical centre is a point within or outside the lens, at which incident rays refract without deviation in its path.

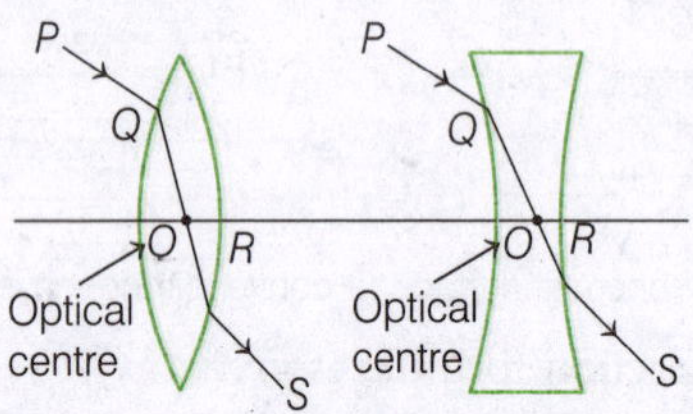

(ii) **Centre of curvature** The centres of the two imaginary spheres of which the lens is a part are called centres of curvature of the lens. A lens has two centres of curvature with respect to its two curved surfaces.

(iii) **Radii of curvature** The radii of the two imaginary spheres of which the lens is a part are called radii of curvature of the lens. A lens has two radii of curvature. These may or may not be equal.

(iv) **Principal axis** The straight line passing through the optical centre and centre of curvature of lens is called principal axis of lens.

(v) **Principal focus** Lens has two principal focus

(a) **First principal focus** It is a point on the principal axis of lens, the rays starting from which (convex lens) or appear to converge at which (concave lens) become parallel to principal axis after refraction.

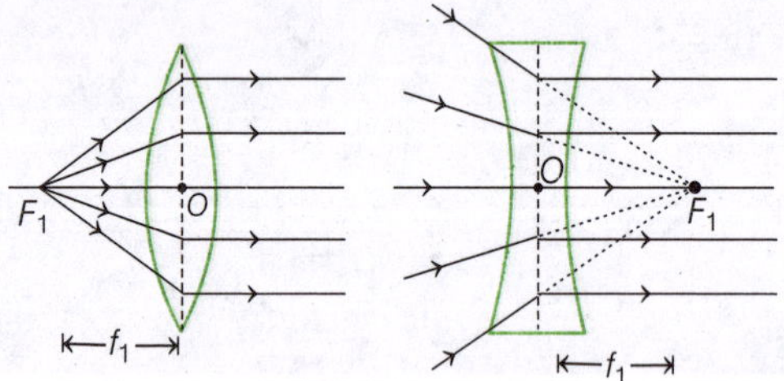

First principal focus

(b) **Second principal focus** It is the point on the principal axis at which the rays coming parallel to the principal axis converge (convex lens) or appear to diverge (concave lens) after refraction from the lens.

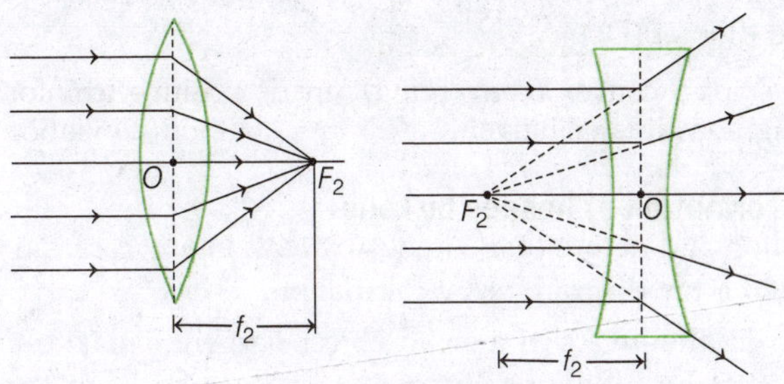

Second principal focus

Both the focuses of convex lens are real, while that of concave lens are virtual.

(vi) **Focal length** The distance between focus and optical centre of lens is called focal length of lens.

(vii) **Aperture** The effective diameter of circular boundary of the lens is called aperture.

Cartesian sign convention for spherical lenses

(i) The principal axis of the spherical surface is taken as X-axis and the optical centre as origin. Here, the principal axis is the diameter extended.

(ii) The direction of the incident light is taken as the positive direction of X-axis and opposite to it is taken as negative.

(iii) The upward direction is taken as positive and the downward direction as negative.

Lens Formula

$$\frac{1}{f} = \frac{1}{v} - \frac{1}{u}$$

where, f = focal length of the lens, u = distance of object and v = distance of image.

Lens Maker's formula, $\frac{1}{f} = (\mu - 1)\left(\frac{1}{R_1} - \frac{1}{R_2}\right)$

where, μ = refractive index of the material of the lens and R_1 and R_2 are radii of curvature of the lens.

Power of a Lens

The reciprocal of the focal length of a lens, when it is measured in metre is called power of a lens.

$$\text{Power of a lens, } (P) = \frac{1}{f\ (\text{metre})}$$

Its unit is diopter (D).

The power of a convex (converging) lens is positive and for a concave (diverging) lens it is negative.

Laws of Formation of Images by Lens

The position and nature of the image by lens, in any case can be obtained either from a ray diagram or by calculation.

To construct the image of a small object perpendicular to the axis of a lens, two of the following three rays are drawn from the top of the object.

(i) A ray parallel to the principal axis after refraction passes through the principal focus or appears to diverge from it.

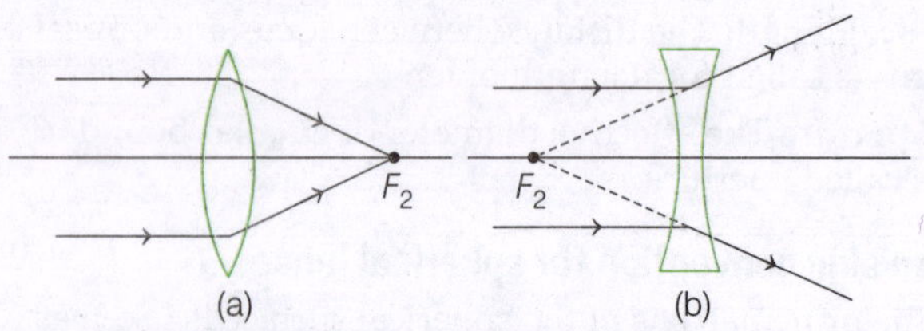

Path of incident ray parallel to principal axis for (a) convex lens (b) concave lens

(ii) A ray through, the optical centre P passes undeviated because the middle of the lens acts like a thin parallel-sided slab.

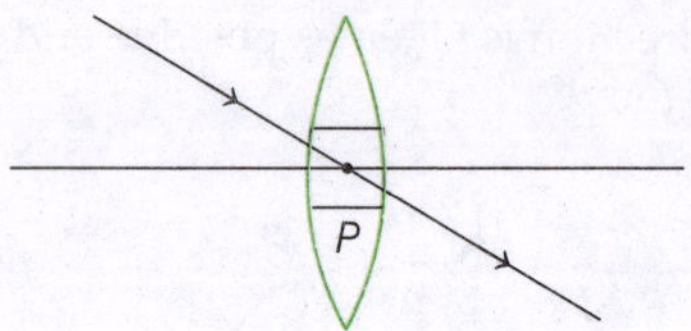

Path of incident ray passing through centre for convex lens

(iii) A ray passing through, the first focus F_1 become parallel to the principal axis after refraction.

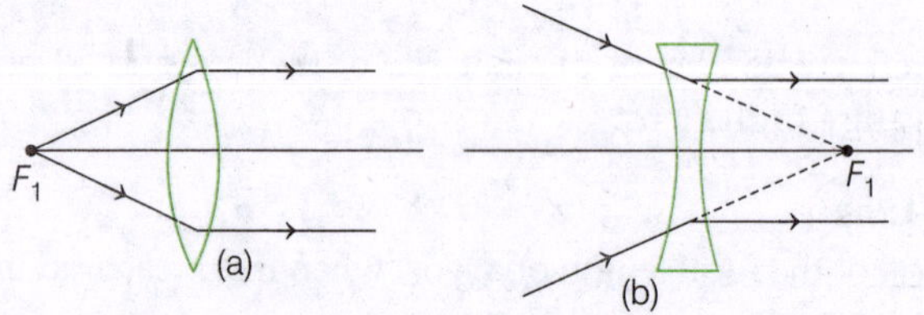

Path incident ray passing through the focus for (a) convex lens (b) concave lens

Image Formation by Lens

1. Image Formation by Convex lens

The image formed by convex lens depends on the position of object. Formation of image by convex lens for different positions of object is shown in the table given below.

Formation of Image by Convex Lenses

S.No.	Position of Object	Ray Diagram	Position of Image	Nature and Size of Image
1.	At infinity	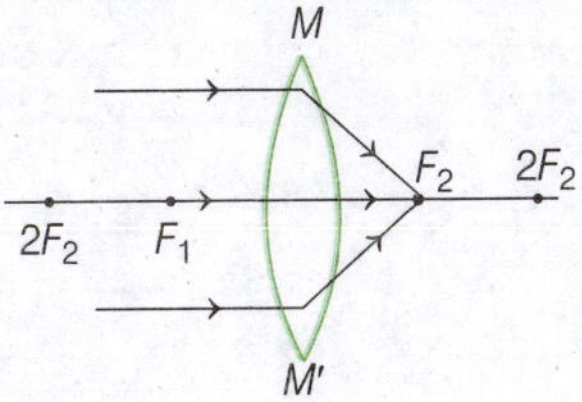	At the principal focus (F_2) or in the focal plane	Real, inverted and extremely diminished
2.	Beyond $2F_1$	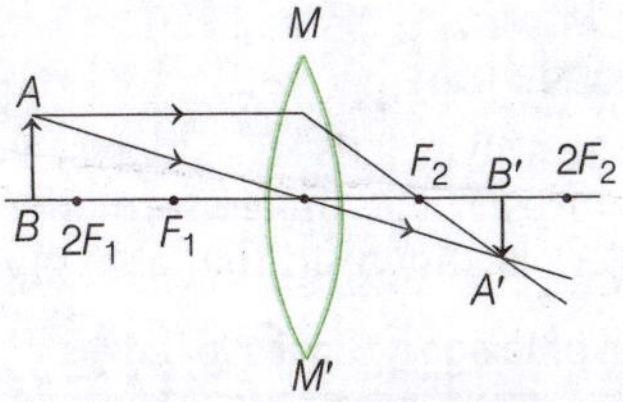	Between F_2 and $2F_2$	Real, inverted and diminished
3.	At $2F_1$	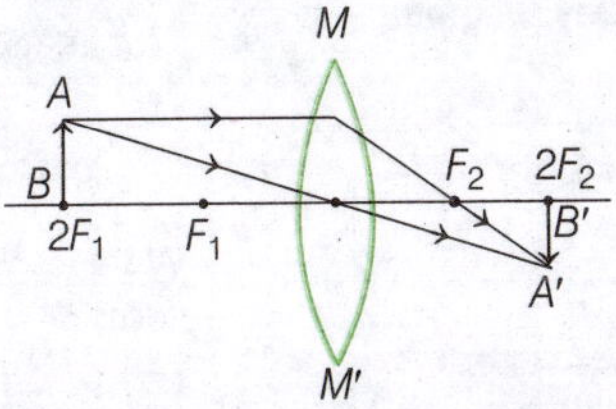	At $2F_2$	Real, inverted and of same size as the object
4.	Between F_1 and $2F_1$	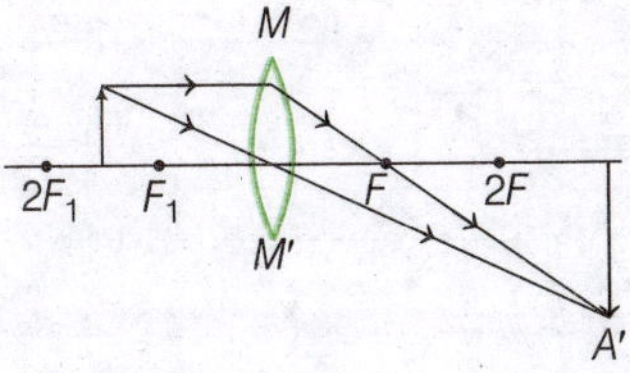	Beyond $2F_2$	Real, inverted and highly magnified

S.No.	Position of Object	Ray Diagram	Position of Image	Nature and Size of Image
5.	At F_1	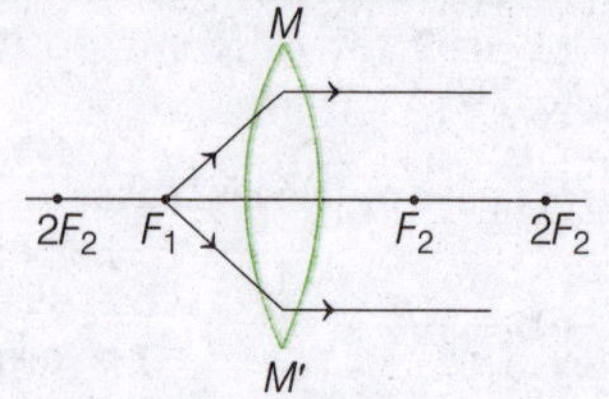	At infinity	Real, inverted and highly magnified
6.	Between F_1 and optical centre	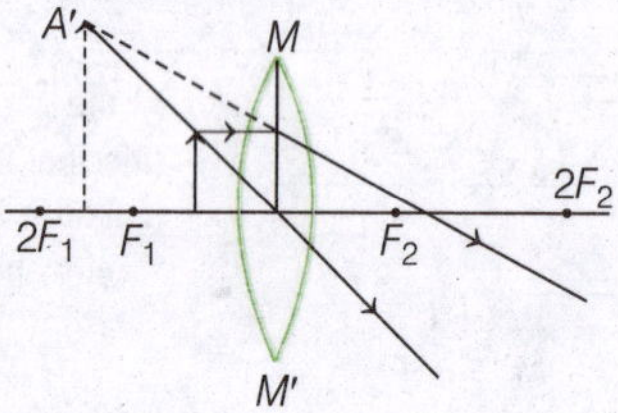	On the same side as the object	Virtual, erect and magnified

2. Image Formation by Concave lens

The image formed by a concave lens is always virtual, erect and diminished (like a convex mirror). The image formation by concave lens for different positions of object is shown in the table given below.

Formation of Image by Concave Lenses

S. No.	Position of Object	Ray Diagram	Position of Image	Nature and Size of Image
1.	At infinity	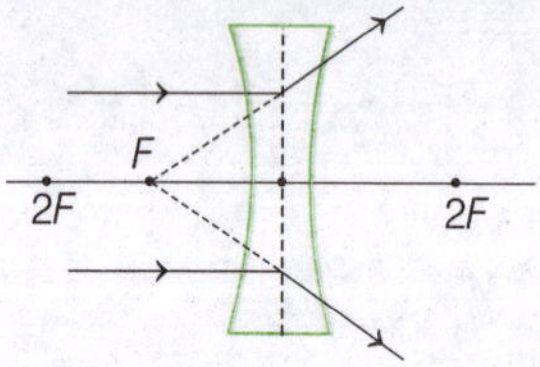	At the focus F	Virtual erect and point size
2.	Anywhere except on the principal axis	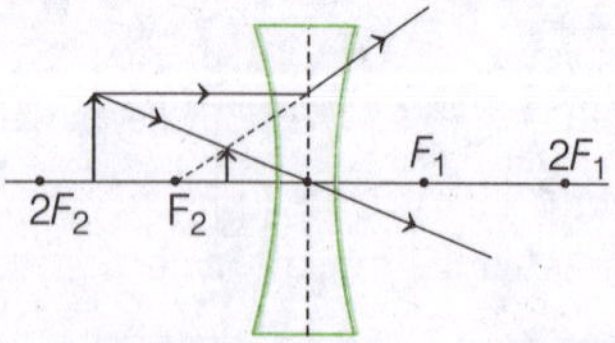	Between the lens and F_2	Virtual, erect, diminished

Focal Length of a Lens Combination

(i) When lenses are in contact

$$\frac{1}{F} = \frac{1}{f_1} + \frac{1}{f_2}$$

Power of the combination, $P = P_1 + P_2$

(ii) When lenses are separated by a distance d

$$\frac{1}{F} = \frac{1}{f_1} + \frac{1}{f_2} - \frac{d}{f_1 f_2}$$

Power of the combination, $P = P_1 + P_2 - dP_1P_2$

Linear and Axial Magnification

Linear magnification, $m = \frac{I}{O} = \frac{v}{u} = \frac{f}{(u+f)}$

For a small sized object placed linearly along the principal axis, its axial (longitudinal) magnification is given by

$$\text{Axial magnification} = \frac{dv}{du} = \left(\frac{v}{u}\right)^2$$

$$= \left(\frac{f}{f+u}\right)^2 = \left(\frac{f-u}{f}\right)^2$$

Focal Length of a Convex Lens by Displacement Method

Focal length of the convex lens

$$f = \frac{a^2 - d^2}{4a}$$

where, a = distance between the image pin and object pin

and d = distance between two positions of lens.

The distance between the two pins should be greater than four times the focal length of the convex lens, *i.e.* $a > 4f$.

Height of the object, $O = \sqrt{I_1 I_2}$.

Cutting of a Lens

(i) If a symmetrical convex lens of focal length f is cut into two parts along its optic axis, then focal length of each part (a plano-convex lens) is $2f$.

However, if the two parts are joined as shown in figure, the focal length of combination is again f.

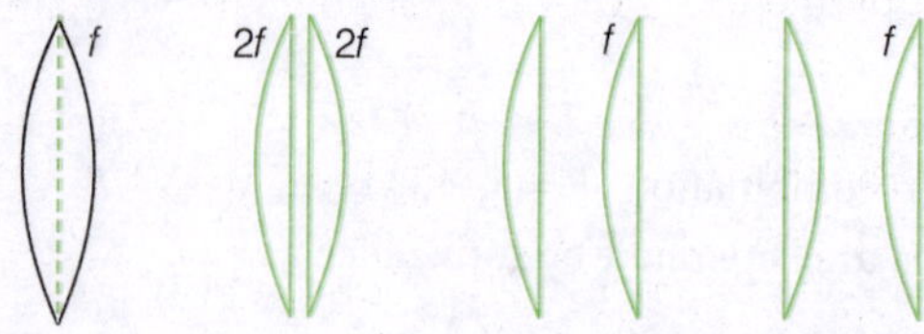

(ii) If a symmetrical convex lens of focal length f is cut into two parts along the principal axis, then focal length of each part remains unchanged as f. If these two parts are joined with curved ends on one side, focal length of the combination is $\frac{f}{2}$. But on joining two parts in opposite sense, the net focal length becomes ∞.

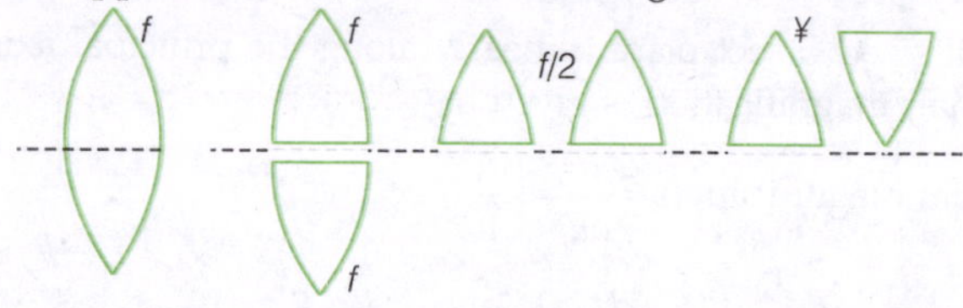

Knowledge Booster

Combination of Lenses and Mirrors

(i) When several lenses or mirrors are combined coaxially, image by first serves as an object for second and so on. The net magnification is given by $m = m_1 \times m_2 \times m_3 \times \ldots$

Direction of incident rays is reversed after every reflection.

(ii) In some cases, object and image are formed at same place after interacting the (lens + mirror) combination. For this, after refraction from lens, rays must retrace their path *i.e.*, must be incident normally on the mirror after refraction from the lens. In other word, we can say that image by lens should be formed at centre of curvature (C) of mirror as shown in figure.

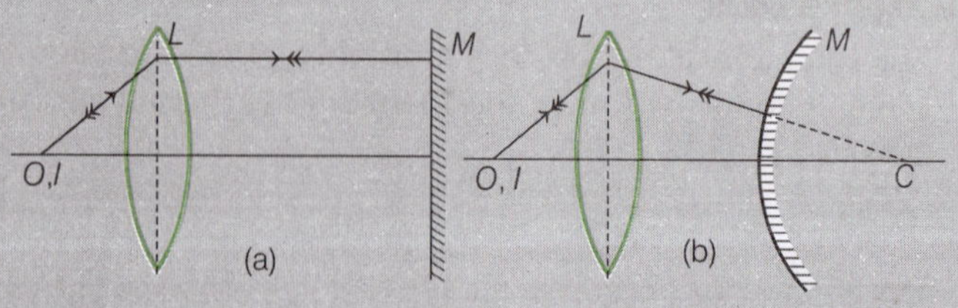

Aberration of Lenses

The image formed by the lens suffer from following two main drawbacks

(i) **Spherical Aberration** Aberration of the lens due to which all the rays passes through the lens are not focussed at a single point and the image of a point object placed on the axis is blurred. This defect is called spherical aberration. It can be reduced by using
(a) lens of large focal lengths (b) plano-convex lenses
(c) crossed lenses
(d) combining convex and concave lens

(ii) **Chromatic Aberration** Image of a white object formed by lens is usually coloured and blurred. This defect of the image produced by lens is called chromatic aberration.

Prism

Prism is uniform transparent medium bounded between two refracting surfaces inclined at an angle.

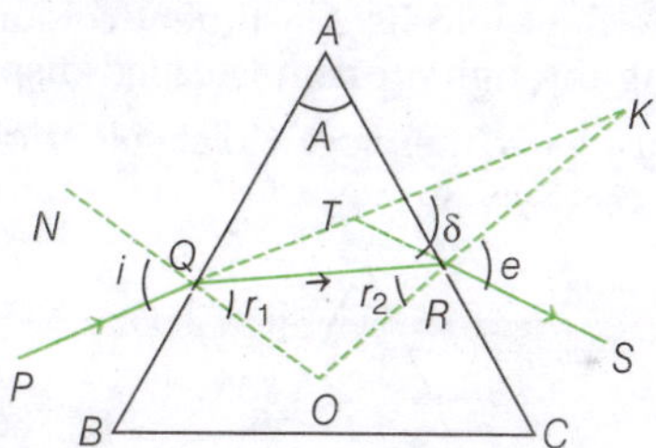

Angle of Deviation

The angle subtended between the direction of incident light ray and emergent light ray from a prism is called angle of deviation (δ).

The angle of emergence of the ray from the second face equals the angle of incidence of the ray on the first face, then deviation produced is minimum.

Value Points

For a prism
- $\sin i = \mu \sin r_1$
- $\mu \sin r_2 = \sin e$
  $r_1 + r_2 = A$
- Angle of deviation, $\delta = i + e - A$

Prism Formula

The refractive index of material of prism, $\mu = \dfrac{\sin\left(\dfrac{A+\delta_m}{2}\right)}{\sin\left(\dfrac{A}{2}\right)}$

where, A = prism angle and δ_m = minimum angle of deviation.

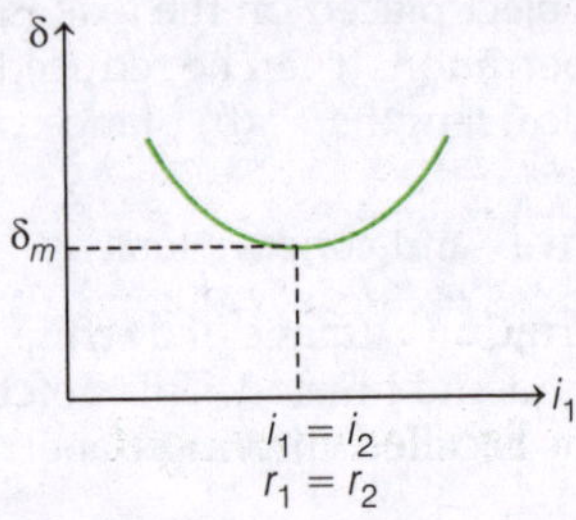

For very small angle prism, $\delta_m = (\mu - 1)A$

Dispersion of Light

The splitting of white light into its constituent colours in the sequence of VIBGYOR, on passing through a prism is called dispersion of light.

The refractive index $\mu_V > \mu_R$, therefore violet colour deviates most and red colour deviates least, *i.e.* $\delta_V > \delta_R$.

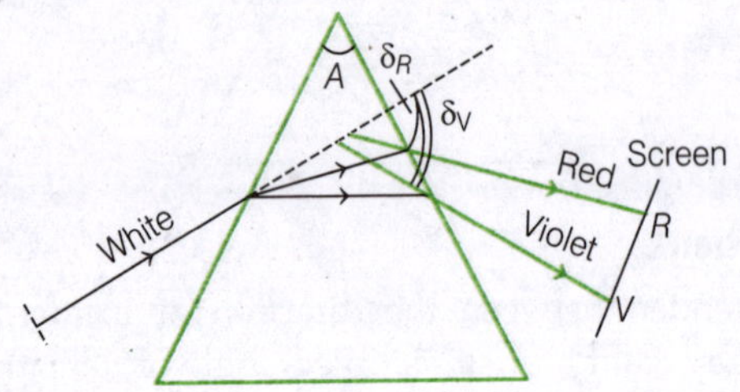

Angular Dispersion

The angle subtended between the direction of emergent violet and red rays of light from a prism is called angular dispersion.

$$\text{Angular dispersion } (\theta) = \delta_V - \delta_R = (\mu_V - \mu_R)A$$

where, δ_V and δ_R are angle of deviation.

$$w = \frac{\theta}{\delta_Y} = \frac{(\mu_V - \mu_R)}{(\mu_Y - 1)}$$

where, $\mu_Y = \dfrac{\mu_V + \mu_R}{2}$ is mean refractive index.

Competition Insight

Scattering of Light

When light passes through a medium in which particles are suspended whose size is of the order of wavelength of light, then light on striking these particles, deviated in different directions. These phenomena is called scattering of light.

According to the Lord Rayleigh, the intensity of scattered light $I \propto \frac{1}{\lambda^4}$

Therefore, red colour of light is scattered least and violet colour of light is scattered most.

Daily Life Examples of Scattering of Light

(i) Blue colour of sky.

(ii) Red colour of signals of danger.

(iii) Black colour of sky in the absence of atmosphere.

(iv) Red colour of sky at the time of sun rise and sun set.

(v) The human eye is most sensitive to yellow colour.

Human Eye

Human eye is an optical instrument which forms real image of the objects on retina.

A human eye has the following main parts

- **Cornea** It is the transparent spherical membrane covering the front of the eye. Light enters the eye through this membrane.
- **Crystalline lens** The eye lens is a convex lens made of a transparent, soft and flexible material like a jelly made of proteins.
- **Iris** It is a dark muscular diaphragm between the **cornea** and the **lens.** It controls the size of the **pupil.**
- **Pupil** It is a small hole between the **iris** through which light enters the eye.
- **Ciliary muscles** They hold the lens in position and help in modifying the curvature of the lens.
- **Retina** It is the light sensitive surface of eye on which the image is formed. It contains light sensitive cells **rods** and **cones.**
- **Optic nerve** It transmits visual information from the **retina** to the **brain.**
- **Sclera** It is an opaque, fibrous, protective, outer layer of an eye containing **collagen** and **elastic fibre.** It is also known as **white part of the eye.**

- **Blind spot** It is the point at which the optic nerve leaves the eye. It contains no rods and cones, so an image formed at this point is not sent to the brain.

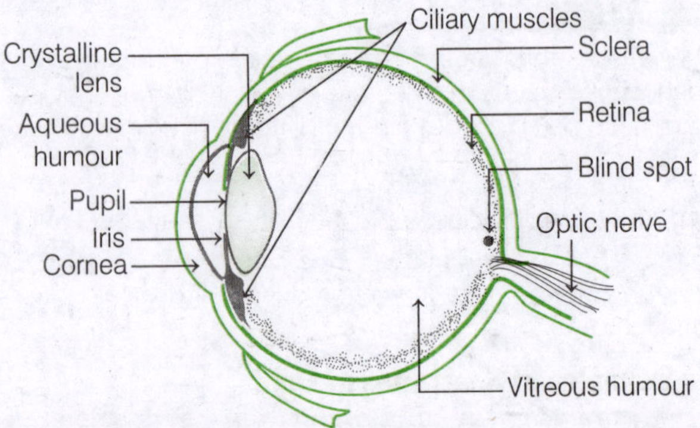

- **Aqueous humour** Behind the cornea, we have a space filled with a transparent liquid called the aqueous humour.
- **Vitreous humour** The space between eye lens and retina is filled with another liquid called vitreous humour.
- **Accommodation of eye** It is the ability of eye lens, to change its focal length to form sharp images of objects at different positions from the eye on the retina of the eye.
- **Range of vision** It is the distance between near point and the far point of an eye. For normal eye, the range of vision is 25 cm to infinity.
- **Near point** It is the nearest position of an object from human eye, so that its sharp images is formed on the retina.

Different defects of vision of human eye are described below

(i) **Myopia or Short-Sightedness** It is a defect of eye due to which a person can see near by objects clearly but cannot see far away objects clearly.

In this defect, the far point of eye shifts from infinity to a nearer distance.

This defect can be removed by using a concave lens of appropriate power.

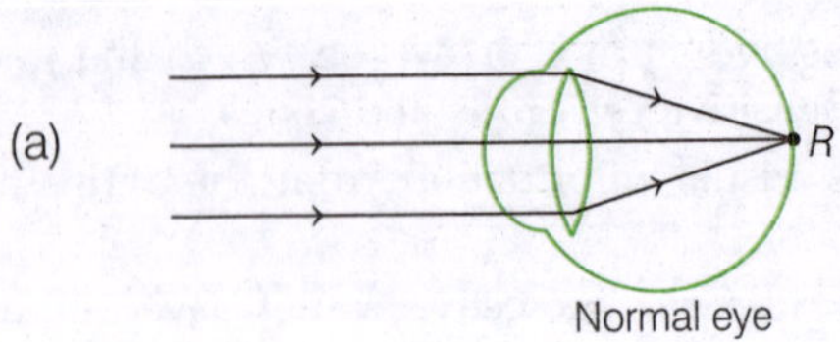

Normal eye

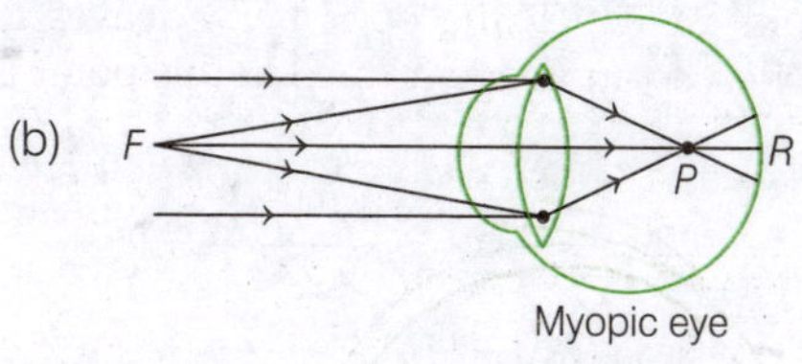

Myopic eye

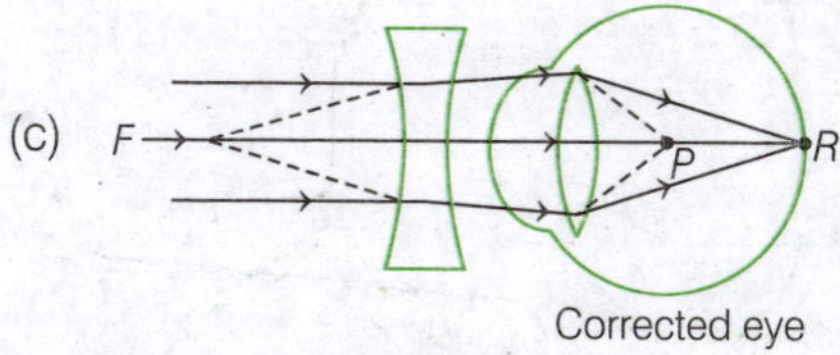

Corrected eye

(ii) **Hypermetropia or Long-Sightedness** In this defect, a person can see far away objects clearly but cannot see near by objects clearly.

In this defect, the near point of eye shifts away from the eye.

This defect can be removed by using a convex lens of appropriate power.

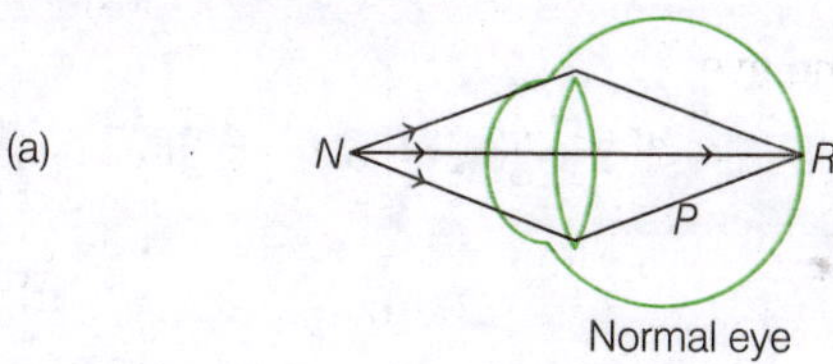

Normal eye

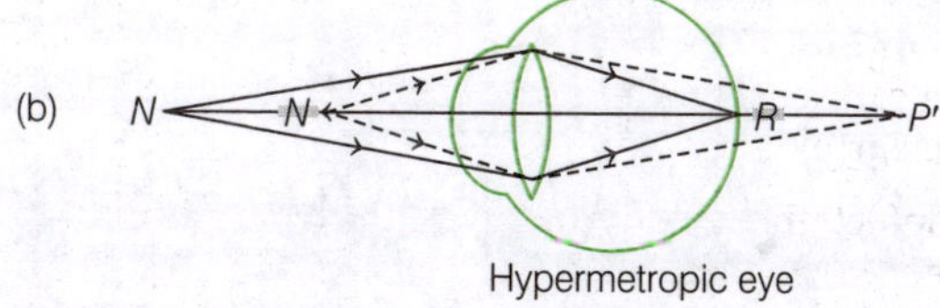

Hypermetropic eye

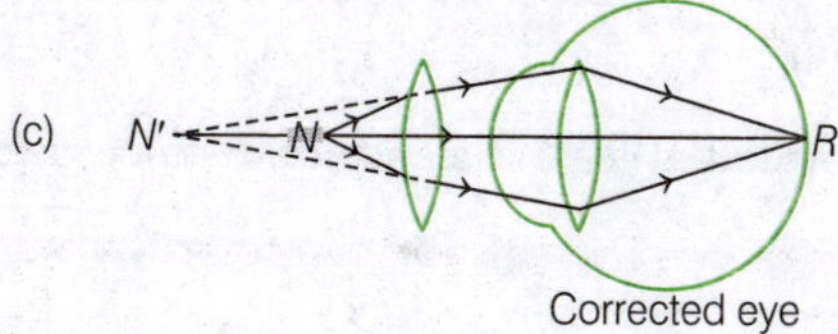

Corrected eye

Competition Insight

- **Astigmatism** In this defect, a person cannot focus on horizontal and vertical lines at the same distance at the same time.

This defect can be removed by using suitable cylindrical lenses.

- **Colour Blindness** In this defect, a person is unable to distinguish between few colours. The reason of this defect is the absence of cone cells sensitive for few colours.
- **Cataract** In this defect, an opaque white membrane is developed on cornea due to which person losts power of vision partially or completely. This defect can be removed by removing this membrane through surgery.

Simple Microscope

It is used for observing magnified images of objects. It consists of a converging lens of small focal length.

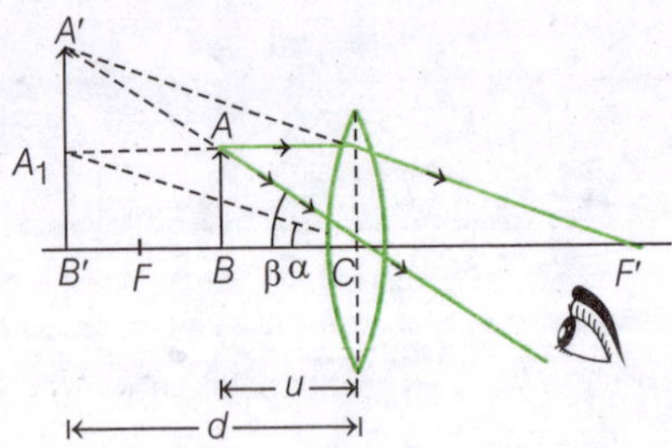

Magnifying Power

(i) When final image is formed at least distance of distinct vision (D), then $M = 1 + \frac{D}{f}$

where, f = focal length of the lens.

(ii) When final image is formed at infinity, then $M = \frac{D}{f}$.

Compound Microscope

It is a combination of two convex lenses called objective lens and eye piece separated by a distance. Both lenses are of small focal lengths but $f_o < f_e$, where f_o and f_e are focal lengths of objective lens and eye piece respectively.

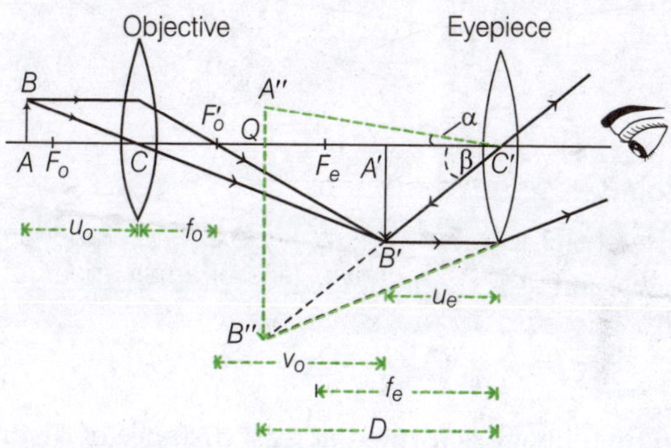

Magnifying Power

(i) When final image is formed at least distance of distinct vision (D), then

$$M = \frac{v_o}{u_o}\left(1 + \frac{D}{f_e}\right)$$

where, v_o = distance of image formed by objective lens

and u_o = distance of object from the objective.

(ii) When final image is formed at infinity, then, $M = \frac{v_o}{u_o} \cdot \frac{D}{f_e}$

Astronomical Telescope

It is also a combination of two lenses called objective lens and eyepiece, separated by a distance.

It is used for observing distinct images of heavenly bodies like stars, planets etc.

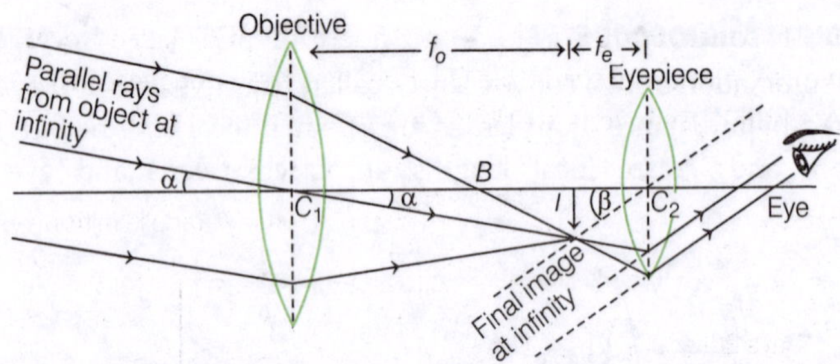

Value Points

Objective lens is a convex lens of large aperture and large focal length while eyepiece is a convex lens of small aperture and small focal length.

Magnifying Power

(i) When final image is formed at least distance of distinct vision (D), then $M = \frac{f_o}{f_e}\left(1 + \frac{D}{f_e}\right)$, where f_o and f_e are focal lengths of objective and eyepiece respectively.

Length of the telescope $(L) = (f_o + u_e)$

where, u_e = distance of object from the eyepiece.

(ii) When final image is formed at infinity, then $M = \frac{f_o}{f_e}$.

Length of the telescope, $(L) = f_o + f_e$

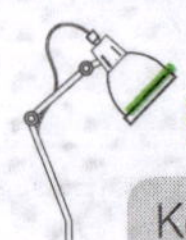

EXPERT Scale Up

Keep these caution points in mind while solving the question

- For large magnifying power of a telescope f_o should be large and f_e should be small.
- For large magnifying power of a microscope $f_o < f_e$ but f_e should be small.

Reflecting Telescope

Reflecting telescope are based upon the same principle except that the formation of images takes place by reflection instead of by refraction. It consists of concave mirror of large aperture and large focal length (objective). A plane mirror is placed between the concave mirror and its focus. A small convex lens works as eye-piece.

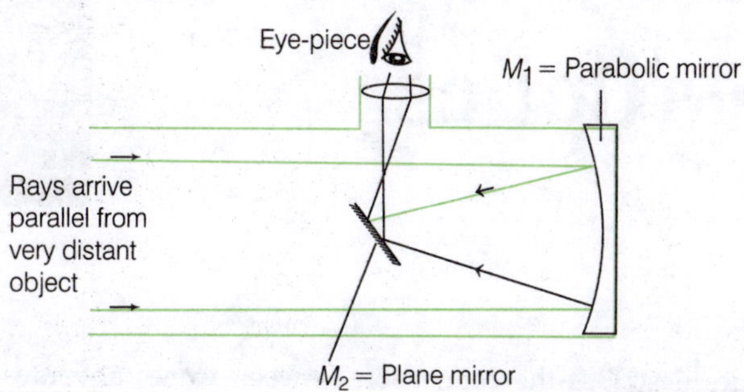

If f_o is focal length of the concave spherical mirror and f_e the focal length of the eye-piece, the magnifying power of the reflecting telescope is given by

$$m = \frac{f_o}{f_e}$$

Competition Insight

Resolving Power

The ability of an optical instrument to produce separate and clear images of two nearby objects is called its resolving power.

Limit of Resolution

The minimum distance between two nearby objects which can be just resolved by the instrument is called its limit of resolution (d).

Resolving power of a microscope $= \frac{1}{d} = \frac{2\mu \sin\theta}{\lambda}$.

where, d = limit of resolution, λ = wavelength of light used,

μ = refractive index of the medium between the objects and objective lens

and θ = half of the cone angle.

Resolving power of a telescope $= \frac{1}{d\theta} = \frac{d}{1.22\,\lambda}$

where, $d\theta$ = limit of resolution, λ = wavelength of light used

and d = diameter of aperture of objective.

Chapter 28

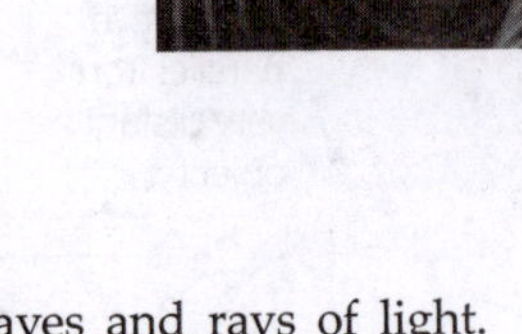

Wave Optics

Wave optics describes the connection between waves and rays of light. According to wave theory of light, the light is a form of energy which travels through a medium in the form of transverse wave motion. The speed of light in a medium depends upon the nature of medium.

Newtons' Corpuscular Theory of Light

Light consists of very small invisible elastic particles called corpuscles, which travel in vacuum with a speed of 3×10^8 m/s.

The size of corpuscular of different colours of light are different.

The theory could explain reflection and refraction.

But it could not explain interference, diffraction, polarisation, photoelectric effect and Compton effect.

The theory failed as it could not explain why light travels faster in a rarer medium than in a denser medium.

Huygens' Wave Theory of Light

Light travel in the form of waves. These waves travel in all direction with the velocity of light.

The waves of light of different colours have different wavelengths.

Huygens' theory could explain reflection, refraction interference, diffraction, polarisation but could not explain photoelectric effect and compton's effect.

Wave theory introduced the concept of wavefront.

Wavefront

A wavefront is defined as the continuous locus of all the particles of a medium, which are vibrating in the same phase.

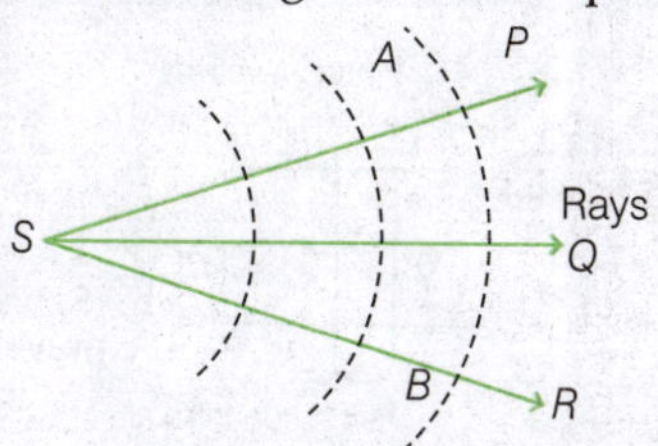

S = source of light, AB = wavefront and SP, SQ and SR are rays of light.

These are of three types

(i) Spherical Wavefront When source of light is a point source, the wavefront is spherical. Amplitude (A) is inversely proportional to distance (x) i.e. $A \propto \frac{1}{x}$.

$\therefore$ Intensity (I) $\propto$ (Amplitude)^2

(ii) Cylindrical Wavefront When source of light is linear in shape, the wavefront is cylindrical.

Amplitude (A) $\propto \frac{1}{\sqrt{x}}$ $\quad \therefore$ Intensity $\propto$ (Amplitude)$^2 \propto \frac{1}{x}$

(iii) Plane Wavefront When the source of light is very far off, the wavefront is plane.

Amplitude (A) $\propto x^0$, Intensity (I) $\propto x^0$

Shape of Wavefront of Reflected and Refracted Wave

The shapes of wavefronts associated with reflected as well as refracted waves.

(i) Shapes of wavefronts before and after reflection from a plane and curved mirrors are as shown below.

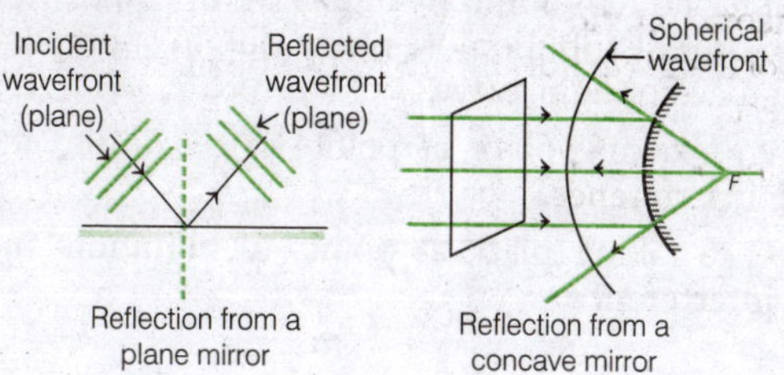

Reflection from a plane mirror

Reflection from a concave mirror

(ii) Shapes of wavefronts before and after refraction from a plane and curved surfaces are as shown below.

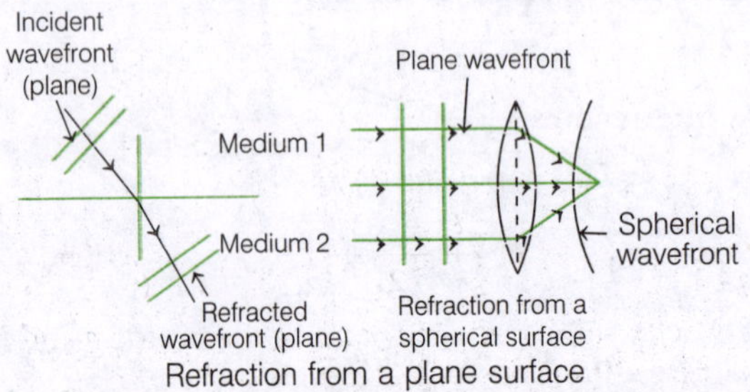

Refraction from a plane surface

Huygens' Principle

(i) Every point on given wavefront (called primary wavefront) acts as a fresh source of new disturbance called secondary wavelets.

(ii) The secondary wavelets travels in all the directions with the speed of light in the medium.

(iii) A surface touching these secondary wavelets tangentially in the forward direction at any instant gives the new (secondary) wavefront that instant.

Superposition of Waves

When two similar waves propagate in a medium simultaneously, then at any point the resultant displacement is equal to the vector sum of displacement produced by individual waves.

$$\mathbf{y} = \mathbf{y}_1 + \mathbf{y}_2$$

Interference of Light

When two light waves of similar frequency having a zero or constant phase difference propagate in a medium simultaneously in the same direction, then due to their superposition maximum intensity is obtained at few points and minimum intensity at other few points. This phenomenon of redistribution of energy due to superposition of waves is called interference of light waves.

The interference taking place at points of maximum intensity is called **constructive interference.**

The interference taking place at points of minimum intensity is called **destructive interference.**

Conditions for Constructive and Destructive Interference

For Constructive Interference

Phase difference, $\phi = 2n\pi$

Path difference, $\Delta x = n\lambda$ where, $n = 0, 1, 2, 3, \ldots$

For Destructive Interference

Phase difference, $\phi = (2n-1)\pi$

Path difference, $\Delta x = \dfrac{(2n-1)\lambda}{2}$ where, $n = 1, 2, 3, \ldots$

If two waves of exactly same frequency and of amplitude a and b interfere, then **amplitude of resultant wave** is given by

$$R = \sqrt{a^2 + b^2 + 2ab\cos\phi}$$

where, ϕ is the phase difference between two waves.

$$R_{max} = (a + b)$$

$$R_{min} = (a - b)$$

Intensity of wave,

$$\therefore \quad I = a^2 + b^2 + 2ab\cos\phi$$

$$= I_1 + I_2 + 2\sqrt{I_1 I_2}\cos\phi$$

where, I_1 and I_2 are intensities of two waves.

Coherent Sources of Light

The sources of light emitting light of same wavelength, same frequency having a zero or constant phase difference are called coherent sources of light.

Incoherent Sources

Two sources of light which do not emit light waves with a constant phase difference are called incoherent sources.

Young's Double Slit Experiment (YDSE)

In this experiment, two points of the same wavefront are used as two coherent sources. Intereference fringes obtained in Young's experiment consists of alternate bright and dark bands. All bright fringes have same intensity and all dark fringes are perfectly dark.

The arrangement of YDSE to produce interference is shown below

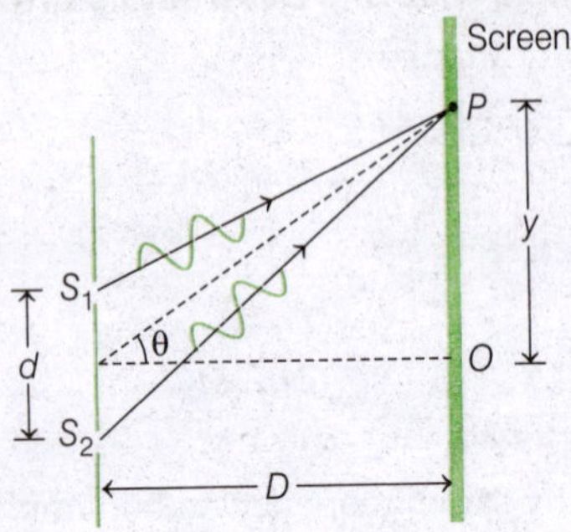

Position of bright fringe, $y_{\text{bright}} = \dfrac{n\lambda}{d} D$

Position of dark fringe, $y_{\text{dark}} = \dfrac{(2n-1)\lambda D}{2d}$

Fringe Width

The distance between the centres of two consecutive bright or dark fringes is called the fringe width, $\beta = \dfrac{\lambda D}{d}$

The angular fringe width is given by $\theta = \dfrac{\lambda}{d} = \dfrac{\beta}{d}$.

where, λ is the wavelength of light, d is the distance between two coherent sources.

Important Points Related with Fringe Width

As we know that fringe width (β) is the distance between two successive maxima or minima. It is given by

$$\beta = \frac{\lambda D}{d} \text{ or } \beta \propto \lambda$$

Two conclusions can be drawn from this relation

(i) If YDSE apparatus is immersed in a liquid of refractive index μ, then wavelength of light and hence fringe width decreases μ times.

$$\beta' = \frac{\beta}{\mu}$$

(ii) If white light is used in place of a monochromatic light, then coloured fringes are obtained on the screen with red fringes of larger size than that of violet because $\lambda_{\text{red}} > \lambda_{\text{violet}}$.

But note that centre is still white because path difference there is zero for all colours. Hence, all the wavelengths interfere constructively. At other places light will interfere destructively for those wavelengths for whom path difference is $\lambda/2, 3\lambda/2, \ldots$, etc, and they will interfere constructively for the wavelengths for whom path difference is $\lambda, 2\lambda, \ldots$, etc.

Shape of fringes on the screen is hyperbolic. But, if the screen is placed at very large distance from slits, then the hyperbola nearly looks straight line in shape.

Angular Width of Fringes

Let angular position of nth bright fringe is θ_n and because of its small value $\tan\theta_n \approx \theta_n$

$$\therefore \quad \theta_n = \frac{Y_n}{D} = \frac{nD\lambda/d}{D} = \frac{n\lambda}{d}$$

Similarly, if angular position of $(n+1)$th bright fringe is θ_{n+1}, then

$$\theta_{n+1} = \frac{Y_{n+1}}{D} = \frac{(n+1)\, D\lambda/d}{D} = \frac{(n+1)\lambda}{d}$$

$\therefore$ Angular width of a fringe,

$$\theta = \theta_{n+1} - \theta_n = \frac{(n+1)\lambda}{d} - \frac{n\lambda}{d} = \frac{\lambda}{d}$$

Also, $$\beta = \frac{D}{d}\lambda$$

$$\therefore \quad \theta = \frac{\lambda}{d} = \frac{\beta}{D}$$

It is independent of n, *i.e.* angular width of all fringes are same.

Intensity of Fringes

Intensity of bright frine $= 4I$ [as $I_1 = I_2 = I$ is YDSE]

Intensity of dark fringe $= 0$

Also, $$\frac{I_1}{I_2} = \frac{a^2}{b^2} = \frac{W_1}{W_2}$$

where, W_1 and W_2 are width of slits, which emanates light of intensity I_1 and I_2.

Maximum Intensity

From above expression, we can see that intensity is maximum at points, where

$$\cos\frac{\phi}{2} = \pm 1 \text{ or } \frac{\phi}{2} = n\pi,\ n = 0, \pm 1, \pm 2, \ldots$$

or $$\phi = 2n\pi \text{ or } \frac{2\pi}{\lambda}\Delta x = 2n\pi$$

or $\Delta x = n\lambda$, we know that this path difference is for maxima. Thus, intensity of bright points are maximum and given by

$$I_{max} = 4I_0$$

Therefore, we can write $I = I_{max} \cos^2 \frac{\phi}{2}$

Minimum Intensity

Minimum intensity on the screen is found at points, where

$$\cos\frac{\phi}{2} = 0 \text{ or } \frac{\phi}{2} = \left(n - \frac{1}{2}\right)\pi$$

(where, $n = \pm 1, \pm 2, \pm 3, \ldots$)

or $$\phi = (2n - 1)\pi$$

or $$\frac{2\pi}{\lambda}\Delta x = (2n - 1)\pi$$

$\Rightarrow$ $$\Delta x = (2n - 1)\frac{\lambda}{2}$$

We know that this path difference corresponds to minima. Thus, intensity of minima are minimum and given by

$$I_{min} = 0$$

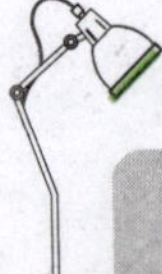

EXPERT Scale Up

- If both the slits are of equal width, $I_1 \approx I_2 = I_0$, then

$$I_{max} = 4I_0 \text{ and } I_{min} = 0$$

- If the slits are of unequal width, then $I_1 \neq I_2$ $I_{min} \neq 0$

Insertion of Transparent Slab in YDSE

When a transparent slab (sheet) of refractive index μ and of thickness t is introduced in one of the path of interfering waves, then fringe pattern shifts in that direction by a distance Y

$$Y = \frac{D}{d}(\mu - 1)t$$

$$= \frac{\beta}{\lambda}(\mu - 1)t$$

where, β = fringe width.

Knowledge Booster

Interference in Thin Flim

Interference effects are commonly observed in thin films, such as thin layers of coil on water or the thin surface of a soap bubble.

The varied colours observed when white light is incident on such films as the result of the interference of waves reflected from the two surfaces of the film.

Let us assume that the light rays travelling in air are nearly normal to the surfaces of the film. Then

(i) The wavelength of light in a medium whose refractive index is μ is

$$\lambda_\mu = \frac{\lambda}{\mu}$$

(ii) If wave is reflected from a denser medium, then it undergoes a phase change 180°.

The path difference betwen the two rays 1 and 2 is $2t$.

Hence, condition of constructive interference will be

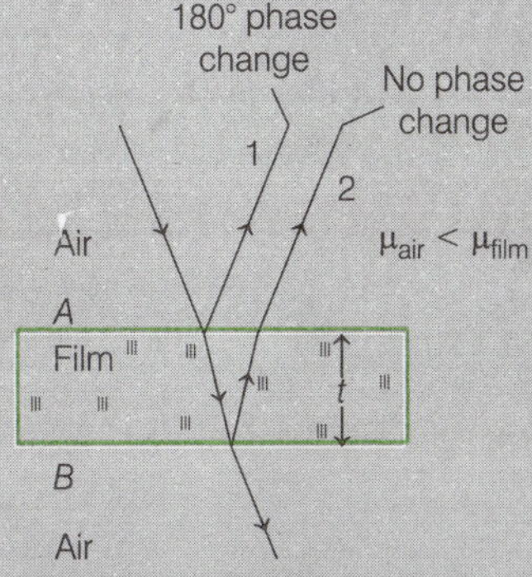

where, $n = 1, 2, 3, \ldots$

$$2t = (2n-1)\frac{\lambda_\mu}{2} \quad \text{or} \quad 2\mu t = \left(n - \frac{1}{2}\right)\lambda \quad \text{as} \quad \lambda_\mu = \frac{\lambda}{\mu}$$

Similarly, condition of destructive interference will be $2\mu t = n\lambda$, where $n = 0, 1, 2, \ldots$

- A soap bubble or oil film on water appears coloured in white light due to interference of light reflected from upper and lower surfaces of soap bubble or oil film.
- In interference fringe pattern, all bright and dark fringes are of same width.

Fresnel's Biprism

It is a combination of two prisms of very small refracting angles placed base to base. It is used to obtain two coherent sources from a single light source.

Llyod's Mirror

The shape of interference fringes obtained from Llyod's mirror are usually hyperbolic.

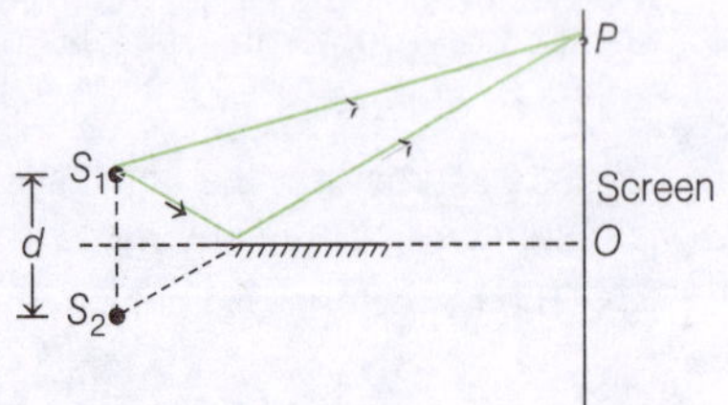

When screen is held at 90° to the line joining foci of the hyperbola, the fringes are circular.

When distance of screen (D) is very large compare to the distance between the slits (d), the fringes are straight.

Diffraction

The bending of light waves around the corners of an obstacle or aperture of the size of the wavelength is called diffraction of light. The phenomenon of diffraction is divided mainly in the following two classes

(a) Fresnel class (b) Fraunhofer class

S.No.	Fresnel Class	Fraunhofer Class
1.	The source is at a finite distance.	The source is at infinite distance.
2.	No opticals are required.	Opticals in the form of collimating lens and focusing lens are required.
3.	Fringes are not sharp and well defined.	Fringes are sharp and well defined.

Fraunhoffer Diffraction at a Single Slit

For Secondary Minima

(a) Path difference $= n\lambda$ (b) Linear distance $= \dfrac{nD\lambda}{a} = \dfrac{nf\lambda}{a}$

where, $\lambda =$ wavelength of light, $a =$ width of single slit, $D =$ distance of screen from the slit and $f =$ focal length of convex lens.

(c) Angular spread $= \dfrac{n\lambda}{a}$ where, $n = 1, 2, 3, \ldots$

For Secondary Maxima

(a) Path difference $= \dfrac{(2n+1)\lambda}{2}$

(b) Linear distance $= \dfrac{(2n+1)D\lambda}{2a} = \dfrac{(2n+1)f\lambda}{2a}$

(c) Angular spread $= \dfrac{(2n+1)\lambda}{2a}$

For Central Maxima

Linear width of central maximum $\dfrac{2D\lambda}{a} = \dfrac{2f\lambda}{a}$

Angular width of central maximum, $2\theta = \dfrac{2\lambda}{a}$

Fresnel's Distance

It is given as, $Z_F = \dfrac{a^2}{\lambda}$, where, a is the size of slit or hole.

Image formation can be explained by ray optics for distance less than Z_F.

 **Knowledge Booster**

Diffraction Grating

- It consists of large number of equally spaced parallel slits. If light is incident normally on a transmission grating, then the direction of principal maxima is given by $d \sin\theta = n\lambda$

  Here, d is the distance between two consecutive slits and is called grating element $n = 1, 2, 3, \ldots$ is the order of principal maxima.
- Diffraction grating is based on combined phenomena of interference and diffraction. It is the results of interference in diffracted waves.
- In diffraction fringe pattern, central bright fringe is brightest and widest and remaining secondary maximas are of gradually decreasing intensities.
- The difference between interference and diffraction is that the interference is the superposition between the wavelets coming from two coherent sources while the diffraction is the superposition between the wavelets coming from the single wavefront.

Polarisation

The phenomenon of restricting of electric vectors of light into a single direction is called **polarisation.** Ordinary light has electric vectors in all possible directions in a plane perpendicular to the direction of propagation of light.

When ordinary light is passed through a tourmaline, calcite or quartz crystal, the transmitted light will have electric vectors in a particular direction parallel to the axis of crystal. This light is then known as plane polarised light.

A plane containing the vibrations of polarised light is called **plane of vibration**. A plane perpendicular to the plane of vibration is called **plane of polarisation**. Polarisation can take place only in transverse waves.

Nicol Prism

A nicol prism is an optical device which is used for producing plane polarised light and analysing light the same.

The nicol prism consists of two calcite crystal cut at 68° with its principal axis joined by a glue called Canada balsam.

Law of Malus

When a beam of completely plane polarised light is incident on an analyser, the intensity of transmitted light from analyser is directly proportional to the square of the cosine of the angle between plane of transmission of analyser and polariser, i.e. $I \propto \cos^2 \theta$

When ordinary light is incident on a polariser the intensity of transmitted light is half of the intensity of incident light.

When a polariser and a analyser are perpendicular to each other, then intensity of transmitted light from analyser becomes 0.

Competition Insight

Brewster's Law

- When unpolarised light is incident at an angle of polarisation (i_p) on the interface separating air from a medium of refractive index μ, then reflected light becomes fully polarised, provided

$$\mu = \tan i_p$$

Here, $$i_p + r = 90°$$

Unpolarised Light Reflected light

Refracted light

Double Refraction

When unpolarised light is incident on a calcite or quartz crystal it splits up into two refracted rays, one of which follows laws of refraction, called **ordinary ray** (O-ray) and other do not follow laws of refraction, called **extraordinary ray** (E-ray). This phenomenon is called double refraction.

Polarisation of Light by Scattering

- The scattering of light can be demonstrated by a simple experiment. A few drops of dilute sulphuric acid is added to a dilute solution of hypo (sodium thiosulphate) prepared in a glass tank.
- A precipitate of fine sulphur particles is formed, the particles grow in size with time. Now, a beam of light from a bright source is sent through the tank. The light scattered by the sulphur particles in a direction at right angles to the incident light appears bluish shown in figure below.

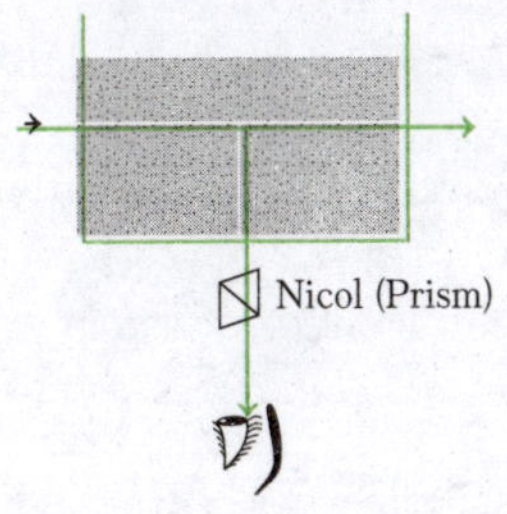

- When the scattered bluish light is seen through an analyser (for example, a rotating Nicol) a variation in intensity with minimum intensity zero is found. This shows that the light scattered in a direction perpendicular to the incident light is plane polarised.

Dichroism

- Few double refracting crystals have a property of absorbing one of the two refracted rays and allowing the other to emerge out. This property of crystal is called dichroism.

Polaroid

It is a polarising film mounted between two glass plates, which is used to produce polarised light.

Uses of Polaroid

(i) Polaroids are used in sun glasses. They protect the eyes from glare.

(ii) The pictures taken by a stercoscopic camera. When seen with the help of polaroid spectacles, it helps in creating three dimensional effect.

(iii) The wind shield of an automobile is made of polaroid. Such a wind shield protects the eyes of the driver of the automobile from the **dazzling light** of the approaching vehicles.

Knowledge Booster

Doppler's Effect in Light

The phenomenon of apparent change in frequency (or wavelength) of the light due to relative motion between the source of light and the observer is called **Doppler's Effect in Light**.

Doppler's Shift

Apparent wavelength > actual wavelength

So, spectrum of the radiation from the source of light shifts towards the red end of spectrum. This is called **red shift**.

However, when waves are received from a source moving towards the observer, there is an apparent decrease in wavelength, this is reffered as **blue shift**

$$\text{Doppler's shift, } \Delta\lambda = \lambda \cdot \frac{v}{c}$$

where, v = speed of source w.r.t. stationary observer

and c = speed of light.

Chapter 29

Electrons, Photons and X-rays

Cathode Rays

Cathode rays are the stream of fast moving electrons in discharge tubes. These rays are produced in a discharge tube at a pressure below 0.01 mm of mercury.

Properties of Cathode Rays

(i) Cathode rays are not electromagnetic rays.

(ii) Cathode rays are deflected by electric field and magnetic field.

(iii) Cathode rays produce heat in metals when they fall on them.

(iv) Cathode rays can pass through thin aluminium or gold foils without puncturing them.

(v) Cathode rays can produce physical and chemical change.

(vi) Cathode rays travel in straight line with high velocity momentum and energy and cast shadow of objects placed in their path.

(vii) On striking the target of high atomic weight and high melting point, they produce X-rays.

(viii) Cathode rays produce fluorescence and phosphorescence in certain substance and hence affect photographic plate.

(ix) Specific charge of an electron was determined by J.J. Thomson using perpendicular magnetic and electric field applied on a beam of electrons, at the same place.

(x) Specific charge of electron $\frac{e}{m} = \frac{E^2}{2VB^2}$

where, E = electric field, B = magnetic field and V = potential difference applied across ends of tube.

(xi) The value of specific charge of an electron is 1.7589×10^{11} C/kg.

(xii) Millikan measured the charge of an electron through his popular oil drop experiment.

(xiii) The charge of the electron as determined by Millikan was found to be 1.602×10^{-19} C.

Positive Rays

Positive rays were discovered by Goldstein. Positive rays are moving positive ions of gas filled in the discharge tube. The mass of these particles is nearly equal to the mass of the atoms of gas.

Properties of Positive Rays

(i) These consists of fast moving positively charged particles.

(ii) These rays are deflected in magnetic and electric fields.

(iii) These rays travel in straight line.

(iv) Speed of positive rays is less than that of cathode rays.

(v) These rays can produce fluorescence and phosphorescence.

Electron Emission

It is the phenomenon of emission of electron from the surface of a metal. The electron emission can be obtained from the following process

(i) Thermionic emission
(ii) Photoelectric emission
(iii) Field emission
(iv) Secondary emission

Photoelectric Effect

The phenomenon of emission of electrons from a metal surface, when radiations of suitable frequency are incident on it, is called photoelectric effect.

Terms Related to Photoelectric Effect

(i) **Work Function** (ϕ) The minimum amount of energy required to eject one electron from a metal surface is called its work function. Its dimensional formula is $[ML^2T^{-2}]$ and unit is J or eV.

(ii) **Threshold Frequency** (v_0) The minimum frequency of light which can eject photoelectron from a metal surface is called threshold frequency of that metal.

Its dimensional formula is $[T^{-1}]$ and unit is Hz.

(iii) **Threshold Wavelength** (λ_{max}) The maximum wavelength of light which can eject photoelectron from a metal surface is called threshold wavelength of that metal.

Relation between work function, threshold frequency and threshold wavelength

$$\phi = h\nu_0 = \frac{hc}{\lambda_{max}}$$

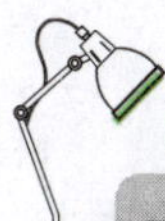

EXPERT Scale Up

For photoelectric emission, energy of incident electromagnetic radiation must be greater than or equal to work function of photosensitive surface.

Laws of Photoelectric Effect

(i) For a given material and a given frequency of incident radiation, the photoelectric current or number of photoelectrons ejected per second is directly proportional to the intensity of the incident light.

(ii) For a given material and frequency of incident radiation, saturation current is found to be proportional to the intensity of incident radiation, whereas the stopping potential is independent of its intensity.

(iii) For a given material, there exists a certain minimum frequency of the incident radiation below which no emission of photoelectrons takes place. This frequency is called **threshold frequency.**

Above the threshold frequency, the maximum kinetic energy of the emitted photoelectrons or equivalent stopping potential is independent of the intensity of the incident light but depends upon only the frequency (or wavelength) of the incident light.

(iv) The photoelectric emission is an instantaneous process. The time lag between the incidence of radiations and emission of photoelectrons is very small, less than even 10^{-9}s.

Einstein's Photoelectric Equation

The maximum kinetic energy of photoelectrons

$$(E_K)_{max} = h\nu - \phi = h(\nu - \nu_0)$$

where, ν is frequency of incident light and ν_0 is threshold frequency.

Stopping Potential

The minimum negative potential given to anode plate at which photoelectric current becomes zero is called stopping potential (V_0).

Maximum kinetic energy of photoelectrons

$$(E_K)_{max} = \frac{1}{2} mv_{max}^2 = eV_0$$

$$= hc\left(\frac{1}{\lambda} - \frac{1}{\lambda_0}\right)$$

where, λ is the wavelength of incident radiation and λ_0 is the threshold wavelength of metal surface.

Dimensional formula of stopping potential is $[ML^2T^{-3}A^{-1}]$ and unit is volt.

Value Points

One photon can emit only one electron from a photosensitive material, no matter how much its energy is.

Graphs related to Photoelectric Effect

(i) Photoelectric current (i) *versus* intensity of incident light (I).

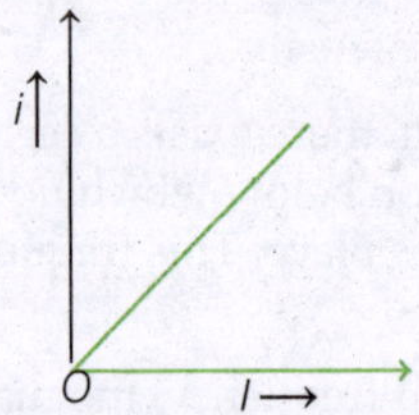

(ii) Variation of photoelectric current (I) *versus* potential for different intensities but constant frequency

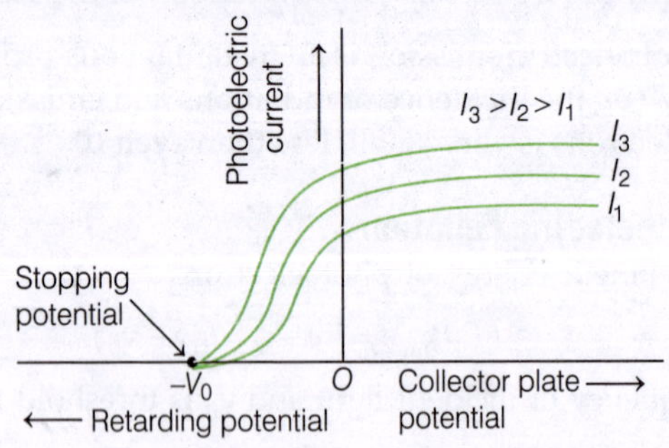

(iii) Variation of photoelectric current (I) *versus* potential for different frequencies but constant intensity of incident radiation

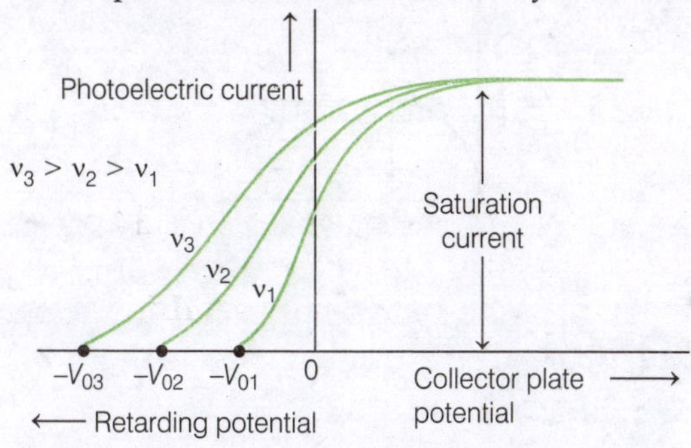

(iv) Stopping potential (V_0) *versus* frequency (ν_0)

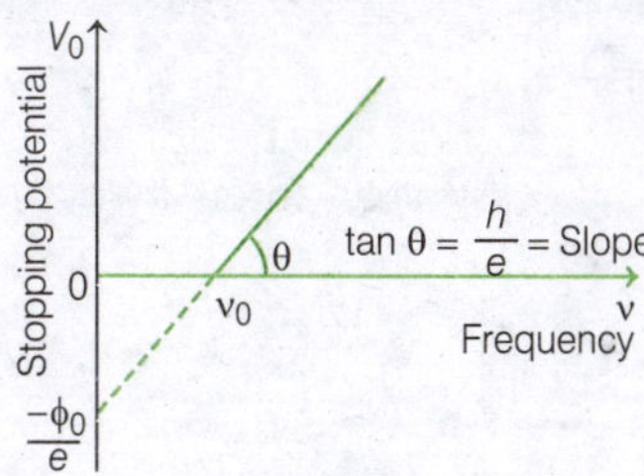

(v) Photoelectric current (i) *versus* frequency (ν)

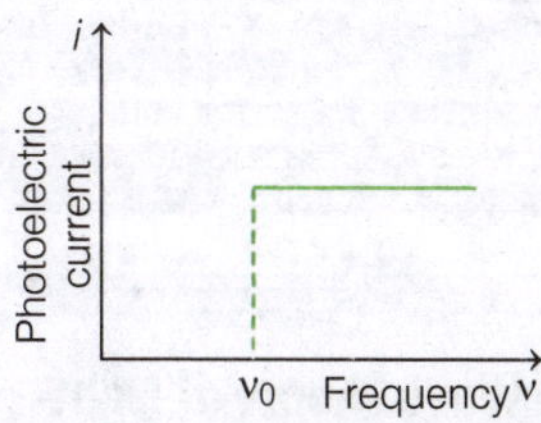

(vi) Stopping potential (V_0) *versus* intensity (I)

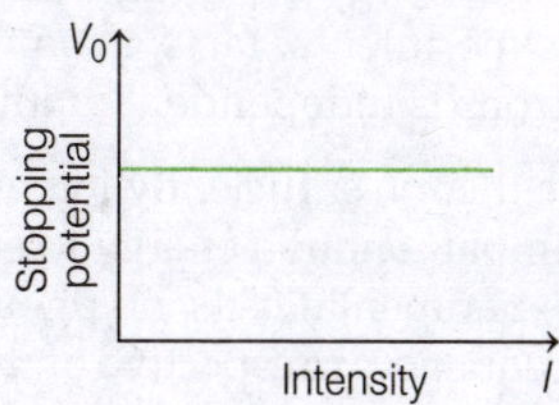

(vii) Photoelectric current (I) *versus* time lag (t)

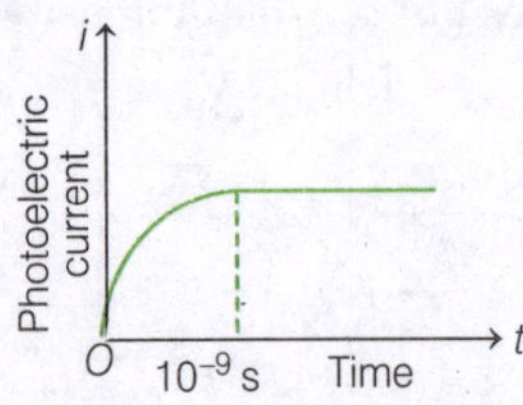

Competition Insight

Photocell

It is a device which converts light energy into electrical energy. It is also called an **electric eye**.

It works on the principle of photoelectric emission.

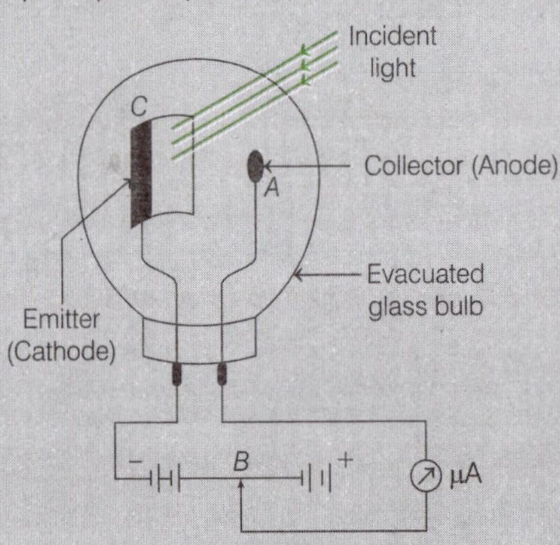

Photoelectric Effect and Wave Theory of Light

(i) According to wave theory, greater the intensity of radiation, greater should be the energy absorbed by each electron. However, as per experimental facts, maximum kinetic energy of ejected photoelectrons is independent of intensity.

(ii) According to wave theory, sufficiently intense beam of radiation should be able to impart enough energy to electrons for ejections. However, as per experimental facts, no photoelectrons takes place below threshold frequency, irrespective of its intensity.

(iii) According to wave theory, it take hours or more for a single electron to come out of metal which contradicts the experimental fact that photoelectric emission is instantaneous.

Planck's Quantum Theory (Particle Nature of Light : The Photon)

In 1990, Max Planck proposed his quantum theory of radiation. According to this theory, the energy of an electromagnetic wave is not continuously distributed over the wavefront, instead of an electromagnetic wave travels in the form of discrete packets or bundles of energy called quanta. One quantum of light radiation is called a **photon**.

The energy of each photon is $E = h\nu$,

where, h is Planck' s constant and ν is frequency of radiation.

The dimensional formula of Planck's constant is $[ML^2 T^{-1}]$ and its SI unit is Js.

The momentum of a photon, $p = \frac{h\nu}{c} = \frac{h}{\lambda}$

Characteristic Properties of Photons

Different characteristic properties of photons are given below

(i) In interaction of radiation with matter, radiation behaves as if it is made up of particles called **photons**.

(ii) A photon travels at a speed of light c in vacuum (*i.e.* 3×10^8 m / s).

(iii) The inertial mass of a photon is given by, $m = \frac{E}{c^2} = \frac{h}{c\lambda} = \frac{h\nu}{c^2}$

(iv) Photons travel in a straight line.

(v) Irrespective of the intensity of radiation, all the photons of a particular frequency ν or wavelength λ have the same energy and momentum.

(vi) Energy of a photon depends upon frequency of the photon, so the energy of the photon does not change when photon travels from one medium to another.

(vii) Wavelength of the photon changes in different media, so velocity of a photon is different in different media.

(viii) Photons are not deflected by electric and magnetic fields. This shows that photons are electrically neutral.

(ix) In a photon-particle collision (such as photoelectron collision), the energy and momentum are conserved. However, the number of photons may not be conserved in a collision.

(x) It has zero rest mass, *i.e.* the photon exist at rest.

Knowledge Booster

Compton Effect

When a monochromatic beam light falls on a target containing free electrons, it is scattered. As a result, the electrons recoil and scattered radiation has wavelength longer than incident one. This effect is called Compton effect.

(i) $\lambda' - \lambda = \lambda =$ Compton shift, $\Delta\lambda = \dfrac{h}{m_0 c}(1 - \cos\phi)$

where, m_0 is rest mass of an electron and c is the speed of light $\dfrac{h}{m_0 c}$.

Compton shift $\Delta\lambda$ is maximum, when $\phi = 180°$.

Recoil electron

Target electron at rest

Incident photon

ϕ

θ

λ_i

Scattered photon

λ_f

Compton scattering

(ii) Kinetic energy of recoil electron, $E_K = \dfrac{hc}{\lambda} - \dfrac{hc}{\lambda'}$

(iii) Direction of recoil electron, $\tan\theta = \dfrac{\lambda \sin\phi}{\lambda' - \lambda\cos\phi}$

(iv) Compton wavelength of electron $= \dfrac{h}{m_0 c} = 0.024$ Å

(v) Maximum Compton shift $(\Delta\lambda)_{max} = \dfrac{2h}{m_0 c} = 0.048$ Å

Dual Nature of Radiation

With the experimental verification, it was proved that light has dual nature, in some phenomena it behaves like wave and in some phenomena it behaves like particle depending upon the dimensions of object with which the particle interacts.

In 1924, French physicist Lewis de-Broglie suggested like radiation, matter too should have dual nature, *i.e.*, the particles like electrons, protons, neutrons, etc, can have particle as well as wave nature.

Matter Waves or de-Broglie Waves

A wave is associated with every moving particle called matter or de-Broglie wave.

Characteristics of Matter Waves

Characteristics of matter waves are given below

(i) Matter waves are not electromagnetic waves in nature.

(ii) Matter waves are non-mechanical waves, *i.e.*, they can travel in vacuum.

(iii) Matter waves are independent of charge, *i.e.*, they are associated with every moving particle (whether charged or uncharged).

(iv) Observation of matter waves is possible only when the de-Broglie wavelength is of the order of size of the particle (*i.e.*, the waves are diffracted).

(v) The phase velocity of the matter waves can be greater than the speed of the light.

(vi) The number of de-Broglie waves associated with nth orbital electron is n.

de-Broglie Wavelength

If a particle of mass m is moving with velocity v, then wavelength of de-Broglie wave associated with it is given by $\lambda = \frac{h}{p} = \frac{h}{mv}$.

For charged particles accelerated through a potential V, $\lambda = \frac{h}{\sqrt{2meV}}$

de-Broglie wavelength associated with various particles

	For charged particle	de-Broglie wavelength
(a)	Electron	$\lambda = \frac{12.27}{\sqrt{V}}$ Å
(b)	Proton	$\lambda = \frac{0.286}{\sqrt{V}}$ Å
(c)	Deuteron	$\lambda = \frac{0.202}{\sqrt{V}}$ Å
(d)	α-particle	$\lambda = \frac{0.101}{\sqrt{V}}$ Å
	For uncharged particle	
(a)	Neutrons	$\lambda = \frac{0.286}{\sqrt{E}}$ Å
(b)	Thermal neutron	$\lambda = \frac{25.17}{\sqrt{T}}$ Å

Competition Insight

Electron Microscope

- Electron microscope is an important application of de-Broglie wave used to study very minute objects like viruses, microbes etc. Like light radiations, electron beams behave as waves but with much smaller wavelength. It uses electric and magnetic field to concentrate electron beam.
- The magnifying power of a microscope is inversely related with the wavelength of radiations used. Here, the electrons are focussed with the help of electric and magnetic lenses. Also, the viewing screen used should be fluorescent so that image produced should be visible.
- An electron microscope can have a very high magnification of $\approx 10^5$.

Davisson-Germer Experiment

- The wave nature of the material particles as predicted by de-Broglie was confirmed by Davisson and Germer (1927) in united states and by GP Thomson (1928) in Scotland.

- This experiment verified the wave nature of electron using Ni crystal.
- Davisson and Germer found that the intensity of scattered beam of electrons was not the same but different at different angles of scattering. It is maximum for diffracting angle 50° at 54 V potential difference.

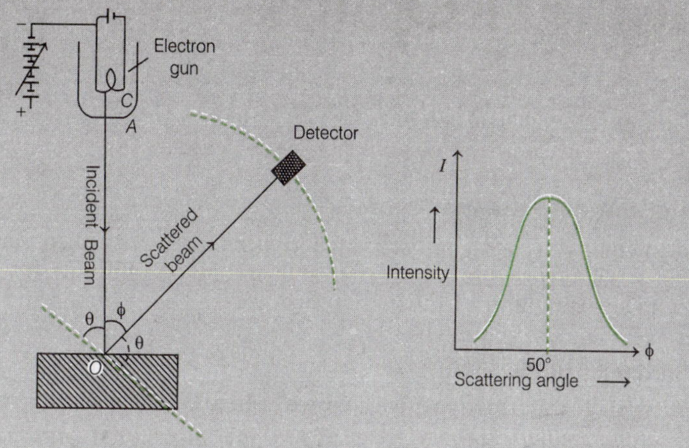

Chapter 30

Atomic Physics

Dalton's Atomic Theory

All elements are consists of very small invisible particles, called atoms. Atoms of same elements are exactly same and atoms of different elements are different.

Thomson's Atomic Model

Every atom is uniformly positive charged sphere of radius of the order of 10^{-10} m, in which entire mass is uniformly distributed and negative charged electrons are embedded randomly. The atom as a whole is neutral.

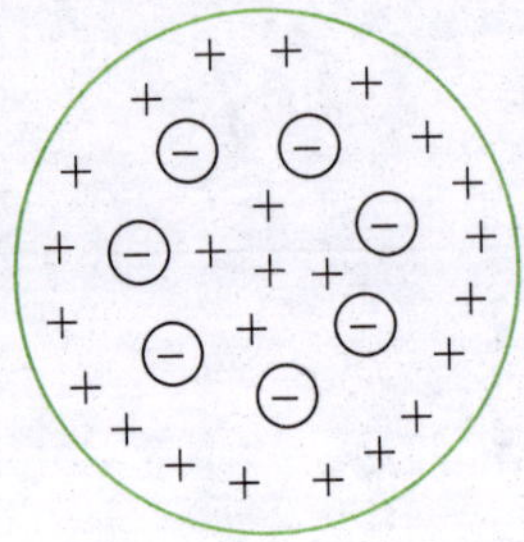

Limitations of Thomson's Atomic Model

(i) It could not explain the origin of spectral series of hydrogen and other atoms.

(ii) It could not explain large angle scattering of α-particle.

Rutherford's Atomic Model

The setup of Rutherford's α-particle scattering experiment is shown in the figure given below

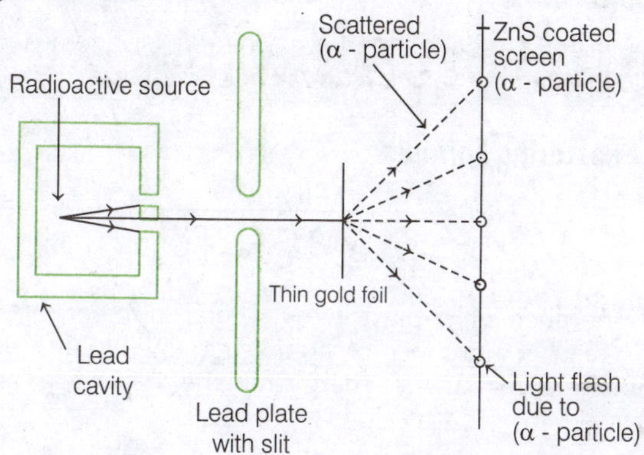

On the basis of this experiment, Rutherford made following conclusions.

(i) The entire positive charge and almost entire mass of the atom is concentrated at its centre in a very tiny region of the order of 10^{-15} m, called nucleus.

(ii) The negatively charged electrons revolve around the nucleus in different orbits.

(iii) The total positive charge on nucleus is equal to the total negative charge on electron. Therefore, atom is overall neutral.

(iv) The centripetal force required by electron for revolution is provided by the electrostatic force of attraction between the electrons and the nucleus.

Distance of Closest Approach

$$r_0 = \frac{1}{4\pi\varepsilon_0} \cdot \frac{2Ze^2}{E_K}$$

where, E_K = kinetic energy of the α-particle.

Impact Parameter

The perpendicular distance of the velocity vector of α-particle from the centre of the nucleus, when the particle is far away from the nucleus is called impact parameter.

$$\text{Impact parameter, } b = \frac{1}{4\pi\varepsilon_0} \cdot \frac{Ze^2 \cot\left(\frac{\theta}{2}\right)}{E_K}$$

where, Z = atomic number of the nucleus,

E_K = kinetic energy of the α-particle and

θ = angle of scattering.

Value Points

For large value of impact parameters, the repulsive forces experienced by the α-particle is weak and *vice-versa*.

Rutherford's Scattering Formula

$$N(\theta) = \frac{N_i nt Z^2 e^4}{(8\pi\varepsilon_0)^2 r^2 E^2 \sin^4\left(\frac{\theta}{2}\right)}$$

where, $N(\theta)$ = number of α-particles, N_i = total number of α-particles reaching the screen, n = number of atoms per unit volume in the foil, Z = atomic number, E = kinetic energy of the α-particle and t = foil thickness.

$$\therefore \qquad N \propto \frac{1}{\sin^4\left(\frac{\theta}{2}\right)}$$

Limitations of Rutherford 's Atomic Model

(i) **About the Stability of Atom** According to Maxwell's electromagnetic wave theory, electron should emit energy in the form of electromagnetic wave during, its orbital motion. Therefore, radius of orbit of electron will decrease gradually and ultimately it will fall in the nucleus.

(ii) **About the Line Spectrum** Rutherford's atomic model cannot explain atomic line spectrum.

Bohr's Atomic Model

Electron can revolve in certain non-radiating orbits called **stationary orbits** for which the angular momentum of electron is an integral multiple of $\left(\frac{h}{2\pi}\right)$.

$$mvr = \frac{nh}{2\pi}$$

where, $n = 1, 2, 3, \ldots$ called principal quantum number.

The radiation of energy occurs only, when any electron jumps from one permitted orbit to another permitted orbit.

Energy of emitted photon, $h\nu = E_2 - E_1$

where, E_1 and E_2 are energies of electron in orbits.

Radius of orbit of electron is given by

$$r = \frac{n^2h^2}{4\pi^2 mK Ze^2}$$

$$\Rightarrow \qquad r \propto \frac{n^2}{Z}$$

where, n = principal quantum number, h = Planck's constant, m = mass of an electron, $K = \frac{1}{4\pi\varepsilon_0}$, Z = atomic number and e = electronic charge.

The radius of the first orbit ($n = 1$) of H-atom is given as

$$r_1 = \frac{h^2\varepsilon_0}{\pi me^2} = 0.53\ \text{Å}$$

This is called Bohr's radius.

Velocity of electron in any orbit is given by

$$v = \frac{2\pi kZe^2}{nh}$$

$$\Rightarrow \qquad v \propto \frac{Z}{n}$$

Frequency of electron in any orbit is given by

$$\nu = \frac{kZe^2}{nhr} = \frac{4\pi^2Z^2e^4mk^2}{n^3h^3}$$

$$\Rightarrow \qquad \nu \propto \frac{Z^2}{n^3}$$

Kinetic energy of electron in any orbit is given by

$$E_K = \frac{2\pi^2me^4Z^2k^2}{n^2h^2} = \frac{13.6\ Z^2}{n^2}\ \text{eV}$$

Potential energy of electron in any orbit is given by

$$E_P = \frac{-4\pi^2me^4Z^2k^2}{n^2h^2} = -\frac{27.2\ Z^2}{n^2}\ \text{eV}$$

Total energy of electron in any orbit is given by

$$E = \frac{-2\pi^2me^4Z^2k^2}{n^2h^2} = -\frac{13.6\ Z^2}{n^2}\ \text{eV}$$

$$\Rightarrow \qquad E \propto \frac{Z^2}{n^2}$$

Competition Insight

Wavelength of radiation emitted in the radiation from orbit n_2 to n_1 is given by

$$\frac{1}{\lambda} = \frac{2\pi^2 mk^2 e^4 Z^2}{ch^3}\left[\frac{1}{n_1^2} - \frac{1}{n_2^2}\right]$$

$$\frac{1}{\lambda} = RZ^2\left[\frac{1}{n_1^2} - \frac{1}{n_2^2}\right]$$

where, $R = \frac{2\pi^2 mK^2 e^4}{ch^3}$

$= 1.097 \times 10^7 \text{ m}^{-1}$

Time period of the electron,

$$T_n = 2\pi\left(\frac{r_n}{v_n}\right) = \frac{4\varepsilon_0^2 n^3 h^3}{me^4}$$

Excitation Energy and Potential

The energy required to take an atom from its lower state to higher state is called excitation energy.

The potential through which an electron should be accelerated to gain higher state is called excitation potential.

Ionisation Energy and Potential

Ionisation energy is the minimum energy needed to ionise an atom. Ionisation energy per unit charge is called ionisation potential.

$$E_{\text{ionisation}} = E_\infty - E_n = \frac{13.6 Z^2}{n^2} \text{ eV}$$

$$\text{Ionisation potential} = \frac{E_{\text{ionisation}}}{e} = \frac{13.6 Z^2}{n^2} \text{ V}$$

de-Broglie's Explanations of Bohr's Second Postulate

According to de-Broglie, a stationary orbit is that which contains an integral number of de-Broglie waves associated with the revolving electrons. For electron revolving in nth orbit of radius r_n.

$$2\pi r_n = n\lambda = \frac{nh}{mv_n} \quad \text{or} \quad mv_n r_n = \frac{nh}{2\pi}$$

Hydrogen Spectrum Series

Each element emits a spectrum of radiation, which is characteristic of the element itself. The spectrum consists of a set of isolated parallel lines and is called the **line spectrum.**

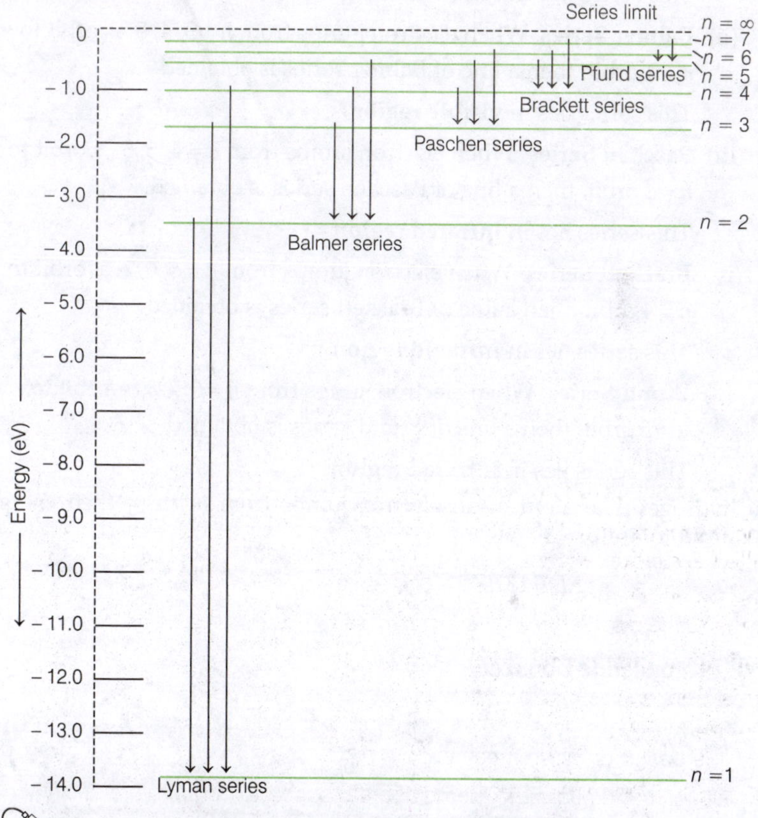

Series limit

$n = \infty$

$n = 7$

$n = 6$

$n = 5$

$n = 4$

$n = 3$

$n = 2$

$n = 1$

Pfund series

Brackett series

Paschen series

Balmer series

Lyman series

Energy (eV)

0, − 1.0, − 2.0, − 3.0, − 4.0, − 5.0, − 6.0, − 7.0, − 8.0, − 9.0, − 10.0, − 11.0, − 12.0, − 13.0, − 14.0

EXPERT Scale Up

- For longest wavelength in any series of hydrogen spectrum, the energy difference in two states showing transition should be minimum.
- For shortest wavelength in any series of hydrogen spectrum, the energy difference in two states showing transition should be maximum.

Hydrogen spectrum contains five series.

(i) **Lyman Series** When electron jumps from $n = 2, 3, 4, \ldots$ orbit to $n = 1$ orbit, then a line of Lyman series is obtained.

This series lies in **ultra violet region.**

(ii) **Balmer Series** When electron jumps from $n = 3, 4, 5, \ldots$ orbit to $n = 2$ orbit, then a line of Balmer series is obtained.

This series lies in **visible region.**

(iii) **Paschen Series** When electron jumps from $n = 4, 5, 6, \ldots$ orbit to $n = 3$ orbit, then a line of Paschen series is obtained.

This series lies in **infrared region.**

(iv) **Brackett Series** When electron jumps from $n = 5, 6, 7, \ldots$ orbit to $n = 4$ orbit, then a line of Brackett series is obtained.

This series lies in **infrared region.**

(v) **Pfund Series** When electron jumps from $n = 6, 7, 8, \ldots$ orbit to $n = 5$ orbit, then a line of Pfund series is obtained.

This series lies in **infrared region.**

In hydrogen like atom, if an electron jumps from n_1 to n_2 then energy required to jump,

$$\Delta E = 13.6 Z^2 \left(\frac{1}{n_1^2} - \frac{1}{n_2^2} \right)$$

 **Knowledge Booster**

Wave Model

It is based on wave mechanics.

Quantum numbers are the numbers required to completely specify the state of the electrons.

In the presence of strong magnetic field, the four quantum numbers are

(i) Principal quantum number (n) can have value 1, 2, ...∞.

(ii) Orbital angular momentum quantum number (l) can have value $0, 1, 2, \ldots, (n-1)$.

(iii) Magnetic quantum number (m_e) which can have values $-l$ to l.

(iv) Magnetic spin angular momentum quantum number (m_s) which can have only two value $\pm \frac{1}{2}$.

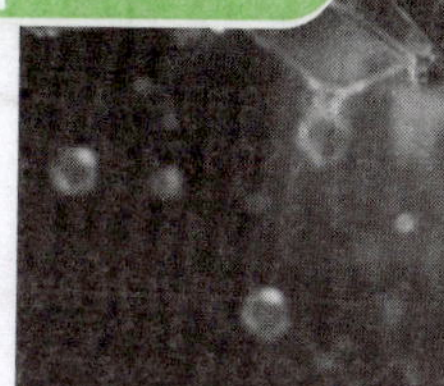

Chapter 31

Nuclear Physics

Nucleus

The entire positive charge and nearly the entire mass of atom is concentrated in a very small space called the nucleus of an atom.

The nucleus consists of protons and neutrons. They are called **nucleons.**

Terms Related to Nucleus

(i) **Atomic Number** The number of protons in the nucleus of an atom of the element is called atomic number (Z) of the element.

(ii) **Mass Number** The total number of protons and neutrons present inside the nucleus of an atom of the element is called mass number (A) of the element.

(iii) **Nuclear Size** The radius of the nucleus $R \propto A^{1/3}$

$$\Rightarrow \quad R = R_0 A^{1/3}$$

where, $R_0 = 1.2 \times 10^{-15}$ m is an empirical constant.

(iv) **Nuclear Density** Nuclear density is independent of mass number and therefore same for all nuclei.

$$\rho = \frac{\text{mass of nucleus}}{\text{volume of nucleus}} \Rightarrow \rho = \frac{3m}{4\pi R_0^3}$$

where, m = average mass of a nucleon.

(v) **Atomic Mass Unit** It is defined as $\frac{1}{12}$th the mass of carbon-12 atom nucleus.

It is abbreviated as amu and often denoted by u. Thus,

$$1 \text{ amu} = \frac{1.992678 \times 10^{-26}}{12} \text{ kg}$$

$$= 1.6 \times 10^{-27} \text{ kg} = 931 \text{ MeV}$$

Isotopes

The atoms of an element having same atomic number but different mass numbers are called isotopes. *e.g.* ${}_1H^1, {}_1H^2, {}_1H^3$ are isotopes of hydrogen.

Isobars

The atoms of different elements having same mass numbers but different atomic numbers are called isobars. *e.g.* ${}_1H^3, {}_2He^3$ and ${}_{11}Na^{22}, {}_{10}Ne^{22}$ are isobars.

Isotones

The atoms of different elements having different atomic numbers and different mass numbers but having same number of neutrons are called isotones. *e.g.* ${}_1H^3, {}_2He^4$ and ${}_6C^{14}, {}_8O^{16}$ are isotones.

Isomers

Atoms having the same mass number and the same atomic number but different radioactive properties are called isomers.

Nuclear Force

The force acting inside the nucleus or acting between nucleons is called nuclear force.

Nuclear forces are the strongest forces in nature.

It is a very short range attractive force.

It is non-central and non-conservative force.

It is independent of charge.

It is 100 times that of electrostatic force and 10^{38} times that of gravitational force.

According to the Yukawa, the nuclear force acts between the nucleons due to continuous exchange of meson particles.

Mass Defect

The difference between the sum of masses of all nucleons (M) and mass of the nucleus (m) is called mass defect.

$$\text{Mass defect } (\Delta m) = M - m$$
$$= [Zm_p + (A - Z)m_n - m_N]$$

Mass Energy Relation

Einstein showed that mass is another form of energy and can convert mass-energy into other forms of energy.

Einstein's mass-energy equivalence relation, $E = mc^2$

Nuclear Binding Energy

The minimum energy required to separate the nucleons upto an infinite distance from the nucleus is called nuclear binding energy.

$$\text{Binding energy, } E_b = [Zm_p + (A - Z)\, m_n - m_N]c^2$$

$$\text{Nuclear binding energy per nucleon} = \frac{\text{Nuclear binding energy}}{\text{Total number of nucleons}}$$

Packing Fraction (*P*)

$$P = \frac{(\text{Exact nuclear mass}) - (\text{Mass number})}{\text{Mass number}} = \frac{M - A}{A}$$

The larger the value of packing friction, greater is the stability of the nucleus.

Binding Energy Curve

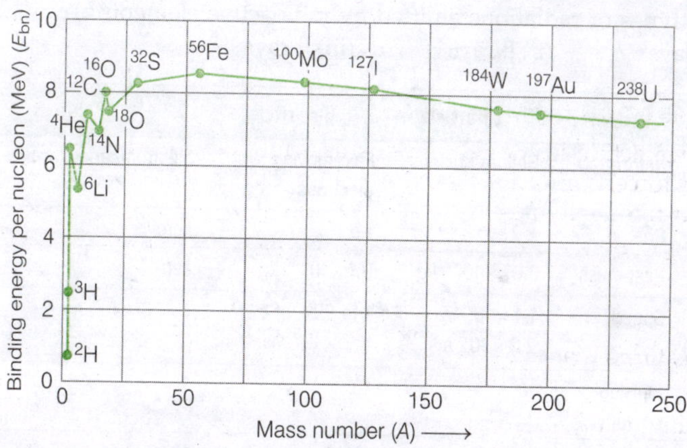

Some features of this curve are given below as

(i) Nuclei having mass number 50 to 80 are most stable.

(ii) Nuclei having mass number more than 80, the average binding energy per nuclei decreases. The nuclei of heavier atoms beyond $_{83}\text{Bi}^{209}$ are radioactive.

(iii) Nuclei having mass number below 20 are comparatively less stable.

(iv) Even-Even nuclei are more stable than their intermediate neighbours.

Value Points

- The nuclei containing even number of protons and even number of neutrons are **most stable**.
- The nuclei containing odd number of protons and odd number of neutrons are **most unstable**.

Radioactivity

The phenomenon of spontaneous emission of radiations by nucleus of some elements is called radioactivity.

This phenomenon was discovered by Henry Becquerel in 1896.

Radiations Emitted by a Radioactive Element

Three types of radiations emitted by radioactive elements are

(i) α-rays (ii) β-rays (iii) γ-rays

S.No.	Property	α-particle	β-particle	γ-rays
1.	Nature	Helium nucleus	Fast moving electrons	Electromagnetic waves
2.	Charge	$+2e$	$-e$	zero
3.	Rest mass	6.67×10^{-27} kg	9.1×10^{-31} kg	zero
4.	Speed	1.4×10^7 to 2.2×10^7 ms^{-1}	1 to 99% of c $= 3 \times 10^8$ ms^{-1}	$c = 3 \times 10^8$ ms^{-1}
5.	Ionising power	10^4	10^2	1
6.	Penetrating power	1	10^2	10^4

- When an α-particle is emitted by a nucleus its atomic number decreases by 2 and mass number decreases by 4.

$$_ZX^A \xrightarrow{\alpha\text{-particle}} {}_{Z-2}Y^{A-4} + {}_2\text{He}^4$$

- When a β-particle is emitted by a nucleus its atomic number is increases by one and mass number remains unchanged.

$$_ZX^A \xrightarrow{\beta\text{-particle}} {}_{Z+1}Y^A + e^- + \overline{\nu}$$

- When a γ-particle is emitted by a nucleus its atomic number and mass number remain unchanged.

Competition Insight

Radioactive Decay Law

The rate of disintegration of radioactive nuclei at any instant is directly proportional to the number of radioactive nuclei present in the sample at that instant.

$$\text{Rate of disintegration} \left(-\frac{dN}{dt}\right) \propto N \text{ or } -\frac{dN}{dt} = \lambda N$$

where, λ is the decay constant.

The number of nuclei present undecayed in the sample at any instant $N = N_0 e^{-\lambda t}$.

where, N_0 is number of nuclei at time $t = 0$ and N is number of nuclei at time t.

Half-life of a Radioactive Element

The time in which the half number of nuclei present initially in any sample decays is called half-life (T) of that radioactive element.

Relation between half-life and disintegration constant is given by

$$T_{1/2} = \frac{\log_e 2}{\lambda} = \frac{0.6931}{\lambda}$$

Average Life or Mean Life (τ)

Average life or mean life (τ) of a radioactive element is the ratio of total life time of all the nuclei and total number of nuclei present initially in the sample.

Relation between average life and decay constant, $\tau = \dfrac{1}{\lambda}$

Relation between half-life and average life, $\tau = 1.44\, T_{1/2}$

The number of nuclei left undecayed after n half-lives is given by

$$N = N_0 \left(\frac{1}{2}\right)^n = N_0 \left(\frac{1}{2}\right)^{\frac{t}{T_{1/2}}}$$

where, $n = \dfrac{t}{T_{1/2}}$, here t = total time.

Activity of a Radioactive Element

The activity of a radioactive element is equal to its rate of disintegration.

$$\text{Activity, } R = \left(-\frac{dN}{dt}\right)$$

Activity of the sample after time t, $R = R_0\, e^{-\lambda t}$

Its SI unit is Becquerel (Bq).

Its other units are Curie and Rutherford.

$$1 \text{ Curie} = 3.7 \times 10^{10} \text{ decay/s}$$

$$1 \text{ Rutherford} = 10^6 \text{ decay/s}$$

Nuclear Reaction

The process by which the identity of a nucleus is changed when it is bombarded by an energetic particle is called nuclear reaction. Its general expression is

$$\underset{\text{(parent nucleus)}}{X} + \underset{\text{(incident particle)}}{a} \longrightarrow \underset{\text{(compound nucleus)}}{c} \longrightarrow \underset{\text{(product nucleus)}}{Y} + \underset{\text{(daughter nucleus)}}{b} + \underset{\text{(energy)}}{Q}$$

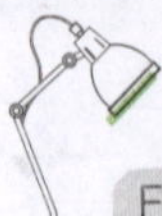

EXPERT Scale Up

For a nuclear reaction, the mass number and atomic number on both sides of reaction should be same.

Q-Value

It means the difference between the rest mass energy of initial constituents and the rest mass energy of final constituents of a nuclear reaction.

Nuclear Energy

The energy released during nuclear reaction is nuclear energy. Two distinct ways of obtaining energy from nucleus are as

(i) Nuclear fission (ii) Nuclear fusion

Nuclear Fission

The process of the splitting of a heavy nucleus into two or more lighter nuclei is called nuclear fission. When a slow moving neutron strikes with a uranium nucleus (${}_{92}U^{235}$), it splits into ${}_{56}Ba^{141}$ and ${}_{36}Kr^{92}$ along with three neutrons and a lot of energy.

$${}_{92}U^{235} + {}_0n^1 \longrightarrow {}_{56}Ba^{141} + {}_{36}Kr^{92} + 3\,{}_0n^1 + \text{energy}$$

Nuclear Chain Reaction

If the particle starting the nuclear fission reaction is produced as a product and further take part in the nuclear fission reaction, then a chain of fission reaction started, which is called nuclear chain reaction.

Nuclear chain reaction are of two types

(i) Controlled chain reaction

(ii) Uncontrolled chain reaction

Knowledge Booster

Nuclear Reactor

The main parts of a nuclear reactor are following

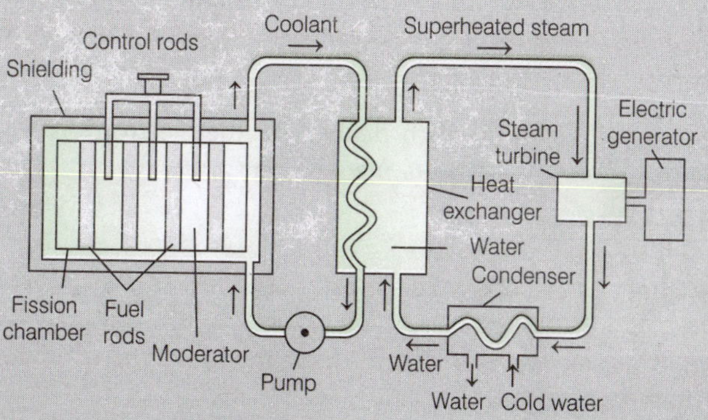

(i) **Fuel** Fissionable materials like $_{92}U^{235}$, $_{92}U^{238}$, $_{94}Pu^{239}$ are used as fuel.

(ii) **Moderator** Heavy water, graphite and baryllium oxide are used to slower down fast moving neutrons.

(iii) **Coolant** The cold water, liquid oxygen etc are used to remove heat generated in the fission process.

(iv) **Control rods** Cadmium or boron rods are good absorber of neutrons and therefore used to control the fission reaction.

Atom bomb's working is based on uncontrolled chain reaction.

Nuclear Fusion

The process of combining of two lighter nuclei to form one heavy nucleus is called nuclear fusion.

When three deuteron nuclei ($_1H^2$) are fused, 21.6 MeV is energy released and nucleus of helium ($_2He^4$) is formed.

$$_1H^2 + {}_1H^2 + {}_1H^2 \longrightarrow {}_2He^4 + {}_1H^1 + {}_0n^1 + 21.6\text{ MeV}$$

In this process, a large amount of energy is released.

Nuclear fusion takes place at very high temperature approximately about 10^7 K and at very high pressure 10^6 atmosphere. Thus, the energy released during nuclear fusion is known as thermonuclear energy. Hydrogen bomb is based on nuclear fusion. The source of sun's energy is the nuclear fusion taking place in the interior of sun.

Chapter 32

Electronics

It is the branch of science which deals with the electron's emission flow and its control through vacuum, gas or semiconductor.

Solid

We know that, each substance is composed of atoms. Substances are mainly classified into three categories namely solids, liquids and gases.

In each solid atoms are at a definite positions and the average distance between them is constant.

Depending upon the internal arrangement of atoms, solids are further divided into two groups.

1. Crystalline Solids

The solid in which the atoms are arranged in a regular order are called the crystalline solids. In other words, we can say that in a crystalline solid, there is periodicity and regularity of its component atoms in all the directions. For example sodium chloride (common salt), diamond, sugar, silver etc are the crystalline solids.

Their atoms are arranged in a definite geometrical shape.

They have a definite melting point.

They are anisotropic, i.e. their physical properties such as thermal conductivity, refractive index etc, are different in different directions.

They are the real solids.

2. Amorphous Solids

The solids in which the atoms do not have a definite arrangement are called the amorphous solids. They are also called the glassy solids. e.g. glass, rubber, plastic, power, etc are the amorphous solids.

They do not have a definite arrangement of its atoms, i.e. they do not have a characteristic geometrical shape.

They do not have a definite melting point.

They are isotropic, *i.e.,* their physical properties such as conductivity of heat refractive index etc, are same in all the directions.

They are not the real solids.

Classification of Solids on the Basis of Conductivity

(i) **Conductor** Conductors are those substances through which electricity can pass easily, e.g. all metals are conductors.

(ii) **Insulator** Insulators are those substances through which electricity cannot pass, e.g. wood, rubber, mica etc.

(iii) **Semiconductor** Semiconductors are those substances whose conductivity lies between conductors and insulators, *e.g.,* germanium, silicon, carbon etc.

Energy Bands of Solids

In a crystal due to interatomic interaction valence electrons of one atom are shared by more than one atom in it. Thus, splitting of energy levels takes place. So, the collection of these closely spaced energy levels is called an energy band.

There are following energy bands in solids

(i) **Valence Band** This energy band contains valence electrons. This band may be partially or completely filled with electrons but never be empty.

The electrons in this band are not capable of gaining energy from external electric field to take part in conduction of current.

(ii) **Conduction Band** This band contains conduction electrons. This band is either empty or partially filled with electrons.

Electrons present in this band take part in the conduction of current.

(iii) **Forbidden Band** This band is completely empty. As temperature increases, forbidden energy gap decreases.

Band gap The minimum energy required to shift an electron from valence band to conduction band is called band gap (E_g).

Classification of Solids on the Basis of Energy Bands

Depending on whether the energy band gap is zero, large or small, the solids may be classified into conductors, insulators and semiconductors, as explained below

1. Conductors (Metals)

In case of metals either the conduction band is partially filled and valence band is partially empty, or conduction band and valence band overlap. In case of overlaping electrons from valence band can easily move into conduction band, thus large number of electrons available for conduction. In case valence band is empty, electrons from its lower level can move to higher level making conduction possible.

This is the reason why resistance of metals is low or the conductivity is high.

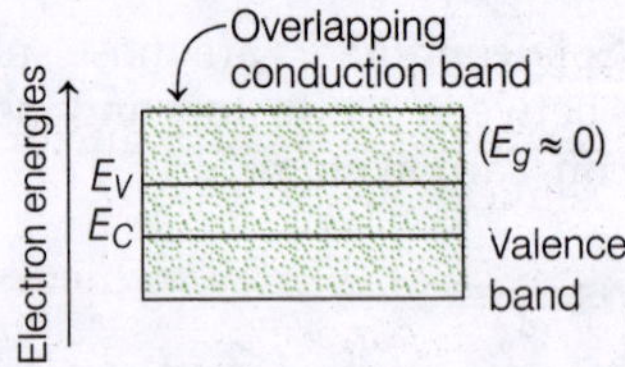

2. Insulators

In insulators, the valence band is completely filled whereas the conduction band is completely empty. As there is no electron in conduction band so no electrical conduction is possible. The energy gap between conduction band and valence band is so large ($E_g > 3$ eV) that no electron in valence band can be provided so much energy from any external source that it can jump this energy gap.

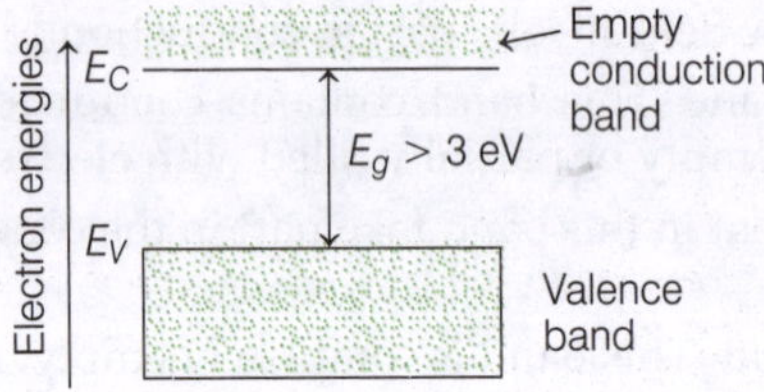

3. Semiconductors

The energy band structure of a semiconductor is shown in figure. It is similar to that of an insulator but with a comparatively small energy gap ($E_g < 3$eV). At absolute zero temperature, the conduction band of semiconductors is totally empty and valence band is completely filled.

Therefore, they are insulators at low temperatures.

However, at room temperature, some electrons in the valence band acquire thermal energy greater than energy band gap and jump over to

the conduction band where they are free to move under the influence of even a small electric field and acquire small conductivity.
Hence the resistance of semiconductor is not as high as that of insulators.

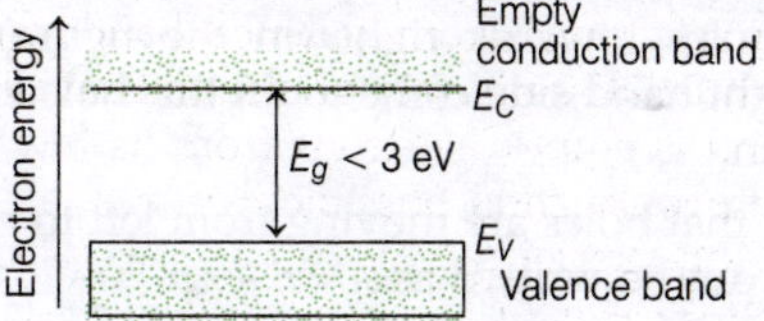

Types of Semiconductor

(i) **Intrinsic Semiconductor** A semiconductor in its pure state is called intrinsic semiconductor.

(ii) **Extrinsic Semiconductor** A semiconductor doped with a suitable impurity to increase its conductivity is called extrinsic semiconductor.

On the basis of doped impurity extrinsic semiconductors are of two types

- ***n*-type Semiconductor** Extrinsic semiconductor doped with pentavalent impurity like As, Sb, Bi, etc in which negatively charged electrons works as charge carrier, is called *n*-type semiconductor. Every pentavalent impurity atom donate one electron in the crystal, therefore it's called a donar atom.
- ***p*-type Semiconductor** Extrinsic semiconductor doped with trivalent impurity like Al, B, etc, in which positively charged holes works as charge carriers, is called *p*-type semiconductor. Every trivalent impurity atom have a tendency to accept one electron, therefore it's called an acceptor atom.

In a doped semiconductor $n_e n_h = n_i^2$, where n_e and n_h are the number density of electrons and holes and n_i is number density of intrinsic carriers, i.e. electrons or holes.

In *n*-type semiconductor, $n_e >> n_h$

In *p*-type semiconductor, $n_h >> n_e$

Electrical Conduction through Semiconductors

When a battery is connected across a semiconductor (whether intrinsic or extrinsic) a potential difference is developed across its ends. Due to the potential difference an electric field is produced inside the semiconductors. A current (although very small) starts flowing through the semiconductor. This current may be due to the motion of (i) free electrons (i_e) and (ii) holes (i_h). Electrons move in opposite direction of electric field while holes move in the same direction.

The motion of holes towards right (in the figure) take place because electrons from right hand side come to fill this hole creating a new hole in their own position.

Thus, we can say that holes are moving from left to right. Thus, current in a semiconductor can be written as, $i = i_e + i_h$

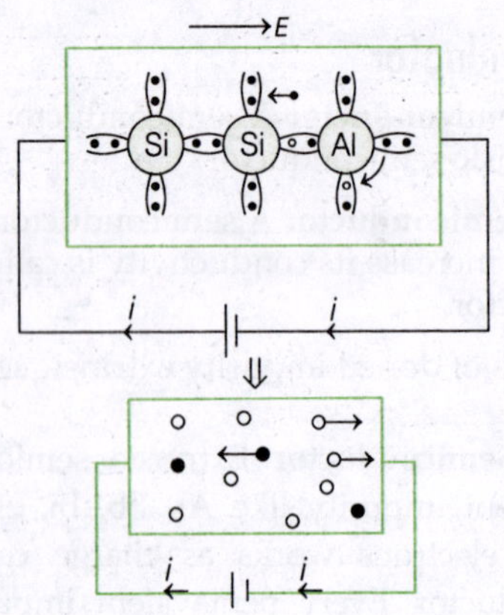

EXPERT Scale Up

The mobility of electrons is much greater than the mobility of holes, therefore *n*-type semiconductor is prefer over *p*-type semiconductor.

Conductivity of semiconductors is given, $\sigma = n_e e \mu_e + n_h e \mu_h$

where n_e and n_h are densities of conduction electrons and holes respectively and μ_e and μ_h are their respective mobilities.

where, $\mu_e = \frac{V_e}{E}, \mu_n = \frac{V_h}{e}$

Electrical conductivity of extrinsic semiconductor is given by

$$\sigma = \frac{1}{\rho} = e(n_e \mu_e + n_h \mu_h)$$

where ρ is resistivity, μ_e and μ_h are mobility of electrons and holes respectively.

Energy gap for Ge is 0.72 eV and for Si, it is 1.1 eV.

p-n Junction and diode

An arrangement consisting a *p*-type semiconductor brought into a close contact with *n*-type semiconductor, is called a *p-n* junction.

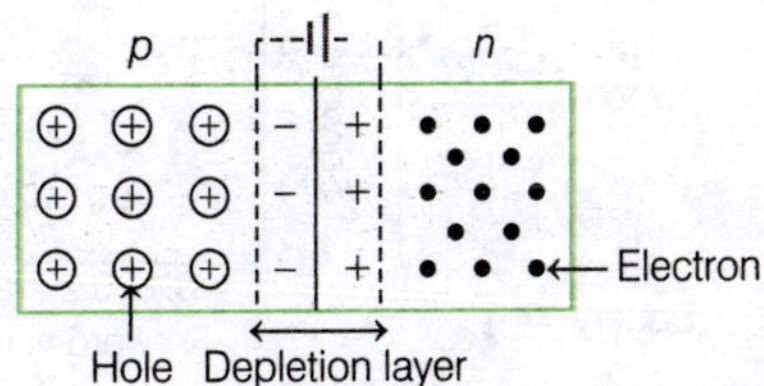

However, if this junction is provided with metallic contacts at the ends for the application of external voltage, then it is called *p-n* junction diode.

p n

p-n junction diode

Terms Related to *p-n* Junction and diode

(i) **Depletion Layer** At *p-n* junction a region is created, where there is no charge carriers. This region is called depletion layer.

The width of this region is of the order of 10^{-6} m.

(ii) **Potential Barrier** The potential difference across the depletion layer is called potential barrier.

Barrier potential for Ge is 0.3 V and for Si is 0.7 V.

(iii) **Forward Biasing** In this biasing, the *p*-side is connected to positive terminal and *n*-side to negative terminal of a battery. In this biasing, forward current flows due to majority charge carriers. The width of depletion layer decreases.

(iv) **Reverse Biasing** In this biasing, the *p*-side is connected to negative terminal and *n*-side to positive terminal of a battery. In this biasing, reverse current flows due to minority charge carriers. The width of depletion layer increases.

Voltage-Current Characteristic Curve of a *p-n* Junction Diode

1. Forward Biased Characteristics

The forward current *versus* forward voltage plot is as shown below

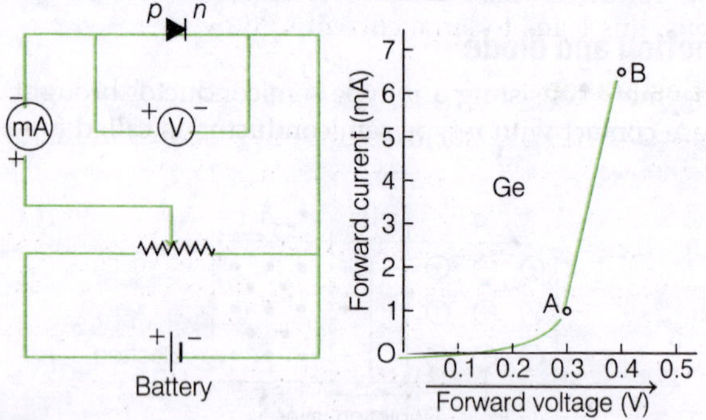

Value Points

The forward voltage beyond which the current through the junction starts increasing rapidly with voltage is called the threshold or knee voltage .

2. Reverse Biased Characteristics

The reverse current *versus* reverse voltage plot is as shown below

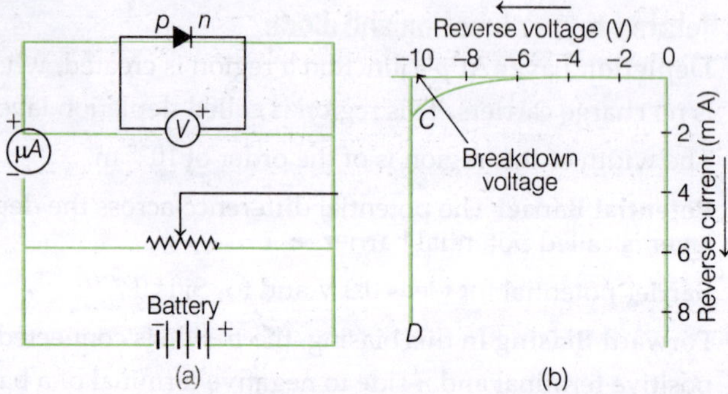

(a) (b)

The reverse current at a certain point is voltage independent upto certain voltage known as **breakdown voltage** and this voltage independent current is called reverse saturation current.

If the reverse biased voltage is too high, then *p-n* junction diode breaks.

(a) Zener Breakdown

With the increase in reverse biased voltage, **E** across the junction also increases. At some point this breaks the covalent bond. Thus, increasing the number of charge carriess, causing large current to flow.

(b) Avalanche Breakdown

High reverse biased voltage, leads to high **E** this causes the minority charge carriers to acquire high velocity while crossing the junction. These carriers by collision breaksdown the covalent bond generating more carries. Thus, this leads to large current to flow.

Dynamic Resistance

The complete *V-I* characterstic of a junction is shown in the figure below

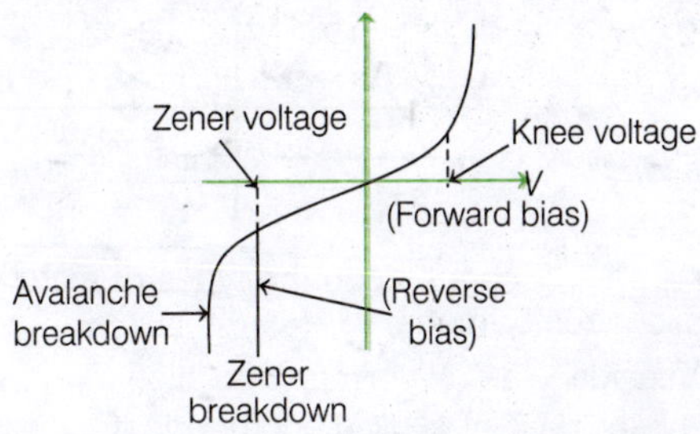

Here, dynamic resistance, $r_d = \dfrac{\Delta V}{\Delta I}$

Competition Insight

Zener Diode

It is a reverse biased heavily doped *p-n* junction diode. It is operated in breakdown region. Its symbol and *V-I* characterstic is shown below as

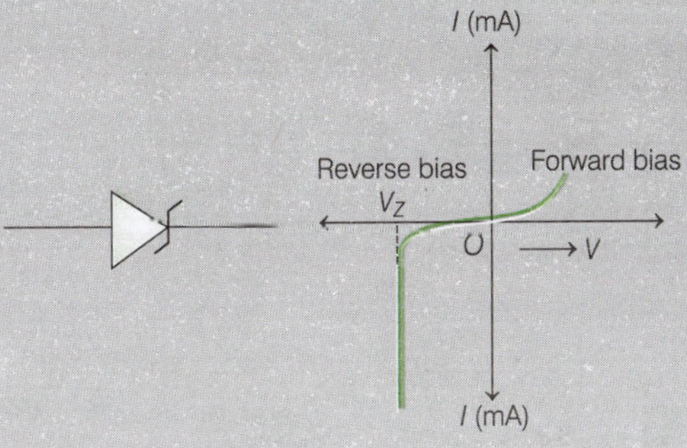

It is also used a voltage regulator.

Light Emitting Diodes (LED)

It is forward biased *p-n* junction diode which emits light when recombination of electrons and holes takes place at the junction.

If the semiconducting material of p-n junction is transparent to light, the light is emitting and the junction becomes a light source, i.e. Light Emitting Diode (LED). Its symbol and V-I characterstic is shown below as

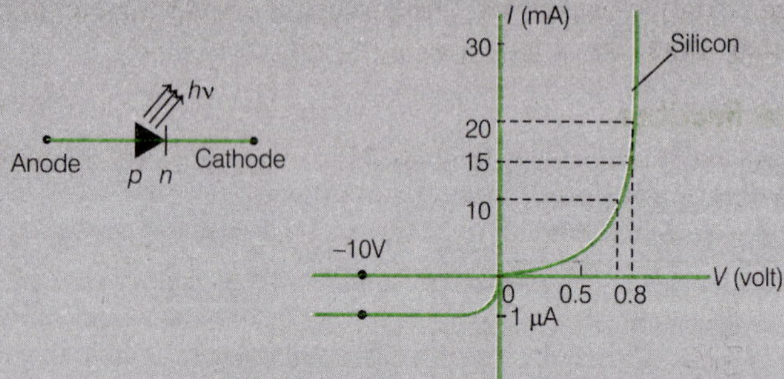

The colour of the light depends upon the types of material used in making the semiconductor diode.

(i) Gallium – Arsenide (Ga-As) – Infrared radiation
(ii) Gallium – Phosphide (GaP) – Red or green light
(iii) Gallium – Arsenide – Phosphide (GaAsP) – Red or yellow light

Photodiode

A photodiode is a special type of junction diode used for detecting optical signals. It is a reverse biased p-n junction made from a photosensitive material. In photodiode, current carriers are generated by photons through photo excitation. Its symbol and V-I characterstic is shown below

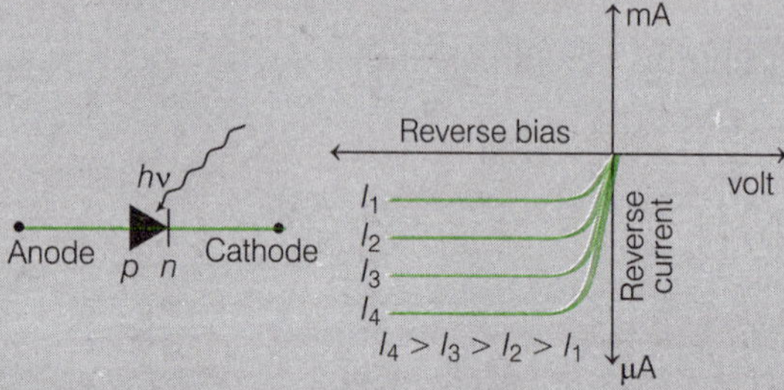

Solar Cell

Solar cell is a p-n junction diode which converts solar energy into electrical energy. Its symbol and V-I characterstic is shown below

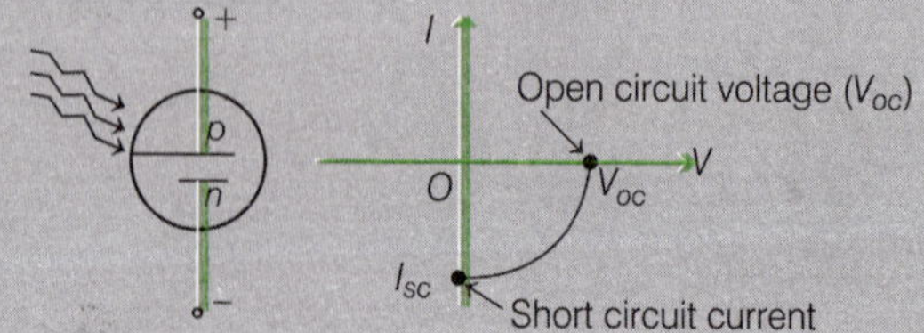

p-n Junction Diode as Rectifier

A device which converts alternating current or voltage into direct current or voltage is known as rectifier. The process of converting AC into DC is called **rectification.**

Half-Wave Rectifier

A half-wave rectifier converts the half cycle of applied AC signal into DC signal. Ordinary transformer may be used here.

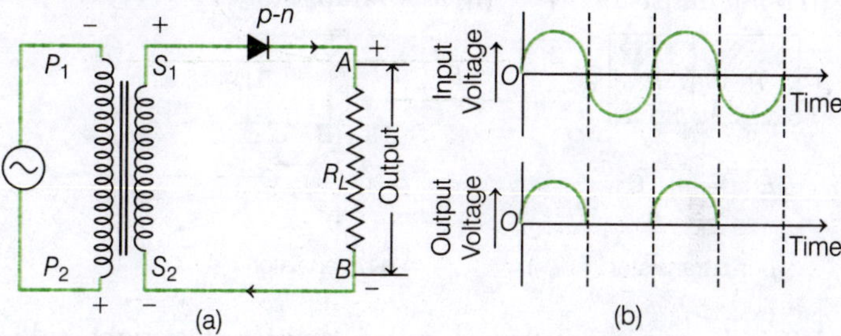

(a) (b)

The ripple frequency (ω) for half wave rectifier is same as that of input AC. Half-wave rectifier converts only one-half of AC input into DC output.

Full-Wave Rectifier

A full-wave rectifier converts the whole cycle of applied AC signal into DC signal. Centre tap transformer is used here.

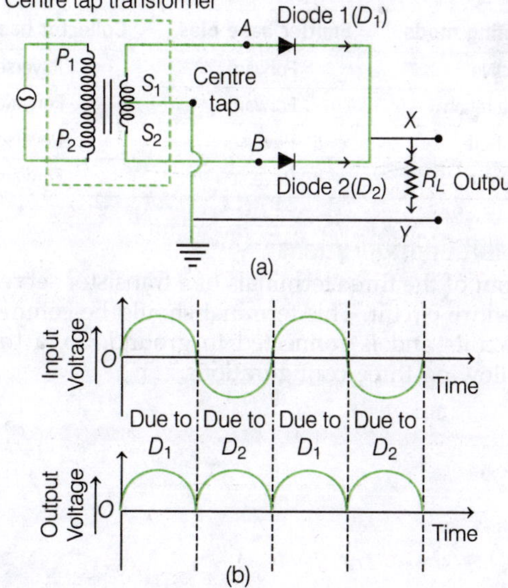

(a)

(b)

The ripple frequency of full-wave rectifier is twice as that of input AC.

Transistor

A transistor is an arrangement obtained by growing a thin layer of one type of semiconductor between two thick layers of other similar type semiconductor.

Types of Transistors

(i) *p-n-p* transistor (ii) *n-p-n* transistor

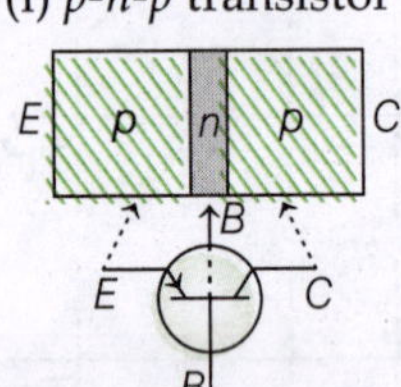

p-n-p transistor

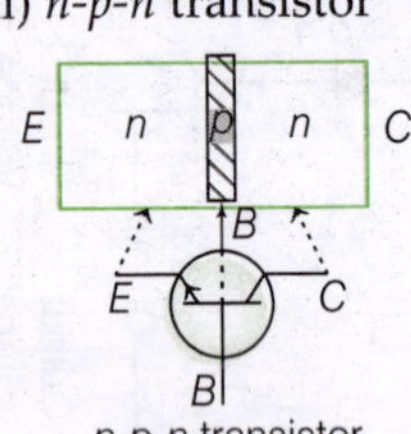

n-p-n transistor

The left side semiconductor is called **emitter,** the right side semiconductor is called **collector** and the thin middle layer is called **base.**

Emitter is highly doped and base is feebly doped.

Biasing of a Transistor

It is defined as the process of applying external voltages to the transistors. Different modes of operation of a transistor is given below

Operating mode	Emitter base bias	Collector base bias
Active	Forward	Reverse
Saturation	Forward	Forward
Cut-off	Reverse	Reverse
Inverse	Reverse	Forward

Transistor Circuit Configurations

One terminal out of the three terminals of a transistor serves as a reference point for the entire circuit. This terminal should be common to the input and output circuits and is connected to ground. So, a transistor can be used in the following three configurations:

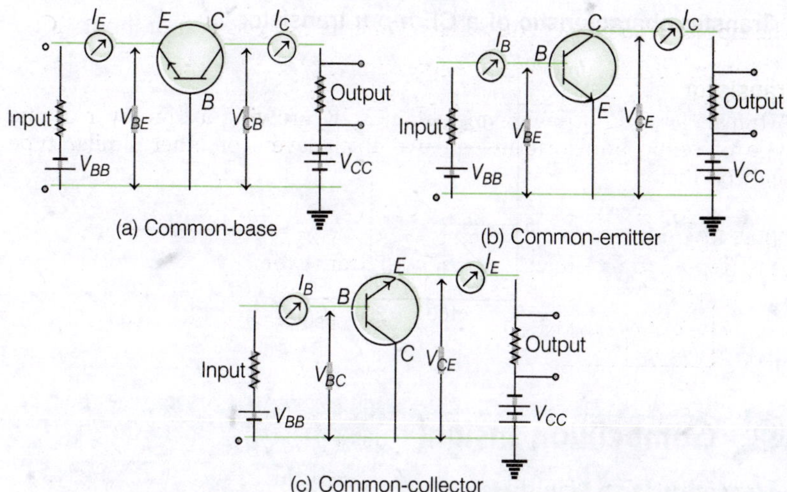

Input characteristic of a CE *n-p-n* transistor

The three types of characterstics curves that can be obtained for the common-emitter configurations are as follows.

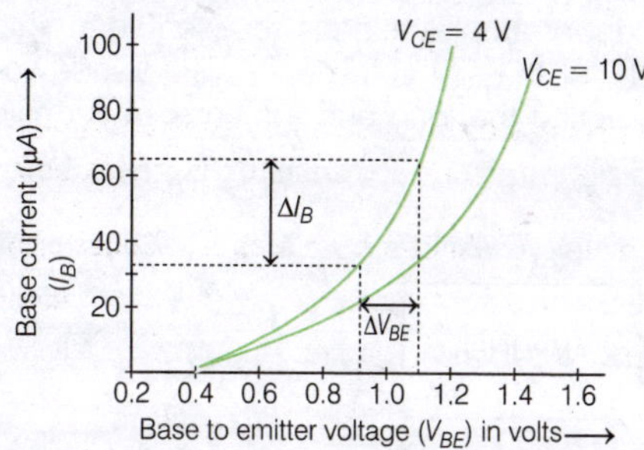

Output characteristic of a CE *n-p-n* transistor

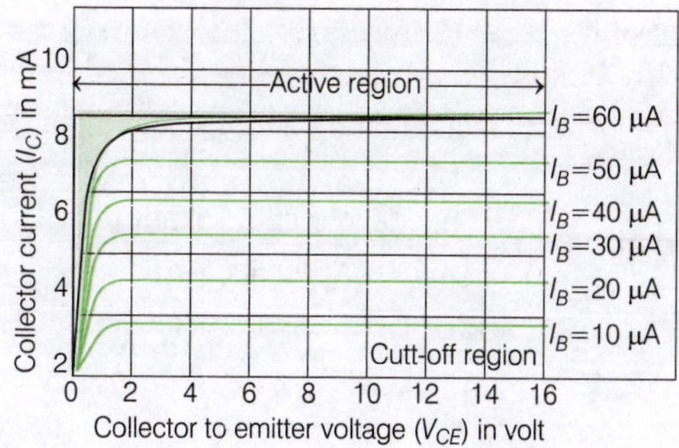

Transfer characteristic of a CE *n-p-n* transistor

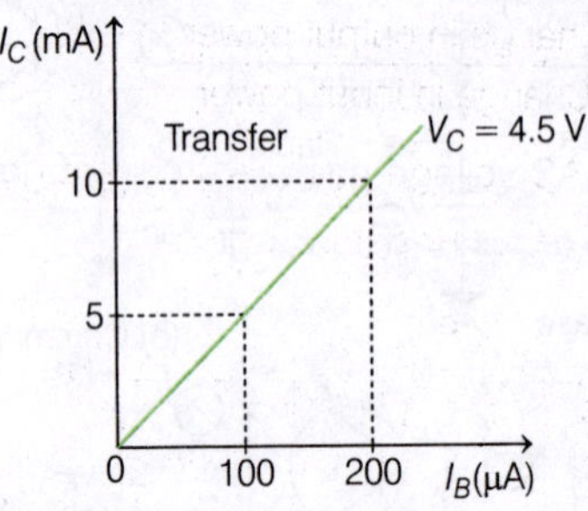

Competition Insight

Transistor as an Amplifier

An amplifier is a device which is used for increasing the amplitude of variation of alternating voltage or current or power.

The amplifier thus produces an enlarged version of the input signal.

The general concept of amplification is repesented in figure. There are two input terminals for the signal to be amplified and two output terminals for connecting the load and a means of supplying power to the amplifier.

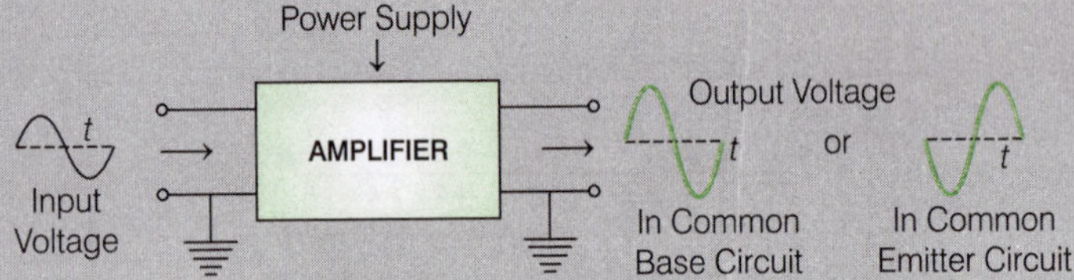

1. Common Base Amplifier

$$\text{AC current gain } (\alpha_{AC}) = \left(\frac{\Delta I_C}{\Delta I_E}\right)_{V_{CB} = \text{constant}}$$

where ΔI_C is change in collector current and ΔI_E change in emitter current.

$$\text{AC voltage gain } (A_V) = \frac{\text{Change in output voltage}}{\text{Change in input voltage}}$$

$$= \alpha_{AC} \times \text{Resistance gain}$$

$$= \alpha_{AC} \times \frac{R_o}{R_i}$$

where, R_o is output resistance of the circuit and R_i is input resistance of the circuit.

$$\text{AC power gain} = \frac{\text{Change in output power}}{\text{Change in input power}}$$

$$= \text{AC voltage gain} \times \text{AC current gain}$$

$$= \alpha_{AC}^2 \times \text{Resistance gain.}$$

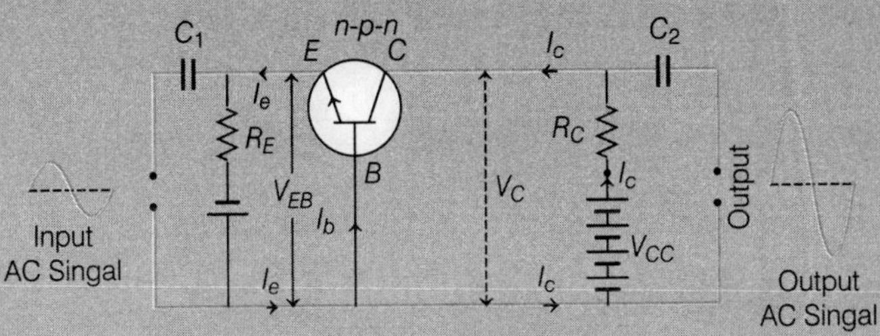

The input and output signals are in the same phase.
There is no amplification in current of a given signal.
There is an amplification in voltage and power of the given signal.

2. Common Emitter Amplifier

$$\text{AC current gain } (\beta_{AC}) = \left(\frac{\Delta I_c}{\Delta I_b}\right)_{V_{CE} = \text{constant}}$$

where ΔI_c is change in collector current, and ΔI_b change in base current.

$$\text{AC voltage gain } (A_V) = \beta_{AC} \times \text{resistance gain}$$

$$\text{AC power gain} = \beta_{AC}^2 \times \text{resistance gain}$$

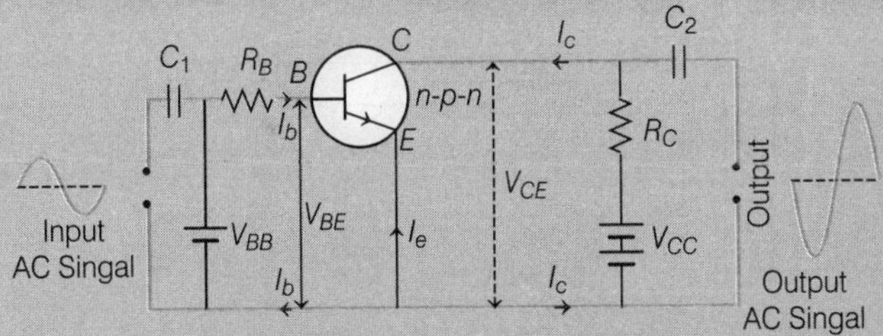

Relation between the current gain of common base and common emitter amplifier, $\beta = \frac{\alpha}{1-\alpha} = \frac{I_c}{I_b}$

The input and output signals are out of phase by π or 180°.
There is amplification in current, voltage and power of the given signal.

Transistor as an Oscillator

An oscillator is an electronic device which produces electric oscillation of constant frequency and amplitude, without any externally applied input signal. It converts DC energy obtained from a battery into AC energy.

Principle of an oscillator

Figure shows the block diagram of an oscillator. An oscillator may be regarded as amplifier which provides its own input signal.

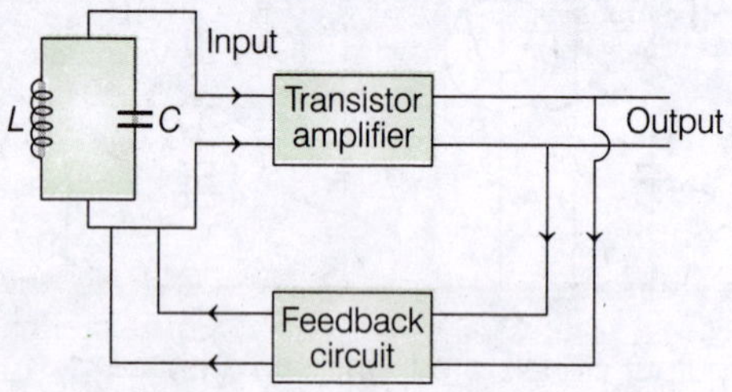

Essential parts of a transistor oscillator are

(i) **Tank Circuit** It is a parallel combination of an inductance L and a capacitance C. The frequency of electric oscillations in the tank circuit is $f = \dfrac{1}{2\pi\sqrt{LC}}$

(ii) **Transistor Amplifier** The amplifier receives the oscillations from the tank circuit and amplifies it.

(iii) **Feedback Circuit** It returns a part of the output power of the transistor amplifier to the tank circuit and produces undamped oscillations. This process is called positive feedback.

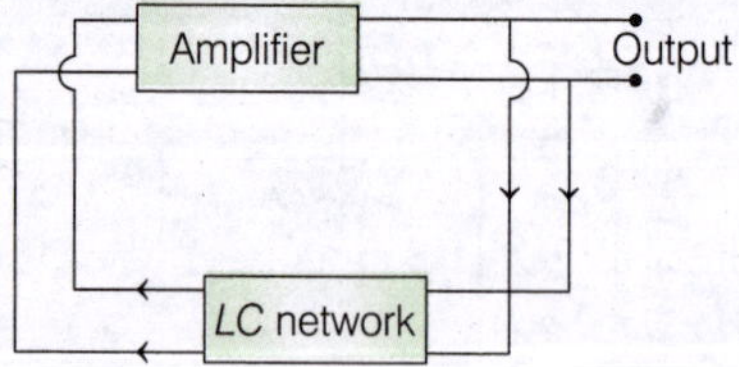

Construction

A basic circuit using a common-emitter n-p-n transistor as an oscillator is given below. A tank circuit (L-C circuit) is connected in the emitter-base circuit. A small coil L called **feedback or tickler** coil is connected in the emitter-collector circuit. The coil L is inductively coupled with the coil L of the tank circuit.

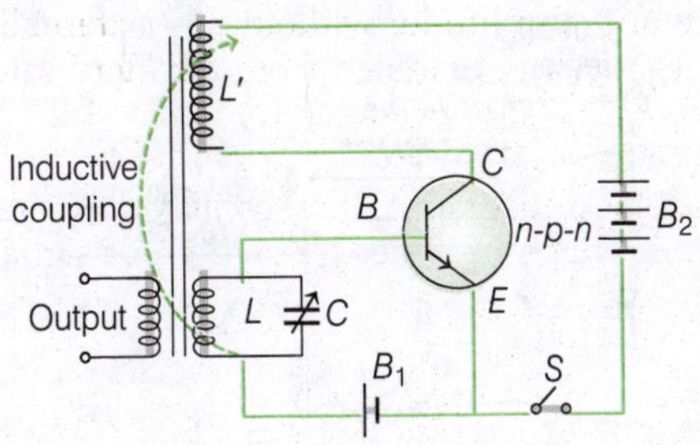

Transistor as a switch

Transistor has an ability to turn things ON and OFF. So, the most common use of transistor in an electronic circuit is as simple switches.

A transistor can be used as a switch because its collector current is directly controlled by the base current.

To understand it properly, letus consider a basic circuit using a common-emitter *n-p-n* transistor as a switch which is given below.

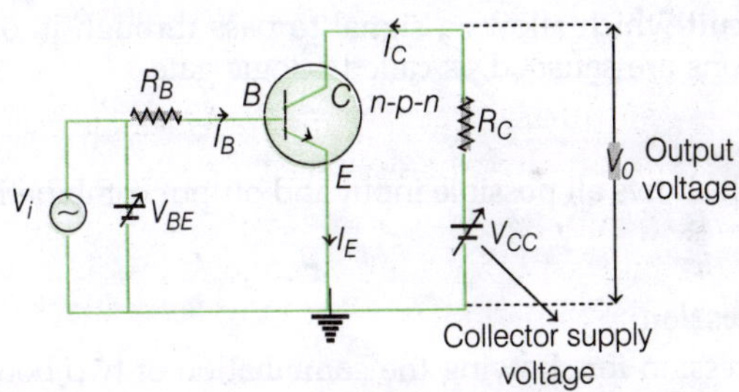

Apply Kirchhoff's voltage rule to the input and output sides of this circuit, we get

$$V_i = I_B \cdot R_B + V_{BE} \qquad (V_i = \text{DC input voltage})$$

and

$$V_o = V_{CC} - I_C \cdot R_C \qquad (V_o = \text{DC output voltage})$$

In case of silicon transistor, if $V_i < 0.6$ V, I_B will be zero, hence, I_C will be zero and transistor will operate in **cut-off state,** and $V_0 = V_{CC}$.

When $V_i > 0.6$ V, some I_B flows, so some I_C flows and transistor will now operate in **active state** and hence output V_0 decreases as the term

$I_C R_C$ increases. With increase in V_i, the I_C increases almost linearly and hence V_0 decreases linearly till its value becomes less than about 1 volt.

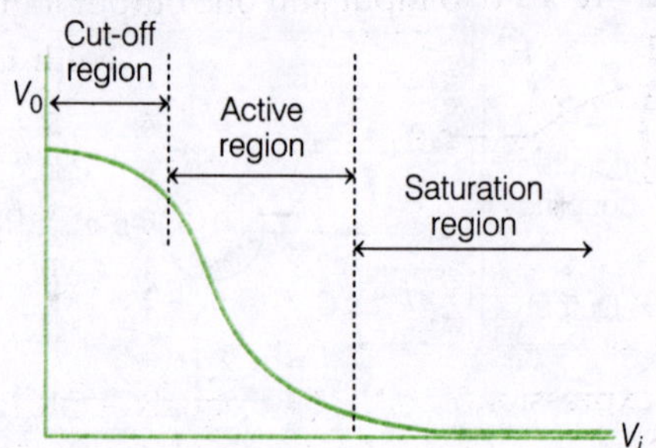

Beyond this, the change becomes non-linear and transistor now goes into the saturation state. When V_i is further increased, V_0 is found to decrease towards zero (however, it may never become to zero).

Now, the operation of transistor as a switch can be understood in the following way. When V_i is low (in cut-off region), V_0 is high. If V_i is high (in saturation region), then V_0 is low, almost zero.

Logic Gate

A digital circuit which allows a signal to pass through it, only when few logical relations are satisfied, is called a logic gate.

Truth Table

A table which shows all possible input and output combinations is called a truth table.

Boolean Expression

It is the expression for showing the combination of two boolean variables resulting into a new boolean variable.

The Boolean expression obey commutative law associative law as well as distributive law.

(i) $A + B = B + A$

(ii) $A \cdot B = B \cdot A$

(iii) $A + (B + C) = (A + B) + C$

de-Morgan's theorems

(i) $\overline{A + B} = \overline{A} \cdot \overline{B}$

(ii) $\overline{A \cdot B} = \overline{A} + \overline{B}$

Basic Logic Gates

(i) **OR Gate** It is a two input and one output logic gate.

Symbol

Truth table

A	B	$Y = A + B$
0	0	0
0	1	1
1	0	1
1	1	1

Boolean expression $Y = A + B$ (Y equals A OR B)

(ii) **AND Gate** It is a two input and one output logic gate.

Symbol

Truth table

A	B	$Y = A \cdot B$
0	0	0
0	1	0
1	0	0
1	1	1

Boolean expression $Y = A \cdot B$ (Y equals A AND B)

(iii) **NOT Gate** It is a one input and one output logic gate.

Symbol

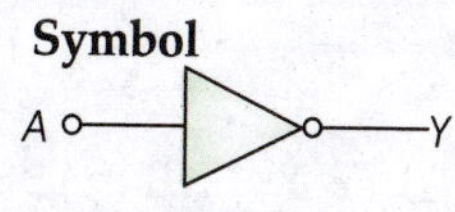

Truth table

A	$Y = \overline{A}$
0	1
1	0

Boolean expression $Y = \overline{A}$ (Y equals NOT A)

Competition Insight

Combination of Gates

(i) **NAND Gate** When output of AND gate is applied as input to a NOT gate, then it is called a NAND gate.

Symbol

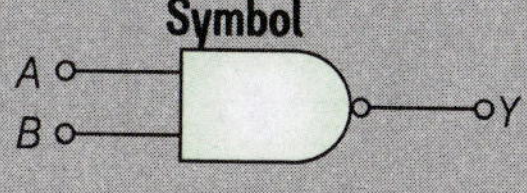

Truth table

A	B	$Y = \overline{A \cdot B}$
0	0	1
0	1	1
1	0	1
1	1	0

Boolean expression $Y = \overline{A \cdot B}$ (Y equals negated of A AND B)

(ii) **NOR Gate** When output of OR gate is applied as input to a NOT gate, then it is called a NOR gate.

Truth table

A	B	Y
0	0	1
0	1	0
1	0	0
1	1	0

Boolean expression $Y = \overline{A + B}$ (Y equals negated of A OR B)

(iii) **XOR gate** It is also called exclusive OR function

Symbol

Truth table

A	B	$\overline{A}$	$\overline{B}$	$A \cdot \overline{B}$	$\overline{A} \cdot B$	$A = A \cdot \overline{B} + \overline{A} \cdot B$
0	0	1	1	0	0	0
0	1	1	0	0	1	1
1	0	0	1	1	0	1
1	1	0	0	0	0	0

Boolean expression

$$Y = A \text{ XOR } B \text{ or } Y = A \oplus B \text{ or } Y = \overline{A}B + A\overline{B}$$

(iv) **XNOR gate** It is also called exclusive NOR function.

Symbol

Truth table

A	B	$Y = \overline{A}\overline{B} + AB$
0	0	1
0	1	0
1	0	0
1	1	1

Boolean expression

$$Y = A \odot B \quad \text{or} \quad Y = \overline{A}\overline{B} + AB$$

Handbook of Physics

Knowledge LIBRARY

Oscillations

Types of Pendulum

(i) Conical Pendulum

- If a simple pendulum is fixed at one end and the bob is rotating in a horizontal circle, then it is called a conical pendulum.

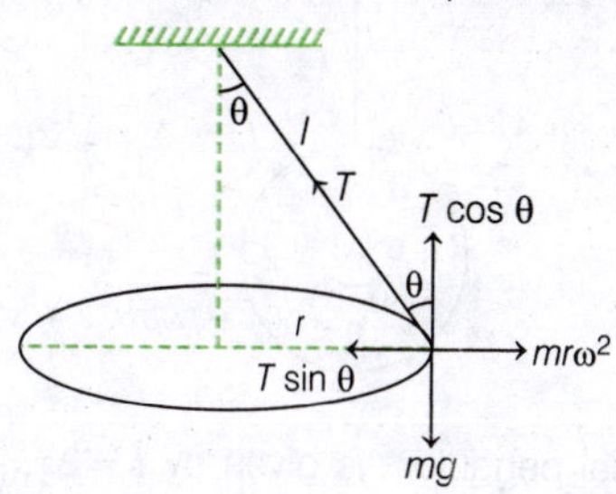

- In equilibrium, $T \sin \theta = mr\omega^2$
- It's time period, $T' = 2\pi \sqrt{\dfrac{mr}{T \sin \theta}}$

(ii) Compound Pendulum

- Any rigid body mounted, so that it is capable of swinging in a vertical plane about some axis passing through it is called a compound pendulum.
- Its time period is given by

$$T = 2\pi \sqrt{\frac{I}{mg\,d}}$$

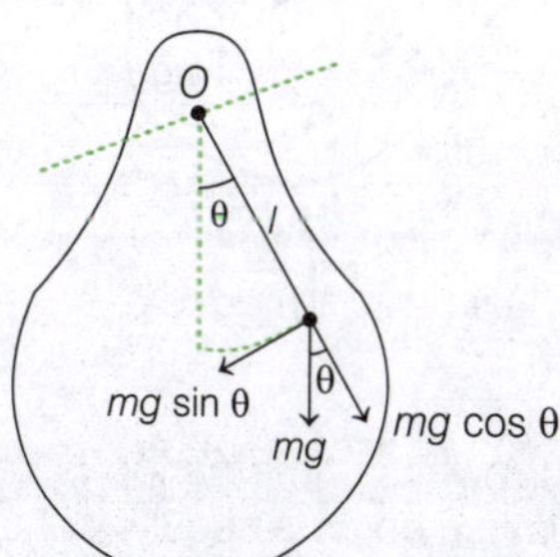

where, I = moment of inertia of the body about an axis passing through the centre of suspension,

m = mass of the body

and d = distance of centre of gravity from the centre of suspension.

(iii) Torsional Pendulum

- It consists of a disc (or some other object) suspended from a wire suspended to a rigid support, which is then twisted and released, resulting in oscillatory motion.

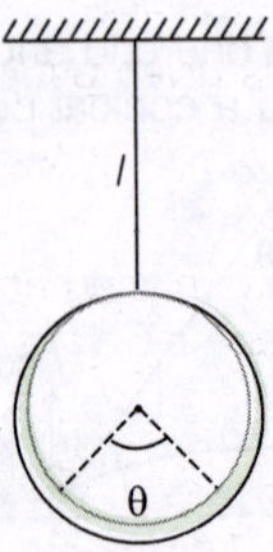

- Time period of torsional pendulum is given by $T = 2\pi\sqrt{\frac{I}{C}}$

where, I = moment of inertia of the body about the axis of rotation and C = restoring couple per unit twist.

(iv) Physical Pendulum

- When a rigid body of any shape is capable of oscillating about an axis (may or may not be passing through it), it constitutes a physical pendulum.

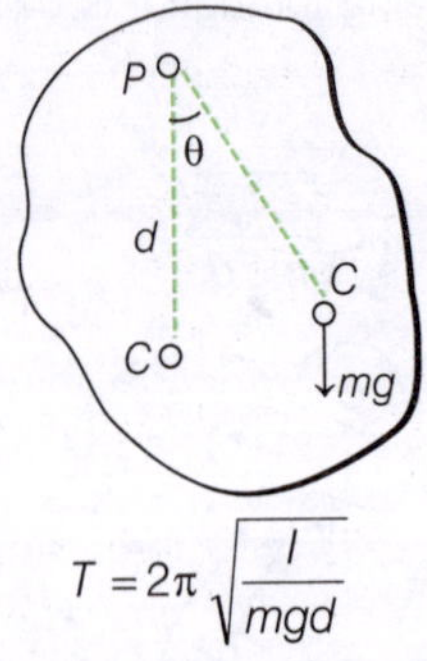

$$T = 2\pi\sqrt{\frac{I}{mgd}}$$

Value Points

- The simple pendulum whose time period is same as that of a physical pendulum is termed as an equivalent simple pendulum.

$$T = 2\pi\sqrt{\frac{I}{mgd}} = 2\pi\sqrt{\frac{l}{g}}$$

- The length of an equivalent simple pendulum is given by $l = \frac{I}{md}$

Oscillations of Liquid in a U-tube

- If a liquid is filled up to height h in both limbs of a U-tube and now liquid is depressed upto a small distance y in one limb and then released, then liquid column in U-tube start executing SHM.
- The time period of oscillation is given by $T = 2\pi\sqrt{\frac{h}{g}}$

Oscillations of Ball in Bowl

- If a small steel ball of mass m is placed at a small distance from O inside a smooth concave surface of radius R and released, it will oscillate about O.

$$T = 2\pi\sqrt{\frac{R}{g}}$$

Oscillations of a Ball in a Tunnel through the Earth

- If a ball moves through a tunnel along a diameter of earth, then due to gravitational force between ball and earth a restoring force is set up, due to which the ball performs SHM, whose time period is given by

$$T = 2\pi\sqrt{R/g}$$

where, R = radius of earth.

Free Oscillations

- When a body which can oscillate about its mean position is displaced from mean position and then released, it oscillates about its mean position.
- These oscillations are called free oscillations and the frequency of oscillations is called **natural frequency.**

Damped Oscillations

- The oscillations in which amplitude decreases with time are called damped oscillations.
- The displacement of the damped oscillator at an instant t is given by

$$x = x_0 e^{-bt/2m}\cos(\omega' t + \phi)$$

where, $x_0 e^{-bt/2m}$ is the amplitude of oscillator which decreases continuously with time t and ω'.

- The mechanical energy E of the damped oscillator at an instant t is given by

$$E = \frac{1}{2}kx_0^2 e^{-bt/m}$$

Forced Oscillations

- Oscillations of any object with a frequency different from its natural frequency under a periodic external force are called forced oscillations.

Resonant Oscillations

- When a body oscillates with its own natural frequency with the help of an external periodic force whose frequency is equal to the natural frequency of the body, then these oscillations are called resonant oscillations.

Lissajous' Figures

- If two SHMs are acting in mutually perpendicular directions, then due to their superpositions the resultant motion, in general, is a curve/loop.
- The shape of the curve depends on the frequency ratio of two SHMs and initial phase difference between them. Such figures are called Lissajous' figures.
- Let two SHMs be of same frequency (*e.g.* $x = a_1 \sin \omega t$ and $y = a_2 \sin (\omega t + \phi)$, then the general equation of resultant motion is found to be

$$\frac{x^2}{a_1^2} + \frac{y^2}{a_2^2} - \frac{2xy}{a_1 a_2} \cos \phi = \sin^2 \phi$$

- The equation represents an ellipse. However, if $\phi = 0°$ or π or $n\pi$, then the resultant curve is a straight inclined line.

Waves

Doppler's Effect

- The phenomena of apparent change in frequency of source due to a relative motion between the source and observer is called Doppler's effect.
  (i) **When Source is Moving and Observer is at Rest** When source is moving with velocity v_S, towards an observer at rest, then apparent frequency

$$n' = n\left(\frac{v}{v - v_S}\right)$$

v_S S → v O

If source is moving away from observer, then

$$n' = n\left(\frac{v}{v + v_S}\right)$$

v_S S → v O

(ii) **When Source is at Rest and Observer is Moving** When observer is moving with velocity v_o, towards a source at rest, then apparent frequency.

$$n' = n\left(\frac{v + v_o}{v}\right)$$

When observer is moving away from source, then

$$n' = n\left(\frac{v - v_o}{v}\right)$$

(iii) **When Source and Observer Both are Moving**

(a) When both are moving in same direction along the direction of propagation of sound, then

$$n' = n\left(\frac{v - v_o}{v - v_s}\right)$$

(b) When both are moving in same direction opposite to the direction of propagation of sound, then

$$n' = n\left(\frac{v + v_o}{v + v_s}\right)$$

(c) When both are moving towards each other, then

$$n' = n\left(\frac{v + v_o}{v - v_s}\right)$$

(d) When both are moving in opposite direction, away from each other, then

$$n' = n\left(\frac{v - v_o}{v + v_s}\right)$$

Transverse Doppler's Effect

- As shown in figure, the position of a source is S and of observer is O. The component of velocity of source towards the observer is $v \cos \theta$. For this situation, the approach frequency (*i.e.* at A) is

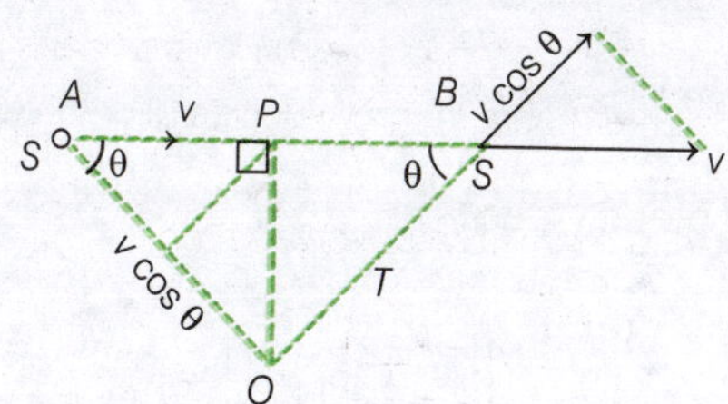

$$n' = \frac{v}{v - v_s \cos\theta} \times n$$

n' which will now be a function of θ so, it will no more be constant.

- Similarly, if then source is moving away from the observer (*i.e.* at *B*) as shown above, with velocity component $v_s \cos\theta$, then

$$n' = \frac{v}{v + v_s \cos\theta} \times n$$

- If $\theta = 90°$, then $v_s \cos\theta = 0$ and there is no shift in the frequency. Thus, at point *P*, Doppler's effect does not occur.

Competition Insight

Effect of motion of medium (air) on apparent frequency

If wind is also blowing with a velocity w, then in this condition the apparent frequency is given by $n' = n\left(\frac{v \pm w \pm v_o}{v \pm w \pm v_s}\right)$

Doppler's effect in reflected sound

- If a source of sound moving towards a stationary wall and there is a stationary observer.
- Then, beat frequency heard by the observer is

$$n_b = \left(\frac{v}{v - v_s} - \frac{v}{v + v_s}\right) n$$

- If car is approaching a wall, then beat frequency heard by the observer in car is $n_b = n\left(\frac{2u}{v - u}\right)$

  where, u is the velocity of car.

Applications of Doppler's Effect

- The measurement from Doppler effect has been used
  - (i) by police to check over speeding of vehicles.
  - (ii) at airports to guide the aircraft.
  - (iii) to study heart beats and blood flow in different parts of the body.
  - (iv) by astrophysicist to measure the velocities of planets and stars.

Limitations of Doppler's Effect

- For supersonic speeds of source or observer, v_s and v_0 should be less $v.v_s < v.v_0 < v$.
- This effect fails when source and observer move at right angles to each other.

Chemical Effect of Electric Current

When a direct current flows through a acidic or basic solution it dissociates into positive and negative ions. This phenomena is called electrolysis and these solutions are called electrolytes.

Some Terms of Electrolysis

(i) **Anode** The electrode connected to the positive terminal of the battery is called an anode.

(ii) **Cathode** The electrode connected to the negative terminal of the battery is called a cathode.

(iii) **Anions** The ions carrying negative charge and move towards the anode in electrolysis are called anions.

(iv) **Cations** The ions carrying positive charge and move towards the cathode in electrolysis are called cations.

(v) **Voltameter** The vessel in which the electrolysis is carried out is called a voltameter.

(vi) **Ionisation** The phenomenon of separation of a molecule into oppositely charged ions is known as ionisation.

Faraday's Laws of Electrolysis

Faraday's laws of electrolysis are of two types

First Law

The mass of the substance liberated during electrolysis at each electrode is directly proportional to the total charge passed through the electrolyte.

$$m \propto q \quad \text{or} \quad m = Zq = ZIt$$

where, Z = Electrochemical equivalent of the substance deposited on electrode,

q = Total charge passed through the electrolyte,

I = Electric current

and t = Time.

Second Law

The mass of each substance liberated at the electrodes in electrolysis by a given amount of charge is proportional to the chemical equivalents of the substances.

$$m \propto E \quad \text{or} \quad \frac{m_1}{m_2} = \frac{E_1}{E_2}$$

where, m_1 and m_2 are masses of the substance liberated on electrodes by passing same amount of current for the same time and E_1, E_2 are chemical equivalents of these substances.

$$\text{Chemical equivalent} = \frac{\text{Atomic weight}}{\text{Valency}}$$

Faraday's constant $(F) = \frac{E}{Z}$

Faraday's constant is equal to the amount of charge required to liberate one chemical equivalent (in gram) of mass of a substance at a electrode during electrolysis.

Faraday's constant, $(F) = Ne$

where, N = Avogadro's number and e = Electronic charge.

or $F = (6.0229 \times 10^{23}) \times (1.602 \times 10^{-19}) = 96487\ C \approx 96500\ C$

Value Points

Uses of Electrolysis

- Electrolysis is used for local anaesthesia. For it current is passed through a nerve, due to which it becomes insensitive to pain.
- Electrolysis is also used for nerve stimulation of polio patients.
- The process of coating an object, that conduct electricity, with another metal is called **electroplating**. The articles of cheap metal are coated with precious metals like silver and gold to make them look attractive.
- The process of coating aluminium with its oxide electrochemically to protect it against corrosion is called **anodising**.

Thermoelectric Effect

Thermocouple

If two wires of different metals are joined at their ends so as to form two junctions, then the resulting arrangement is known as thermocouple.

Uses of Thermocouple

(a) Thermometer to measure temperature.

(b) Thermoelectric current-meter to measure current.

(c) Thermoelectric generator.

(d) Thermoelectric refrigerator.

Seebeck Effect

When the two junctions of a thermocouple are kept at different temperatures, then an emf is produced between the junctions, which is called thermo emf and this phenomena is called seebeck effect.

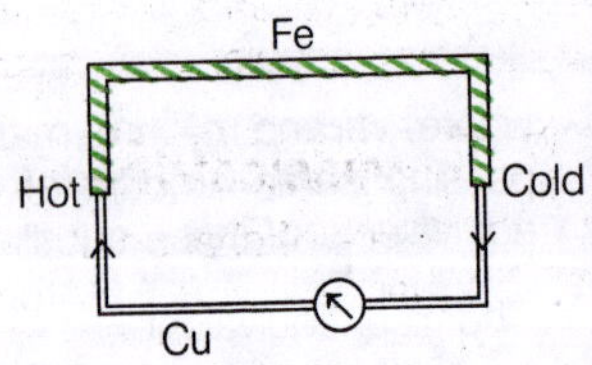

Thermoelectric Series or Seebeck Series

Seebeck form a series of metals for which thermoelectric current flows in a thermocouple through the hot junction from a metal occuring earlier, to a metal occuring later in series.

The series is given below

Bi, Ni, Co, Pd, Pt, Cu, Mn, Hg, Pb, Sn, Au, Zn, Cd, Fe, Sb, Te, Fe, Mo and Cr.

Neutral Temperature (T_n)

The temperature of the hot junction at which thermo emf in a thermocouple is maximum is called neutral temperature. The value of neutral temperature is constant for thermocouple. Its value depends upon the nature of material forming the thermocouple and independent of temperature of cold junction.

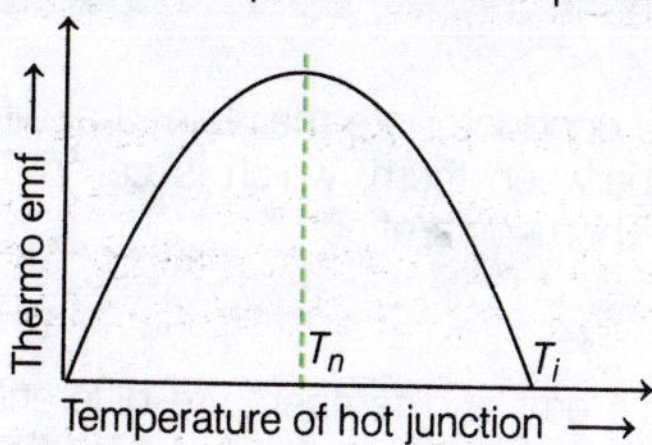

Temperature of Inversion (T_i)

The temperature of the hot junction at which the thermo emf in a thermocouple becomes zero and beyond it, reverses its direction is called temperature of inversion. Its value depends upon the temperature of the cold junction as well as the nature of the materials forming the thermocouple.

Relation between neutral temperature (T_n) and temperature of inversion (T_i) is given by

$$T_n = \frac{T_i + T_0}{2}$$

where, T_0 is the temperature of **cold junction.**

When cold junction is at 0°C, then thermo emf changes with temperature of hot junction (T) as follows

$$E = \alpha T + \frac{1}{2}\beta T^2$$

where, α and β are constants depending upon nature of metals forming thermocouple.

Thermoelectric Power

The rate of change of thermo emf with temperature is called thermoelectric power.

Thermoelectric power, $S = \frac{dE}{dt} = \alpha + \beta T$

Peltier Effect

When current is passed through a thermocouple, then heat is generated at its one junction and absorbed at another junction. This phenomena is called Peltier effect.

Peltier effect is the reverse effect of seebeck effect.

Peltier Coefficient

The ratio of heat energy absorbed or evolved at a junction of a thermocouple to the charge flowing through it called Peltier coefficient.

$$\text{Peltier coefficient, } \pi = \frac{\text{Peltier heat}}{\text{Charge flowing}}$$

Its SI unit is JC^{-1}.

Thomson's Effect

If two parts of a single conductor are maintained at different temperatures, then an emf is produced between them, which is called **Thomson's emf** and this phenomena is called Thomson's effect.

Thomson's Coefficient

The ratio of Thomson's emf and temperature difference between two points is called Thomson's coefficient.

$$\text{Thomson's coefficient, } (\sigma) = \frac{dV}{dT}$$

where, dV = Potential difference between two points

and dT = Temperature difference between the two same points.

Thermopile

It is a combination of a large number of thermocouples in series. It is used to detect the heat radiation and to note small variation or difference in temperature.

Deflection Magnetometer

It is a device used to determine M and H. Its working is based on tangent law. Deflection magnetometer can be used into two settings

(i) **Tangent A setting** In this setting, the arms of the magnetometer are along East-West and magnet is parallel to the arms.

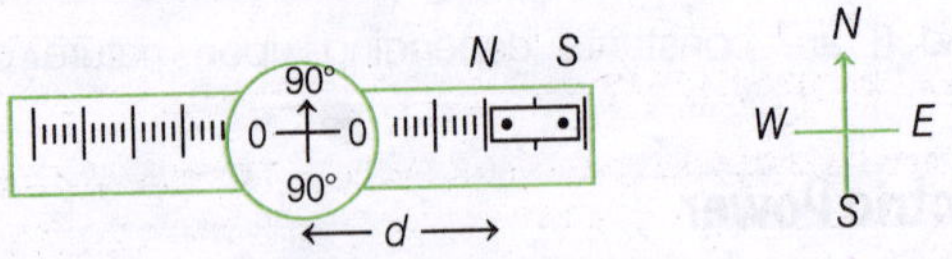

In equilibrium, $B = H \tan \theta$

$$\frac{\mu_0}{4\pi} \cdot \frac{2M}{d^3} = H \tan \theta$$

(ii) **Tangent *B* setting** In this setting, the arms of the magnetometer are along North-South and magnet is perpendicular to these arms.
In equilibrium,

$$B = H \tan \theta$$

$$\frac{\mu_0}{4\pi} \cdot \frac{M}{d^3} = H \tan \theta$$

In above setting, the experiment can be performed in two ways

(a) **Deflection method** In this method, one magnet is used at a time and deflection in galvanometer is observed.

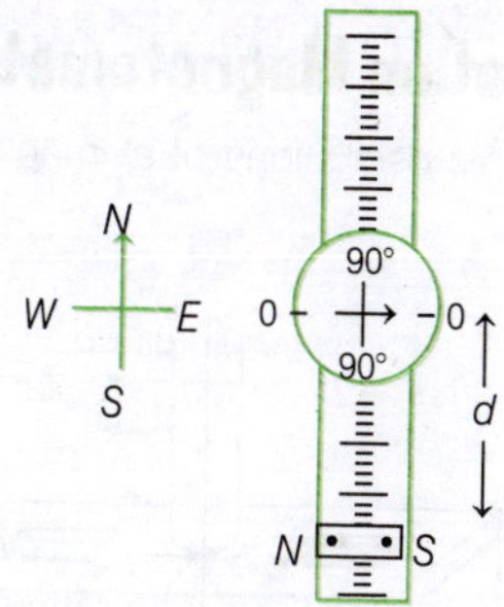

Ratio of magnetic dipole moments of the magnets, $\frac{M_1}{M_2} = \frac{\tan \theta_1}{\tan \theta_2}$

where, θ_1 and θ_2 are mean values of deflection for two magnets.

(b) **Null method** In this method, both magnets are used at a time and no deflectioin condition is obtained. If magnets are at distances d_1 and d_2, then $\frac{M_1}{M_2} = \left(\frac{d_1}{d_2}\right)^3$

Tangent Galvanometer

It is a device used for detection and measurement of low electric currents. Its working is based on tangent law.

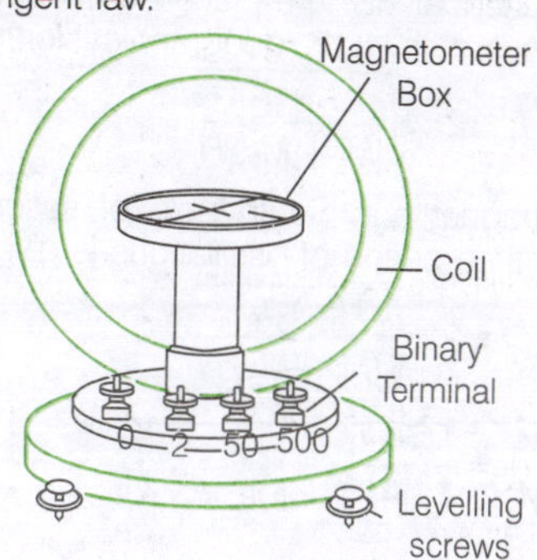

If θ is the deflection produced in galvanometer when I current flows through it, then

$$I = \frac{2R}{N\mu_0} H \tan\theta = \frac{H}{G} \tan\theta = K \tan\theta$$

where, $G = \frac{N\mu_0}{2R}$ is called **galvanometer constant** and $K = \frac{H}{G}$ is called **reduction factor** of tangent galvanometer.

Here, N is number of turns in the coil and R is radius of the coil.

Tangent galvanometer is also called moving magnet type galvanometer.

Vibration Magnetometer

It is based on simple harmonic oscillations of a magnet suspended in uniform magnetic field.

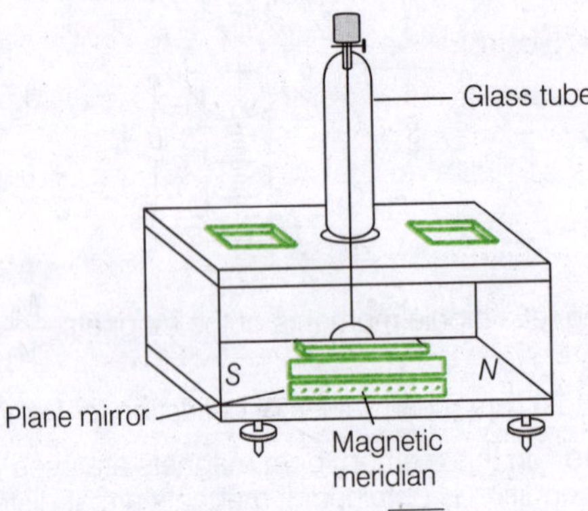

Time period of vibrations is given by, $T = 2\pi\sqrt{\frac{I}{MH}}$

where, I = moment of inertia of the magnet,

M = magnetic dipole moment of the magnet

and H = horizontal component of earth's magnetic field.

When two magnets of unequal size are placed one above the other and North poles of both magnets are towards geographic North, then time period of oscillations is given by, $T_1 = 2\pi\sqrt{\frac{I_1 + I_2}{(M_1 + M_2)H}}$

If North pole of first magnet and South pole of second magnet is towards geographic North, then time period of oscillations is given by

$$T_2 = 2\pi\sqrt{\frac{(I_1 + I_2)}{(M_1 - M_2)H}}$$

Then, $$\frac{M_1}{M_2} = \frac{T_2^2 + T_1^2}{T_2^2 - T_1^2}$$

X-rays

When cathode rays strike on a heavy metal of high melting point, then a very small fraction of its energy converts into a new type of waves called X-rays. X-rays were discovered by **Roentgen**.

Properties of X-rays

(i) X-rays are electromagnetic waves of wavelengths ranging from 0.1 Å to 100 Å and frequencies ranging from 10^{16} Hz to 10^{18} Hz.

(ii) Soft X-rays have greater wavelength and lower frequency.

(iii) Hard X-rays have lower wavelength and higher frequency.

(iv) X-rays are produced in coolidge tube.

(v) Molybdenum and tungsten provide suitable targets. These elements have large atomic number and high melting point for the purpose.

(vi) The intensity of X-rays depends on the heating voltage or filament current.

(vii) The kinetic energy of X-ray photons depends upon the voltage applied across the ends of coolidge tube.

(viii) If total energy of fast moving electron transfer to X-ray photon, then its energy $eV = h\nu = \frac{hc}{\lambda}$.

(ix) Wavelength of emitted X-rays is given by $\lambda = \frac{hc}{eV}$,

where h = Planck's constant, c = speed of light, e = electronic charge and V = potential difference applied across the ends of the tube.

(x) Absorption of X-rays $I = I_0 e^{-\mu x}$, where I_0 = initial intensity of X-rays, I = final intensity of emergent X-rays, x = thickness of material and μ = absorption coefficient.

Classification of X-rays

X-rays are of two types, continuous and characteristic. While the former depends only on the accelerating voltage V, the later depends on the target used.

(i) **Continuous X-rays** The continuous X-rays (or bremsstrahlung X-rays) produced at a given accelerating potential V vary in wavelength, but none has a wavelength shorter than a certain value λ_{min}. This minimum wavelength corresponds to the maximum energy of the X-rays which in turn is equal to the maximum kinetic energy qV or eV of the striking electrons. Thus,

$$\frac{hc}{\lambda_{min}} = eV \quad \text{or} \quad \lambda_{min} = \frac{hc}{eV}$$

After substituting values of h, c and e, we obtain the following simple formula for λ_{min}.

$$\lambda_{min} \text{ (in Å)} = \frac{12375}{V} \quad \ldots\text{(i)}$$

If V is increased, then λ_{min} decreases. This wavelength is also known as the **cut-off wavelength** or the **threshold wavelength**.

(ii) **Characteristic X-rays** Some of the fast moving electrons with high velocity penetrate the surface atoms of the target material and knock out the electrons even from the inner most shells of atom. Now, a vacancy is created at that place.

Electrons from higher shell jumps to fill the created vacancy. When the electron jumps from a higher energy level E_2 to lower energy orbit E_1, it radiates energy $(E_2 - E_1)$. Thus, this energy difference is radiated in the form of X-rays of very small but definite wavelength which depends upon target material. The X-ray spectrum consists of sharp lines and is called **characteristic X-ray spectrum**.

Diffraction of X-rays

X-rays can be diffracted by crystals following **Bragg's law**. According to this

$$2d \sin \theta = n\lambda$$

where, $n = 1, 2, 3, \ldots$, d = spacing of crystal planes
and θ = angle of diffraction.

X-rays Spectrum

The energy spectrum of X-rays is a line spectrum, containing following series

(i) ***K*-series** When electrons of any higher orbit ($n = 2, 3, 4, \ldots$) jump to first orbit ($n = 1$), then K-series of X-rays are produced.

(ii) ***L*-series** When electrons of higher orbit ($n = 3, 4, 5, \ldots$) jump to second orbit ($n = 2$), then L-series of X-rays are produced.

(iii) ***M*-series** When electrons of higher orbit ($n = 4, 5, 6, \ldots$) jump to third orbit ($n = 3$), then M-series of X-rays are produced.

First lines of these series are called K_α, L_α, M_α and second lines of these series are called K_β, L_β, M_β.

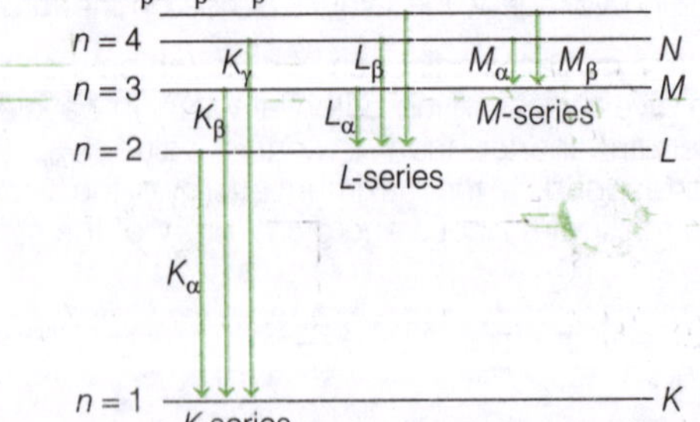

The energy of X-ray radiation as

$$\Delta E = Rhc(Z-b)^2\left[\frac{1}{n_1^2}-\frac{1}{n_2^2}\right]$$

$$\nu = Rc(Z-b)^2\left[\frac{1}{n_1^2}-\frac{1}{n_2^2}\right]$$

Moseley's Law

The frequency of X-rays is given by $\nu = a(Z-b)^2$

where, a and b are constants and Z is atomic number of element.

$$\nu \propto Z^2$$

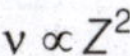

Value Points

Uses of X-rays

Uses of X-rays are given below

(i) X-rays are used for medical imaging.

(ii) X-rays are used in treating cancer.

(iii) They are useful for determining crystal structure by X-ray crystallography.

(iv) X-rays are useful for airport security.

(v) In art, the change occurring in old oil paintings can be examined by X-rays.

(vi) X-rays are used in laboratories for materials characterisation.

DC Motor

It is a device which converts electrical energy into mechanical energy. Its working is based on the fact that when a current carrying coil is placed in uniform magnetic field a torque acts on it.

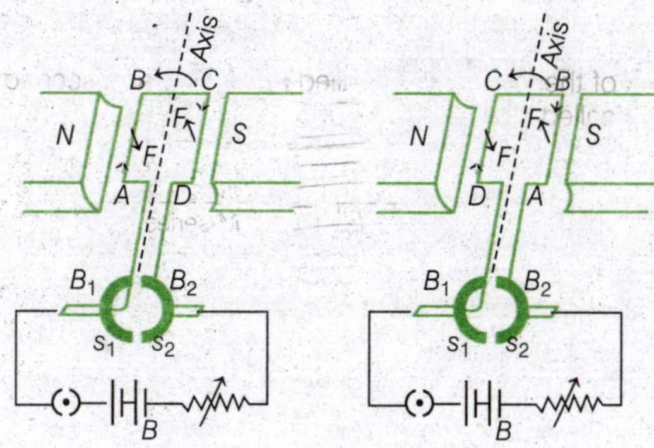

Torque acting on a current carrying coil placed in uniform magnetic field

$$\tau = NBIA \sin \theta$$

When armature coil rotates a back emf is produced in the coil.

Efficiency of a motor, $\eta = \dfrac{\text{Back emf}}{\text{Applied emf}} = \dfrac{E}{V}$

Communication

Faithful transmission of information from one place to another place is called communication.

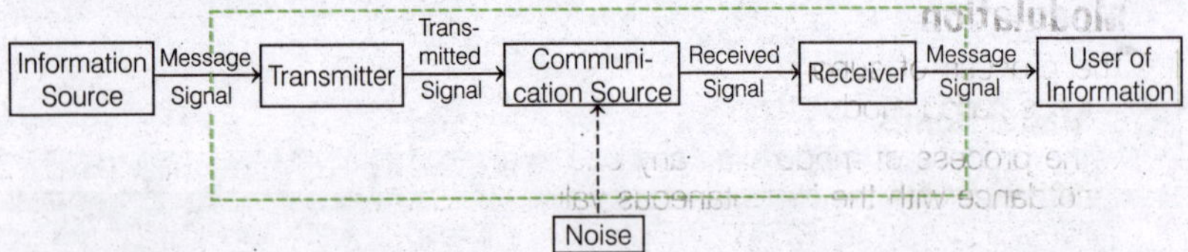

Communication System

A communication system contains three main parts

(i) **Transmitter** It processes and encodes the informations and make it suitable for transmission.

(ii) **Communication Channel** The medium through which information propagates from transmitter to receiver is called communication channel.

(iii) **Receiver** It receives and decodes the signal.

Message Signals

A time varying electrical signal generated by a transducer out of original signal is called message signal. It is a single valved function of time that conveys information.

The message signal for communication can be analog signals or digital signals.

Message signals are of two types

(i) **Analog Signal** A signal in which current or voltage changes it's magnitude continuously with time, is called an analog signal.

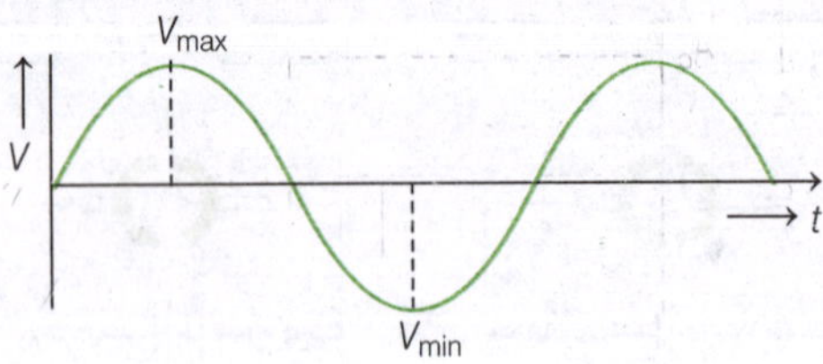

(i) **Digital Signal** A signal in which current or voltage have only two values, is called a digital signal.

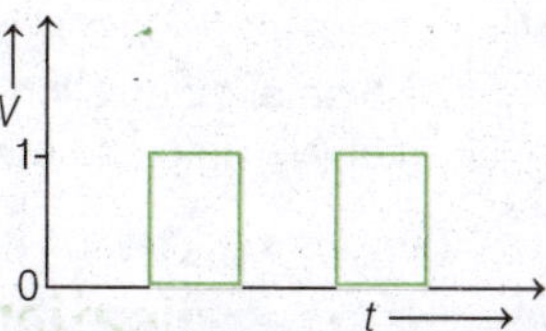

An analog signal can be constructed into a digital signal and *vice-versa*.

Modulation

The process of superimposing the audio signal over a high frequency carrier wave is called modulation.

In the process of modulation any one characteristic of carrier wave is varied in accordance with the instantaneous value of audio signal (modulating signal).

Value Points

Need for Modulation

(i) Energy carried by low frequency audio waves (20 Hz to 20000 Hz) is very small.

(ii) For efficient radiation and reception of signal, the transmitting and receiving antennas should be very high approximately 5000 m.

(iii) The frequency range of audio signal is so small that overlapping of signals create a confusion.

Types of Modulation

(i) **Amplitude Modulation** In this type of modulation, the amplitude of high frequency carrier wave is varied in accordance to instantaneous amplitude of modulating signal.

Band width required for amplitude modulation

= Twice the frequency of the modulating signal.

$$\text{Modulation index, } \mu = \frac{\text{Change in amplitude of carrier wave}}{\text{Amplitude of carrier wave}}$$

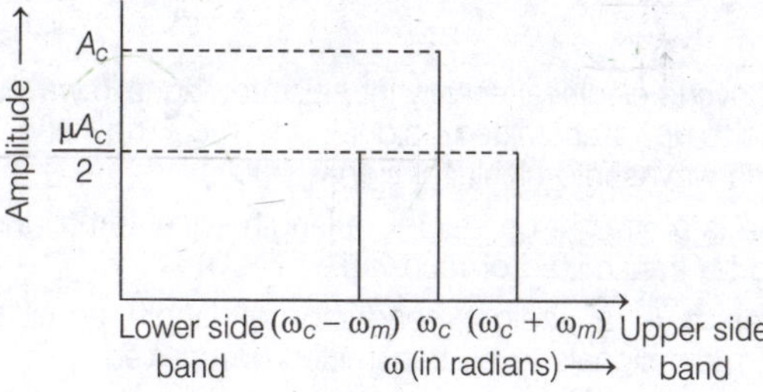

(ii) **Frequency Modulation** In this type of modulation, the frequency of high frequency carrier wave is varied in accordance to instantaneous frequency of modulating signal.

(iii) **Pulse Modulation** In this type of modulation, the continuous waveforms are sampled at regular intervals. Information is transmitted only at the sampling times.

 **Value Points**

Frequency modulation has greater noise immunity than amplitude modulation.

Demodulation

The process of separating of audio signal from modulated signal is called demodulation.

Bandwidth

The type of communication system needed for a given signal depends on the band of frequencies. Bandwidth of these bands is given by difference of highest and lowest frequency within the band. Various transmission media used for communication with their range is listed below

Services	Frequency bands	Remarks
Standard AM broadcast	540-1600 kHz	Radio broadcast
FM broadcast	88-108 MHz	Music channel
Television	54-72 MHz	VHF (Very High Frequencies)
	76-88 MHz	TV
	174-216 MHz	UHF (Ultra High Frequencies)
	420-890 MHz	TV
Cellular	896-901 MHz	Mobile to base station
Mobile radio	840-935 MHz	Base station to mobile
Satellite	5.925-6.425 GHz	Uplink
Communication	3.7-4.2 GHz	Downlink

Antenna

An antenna converts electrical energy into electromagnetic waves at transmitting end and pick up transmitted signal at receiving end and converts electromagnetic waves into electrical signal.

Hertz Antenna is a straight conductor of length equal to half the wavelength of radio signal to be transmitted or received.

Marconi Antenna is a straight conductor of length equal to quater of a wavelength of radio signals to be transmitted or received.

Propagation of Electromagnetic Waves

In communication using radio waves between two places, the electromagnetic waves are radiated out by the transmitter antenna at one place which travel through the space and reach the receiving antenna at the other place. With reference to the frequency range and wavelength range, the radio waves have been divided into various categories shown in table.

Frequency Range and Wavelength Range of Radio Waves with its uses

S. No.	Frequency band	Frequency range	Wavelength range	Main use
1.	Very-Low Frequency (VLF)	3 kHz to 30 kHz	10 km to 100 km	Long distance point to point communication
2.	Low Frequency (LF)	30 kHz to 300 kHz	1 m to 10 km	Marine and navigational purposes
3.	Medium Frequency (MF)	300 kHz to 3 MHz	100 m to 1 km	Marine and broadcasting purposes
4.	High Frequency (HF)	3 MHz to 30 MHz	10 m to 100 m	Communication of all types
5.	Very-High Frequency (VHF)	30 MHz to 300 MHz	1 m to 10 m	T V Radar and air navigation
6.	Ultra-High Frequency (UHF)	300 MHz to 3000 MHz	10 cm to 1 m	Radar and microwave communication
7.	Super-High-Frequency (SHF)	3 GHz to 30 GHz	1 cm to 1 cm	Radar, Radio relays and navigation purposes
8.	Extremely-High-Frequency (EHF)	30 GHz to 300 GHz	1 mm to 1 cm	Optical fibre communication

Earth's Atmosphere

The gaseous envelope surrounding the earth is called earth's atmosphere. It contains the following layers.

(i) **Troposphere** This region extends upto a height of 12 km from earth's surface.

(ii) **Stratosphere** This region extends from 12 km to 50 km. In this region, most of the atmospheric ozone is concentrated from 30 to 50 km. This layer is called ozone layer.

(iii) **Mesosphere** The region extends from 50 km to 80 km.

(iv) **Ionosphere** This region extends from 80 km to 400 km.

In ionosphere the electron density is very large in a region between 90 km and 150 km from earth's surface which extends vertically for a few kilometres. This layer is called **Kennelly Heaviside layer.**

In ionosphere a layer having large electron density is found at height 250 km from earth's surface is called **Appleton layer.**

There are four main layers in earth's atmosphere having high density of electrons and positive ions, produced due to ionisation by the high energy particles coming from sun, star or cosmos. These layers play their effective role in space communication. These layers are *D, E,* F_1 and F_2.

(i) ***D*-layer** is at a virtual height of 65 km from surface of earth and having electron density $\approx 10^9$ m^{-3}.

(ii) ***E*-layer** is at a virtual height of 100 km, from the surface of earth, having electron density $\approx 2 \times 10^{11}$m^{-3}.

(iii) **F_1-layer** is at a virtual height of 180 km from the surface of earth, having electron density $\approx 3 \times 10^{11}$m^{-3}.

(iv) **F_2-layer** is at a vertical height of about 300 km in night time and about 250 to 400 km in day time. The electron density of this layer is $\approx 8 \times 10^{11}$m^{-3}.

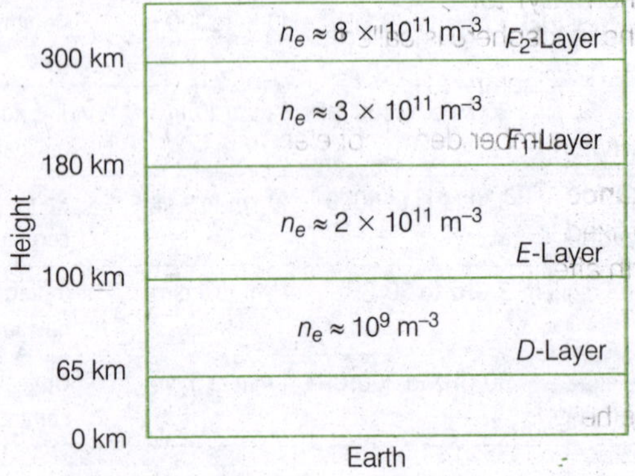

Propagation of Radio Waves

The three modes are discussed below

(i) **Ground Wave or Surface Wave Propagation** It is suitable for low and medium frequency upto 2 MHz. It is used for local broad casting.

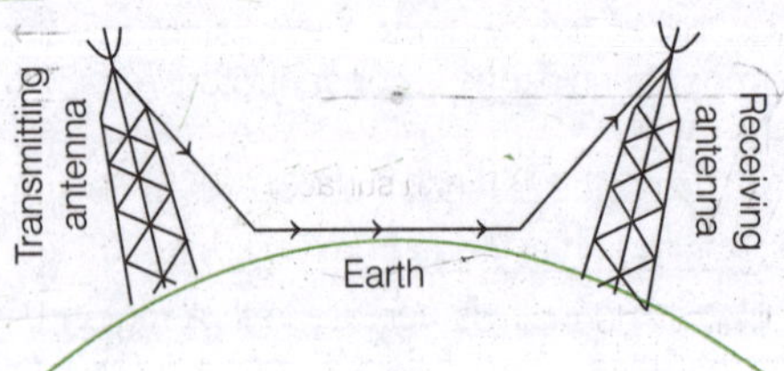

(ii) **Sky Wave Propagation** It is suitable for radiowaves of frequency between 2 MHz to 30 MHz. It is used for long distance radio communication.

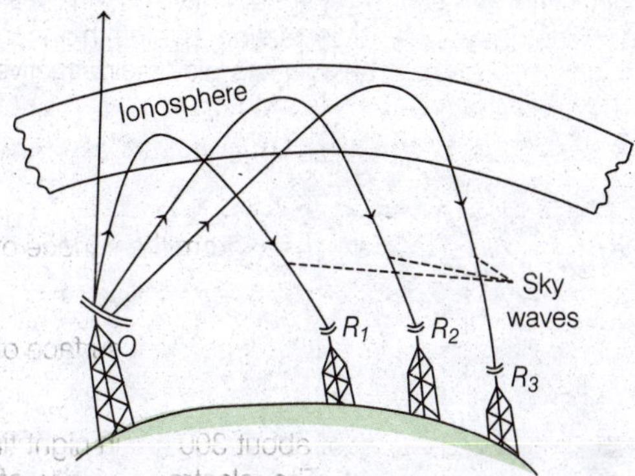

Critical Frequency The highest frequency of radio wave which when sent straight (normally) towards the given layer of ionosphere gets reflected back by the ionosphere is called critical frequency.

$$\text{Critical frequency, } \nu_c = 9\,(N_{max})^{1/2}$$

where, N_{max} = number density of electrons/metre^3.

Skip Distance The minimum distance from the transmitter at which a sky wave of a fixed frequency but not more than critical frequency is sent back to the earth after reflection from the ionosphere.

$$\text{Skip distance } (D_{skip}) = 2h\sqrt{\left(\frac{\nu_{max}}{\nu_c}\right)^2 - 1}$$

where, h is height of reflecting layer of atmosphere,

ν_{max} is maximum frequency of electromagnetic waves and

ν_c is critical frequency.

(iii) **Space Wave Propagation** It is suitable for 30 MHz to 300 MHz. It is used in television communication and radar communication. It is also called line of sight communication.

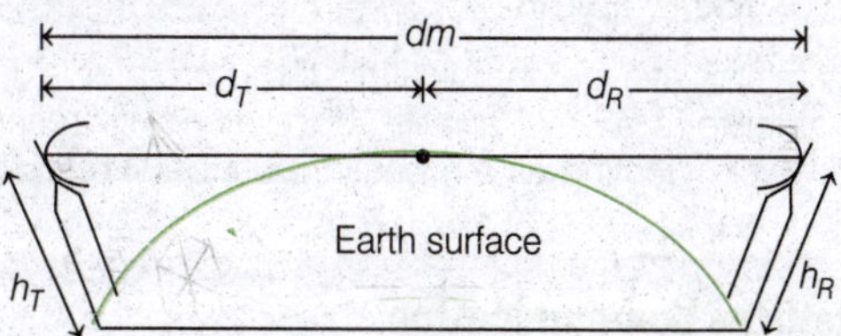

- Range is limited due to curvature of earth. If h be the height of the transmitting antenna, then signal can be received upto a maximum distance $d = \sqrt{2Rh}$

- If height of transmitting and receiving antennas be h_T and h_R respectively. The effective range will $d = \sqrt{2Rh_T} + \sqrt{2Rh_R}$

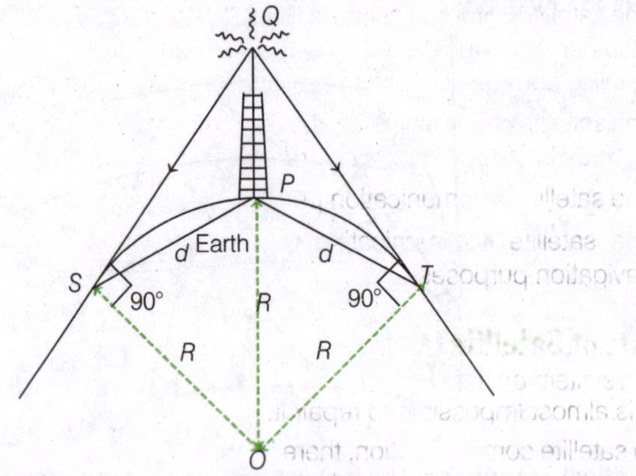

The variation in the strength of a signal at receiver due to interference of waves, is called fading.

Microwave Propagation

Microwave communication is used in radar to locate the flying objects in space.

These waves can be transmitted as beam signals in a particular direction, much better than radiowave.

There is no diffraction of microwave around corners of an obstacle which happens to lie along its passage.

Satellite Communication

It is carried out between a transmitter and a receiver through a satellite. A geostationary satellite is utilised for this purpose, whose time period is 24 hours.

A communication satellite is a space craft, provided with microwave receiver and transmitter. It is placed in an orbit around the earth.

The India remote sensing satellites are

IRS-IA, IRS-IB and IRS-IC

The line-of-sight microwave communication through satellite is possible if the communication satellite is always at a fixed location with respect to the earth, *e.g.*, the satellite which is acting as a repeater must be at rest with respect to the earth.

Merits of Satellites Communication

1. The satellite communication covers wide area for broadcasting as compared to other communication systems i.e. it has wide coverage range.

2. The satellite communication is also used effectively in mobile communication.
3. The satellite communication is found to be much economical as compared to other communication systems on earth. Infact, the cost involved in satellite communication is independent of the distance.
4. The satellite communication is most cost effective in remote and hilly areas, such as Ladakh, Himachal Pardesh etc.
5. The satellite communication permits transmission of data at high rate.
6. The satellite communication is very accurate for search, rescue and navigation purposes.

Demerits of Satellite Communication

1. If a system on the satellite goes out of order due to environmental stresses, it is almost impossible to repair it.
2. In satellite communication, there is a time delay between transmission and reception, due to extremely large communication path length (greater than 2×36000 km). This delay causes a time gap while communicating.

Competition Insight

Optical Communication

System of communication operating in optical range of frequencies (i.e. 1-1000 THz) is termed as optical communication. For this type of communication, optical fibres are used.

An optical fibre is a long thread consisting of a central core of glass or plastic of uniform refractive index. It is surrounded by a cladding of material of refractive index less than that of the core and a protective jacket of insulating material.

There are three types of optical fibre configuration

(i) Single mode step index fibre
(ii) Multi mode step index fibre
(iii) Multi mode graded index fibre.

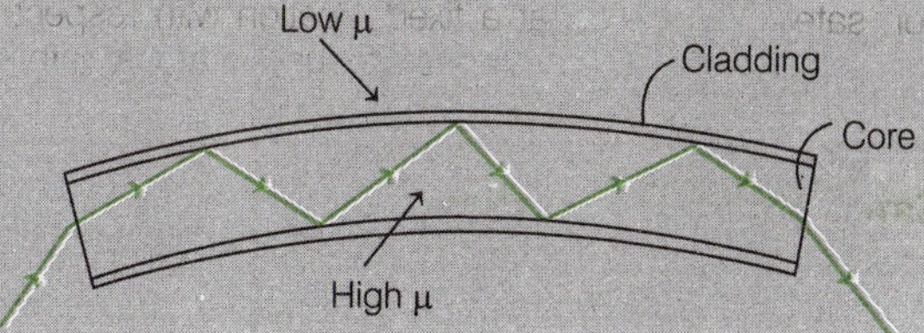

Applications of Optical Fibres

1. A bundle of optical fibres is called light pipe. This pipe can transmit an image. Since the pipe is flexible, it can be twisted in any desired manner. Hence it is used in medical and optical examination of even the inaccessible parts of human body, *e.g.*, in endoscopy.
2. Optical fibres are used in transmission and reception of electrical signals by coverting them first into light signals.
3. Optical fibres are used in telephone and other transmitting cables. Each fibre can carry upto 2000 telephone messages without much loss of intensity.

LED and Diode Laser in Communication

Light Emitting Diode (LED) and diode laser are preferred sources for optical communication links to the following features.

(i) Each produces light of suitable power required in optical communication. Diode laser provides light which is monochromatic and coherent. This light is obtained as a parallel beam. It is used in very long distance transmission.

(ii) LED provides almost monochromatics light. This is suitable for small distance transmission. It is infact, a low cost device as compared to diode lasers.

Internet Telephony

Modem

The term modem is contraction of the term modulator and demodulator. Modem is a device which can modulate as well as demodulate the signal. It connects one computer to another through ordinary telephone lines.

The Internet

Internet permits communication and sharing of all types of information between any two or more computers connected through a large and complex network.

The exchange of information on internet is very fast (at the speed of light) as electronic signals (messages) of computers are communicated through electromagnetic waves.

Application of internet include: internet surfing, E-mails, file transfer, E-banking, E-commerce, E-booking and social networking.

Fax (Facsimile Telegraphy)

The electronic reproduction of a document at a distant place is called FAX.

Mobile Telephony

Mobile phone can wirelessly send and receive radio frequency signals. The central concept of this system is to divide the service area into a suitable number of cells centred office called MTSO (Mobile Telephone Switching Office).

Mobile phones operate typically in UHF of frequencies (about 800-950 MHz).

Global Positioning System (GPS)

GPS is a space based satellite navigation system that provides accurate information about time and location anywhere on or near the earth.

GPS is a method of identifying location or position of any point (or a person) on the earth using a system of 24 satellites, which are continuously orbiting, monitoring and mapping the earth surface.

Every such satellite orbits around the earth twice a day at a distance of about 20,000 km from it.

The orbits of these satellites are aligned in such a way that atleast four of them always keep looking any given point on the earth surface.

Universe

Solar System

The sun and all the objects moving around it taken together is called solar system.

Solar system consists of the sun, the eight planets and other heavenly bodies like asteroids and comets etc.

Nearest star from the earth other than the sun is alpha centauri.

Sun

The sun is a typical example of a star.

Seventy per cent of sun's mass is hydrogen, twenty eight per cent helium and two per cent heavier elements from lithium to uranium.

The sun's mass is about 2×10^{30} kg which is more than 3×10^5 times that of the earth and radius is 6.96×10^5 km.

The source of sun's energy is the process of nuclear fusion taking place in it.

The sun rotates about its axis and completes one rotation in 24.47 days at its equator.

Photosphere

It is the inner part of sun which appears as a bright disc. It is a denser mixture of gases and vapours. Its thickness is about 500 km and its temperature is about 6000 K.

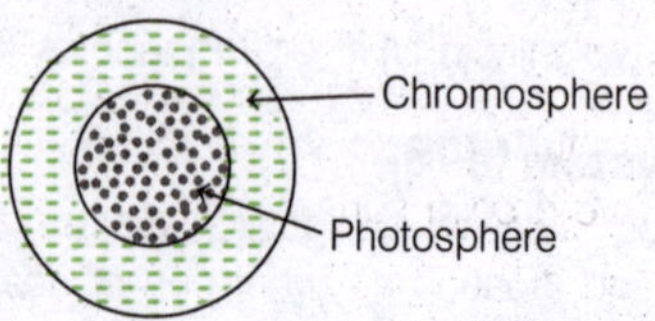

Chromosphere

It is the outer part of sun, just above the photosphere. It is a rarer mixture of gases and vapours.

Planets

The heavenly bodies which revolve around the sun in a fixed orbits are called planets.

There are eight planets in solar system

(i) **Mercury** Nearest and smallest planet of the solar system. Life is not possible on mercury.

(ii) **Venus** Also called morning star and the evening star, as it is brightest amongst all. Venus is the closest planet to the earth. It is one of the hottest planet of our solar system. It rotates from east to west on its axis.

(iii) **Earth** It is the only planet which contains suitable conditions for evolution and survival of life. It has only one natural satellite named **moon.**

(iv) **Mars** It has traces of O_2 but percentage of O_2 is not sufficient for evolution and survival of life.Mars is also called red planet. The temperature of mars varies from $-153°C$ to $20°C$. It has two satellites known as **phobos** and **deimos**.

(v) **Jupiter** Largest planet of the solar system. Jupiter has 95 satellites. Its temperature is about -140 °C. Also, no life is possible on the jupiter.

(vi) **Saturn** It has rings around it. Saturn is the second largest planet of the solar system having maximum number of satellite. Its temperature is about $-180°C$.

(vii) **Uranus** It rotates from east to west on it axis. Uranus appears green due to the large amount of methane and ammonia clouds in its atmosphere. Its temperature is about $-195°C$. It has 28 satellites.

(viii) **Neptune** It has no special characteristic. Neptune is very far away from the sun. It has two satellites.

Note The ninth planet pluto is now taken as a dwarf planet.

Terrestrial Planets

The four planets nearest to the sun, Mercury, Venus, Earth and Mars are called **terrestrial planets.**

These planets have well defined surface of rocks and soil.

Jovian Planets

The four planets Jupiter, Saturn, Uranus and Neptune are called **jovian planets**.

These planets do not have a solid surface.

The Moon

It is the natural satellite of the earth.

It revolves around the earth once in 27.33 days.

Diameter is 3476 km.

Distance from the earth is 384400 km.

Mass of the moon is 0.0123 times the mass of the earth.

Maximum temperature at day is 117°C and at night is –171°C.

Competition Insight

Eclipses

It is the total or partial obscuration of light from a celestial body as it passes through the shadow of another body.

Eclipse occurs when the sun, moon and earth lie in straight line.

(i) **Solar eclipse** When moon passes between the earth and the sun, cutting off the light of the sun from the earth.

Solar eclipse may be partial, total or annular.

(ii) **Lunar eclipse** When the earth comes between the sun and the moon a full moon during rotation in their respective orbits.

A ring shaped lunar eclipse is not possible because the size of the moon is less than that of the earth.

Asteroids (Minor Planets)

The small, rocky, irregularly shaped objects revolving around the sun are called asteroids or minor planets.

There is a belt of asteroids between the orbits of mars and Jupiter.

The largest asteroid is Ceres.

Asteroids can have moon too. The asteroid Ida has its moon Dactyl.

Meteoroids

Small pieces of rock travelling through space are called meteroids. These are fragments from an asteroid, a comet, a moon, mars, etc.

Meteors

When a meteroid enter earth's atmosphere, it heats up due to friction. The hot vapours give off light before cooling down. A streak of light caused by a vaporising meteoroid is called a meteor or a shooting star.

Meteorite

A meteoroid that hits the ground is called a meteorite.

Comets

Comets are objects which move in highly elongated orbits around the sun. They are made up of frozen gases and rocks. They have a long tail which always points away from the sun.

Inner Structure of the Earth

The earth is made up of three different layers

(i) **Crust** It is the thinnest and outermost layer. It is about 10 km thick under the oceans and could be up to 45 km thick under the continents.

(ii) **Mantle** It lies below the crust. It extends up to a depth of about 3000 km. The temperature inside the mantle is about 1000°C.

(iii) **Core** It is the innermost part of earth. It is made up of iron mostly. The outer part of core is in molten state have a temperature about 4000°C and inner part is in solid state because of very high pressure.

Stars

(a) The heavenly objects which shine like the sun due to their own energy are called stars.

(b) The sun is the nearest star to the earth. After the sun, alpha centauri is the next nearest star to the earth.

(c) A person can see nearly 5000 stars with the naked eye on a clear night.

(d) In addition to these stars, many groups of bright and faint stars called **constellations** can be see in the sky.

(e) The space between stars is almost empty with traces of interstellar gas and dust.

Brightness of Stars

(a) The brightness of stars is represented through a system of magnitudes.

(b) The Greek astronomer Hipparchus considered the brightest visible stars as first magnitude stars. Those about one-half as bright were called second magnitude stars and so on; the sixth magnitude stars which were the faintest stars in the sky.

(c) The magnitude scale is now defined so that a magnitude difference of 5 corresponds exactly to a factor of 100 in the amount of light energy arriving at the earth.

(d) It now follows that if l_1 and l_2 are the brightness values of two stars of magnitudes m_1 and m_2 respectively, then

$$\frac{l_1}{l_2} = 100^{(m_2 - m_1)/5}$$

Taking log of both sides, we get

$$\log\left(\frac{l_1}{l_2}\right) = \left(\frac{m_1 - m_2}{5}\right)\log 100 = \left(\frac{m_2 - m_1}{5}\right)2$$

or $$(m_2 - m_1) = \frac{5}{2}\log\left(\frac{l_1}{l_2}\right) = -2.5\log\left(\frac{l_2}{l_1}\right)$$

If $l_1 = l_0$, the brightness of a star of zero magnitude, i.e. $m_1 = 0$,

then $$m_2 = -2.5\log\left(\frac{l_2}{l_0}\right)$$

So, in general; $$m = -2.5\log\left(\frac{l}{l_0}\right)$$

(e) This shows that the stars which are brighter than the standard one have negative magnitude values. Thus, a star having magnitude -5 will be 100 times more brighter than a star of zero magnitude. The value of m for the sun is nearly -26.5

Life Cycle of a Star

Birth of a Star

(a) Interstellar dust and gas present in outer space come together under gravitational force to from a cloud.

(b) When the cloud of dust and gas grows to a large size (of the order of 1000 solar masses) it starts contracting under the efffect of gravitational force. As a result of contraction, the cloud heats up and starts radiating. This in turn causes further contraction and results in further heating up of the cloud. This process repeats again and again till the temperature of the central core rises to about 10^7 K.

(c) When this temperature is attained, the fusion of hydrogen atoms into helium atoms is initiated with the release of energy. This energy keeps the star shining. The dwarf stars which from more than 90% of the whole population are found to be in this stage of evolution.

Death of a Star

Phase I

(i) When the hydrogen in the core of the star is exhausted it heads towards its death.

(a) With complete conversion of hydrogen atom into helium atoms, the core of the star starts contracting again with a consequent rise of temperature.

(b) With the rises in temperature, the outer layers of the star expand and the size of the star increases.

(c) With the successive contraction of the core and the expansion of the outer layers, the temperature of the outer layers falls to make the star appear red. At this state, it is called **red giant**.

(d) At this stage, the release of energy in the star is so large and rapid that a violent explosion called **nova** or **super nova** occurs and throws out a large portion of outer layers back into outer space leaving behind the core of the star.

Phase II

(ii) This decay of the star is called the **death of a star**. The core that remains behind may end up as one of the following corpses
white dwarf, neutron star and black hole.

(a) When the original mass of the star ≤ 1.4 solar mass, the core of the star tends to die as white dwarf which just cools off slowly, changing its colour from white through yellow to red and finally becomes black. This mass limit of 1.4 solar mass is called **Chandra Shekher limit**.

(b) When the mass of the star is between 1.4 to 5 solar masses, the core of the star tends to die as neutron star.

(c) When the mass of the star is more than 5 solar masses, the core continues to contract; continuously as a result of explosion, the core tends to die as a black hole.

Value Points

Black Hole

It is a region in space in which the gravitational force is so great that no object (even light) can escape from it.

Galaxy

A huge group of stars and other celestial bodies bound together by gravity is called a galaxy.

There are over 100 billion (10^{11}) galaxies in the universe.

Our galaxy is called **Milky Way Galaxy**.

Milky Way Galaxy is a spiral galaxy.

There are 250 billion stars in our milky way galaxy.

Constellation

A group of stars forming a recognisable pattern is called a constellation.

Few constellations are Ursa Major (great bear), Leo (lion), Pisces (fish), Taurus (bull), Hercules (a hero), Orion (a hunter) etc.

Ursa Major have seven brightest stars forms a shape of great bear.

The Big-Bang Theory

About 15 billion years ago, the whole matter of the universe was concentrated in a highly dense small region. A sudden explosion broke this region into pieces which start to move away from each other. The instant of this explosion is called the big bang. Therefore, the universe is expanding continuously.

handbook
Appendices

Appendices

The Greek Alphabet

Alpha	Α	α
Beta	Β	β
Gamma	Γ	γ
Delta	Δ	δ
Epsilon	Ε	ε
Zeta	Ζ	ζ
Eta	Η	η
Theta	Θ	θ
Iota	Ι	ι
Kappa	Κ	κ
Lambda	Λ	λ
Mu	Μ	μ
Nu	Ν	ν
Xi	Ξ	ξ
Omicron	Ο	ο
Pi	Π	π
Rho	Ρ	ρ
Sigma	Σ	σ
Tau	Τ	τ
Upsilon	Υ	υ
Phi	Φ	ϕ
Chi	Χ	χ
Psi	Ψ	ψ
Omega	Ω	ω

Common SI Prefixes and Symbols for Multiples and Sub-multiples

Multiple			Sub-multiple		
Factor	Prefix	Symbol	Factor	Prefix	Symbol
10^{18}	Exa	E	10^{-18}	atto	a
10^{15}	Peta	P	10^{-15}	femto	f
10^{12}	Tera	T	10^{-12}	pico	p
10^{9}	Giga	G	10^{-9}	nano	n
10^{6}	Mega	M	10^{-6}	micro	μ
10^{3}	kilo	k	10^{-3}	milli	m
10^{2}	Hecto	h	10^{-2}	centi	c
10^{1}	Deca	da	10^{-1}	deci	d

Some Important Constants

Name	Symbol	Value
Speed of light in vacuum	c	2.9979×10^{8} ms^{-1}
Charge of electron	e	1.602×10^{-19} C
Gravitational constant	G	6.673×10^{-11} Nm^{2}kg^{-2}
Planck constant	h	6.626×10^{-34} Js
Boltzmann constant	k	1.381×10^{-23} JK^{-1}
Avogadro number	N_A	6.022×10^{23} mol^{-1}
Universal gas constant	R	8.314 J mol^{-1} K^{-1}
Mass of electron	m_e	9.110×10^{-31} kg
Mass of neutron	m_n	1.675×10^{-27} kg
Mass of proton	m_p	1.673×10^{-27} kg
Electron-charge to mass ratio	e/m_e	1.759×10^{11} C/kg
Faraday constant	F	9.648×10^{4} C/mol
Rydberg's constant	R	1.097×10^{7} m^{-1}
Stefan-Boltzmann constant	σ	5.670×10^{-8} W m^{-2} K^{-4}
Permittivity of free space	ε_0	8.854×10^{-12} C^{2}N^{-1} m^{-2}
Mechanical equivalent of heat	J	4.186 J cal^{-1}
Standard atmospheric pressure	1 atm	1.013×10^{5} Pa
Electron-volt	1 eV	1.602×10^{-19} J
Unified atomic mass unit	1 u	1.661×10^{-27} kg
Energy equivalent of 1 u	uc^2	931.5 MeV

Important Conversion Factors

Length

- 1 km = 0.6215 mi
- 1 mi = 1.609 km
- 1 m = 1.0936 yd = 3.281 ft = 39.37 in
- 1 in = 2.54 cm
- 1 ft = 12 in = 30.48 cm
- 1 yd = 3 ft = 91.44 cm = 36 inch
- 1 light year = 1 ly = 9.461×10^{15} m
- 1 Å = 0.1 nm

Area

- 1 $m^2 = 10^4$ cm^2
- 1 km^2 = 0.3861 mi^2 = 247.1 acres
- 1 in^2 = 6.4516 cm^2
- 1 ft^2 = 9.29×10^{-2} m^2
- 1 m^2 = 10.76 ft^2
- 1 acre = 43560 ft^2
- 1 mi^2 = 640 acres = 2.590 km^2

Volume

- 1 $m^3 = 10^6$ cm^3
- 1 L = 1000 cm^3 = 10^{-3} m^3
- 1 gal = 3.786 L
- 1 gal = 4 qt = 8 pt = 128 oz = 231 in^3
- 1 in^3 = 16.39 cm^3
- 1 ft^3 = 1728 in^3 = 28.32 L = 2.832×10^4 cm^3

Speed

- 1 km h^{-1} = 0.2778 m s^{-1} = 0.6215 mi h^{-1}
- 1 mi h^{-1} = 0.4470 m s^{-1} = 1.609 km h^{-1}
- 1 mi h^{-1} = 1.467 ft s^{-1}

Magnetic Field

- 1 G = 10^{-4} T
- 1 T = 1 Wb m^{-2} = 10^4 G

Angle and Angular Speed

- π rad = 180°
- 1 rad = 57.30°
- 1° = 1.745×10^{-2} rad
- 1 rev min^{-1} = 0.1047 rad s^{-1}
- 1 rad s^{-1} = 9.549 rev min^{-1}

Mass

- 1 kg = 1000 g
- 1 tonne = 1000 kg = 10^9 mg
- 1 u = 1.6606×10^{-27} kg
- 1 kg = 6.022×10^{26} u
- 1 slug = 14.59 kg
- 1 kg = 6.852×10^{-2} slug
- 1 u = 931.50 MeV/c^2

Density

- 1 g cm^{-3} = 1000 kg m^{-3} = 1kg L^{-1}

Force

- 1 N = 0.2248 lbf = 10^5 dyne
- 1 lbf = 4.4482 N
- 1 kgf = 2.2046 lbf

Time

- 1 h = 60 min = 3.6 ks
- 1 d = 24 h = 1440 min = 86.4 ks
- 1 y = 365.24 d = 31.56 Ms

Pressure

- 1 Pa = 1 Nm^{-2}
- 1 bar = 100 kPa
- 1 atm = 101.325 kPa = 1.01325 bar
- 1 atm = 14.7 lbf/in^2 = 760 mm Hg = 29.9 in Hg = 33.8 ft H_2O
- 1 lbf in^{-2} = 6.895 kPa
- 1 torr = 1 mm Hg = 133.32 Pa

Energy

- 1 kWh = 3.6 MJ
- 1 cal = 4.186 J
- 1 ft lbf = 1.356 J = 1.286 $\times 10^{-3}$ Btu
- 1 L atm = 101.325 J
- 1 L atm = 24.217 cal
- 1 Btu = 778 ft lb = 252 cal = 1054.35 J
- 1 eV = 1.602 $\times 10^{-19}$ J
- 1 u c^2 = 931.50 MeV
- 1 erg = 10^{-7} J

Power

- 1 horse power, hp = 550 ft lbf/s = 745.7 W
- 1 Btu min^{-1} = 17.58 W
- 1 W = 1.341 $\times 10^{-3}$ hp = 0.7376 ft lbf/s

Thermal Conductivity

- 1 W $m^{-1}K^{-1}$ = 6.938 Btu in/hft^2°F
- 1 Btu in/hft^2°F = 0.1441 W/m-K

Derived Units in SI System

Physical Quantity	SI Unit	
	Name	Symbol
Area	square metre	m^2
Volume	cubic metre	m^3
Speed, velocity	metre per second	m/s or ms^{-1}
Angular velocity	radian per second	rad/s or rad s^{-1}
Acceleration	metre per second square	m/s^2 or ms^{-2}
Angular acceleration	radian per second square	rad/s^2 or rad s^{-2}
Wave number	per metre	m^{-1}
Density, mass density	kilogram per cubic metre	kg/m^3 or kg m^{-3}
Current density	ampere per square metre	A/m^2 or A m^{-2}
Magnetic field strength, magnetic intensity, magnetic moment density	ampere per metre	A/m or A m^{-1}
Concentration (an amount of substance)	mole per cubic metre	mol/m^3 or mol m^{-3}
Specific volume	cubic metre per kilogram	m^3/kg or m^3kg^{-1}
Luminance, intensity of illumination	candela per square metre	cd/m^2 or cd m^{-2}
Kinematic viscosity	square metre per second	m^2/s or m^2s^{-1}
Momentum	kilogram metre per second	kg m s^{-1}
Moment of inertia	kilogram square metre	kg m^2
Radius of gyration	metre	m
Linear/superficial/volume expansivities	per kelvin	K^{-1}
Flow rate	cubic metre per second	m^3s^{-1}

SI Derived Units with Special Names

Physical Quantity	SI Unit			
	Name	Symbol	Expression in Terms of Other Units	Expression in Terms of SI Base Units
Frequency	hertz	Hz	—	s^{-1}
Force	newton	N	—	$kg\ m\ s^{-2}$
Pressure, stress	pascal	Pa	N/m^2 or $N\ m^{-2}$	$kg\ m^{-1}s^{-2}$
Energy, work, quantity of heat	joule	J	N m	$kg\ m^2\ s^{-2}$ or $kg\ m^2/s^2$
Power, radiant flux	watt	W	J/s or $J\ s^{-1}$	$kg\ m^2\ s^{-3}$
Quantity of electricity, electric charge	coulomb	C	—	A s
Electric potential, potential difference, electromotive force	volt	V	W/A or $W\ A^{-1}$	$kg\ m^2\ s^{-3}A^{-1}$ or $kg\ m^2/s^3A$
Capacitance	farad	F	C/V	$A^2s^4\ kg^{-1}\ m^{-2}$
Electric resistance	ohm	Ω	V/A	$kg\ m^2\ s^{-3}A^{-2}$
Conductance	siemens	S	A/V	$m^{-2}kg^{-1}\ s^3A^2$
Magnetic flux	weber	Wb	V s or J/A	$kg\ m^2\ s^{-2}A^{-1}$
Magnetic field, magnetic flux density	tesla	T	Wb/m^2	$kg\ s^{-2}A^{-1}$
Inductance	henry	H	Wb/A	$kg\ m^2\ s^{-2}A^{-2}$
Luminous flux, luminous power	lumen	lm	—	cd/sr
Illuminance	lux	lx	lm/m^2	m^{-2} cd sr
Activity (of a radio nuclide/radioactive source)	becquerel	Bq	—	s^{-1}
Absorbed dose, absorbed dose index	gray	Gy	J/kg	m^2/s^2 or m^2s^{-2}

SI Derived Unit Represented in terms of SI Unit with Special Names

Physical Quantity	SI Unit	
	Symbol	SI
Magnetic moment	$J\ T^{-1}$	$m^2\ A$
Dipole moment	C m	m A s
Kinematic viscosity	Pa s or $N\ s\ m^{-2}$	$kg\ m^{-1}s^{-1}$
Couple, Moment of force	Nm	$kg\ m^2\ s^{-2}$
Surface tension	N/m or $N\ m^{-1}$	$kg\ s^{-2}$

Physical Quantity	SI Unit	
	Symbol	SI
Thermal flux density	W/m^2	$kg\ s^{-3}$
Heat-capacity, Entropy	J/K	$kg\ m^2\ s^{-2}K^{-1}$
Specific heat capacity, Specific entropy	J/kg K	$m^2\ s^{-2}\ K^{-1}$
Specific energy, Latent heat	J/kg or $J\ kg^{-1}$	$m^2\ s^{-2}$
Radiation/radiant intensity	W/sr or $W\ sr^{-1}$	$kg\ m^2\ s^{-3}\ sr^{-1}$
Thermal conductivity	W/m K or $W\ m^{-1}K^{-1}$	$kg\ m\ s^{-3}\ K^{-1}$
Energy-density	J/m^3 or $J\ m^{-3}$	$kg\ m^{-1}\ s^{-2}$
Electric field intensity	V/m or $V\ m^{-1}$	$kg\ m\ s^{-3}A^{-1}$
Electric charge density	C/m^3 or $C\ m^{-3}$	$m^{-3}\ s\ A$
Permittivity	F/m or $F\ m^{-1}$	$kg^{-1}m^{-3}s^4A^2$
Permeability	H/m or $H\ m^{-1}$	$kg\ m\ s^{-2}A^{-2}$
Molar energy	J/mol or $J\ mol^{-1}$	$kg\ m^2s^{-2}mol^{-1}$
Angular momentum, Planck's constant	J-s	$kg\ m^2s^{-1}$
Molar entropy, Molar heat capacity	J/mol K or $J\ mol^{-1}\ K^{-1}$	$kg\ m^2\ s^{-2}K^{-1}mol^{-1}$
Exposure time (X- and γ-rays)	C/kg or $C\ kg^{-1}$	$kg^{-1}\ s\ A$
Absorbed dose rate	Gy/s or $Gy\ s^{-1}$	$m^2\ s^{-3}$
Compressibility	Pa^{-1}	$kg^{-1}\ m\ s^2$
Coefficient of Elasticity	N/m^2 or $N\ m^{-2}$	$kg\ m^{-1}s^{-2}$
Pressure gradient	Pa/m or $N\ m^{-3}$	$kg\ m^{-2}s^{-2}$
Gravitational potential	J/kg or $J\ kg^{-1}$; N m/kg or $N\ m\ kg^{-1}$	$m^2\ s^{-2}$
Impulse	N s	$kg\ m\ s^{-1}$
Angular impulse	Nm s	$kg\ m^2s^{-1}$
Specific resistance	Ω m	$kg\ m^3s^{-3}A^{-2}$
Surface energy	J/m^2 or $J\ m^{-2}$; N/m or $N\ m^{-1}$	$kg\ s^{-2}$

Important Scientific Instruments & their use

Altimeter It measures altitudes and is used in aircrafts.

Ammeter It measures strength of electric current (in ampere).

Audiometer It measures intensity of sound.

Barometer It measures atmospheric pressure.

Binocular It is used to view distant objects.

Burette	It is used to deliver any required volume of a liquid upto its maximum capacity
Calorimeter	It measures quanitity of heat.
Cardiogram	It traces movements of the heart, recorded on a cardiograph.
Chronometer	It determines longitude of a place kept on board ship.
Cinematography	It is an instrument used in Cinema making to throw on screen and enlarged image of photograph.
Dynamo	It converts mechanical energy into electrical energy.
Dynamometer	It measures electrical power.
Electrometer	It measures electricity.
Electroscope	It detects presence of an electric charge.
Endoscope	It examines internal parts of the body.
Fathometer	It measures the depth of the ocean.
Galvanometer	It measures the electric current of low magnitude.
Hydrometer	It measures the specific gravity of liquids.
Hygrometer	It measures humidity in air.
Hydrophone	It measures sound under water.
Lactometer	It determines the purity of milk.
Manometer	It measures the pressures of gases.
Mariner's compass	It is an instrument used by the sailors to determine the direction.
Microphone	It converts the sound waves into electrical vibration and to magnify the sound.
Microscope	It is used to obtain magnified view of small objects.
Odometer	An instrument by which the distance covered by wheeled vehicles is measured.
Phonograph	It is used for producing sound.
Photometer	It compares the luminous intensity of the source of light.
Periscope	It is used to view objects above sea level (Used in sub-marines).
Radar	It is used for detecting the direction and range of an approaching plane by means or radio microwaves.
Radiometer	It mesures the emission of radiant energy.
Screw gauge	It is used to measure thickness of a thin glass plate and diameter of a thinwire or a small sphere.
Seismograph	It measures the intensity of earthquake shocks.
Salinometer	It determines salinity of solution.

Sonometer To measure frequency of a tunning fork.

Spectrometer It is an instrument for measuring the energy distribution of a particular type of radiation.

Speedometer It is an instrument placed in a vehicle to record its speed.

Sphygmomanometer It measures blood pressure.

Spherometer It measures the curvaturs of surfaces.

Stereoscope It is used to view two dimensional pictures.

Stethoscope An instrument which is used by the doctors to hear and analyse heart and lung sounds.

Straboscope It is used to view rapidly moving objects.

Tachometer An instrument used in measuring speeds of aeroplanes and motor boats.

Telescope It views distant objects in space.

Thermometer This instrument is used for the measurement of temperatures.

Thermostat It regulates the temperature at a particular point.

Voltmeter It measures the electric potential difference between two points.

Vernier callipers To measure lengths accurately.

Inventions and Discoveries

Invention	Year	Inventor	Country
Adding machine	1642	Blaise Pascal and Wihelm Schickard	France
Aeroplane	1903	Orville and Wilbur Wright	USA
Air conditioning	1902	Carrier	USA
Airplane (Jet engine)	1939	Ohain	Germany
Airship (Non-rigid)	1852	Henri Giffard	France
Atomic bomb	1945	J Robert Oppenheimer	USA
Ball-point pen	1888	John J Loud	USA
Barometer	1644	Evangelista Torricelli	Italy
Battery (Electric)	1800	Alessandro Volta	Italy
Bicycle	1839-40	Kirkpatrick Macmillan	Britain
Bicycle tyres (Pneumatic)	1888	Johan Boyd Dunlop	Britain
Bifocal lens	1780	Benjamin Franklin	USA
Bleaching powder	1798	Tennant	Britain
Busnen burner	1855	R Willhelm von Bunsen	Germany

Invention	Year	Inventor	Country
Burglar alarm	1858	Edwin T Holmes	USA
Camera (Kodak)	1888	Walker Eastman	USA
Car (Steam)	1769	Nicolas Cugnot	France
Car (Petrol)	1888	Karl Benz	Germany
Carburetor	1876	Gottlieb Daimler	Germany
Cassette (Videotape)	1969	Sony	Japan
Cement (Portland)	1824	Joseph Aspdin	Britain
Cinema	1895	Nicolas and Jean Lumiere	France
Clock (Mechanical)	1725	I-Hsing and Liang Ling-Tsan	China
Clock (Pendulum)	1656	Christian Huygens	Netherlands
Compact disc	1972	RCA	USA
Compact disc player	1979	Sony, Philips	Japan, Netherlands
Computer (Laptop)	1987	Sinclair	Britain
Computer (Mini)	1960	Digital Corp	USA
Diesel engine	1895	Rudolf Diesel	Germany
Dynamo	1832	Hypolite Pixii	France
Electric flat iron	1882	H W seeley	USA
Electric light bulb	1879	Thomas Alva Edison	USA
Electric motor (DC)	1873	Zenobe Gramme	Belgium
Electri motor (AC)	1888	Nikola Tesla	USA
Electric iron	1882	Henry W Seeley	USA
Electric washing machine	1906	Alva J Fisher	USA
Electro-magnet	1824	William Sturgeon	Britain
Electroplating	1805	Luigi Brugnatelli	Italy
Electronic computer	1824	Dr Alan M Turing	Britain
Facsimile machine	1843	Alexander Bain	Britain
Fibre optics	1955	Kepany	Britain
Film (Moving outlines)	1885	Louis Prince	France
Film (Talking)	1922	J Engl, J Mussolle and H Vogt	Germany
Galvanometer	1834	Andre-Marie Ampere	France
Gramophone	1878	Thomos Alva Edison	USA
Helicopter	1924	Etienne Oehmichen	France

Invention	Year	Inventor	Country
Hydrogen Bomb	1952	Edward Teller	USA
Intelligence testing	1905	Simon Binet	France
Jet engine	1937	Sir Frank Whittle	Britain
Laser	1960	Theodore Maiman	USA
Launderette	1934	J F Cantrell	USA
Lift (Mechanical)	1852	Elisha G Otis	USA
Lighting conductor	1752	Benjamin Franklin	USA
Loudspeaker	1900	Horace Short	Britain
Machine gun	1918	Richard Gatling	Britain
Magnetic recording tape	1928	Fritz Pfleumer	Germany
Microphone	1876	Alexander Graham Bell	USA
Microscope (Comp.)	1590	Z Jansseen	Netherlands
Microscope (Elect.)	1931	Ruska Knoll	Germany
Microwave oven	1947	Percy Le Baron Spencer	USA
Motor cycle	1885	G Daimler	Germany
Movie projector	1893	Thomas Edison	USA
Neon lamp	1910	Georges Claude	France
Neutron bomb	1958	Samuel Cohen	USA
Optical fibre	1955	Narinder Kapany	Germany
Pacemaker	1952	Zoll	USA
Photoelectric cell	1893	Julius Elster, Hans F Geitel	Germany
Photography (On metal)	1826	J N Niepce	France
Photography (On paper)	1835	WH Fox Talbot	Britain
Photography (On film)	1888	John Carbutt	USA
Piano	1709	Cristofori	Italy
Pistol, revolver	1836	Colt	USA
Radar	1922	A H Laylor and Leo C Young	USA
Radiocarbon dating	1947	Libby	USA
Radio telegraphy	1864	Dr Mohlon Lommis	USA
Radio telegraphy (Trans Atlantic)	1901	G Marconi	Italy
Rayon	1883	Sir Joseph Swan	Britain
Razor (Electric)	1931	Col Jacob Scick	USA
Razor (Safety)	1895	King C Gillatte	USA
Refrigerator	1850	James Harrison, Alexander catlin	USA

Invention	Year	Inventor	Country
Rubber (Latex foam)	1928	Dunlop Rubber Co.	Britain
Rubber (Vulcanised)	1841	Charles Goodyear	USA
Rubber (Waterproof)	1823	Charles Macintosh	Britain
Safety pin	1849	Walter Hunt	USA
Ship (Steam)	1775	I C Perier	France
Ship (Turbine)	1894	Hon Sir C Parsons	Britain
Steam engine	1698	Thomas Savery	Britain
Steam engine (Piston)	1712	Thomas Newcomen	Britain
Steam engine (Condenser)	1765	James Watt	Britain
Steel (Stainless)	1913	Harry Brearley	Britain
Stethoscope	1819	Laennec	France
Submarine	1776	David Bushnell	USA
Super computer	1976	J H Van Tassel	USA
Tank	1914	Sir Emest D Swington	Britain
Tape recorder	1899	Fessenden Poulsen	Denmark
Telegraph	1787	M Lammond	France
Telegraph code	1837	Samuel F B Morse	USA
Telephone (Cellular)	1947	Bell Labs	USA
Telephone (Imperfect)	1849	At tonio Meucci	Italy
Telephone (Perfected)	1876	Alexander Graham Bell	USA
Telescope	1608	Hans Lippershey	Netherlands
Television (Mechanical)	1926	John Logic Baird	Britain
Television (Electronic)	1927	P T Farnsworth	USA
Television (Colour)	1928	John Logie Baird	Britain
Transistor	1948	Bardeen, Shockley and Brattain	USA
Transistor radio	1948	Sony	Japan
Uranium Fission (Atomic reactor)	1942	Szilard Fermi	USA
Vacuum cleaner (Elec.)	1907	Spangler	USA
Video tape	1956	Charles Ginsberg	USA
Washing machine (Elec.)	1907	Hurley Machine Co.	USA
Pocket Watch	1462	Bartholomew Manfredi	Italy
Wireless (Telegraphy)	1896	G Marconi	Italy

Important Formulae

Chapter-1 Units and Measurement

1. Area = Length × Breadth
2. Volume = Length × Breadth × Height
3. $\text{Density} = \dfrac{\text{Mass}}{\text{Volume}}$
4. $\text{Speed} = \dfrac{\text{Distance}}{\text{Time}}$
5. $\text{Absolute error } (a_m) = \dfrac{a_1 + a_2 + a_3 + \ldots a_n}{n}$
6. $\text{Mean absolute error } (\Delta\bar{a}) = \dfrac{|\Delta a_1| + |\Delta a_2| + \ldots + |\Delta a_n|}{n}$
7. $\text{Relative error} = \dfrac{\text{Mean absolute error } (\Delta\bar{a})}{\text{Absolute error}(a_m)}$
8. $\text{Percentage error} = \dfrac{\Delta\bar{a}}{a_m} \times 100\%$
9. Error in addition or subtraction
$$\Delta x = \pm(\Delta a + \Delta b)$$
10. Error in multiplication or division
$$\frac{\Delta x}{x} = \pm\left(\frac{\Delta a}{a} + \frac{\Delta b}{b}\right)$$

Chapter-2 Scalar and Vectors

11. Scalar product of orthogonal unit vectors
$$\hat{\mathbf{i}}\cdot\hat{\mathbf{i}} = \hat{\mathbf{j}}\cdot\hat{\mathbf{j}} = \hat{\mathbf{k}}\cdot\hat{\mathbf{k}} = 1$$
and $$\hat{\mathbf{i}}\cdot\hat{\mathbf{j}} = \hat{\mathbf{j}}\cdot\hat{\mathbf{k}} = \hat{\mathbf{k}}\cdot\hat{\mathbf{i}} = 0$$
12. Scalar product in cartesian coordinates
$$\mathbf{A}\cdot\mathbf{B} = A_x B_x + A_y B_y + A_z B_z$$
13. Vector product of orthogonal unit vectors
$$\hat{\mathbf{i}}\times\hat{\mathbf{i}} = \hat{\mathbf{j}}\times\hat{\mathbf{j}} = \hat{\mathbf{k}}\times\hat{\mathbf{k}} = 0$$
and $$\hat{\mathbf{i}}\times\hat{\mathbf{j}} = \hat{\mathbf{k}},\ \hat{\mathbf{j}}\times\hat{\mathbf{k}} = \hat{\mathbf{i}},\ \hat{\mathbf{k}}\times\hat{\mathbf{i}} = \hat{\mathbf{j}}$$
14. Vector product in cartesian coordinates
$$\mathbf{A}\times\mathbf{B} = (A_y B_z - A_z B_y)\,\hat{\mathbf{i}} - (A_x B_z - B_x A_z)\,\hat{\mathbf{j}} + (A_x B_y - A_y B_x)\,\hat{\mathbf{k}}$$

Chapter-3 Motion in a Straight Line

15. Instantaneous speed = $\lim_{\Delta t \to 0} \frac{\Delta s}{\Delta t}$

16. Velocity = $\frac{\text{Displacement}}{\text{Time taken}}$

17. Acceleration = $\frac{\text{Change in velocity } (\Delta v)}{\text{Time interval } (\Delta t)}$

18. Equations of Motion

    (i) $v = u + at$

    (ii) $s = ut + \frac{1}{2}at^2$

    (iii) $v^2 = u^2 + 2as$

    (iv) Distance travelled in nth second

$$S_n = u + \frac{a}{2}(2n - 1)$$

Chapter-4 Motion in a Plane

19. Equation of the path of projectile

$$y = x\tan\theta - \frac{g}{2u^2\cos^2\theta} \cdot x^2$$

20. Time of flight, $T = \frac{2u\sin\theta}{g}$

21. Maximum height, $H = \frac{u^2\sin^2\theta}{2g}$

22. Horizontal range, $R = \frac{u^2\sin 2\theta}{g} \Rightarrow R_{\text{max}} = \frac{u^2}{g}$

23. Angular displacement $(\Delta\theta) = \frac{\text{Linear displacement}}{\text{Radius}}$

24. Angular velocity $(\omega) = \frac{\text{Angular displacement}}{\text{Time interval}}$

25. Angular acceleration $(\alpha) = \frac{\text{Change in angular velocity}}{\text{Time taken}}$

26. Relation between angular velocity and linear velocity; $v = r\omega$

27. Relation between angular acceleration and linear acceleration; $a = r\alpha$

28. Centripetal acceleration, $a = \frac{v^2}{r} = r\omega^2$

Chapter-5 Laws of Motion

29. Centripetal force, $F = \frac{mv^2}{r} = mr\omega^2$

30. Force, $F = m \cdot a$

31. Linear momentum, $p = mv$

32. Impulse = Force × Time = Change in momentum

33. Force = Mass × Acceleration

34. Weight = Mass × Acceleration due to gravity

35. Thrust on the rocket at any instant, $F = -u \frac{dM}{dt}$

36. Limiting friction $(f_s) = \mu_s \times R$ (normal reaction)

37. Kinetic friction $(f_K) = \mu_K \times R$

38. Maximum speed of a car on a level road; $v_{max} = \sqrt{\mu_s Rg}$

39. Maximum speed of a car on a banked road;

$$v_{max} = \left[Rg \left(\frac{\mu_s + \tan\theta}{1 - \mu_s \tan\theta} \right) \right]^{1/2}$$

For $\mu_s = 0$, $v_{max} = [Rg \tan\theta]^{1/2}$

Chapter-6 Work, Energy and Power

40. Work = Force × Displacement × $\cos\theta$

41. Power = Rate of doing work = $\frac{\text{Work done}}{\text{Time taken}}$

42. Kinetic energy = $\frac{1}{2} mv^2 = \frac{p^2}{2m}$

43. Gravitational potential energy = mgh

44. Elastic potential energy = $\frac{1}{2} kx^2$

45. Work-Energy theorem

$$W = \int_{v_1}^{v_2} F \cdot ds$$

$$= \frac{1}{2} m v_2^2 - \frac{1}{2} m v_1^2 = K_f - K_i$$

$$= \Delta KE$$

46. Mass-Energy Equivalence, $E = \Delta mc^2$

Chapter-7 Rotational Motion

47. Centre of mass of system of n-particles

$$\mathbf{r}_{CM} = \frac{m_1 \mathbf{r}_1 + m_2 \mathbf{r}_2 + \ldots + m_n \mathbf{r}_n}{m_1 + m_2 + \ldots + m_n} = \sum_{i=1}^{n} \frac{m_i \mathbf{r}_i}{\Sigma m_i}$$

48. Moment of force = Force × Perpendicular distance

49. Moment of inertia , $I = MK^2$

50. Radius of gyration , $K = \sqrt{\frac{r_1^2 + r_2^2 + \ldots + r_n^2}{n}}$

51. Torque = Moment of inertia × Angular acceleration

52. Rotational kinetic energy $(K) = \frac{1}{2} I\omega^2$

53. Kinematical equations in circular motion

(i) $\omega = \omega_0 + \alpha t$ (ii) $\theta = \omega_0 t + \frac{1}{2} \alpha t^2$

(iii) $\omega^2 = \omega_0^2 + 2\alpha\theta$

Chapter-8 Gravitation

54. Relation between universal gravitational constant (G) and acceleration due to gravity (g); $g = \frac{GM}{R^2}$

55. Gravitational field, $E = \frac{F}{m} = \frac{GM}{r^2}$

56. Gravitational potential, $V = \frac{W}{m} = -\frac{GM}{r}$

57. Gravitational potential energy, $U = -\frac{GMm}{r}$

58. Time period of satellite, $T = 2\pi \sqrt{\frac{r^3}{GM}}$

59. Orbital velocity, $v_o = \sqrt{\frac{GM}{r}} = R\sqrt{\frac{g}{R+h}}$

60. Energy of a satellite in orbit, $E = -\frac{GMm}{2r}$

61. Binding energy $= \frac{+GMm}{2r}$

62. Escape velocity, $v_e = \sqrt{\frac{2GM}{R}} = \sqrt{2gR} = \sqrt{\frac{8\pi\rho GR^2}{3}}$

63. Relation between escape velocity and orbital velocity;

$$v_e = \sqrt{2}\ v_o$$

64. Inertial mass $= \frac{\text{Force}}{\text{Acceleration}}$

65. Gravitational mass $= \frac{\text{Weight of body}}{\text{Acceleration due to gravity}}$

Chapter-9 Mechanical Properties of Solids

66. Stress $= \frac{\text{Restoring force}}{\text{Area}}$

67. Strain $= \frac{\text{Change in configuration}}{\text{Original configuration}}$

68. Hooke's Law,

Stress = Modulus of elasticity × Strain

69. Young's Modulus of elasticity, $Y = \frac{\text{Normal stress}}{\text{Longitudinal strain}}$

70. Bulk modulus of elasticity, $K = \frac{\text{Normal stress}}{\text{Volumetric strain}}$

71. Modulus of rigidity, G or $S = \frac{\text{Tangential stress or Shear stress}}{\text{Shearing strain}}$

72. Compressibility $= \frac{1}{\text{Bulk modulus}}$

73. Elastic potential energy in a stretched wire

$$= \frac{1}{2}(\text{stress}) \times \text{strain} \times \text{volume of the wire}$$

74. Elastic potential energy per unit volume

$$= \frac{1}{2} \times \text{stress} \times \text{strain}$$

$$= \frac{1}{2} \times \text{Young's modulus} \times (\text{strain})^2$$

75. Elastic potential energy of a stretched spring $= \frac{1}{2} kx^2$

76. Thermal stress $= \frac{F}{A} = Y\alpha\Delta\theta$

77. Poisson's ratio $(\sigma) = \frac{\text{Lateral strain}}{\text{Longitudinal strain}}$

Chapter-10 Mechanical Properties of Fluids

78. Pressure exerted by the liquid, $p = h\rho g$

79. Density of a mixture of substances, $\rho = \dfrac{m_1 + m_2}{\left(\dfrac{m_1}{\rho_1}\right) + \left(\dfrac{m_2}{\rho_2}\right)}$

80. Viscous force $(F) = -\eta\, A \frac{dv}{dx}$

81. Stoke' law, $F = 6\pi\eta rv$

82. Terminal velocity

$$v_t = \frac{2}{9} \cdot \frac{r^2 (\rho - \sigma) g}{\eta}$$

83. Critical velocity $v_c = \frac{k\eta}{r\rho}$

84. Equation of continuity

$$a_1 v_1 = a_2 v_2 \quad \Rightarrow \quad av = \text{constant}$$

85. Bernoulli's theorem, $p + \frac{1}{2} \rho v^2 + \rho gh = \text{constant}$

86. Rate of flow of liquid in venturimeter;

$$v = a_1 a_2 \sqrt{\frac{2gh}{a_1^2 - a_2^2}}$$

87. Surface tension $= \frac{\text{Force}}{\text{Length}} = \frac{\text{Work done}}{\text{Change in area}}$

88. Surface energy = Surface tension × Increase in surface area.

89. Ascent of a liquid column in a capillary tube:

$$h = \frac{2s\cos\theta}{r\rho g} - \frac{r}{3}$$

(Factor $r/3$ can be neglected for a narrow tube)

90. Zurin's law, $Rh = \text{constant} \Rightarrow R_1h_1 = R_2h_2$

Chapter-11 Thermal Properties of Matter

91. Relation between different scales of temperatures

$$\frac{C}{100} = \frac{F-32}{180} = \frac{K-273}{100} = \frac{R}{80}$$

92. Thermal (heat) capacity, $Q = mc \times \Delta T$.

93. Water equivalent; $W = ms$ = heat capacity of a body

94. Latent heat, $Q = mL$

95. Principle of calorimetry,

Heat lost = Heat gained

96. Coefficient of linear expansion, $\alpha = \dfrac{\Delta l}{l \times \Delta t}$

97. Coefficient of superficial expansion

$$\beta = \frac{\Delta A}{A \times \Delta t}$$

98. Coefficient of cubical expansion

$$\gamma = \frac{\Delta V}{V \times \Delta t}$$

99. Relation between coefficient of linear, superficial and cubical expansions

$$\beta = 2\alpha \text{ and } \gamma = 3\alpha$$

$$\therefore \quad \alpha : \beta : \gamma = 1 : 2 : 3$$

Chapter-12 Kinetic Theory of Gases

100. Boyle's law

$$pV = \text{constant}$$

$$p_1V_1 = p_2V_2$$

101. Charles' law

$$\frac{V}{T} = \text{constant}$$

$$\frac{V_1}{T_1} = \frac{V_2}{T_2}$$

102. Standard gas equation

$$pV = nRT$$

103. van der Waals' gas equation

$$\left(p + \frac{a}{V^2}\right)(V - b) = RT$$

104. Pressure due to an ideal gas

$$p = \frac{1}{3}\frac{mn}{V}c^2 = \frac{1}{3}\rho c^2$$

105. Average speed of molecules of a gas

$$v = \sqrt{\frac{8kT}{\pi m}} = \sqrt{\frac{8RT}{\pi M}}$$

106. The most probable speed of molecules of a gas

$$v_{mp} = \sqrt{\frac{2kT}{m}} = \sqrt{\frac{2RT}{M}}$$

107. Degree of freedom

f or $N = 3$ (Number of particles) – Number of independent relation.

108. Specific heat of a gas at constant volume

$$C_V = \frac{f}{2}R$$

109. Specific heat of a gas at constant pressure

$$C_p = \left(\frac{f}{2} + 1\right)R$$

110. Ratio of specific heats of a gas at constant pressure and at constant volume

$$\gamma = \left(1 + \frac{2}{f}\right)$$

111. Mean free path, $\lambda = \dfrac{kT}{\sqrt{2}\,\pi\sigma^2 p}$

Chapter-13 Thermodynamics

112. Work done by a thermodynamic system

$$W = p \times \Delta V$$

113. First law of thermodynamics

$$\Delta Q = \Delta U + \Delta W$$

114. Efficiency of the cycle

$$\eta = \frac{\text{Work done}}{\text{Heat supplied}}$$

115. Slope of the adiabatic curve

$$= \gamma \times \text{slope of the isothermal curve}$$

116. Isothermal modulus of elasticity, $E_S = p$

117. Adiabatic modulus of elasticity, $E_T = \gamma p$

118. Ratio between adiabatic and isothermal modulus

$$\frac{E_T}{E_S} = \gamma = \frac{C_p}{C_V}$$

119. Thermal efficiency of a heat engine

$$\eta = \frac{\text{Work done / cycle}}{\text{Total amount of heat absorbed / cycle}}$$

$$= 1 - \frac{Q_2}{Q_1} = 1 - \frac{T_2}{T_1}$$

120. Coefficient of performance of refrigerator

$$\beta = \frac{Q_2}{W} = \frac{Q_2}{Q_1 - Q_2} = \frac{T_2}{T_1 - T_2}$$

121. Relation between efficiency (η) and coefficient of performance (β)

$$\beta = \frac{1 - \eta}{\eta}$$

122. Temperature gradient $= \dfrac{\text{Change in temperature}}{\text{Perpendicular distance}} = -\dfrac{\Delta\theta}{\Delta x}$

123. The amount of heat flow in a conducting rod, $Q = \dfrac{KA\Delta\theta t}{l}$

124. Thermal resistance, $R = \dfrac{\Delta\theta}{H} = \dfrac{l}{KA}$

Chapter-14 Simple Harmonic Motion

125. Frequency $= \dfrac{1}{\text{Time period}}$

126. Angular frequency

$$\omega = 2\pi\nu$$

127. Velocity of a particle executing SHM

$$v = \omega\sqrt{(a^2 - y^2)}$$

128. Acceleration of a particle executing SHM

$$a = -\omega^2 y$$

129. Time period in SHM

$$T = 2\pi\sqrt{\frac{\text{Displacement}}{\text{Acceleration}}}$$

130. Time period of the simple pendulum

$$T = 2\pi\sqrt{\frac{l}{g}}$$

131. Restoring force $(F) = -$ Force constant of spring × distance

$$= -ky$$

132. Time period of a loaded spring

$$T = 2\pi\sqrt{\frac{m}{k}}$$

Chapter-15 Waves

133. Wave velocity, $v = f\lambda$

134. Velocity of longitudinal (sound) waves, $v = \sqrt{\dfrac{E}{\rho}}$

135. Newton's formula for isothermal process, $v = \sqrt{\dfrac{E_S}{\rho}} = \sqrt{\dfrac{p}{\rho}}$

136. Laplace's correction for adiabatic process

$$v = \sqrt{\frac{E_T}{\rho}} = \sqrt{\frac{\gamma p}{\rho}}$$

137. Speed of transverse motion

$$v = \sqrt{\frac{T}{m}}$$

138. Plane progressive simple harmonic wave

$$y = a\sin 2\pi\left(\frac{t}{T} - \frac{x}{\lambda}\right)$$

$$= a\sin\frac{2\pi}{\lambda}(vt - x)$$

Chapter-16 Electrostatics

139. Quantization of charge

$$Q = \pm\, ne$$

140. Coulomb's law of electrostatics

$$F = \frac{1}{4\pi\varepsilon_0}\cdot\frac{q_1 q_2}{r^2}$$

141. Electric field intensity

$$\mathbf{E} = \lim_{q_0 \to 0}\frac{\mathbf{F}}{q_0}$$

142. Electric field intensity due to a point charge q

$$E = \frac{1}{4\pi\varepsilon_0}\cdot\frac{q}{r^2}$$

143. Electric potential $V = \dfrac{W}{q}$

144. Electric potential due to a point change q

$$V = \frac{1}{4\pi\varepsilon_0}\cdot\frac{q}{r}$$

145. Potential gradient $= \dfrac{dV}{dr}$

146. Relation between potential gradient and electric field intensity

$$E = -\left(\frac{dV}{dr}\right)$$

147. Electric flux $(\phi_E) = \mathbf{E}\cdot\mathbf{ds}$

148. Gauss' theorem

$$\phi_E = \oint_s \mathbf{E} \cdot \mathbf{ds} = \frac{1}{\varepsilon_o} \Sigma q_{\text{enclosed}}$$

149. Electric dipole moment

$$\mathbf{p} = q \times 2\,\mathbf{l}$$

150. Torque

$$\tau = Ep\sin\theta = \mathbf{p} \times \mathbf{E}$$

151. Work done of an electric dipole

$$W = pE\,(\cos\theta_1 - \cos\theta_2)$$

152. Potential energy of an electric dipole

$$U = -\,pE\cos\theta$$

153. Potential energy of charge system

$$U = \frac{1}{4\pi\varepsilon_o} \cdot \frac{q_1 q_2}{r}$$

154. Capacitance of a conductor, $C = \dfrac{q}{V}$

155. Capacitance of an isolated spherical conductor

$$C = 4\pi\varepsilon_o R$$

Chapter-17 Current Electricity

156. Electric current, $I = \dfrac{q}{t}$

157. Drift velocity, $v_d = \dfrac{eE\tau}{m} = \dfrac{eV\tau}{ml}$

158. Relation between electric current and drift velocity, $v_d = \dfrac{I}{Ane}$

159. Mobility of electron, $\mu = \dfrac{v_d}{E}$

160. Ohm's law; $I \propto V$

$\Rightarrow$ $V = IR$

161. Electrical resistance, $R = \dfrac{ml}{ne^2 A\tau} = \dfrac{V}{I}$

162. Resistivity, $\rho = \dfrac{m}{ne^2\tau} = \dfrac{1}{\sigma}$

163. Relation between current density (J) and electrical conductivity (σ)

$$J = \sigma E$$

164. Electromotive force (emf) of a cell

$$E = \frac{W}{q}$$

165. Terminal potential difference

$$V = \frac{W}{q}$$

166. Relation between E, V and internal resistance of a cell

$$E = V + Ir$$

167. Principle of Wheatstone bridge, $\frac{P}{Q} = \frac{R}{S}$

168. Principle of Meter bridge, $\frac{R}{S} = \frac{l_1 \text{ (length of wire)}}{100 - l_1}$

169. Joule's law, $H = I^2 Rt = \frac{V^2 \cdot t}{R}$ joule

or $$H = \frac{I^2 Rt}{4.18} = \frac{V^2 t}{4.18 R} \text{ calories}$$

170. Electric power $P = VI = I^2 R = \frac{V^2}{R}$

171. Electric energy

$$W = V.q = VIt = I^2 Rt = \frac{V^2 t}{R}$$

Chapter-18 Magnetic Effect of Current

172. Biot Savart's law

$$\mathbf{dB} = \frac{\mu_0}{4\pi} \frac{\mathbf{I dl} \times \mathbf{r}}{r^3} \Rightarrow dB = \frac{\mu_0}{4\pi} \cdot \frac{Idl \sin\theta}{r^2}$$

173. Magnetic dipole

$$|M| = NiA$$

174. Ampere's circuital law

$$\oint \mathbf{B} \cdot \mathbf{d}l = \mu_0 I$$

175. Magnetic field inside the turns of toroid

$$B = \mu_0 n I$$

176. Radius of circular path

$$r = \frac{mv}{Bq}$$

177. Torque acting on a current carrying coil placed inside a uniform magnetic field

$$\tau = NBIA \sin\theta$$

178. Current sensitivity

$$I_s = \frac{\theta}{I} = \frac{NBA}{K}$$

179. Voltage sensitivity

$$V_s = \frac{\theta}{V} = \frac{NBA}{KR}$$

180. Principle of ammeter, $S = \left(\frac{I_g}{I - I_g}\right) G$

181. Principle of voltmeter

$$V = I_g (G + R)$$

Chapter-19 Magnetism and Matter

182. Coulomb's law for magnetic poles

$$F = \frac{\mu_0}{4\pi} \cdot \frac{m_1 m_2}{r^2}$$

183. Magnetic dipole moment

$$\mathbf{M} = \mathbf{m}\,(2l)$$

184. Torque acting on a magnetic dipole

$$\tau = \mathbf{M} \times \mathbf{B} = MB \sin\theta$$

185. Potential energy of a magnetic dipole

$$U = W = -MB\cos\theta = -\mathbf{M} \cdot \mathbf{B}$$

186. Magnetic flux, $\phi = \mathbf{B} \cdot \mathbf{A} = BA \cos\theta$

187. Magnetic induction, $B = \frac{\phi}{A} = \mu_0 (H + I)$

188. Magnetic permeability, $\mu = \frac{B}{H}$

189. Magnetising force or Magnetic intensity, $H = \frac{B}{\mu}$

190. Intensity of magnetisation

$$\mathbf{I} = \frac{\mathbf{M}}{\mathrm{V}} = \frac{m}{A}$$

191. Magnetic susceptibility, $\chi_m = \frac{I}{H}$

192. Relation between magnetic permeability and susceptibility

$$\mu = \mu_0 (1 + \chi_m)$$

193. Curie law in magnetism, $\chi_m \propto \frac{1}{T}$

$$\chi_m T = \text{constant}$$

Chapter-20 Electromagnetic Induction

194. Motional emf, $E = \mathbf{B} \cdot \mathbf{v} \times l = Bvl$

195. Coefficient of self-induction, $L = \frac{\phi}{I} = \frac{\mu_0 N^2 A}{l} = \mu n^2 Al$

196. Coefficient of mutual induction, $M = \frac{\phi}{I}$

197. Mutual induction of two long coaxial solenoids

$$M = \frac{\mu_0 N_1 N_2 A}{l} = \mu_0 n_1 n_2 Al$$

198. Growth of current in an inductor

$$I = I_0 (1 - e^{-Rt/L})$$

199. Decay of current in an inductor, $I = I_0 e^{-Rt/L}$

Chapter-21 Alternating Current

200. Instantaneous value of alternating current

$$I = I_0 \sin \omega t$$

201. Inductive reactance

$$X_L = L\omega = L \cdot 2\pi f = \frac{L \cdot 2\pi}{T}$$

202. Capacitive reactance

$$X_C = \frac{1}{C\omega} = \frac{1}{C \cdot 2\pi f} = \frac{T}{C \cdot 2\pi}$$

203. Impedance of an AC circuit

$$Z = \sqrt{R^2 + (X_L - X_C)^2}$$

204. Average power in AC circuit

$$P_{av} = V_{rms} \cdot i_{rms} \cdot \cos\theta$$

205. Resonant frequency, $f = \dfrac{1}{2\pi\sqrt{LC}}$

206. *Q*-factor or sharpness at resonance

$$Q = \frac{1}{R}\sqrt{\frac{L}{C}}$$

207. Induced emf produced by the AC generator

$$e = NBA\omega \sin\omega t = e_o \sin\omega t$$

208. Torque acting on a current carrying coil

$$\tau = NBIA \sin\theta$$

209. Transformation ratio

$$K = \frac{N_S}{N_P} = \frac{E_S}{E_P} = \frac{I_P}{I_S}$$

Chapter-22 Ray Optics

210. Mirror formula, $\dfrac{1}{f} = \dfrac{1}{v} + \dfrac{1}{u}$

211. Relation between focal length and radius of curvature, $f = \dfrac{R}{2}$

212. The power of a mirror, $P = \dfrac{1}{f(\text{metre})} = \dfrac{100}{f(\text{cm})}$

213. Newton's formula for a concave mirror

$$f = \sqrt{x_1 x_2}$$

214. Linear magnification, $m = \dfrac{I}{O} = -\dfrac{v}{u}$

215. Snell's law, $\dfrac{\sin i}{\sin r} = \text{constant } ({}_1\mu_2)$

216. Refractive index of a medium $(\mu) = \dfrac{c}{v}$

217. Relative refractive index

$$ {}_1\mu_2 = \frac{v_1}{v_2} $$

218. Refractive index of denser medium

$$ \mu = \frac{1}{\sin C} $$

219. Lens formula, $\frac{1}{f} = \frac{1}{v} - \frac{1}{u}$

220. Lens Maker's formula, $\frac{1}{f} = (\mu - 1)\left(\frac{1}{R_1} - \frac{1}{R_2}\right)$

221. Linear magnification for lens

$$ m = \frac{I}{O} = \frac{v}{u} $$

222. Focal length of a convex lens by displacement method

$$ f = \frac{a^2 - d^2}{4a} $$

223. Height of the object, $O = \sqrt{I_1 I_2}$

224. Prism formula

$$ \mu = \frac{\sin\left(\frac{A + \delta_m}{2}\right)}{\sin\left(\frac{A}{2}\right)} $$

Chapter-23 (Wave Optics)

225. Interference fringe width, $\beta = \frac{D\lambda}{d}$

226. Law of Malus, $I \propto \cos^2 \theta$

227. Brewster's law, $\mu = \tan i_p$

Chapter-24 Dual Nature of Rodiation and Matter

228. Energy of a photon, $E = h\nu$

229. Momentum of a photon

$$ p = \frac{h\nu}{c} = \frac{h}{\lambda} $$

230. Relation between work function, threshold frequency and threshold wavelength

$$\phi = h\nu_o = \frac{hc}{\lambda_{max}}$$

231. Einstein's photoelectric equation

$$(E_K)_{max} = h\nu - \phi = h(\nu - \nu_o)$$

232. Maximum kinetic energy of photo electrons

$$(E_k)_{max} = \frac{1}{2}mv_{max}^2 = eV_o$$

233. de-Broglie wavelength

$$\lambda = \frac{h}{p} = \frac{h}{mv} = \frac{h}{\sqrt{2meV}}$$

234. Bragg's law, $2d\sin\theta = n\lambda$

Chapter-25 Atoms

235. Distance of closest approach

$$r_0 = \frac{1}{4\pi\varepsilon_0} \cdot \frac{2ze^2}{E_K}$$

236. Impact parameter

$$b = \frac{1}{4\pi\varepsilon_0} \cdot \frac{Ze^2 \cot\left(\frac{\theta}{2}\right)}{E_K}$$

237. Radius of orbit of electron

$$r = \frac{n^2h^2}{4\pi^2 mkZe^2}$$

238. Velocity of electron in any orbit

$$v = \frac{2\pi\, kZe^2}{nh}$$

239. Frequency of electron in any orbit

$$\nu = \frac{kZe^2}{nhr} = \frac{4\pi^2 Z^2 e^4 mk^2}{n^3h^3}$$

240. Kinetic energy of electron in any orbit

$$E_k = \frac{2\pi^2 me^4 Z^2 k^2}{n^2 h^2} = \frac{13.6 Z^2}{n^2} \text{ eV}$$

241. Potential energy of electron in any orbit

$$E_p = -\frac{4\pi^2 me^4 Z^2 k^2}{n^2 h^2} = -\frac{27.2 Z^2}{n^2} \text{ eV}$$

242. Total energy of electron in any orbit

$$E = \frac{-2\pi^2 me^4 Z^2 k^2}{n^2 h^2} = \frac{-13.6 Z^2}{n^2} \text{ eV}$$

Chapter-26 Nuclei

243. Radius of the nucleus $R \propto A^{1/3}$

$\Rightarrow$ $$R = R_0 A^{1/3}$$

244. Nuclear density

$$\rho = \frac{\text{Mass of nucleus}}{\text{Volume of nucleus}} = \frac{3m}{4\pi R_0^3}$$

245. Mass defect $\Delta m = M - m = [Zm_p + (A - Z)m_n - m_N]$

246. Nuclear binding energy $= (\Delta m)c^2$

$$= [Zm_p + (A - Z)m_n - m_N]c^2$$

247. Nuclear binding energy per nucleon

$$= \frac{\text{Nuclear binding energy}}{\text{Total number of nucleons}}$$

$$= \frac{[Zm_p + (A - Z)m_n - m_N]c^2}{A}$$

248. Packing fraction, $P = \frac{\text{(Exact nuclear mass)} - \text{(Mass number)}}{\text{Mass number}}$

249. Rate of disintegration

$$\frac{-dN}{dt} \propto N \Rightarrow \frac{-dN}{dt} = \lambda N$$

250. Relation between half-life and disintegration constant

$$T_{1/2} = \frac{\log_e 2}{\lambda} = \frac{0.6931}{\lambda}$$

Chapter-27 Semiconductor Electronics

251. Electrical conductivity of extrinsic semiconductor

$$\sigma = \frac{1}{\rho} = e(n_e\mu_e + n_h\mu_h)$$

252. Relation between the current gain of common base and common emitter amplifier

$$\beta = \frac{\alpha}{1-\alpha} = \frac{I_C}{I_B}$$

Chapter-28 EM Waves

253. Displacement current,

$$I_D = \varepsilon_0 \cdot \frac{d\phi_E}{dt}$$

254. Ampere-Maxwell law

$$\oint \mathbf{B} \cdot d\mathbf{l} = \mu_0 (I + I_D)$$

255. Average electric energy density

$$U_E = \frac{1}{2}\varepsilon_0 E^2 = \frac{1}{4}\varepsilon_0 E_0^2$$

256. Average magnetic energy density

$$U_B = \frac{1}{2}\frac{B^2}{\mu_0} = \frac{1}{4}\frac{B_0^2}{\mu_0}$$

Chapter-29 Communication System

257. Critical frequency, $\nu_c = 9(N_{\max})^{1/2}$

258. Skip distance $(D_{\text{skip}}) = 2h\left(\frac{v_{\max}}{v_c}\right)^2 - 1$

259. Effective range in space wave propagation

$$d = \sqrt{2Rh_T} + \sqrt{2Rh_R}$$

Noble Prizes in Physics

Year	Laureate	Country	Rationale
2024	John Hopfield	USA	For foundational discoveries and inventions that enable machine learning with artificial neural network.
	Geoffrey E. Hinton	United Kingdom	
2023	Pierre Agostini	USA	For experimental methods that generate attosecond pulses of light for the study of electron dynamics in matter.
	Ferenc Krausz	Hungary	
	Anne L'Huillier	France	
2022	Alain Aspect	France	For experiments with entangled photons, establishing the violation of Bell inequalities and pioneering quantum information science.
	John Clauser	USA	
	Anton Zeilinger	Austria	
2021	Syukuro Manabe	Japan	For the physical modelling of Earth's climate, quantifying variability and reliably predicting global warming.
	Klaus Hasselmann	Gemany	
	Giorgio Parisi	Italy	For the discovery of the interplay of disorder and fluctuations in physical systems from atomic to planetary scales.
2020	Roger Penrose	United Kingdom	For the discovery that black hole formation is a robust prediction of the general theory of relativity.
	Reinhard Genzel	Germany	For the discovery of a supermassive compact object at the centre of our galaxy.
	Andrea Ghez	USA	
2019	James Peebles	Canada	contributions to our understanding of the evolution of the universe and Earth's place in the cosmos .
	Michel Mayor	Switzerland	For theoretical discoveries in physical cosmology.
	Didier Queloz	Switzerland	Cor the discovery of an exoplanet orbiting a solar-type star.
2018	Arthur Ashkin	America	For the invention of the optical tweezers and their applications to biological systems.
	Gerard Mourou	French	For their method of generating high-intensity, ultra short optical pulses.
	Donna Strickland	Canada	

Year	Laureate	Country	Rationale
2017	Rainer Weiss Barry C. Barish Kip S. Thorne	Germany America USA	For decisive contributions to the LIGO detector and the observation of gravitational waves.
2016	David J. Thouless F. Duncan. M Haldane J. Michael Kosterlitz	United Kingdom United Kingdom United Kingdom	For theoretical discoveries of topological phase transitions and topological phases of matter.
2015	Takaaki Kajita Arthur B. Mc Donald	Japan Canada	For the discovery of neutrino oscillations which shows that neutrinos have mass.
2014	Shuji Nakamura, Isamu Akasaki Hiroshi Amano	Japan United States Japan	For the invention of efficient blue light emitting diodes which has enabled bright and energy - saving white light sources.
2013	Francois Englert Peter W. Higgs	Belgium United Kingdom	For the theoretical discovery of a mechanism that contributes to our understanding of the origin of mass of sub-atomic particles and which recently was confirmed through the discovery of the predicted fundamental particle by the ATLAS and CMS experiments at CERN's large Hadron Collider.
2012	Serge Haroche David J. Wineland	France United States	For ground-breaking experimental methods that enable measuring and manipulation of individual quantum systems.
2011	Saul Perlmutter Brian P. Schmidt Adam G. Riess	United States Australia United States	For the discovery of the accelerating expansion of the Universe through observations of distant supernovae
2010	Andre Geim Konstantin Novoselov	United Kingdom United Kingdom	For ground-breaking experiments regarding the two-dimensional material graphene
2009	Charles K. Kao	Hong Kong United Kingdom United States	For ground-breaking achievements concerning the transmission of light in fibers for optical communication
	Willard S. Boyle George E. Smith	Canada United States United States	For the invention of an imaging semiconductor circuit -the CCD sensor
2008	Makoto Kobayashi Toshihide Maskawa	Japan Japan	For the discovery of the origin of the broken symmetry which predicts the existence of at least three families of quarks in nature
	Yoichiro Nambu	Japan United States	For the discovery of the mechanism of spontaneous broken symmetry in subatomic physics

Year	Laureate	Country	Rationale
2007	Albert Fert Peter Grunberg	France Germany	For the discovery of giant magnetoresistance
2006	John C. Mather George F. Smoot	United States United States	For their discovery of the blackbody form and anisotropy of the cosmic microwave background radiation
2005	Roy J. Glauber	United States	For his contribution to the quantum theory of optical coherence
	John L. Hall Theodor W. Hansch	United States Germany	For their contributions to the development of laser based precision spectroscopy, including the optical frequency comb technique
2004	David J. Gross Hugh David Politzer Frank Wilczek	United States United States United States	For the discovery of asymptotic freedom in the theory of the strong interaction
2003	Alexei Alexeyevich Abrikosov Vitaly Lazarevich Ginzburg Anthony James Leggett	Russia United States Russia United Kingdom United States	For pioneering contributions to the theory of superconductors and superfluids
2002	Raymond Davis, Jr. Masatoshi Koshiba	United States Japan	For pioneering contributions to astrophysics, in particular for the detection of cosmic neutrinos
	Riccardo Giacconi	Italy United States	For pioneering contributions to astrophysics, which have led to the discovery of cosmic X-ray sources
2001	Eric Allin Cornell Carl Edwin Wieman Wolfgang Ketterle	United States United States Germany	For the achievement of Bose-Einstein condensation in dilute gases of alkali atoms, and for early fundamental studies of the properties of the condensates
2000	Zhores Ivanovich Alferov Herbert Kroemer	Russia Germany	For developing semiconductor hetero structures used in high speed and optoelectronics
	Jack St. Clair Kilby	United States	For his part in the invention of the integrated circuit

Researchers and their Discoveries

1. **Andre-Marie Ampere** *Father of electrodynamics.*
2. **Albert Einstein Explained** Brownian motion and *photoelectric effect,* contributed to theory of atomic spectra, formulated *theories of special and general relativity*.
3. **Arthur Compton** Discovered the *increase in wavelength of X-rays* when scattered by an electron.

4. **Aage Bohr** Contributed to theoretical understanding of collective motion and particle motion in *atomic nuclei*.
5. **Arnold Sommerfeld** Generalized the circular orbits of the atomic Bohr model to elliptical orbits, introduced the concept of the *magnetic quantum number*, used statistical mechanics to explain the electronic properties of metals.
6. **Blaise Pascal** Discovered that pressure applied to an enclosed fluid remains undiminished as it is transmitted to every part of the fluid and to the walls of its container (*Pascal's principle*).

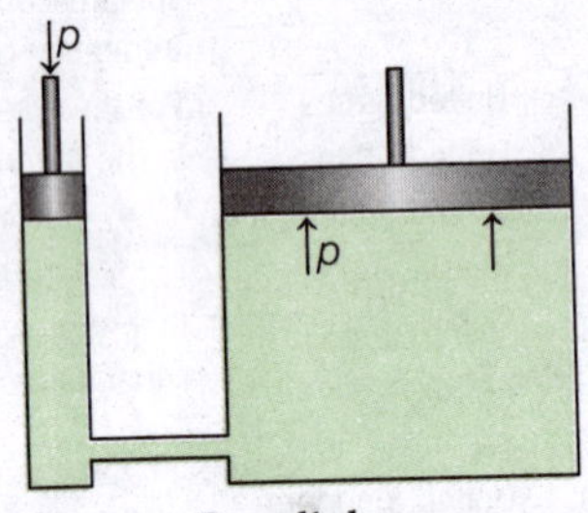

Pascal's law

7. **Benjamin Franklin** The first American physicist, characterized two kinds of *electric charge*, which he named *positive* and *negative*.
8. **Christiaan Huygens'** Proposed a simple *geometrical wave theory of light*, now known as *Huygens' principle*; pioneered use of the pendulum in clocks.
9. **Charles Augustin de Coulomb** Experiments on elasticity, electricity and magnetism, established experimentally nature of *the force between two charges*.
10. **Count Alessandro Volta** Pioneer in study of electricity, *invented the first electric battery*.

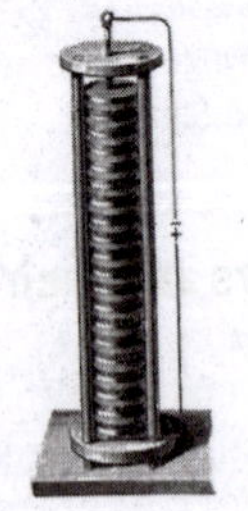
Electric battery

11. **Christian Doppler** Experimented with *sound waves;* derived an expression for the apparent change in wavelength of a wave due to relative motion between the source and observer.
12. **Daniel Bernoulli** Developed the fundamental relationship of *fluid flow* now known as *Bernoulli's principle.*

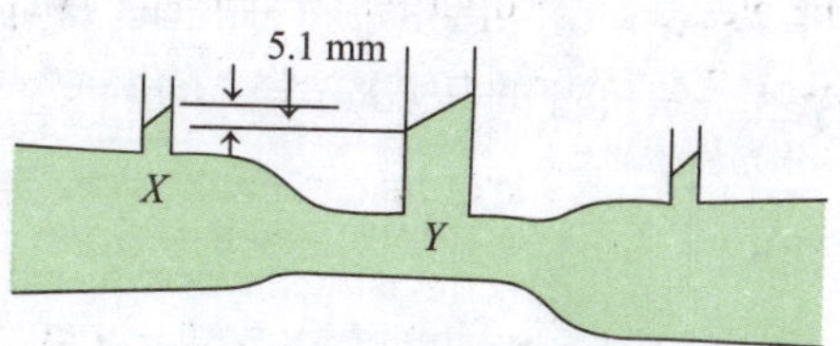

Venturimetre

13. **Enrico Fermi** Performed experiments leading to first self-sustaining *nuclear chain reaction,* developed a theory of *beta decay* that introduced the weak interaction, derived the statistical properties of gases that obey the Pauli exclusion principle.
14. **Frederic Joliot-Curie** Co-discovered artificial *radioactivity.*
15. **Galileo Galilei** Performed fundamental observations, experiments and mathematical analysis in *astronomy and physics*; discovered **mountains** *and craters on the moon, the phases of Venus,* and the four largest *satellites of Jupiter: Io, Europa, Callisto, and Ganymede.*
16. **George Ohm** Discovered that current flow through conductor is directly proportional to potential difference and inversely proportional to resistance (*Ohm's law*).
17. **Guglielmo Marconi** Invented the first practical system of *wireless telegraphy.*
18. **George E. Smith** Co-invented the *CCD (charge-coupled device).*
19. **Henry Cavendish** Discovered and studied hydrogen; *first to measure Newton's gravitational constant*; calculated mass and mean density of Earth.
20. **Hans Christian Oersted** Discovered that a *current in a wire can produce magnetic effects.*
21. **Hermann von Helmholtz** Developed first law of thermodynamics, a *statement of conservation of energy.*
22. **Heinrich Hertz** Worked on electromagnetic phenomena; *discovered radio waves* and the photoelectric effect.

23. **Henry Moseley** Developed the *modern form of the periodic table* of elements *based on their atomic numbers.*
24. **Homi Jehangir Bhabha** Initiated *nuclear research* programs in India; carried out experiments in *cosmic rays*; calculated cross-section for *elastic electron-positron scattering.*
25. **Irene Joliot-Curie** Co-discovered artificial *radioactivity.*
26. **James Watt** Invented the modern condensing *steam engine* and a *centrifugal governor.*
27. **Joseph Fourier** Established the *differential equation governing heat diffusion* and solved it by devising an infinite series of sines and cosines capable of approximating a wide variety of functions.
28. **Jean-Baptiste Biot** Studied *polarization of light*; co-discovered that *intensity of magnetic field* set up by a current flowing through a wire varies inversely with the distance from the wire.
29. **Johann Carl Friedrich Gauss** Formulated separate electrostatic and electrodynamical laws, including *Gauss's law*; contributed to development of number theory, differential geometry, potential theory, theory of terrestrial magnetism, and methods of calculating planetary orbits.
30. **Joseph Henry** Performed extensive fundamental studies of electromagnetic phenomena; *devised first practical electric relay and doorbell.*

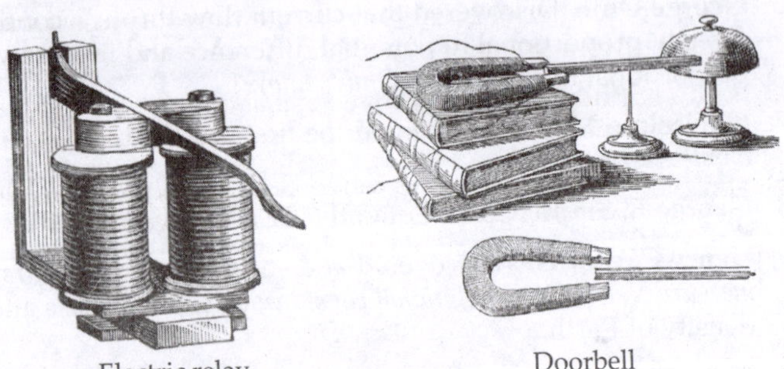

Electric relay

Doorbell

31. **James Prescott Joule** Discovered *mechanical equivalent of heat.*
32. **Jean-Bernard-Léon Foucault** Accurately measured *speed of light*; invented the *gyroscope*; demonstrated the Earth's rotation.
33. **Johann Balmer** Developed empirical formula to describe *hydrogen spectrum.*

34. **James Clerk Maxwell** Propounded the theory of *electromagnetism*; developed the *kinetic theory of gases*.
35. **Josef Stefan** Studied *blackbody radiation*.
36. **Josiah Gibbs** Developed *chemical thermodynamics*; introduced concepts of *free energy* and *chemical potential*.
37. **John Henry Poynting** Demonstrated that the energy flow of electromagnetic waves could be calculated by an equation (now called *Poynting vector*).
38. **Janne Rydberg** Analyzed the spectra of many elements; discovered many line series were described by a formula that depended on a universal constant (*the Rydberg constant*).
39. **Johannes van der Waals** Worked on *equations of state for gases and liquids*.
40. **Leonard Euler** Made fundamental contributions to *fluid dynamics*, lunar orbit theory (tides), and mechanics; also contributed prolifically to all areas of classical mathematics.
41. **Lord Rayleigh (born John William Strutt)** Discovered argon; explained how *light scattering* is responsible for the red colour of sunset and the blue colour of the sky.
42. **Lord Ernest Rutherford** Theorized existence of the atomic nucleus based on results of the *alpha-scattering experiment* performed by Hans Geiger and Ernest Marsden; developed theory of Rutherford scattering (scattering of spinless, pointlike particles from a Coulomb potential).
43. **Ludwig Boltzmann** Developed *statistical mechanics* and applied it to the kinetic theory of gases.
44. **Michael the Faraday** Discovered *electromagnetic induction* and devised *first electrical transformer*.

Electric transformer

45. **Max Planck** Formulated the *quantum theory;* explained wavelength distribution of *blackbody radiation.*

46. **Marie Curie** Discovered *radioactivity of thorium;* co-discovered radium and polonium.

47. **Nikola Tesla** Created the concept of *alternating current.*

48. **Niels Bohr** Contributed to the *quantum theory* and the theory of *nuclear reactions* and *nuclear fission.*

49. **Osborne Reynolds** Contributed to the fields of *hydraulics* and *hydrodynamics;* developed mathematical framework for turbulence and introduced the *Reynolds number,* which provides a criterion for dynamic similarity and correct modeling in many fluid flow experiments.

50. **Sir Isaac Newton** Developed theories of *gravitation* and *mechanics,* and invented differential calculus.